Historiography, Empire and the Rule of Law

Imagined Constitutions, Remembered Legalities

Ian Duncanson

Routledge
Taylor & Francis Group
a GlassHouse book

First published 2012
by Routledge
2 Park Square, Milton Park, Abingdon, Oxon OX14 4RN

Simultaneously published in the USA and Canada
by Routledge
711 Third Avenue, New York, NY 10017

A GlassHouse Book

First issued in paperback 2013

Routledge is an imprint of the Taylor & Francis Group, an informa business

British Library Cataloguing in Publication Data
A catalogue record for this book is available from the British Library

Library of Congress Cataloging in Publication Data
Duncanson, Ian.
Historiography, empire, and the rule of law : imagined constitutions, remembered legalities / Ian Duncanson.
p. cm.
1. Rule of law. 2. Legal positivism. 3. Historiography. I. Title.
K3171.D86 2012
340'.11—dc22

2011013938

ISBN 13: 978–0–415–67886–5 (hbk)
ISBN 13: 978–0–415–72017–5 (pbk)
ISBN 13: 978–0–203–80244–1 (ebk)

Typeset in Times New Roman
by Keystroke, Station Road, Codsall, Wolverhampton

In memory of Sandy Duncanson,
8.4.1973–25.6.2010

For JEG and KD

Contents

Acknowledgements

Too much is owed to too many people to mention all of them. For encouragement of my earlier work, I owe a debt to the late Sir Neil MacCormick, MEP and Professor of Jurisprudence at the University of Edinburgh. More lately, I thank colleagues and friends at the Law and Society Association of Australia and New Zealand, most especially Luke MacNamara and Rick Moer of the Legal Extensions Program at the University of Wollongong. David Sugarman of the University of Lancaster proved an encouragement. Wes Pue, at UBC has been a great support, both at a distance and in providing me with a home at Green College, UBC, electronic facilities and access to the university's excellent libraries. Wes provided remarkable light in what were, for me, some dark times. The Sociolegal Research Centre at Griffith University has funded conference travel and other resources.

Phillip Darby, of the Institute for Postcolonial Studies, University of Melbourne, and my doctoral supervisor, provided both enthusiastic reinforcement of what I was attempting whilst restraining some of my quirkier ideas on numerous occasions over sherry on his delightful roof garden overlooking the Institute. I was very proud to have such a learned and humorous scholar undertake supervision of my work.

I owe most to my friend, colleague and wife, Judith Grbich, a genius with titles and technicalities, and with whom I have had long discussions about intellectual matters concerning our work over the years. Scholarly impasses, after many hours of conversations were always resolved with, "write what you think, remembering that everything is open to dispute and nothing is final": a timely injunction in the gloomy and sometimes oppressive era of the modern university.

From my late son, I learned that great things can be gained in the direst circumstances.

Foreword

These are perilous times – perhaps not unlike those times that Thomas Paine characterized as trying men's souls. But they cannot be tackled with hollow and empty categories. States of exception are apparently everywhere and permanent. Torture is no longer anathema to a liberal legal order, but regulated within the horizon of a 'ticking bomb'. National sovereignty is reasserted by progressives as the response to rapacious capitalism. The political subject, if she survived the many proclamations of her demise, is reduced to an opaque 'figure' of political philosophy. Empire, we are told, is an infinite order with no 'outside'. Much of this inanity in political and legal thinking could have been avoided if there was some attention to historical specificity when thinking law, the subject, sovereignty, or Empire. That is the major corrective offered by this book.

Empire was an enterprise through which imperial states learnt to govern themselves by governing others. With close attention to the British Empire, and the English in particular within that formation, this book examines how imperial law was a process of *learning-to-be*. The book asks how subjects were constituted and re-constituted through education and legislation – in the metropolis *and* the outer reaches of empire. The result is an elaborate and historically rich account of how statecraft is contingent on the rule of law. Taking up classic concerns of jurisprudence and legal theory – Duncanson shatters their torpidity by deploying Lacan and Foucault to explain how legality constitutes the subject. At the heart of imperial legality is a constitutional imaginary folded into the educative aspirations of legislation. This process is not only of significance to the study of the British Empire, but also to all postcolonial polities constituted by that order of rule. This book is thus essential reading for any scholar or student of empire and imperialism, constitutions and constitutionalism, or utilitarianism, liberalism, and the rule of law.

Stewart Motha
Reader in Law, Kent Law School
University of Kent, UK

Preface

> For really I think that the poorest he that is in England hath a right to live as the greatest he; and therefore truly sir, I think it's clear that every man that is to live under a government ought first by his own consent to put himself under that government; and I do think that the poorest man in England is not at all bound in a strict sense to a government that he has not had a voice to put himself under. I should doubt whether I was an Englishman or no, that I should doubt of these things.
>
> Colonel Rainsborough, in ASP Woodhouse (ed), *Puritanism and Liberty: Being The Army Debates 1647–9, from the Clarke Manuscripts*, London, Dent (1938), 53.

> I deplore the neglect of Civil War battlefields. I'd really like to see Naseby commemorated as Bosworth is. It's incomparably more significant. Bosworth was just a change of dynasty. Naseby changed the world men and women lived in.
>
> Diane Purkiss, *The English Civil War: A People's History*, London, Harper (2006), Q&A section, 4.

Very little in the histories of political communities or the means of their constitution as such has a clear beginning, and historiography which suggests otherwise strays away from the controversies endemic to the discourses of the humanities and sciences into the land of mythology and fantasy. Nevertheless, we are familiar from the work of Thomas Kuhn with the idea of *moments* in which, for some scholars and others, different ways of seeing, living and acting in the world suddenly seem possible.[1] Establishing the plausibility of such differences is seldom unaccompanied by bitter, occasionally violent, resistance from those who prefer the *status quo*, and there is no iron law of progress to determine whether or not they are correct to do so.

1 Thomas Kuhn, *The Structure of Scientific Revolutions*, 2nd edn, Chicago, IL, University of Chicago Press (1970).

In political and constitutional affairs, seventeenth century England was a moment in which differences were glimpsed. It has to be contrasted with other events in western history. As Purkiss observes in the opening quotation, whilst the Battle of Bosworth, (famous from the closing scenes of Shakespeare's *Richard III*), replaced the dynasty of York with that of the Tudors; and, we might add, whilst treaties like those between Protestant and Catholic powers at Augsburg (1555) and Westphalia (1648) on mainland Europe also actually changed the constitutional practice of monarchy little, the politico-religious outcomes in seventeenth century England altered, in Kuhn's term, the paradigm through which politics began to be practiced. The European mainland treaties established that dynasties chose the religious practices to be followed by their subjects and to respect each others' choices. Although some international lawyers trace the modern state system, at least to Westphalia, this is, we shall see, contested. The dynasties were not states in any modern sense. By contrast with the events that led to them, the period from the English Petition of Right of 1628, through the Parliamentary victories at Naseby and Marston Moor (which Purkiss mentions elsewhere), to its Revolution of 1688 created, or at least deployed, a new vocabulary in which government could and would everywhere eventually be conceived. However miserably put into practice, by 2000, popular sovereignty and equality before the law were seldom denied in theory. Seventeenth century English Whigs, military and civilian, remembered, and some had called for, popular sovereignty, but even those who by 1688 shuddered at the prospect, had created a language in which such an idea could be thought.

And here we encounter several puzzles. The participants in the revolutions settled by the English, abetted by the southern Scots, and followed, as we shall see, a century later by the Americans, saw themselves, so far as their rulers were concerned, as revolutionaries in the old sense of returning to the past – the English to the Saxon freedoms of Tacitus' German imaginings; the Americans to the life of the freeborn Englishman. Their revolutions were actually breaks from the past. New, innovatory and potentially encompassing constitutions emerged, but in the language of the old. The revolutions of France and Russia, as Hannah Arendt has commented,[2] were revolutions in the new sense, aspirations to a new utopian beginning, which, in the event, however, led back to the Bourbon-like absolutism of the Terror and the Napoleons in France, and to the Romanov-like Leninism and Stalinism of post-1917 Russia.

A second puzzle: Westphalia did not, if we follow Teschke,[3] produce states, but merely endorsed cumbrous dynasties, but what did the Glorious Revolution of 1688 produce for England, soon, after the Union, to become Great Britain? John Brewer's is a nice title,[4] but it does not, in my view, reflect the constitutional

2 Hannah Arendt, *On Revolution*, Harmondsworth, Penguin Books (1952).

3 Benno Teschke, *The Myth of 1648: Class, Geopolitics and the Making of Modern International Relations*, London, Verso (2003).

4 John Brewer, *The Sinews of Power: War, Money and the English State 1688–1783*, London, Unwin Hyman (1989).

aspirations of Britain's contemporary rulers: security of landed title, fiscal and commercial efficiency and the economical possibility to "balance" Europe to avert threats to these accomplishments, just as they balanced government power at home with the gentlemanly apparatus of Parliament and common law, an oligarchy in perpetual negotiation with its own factions and with the common people, but not – god forbid – a state, with all its connotations of overbearing power. Arthur Cash has neatly encapsulated the widespread mistrust of George III's centralizing ministries of the 1760s and its connection with American secession.[5] In Great Britain, the Wilkes affair may have been one of the last gasps of the common law's protection of white male, and potentially others' rights. His use of the courts to resist executive power was an inspiration to the supporters of the Americans.

However, while an important concern in the text that follows is the English disruption of Absolutism in the seventeenth century and the social, religious and cultural accommodations prerequisite to preserving the gains it achieved, another concern is the corrosive yet not fatal impact of empire on civil rights. And this is really the final puzzle my text pursues and it can do so only adequately in the wake of much more profound historical research, gesturing, perhaps, to future assessments of the trajectory of the American empire anticipated by Benjamin Franklin[6] in the 1770s, as it expanded through first nation lands, continental territory claimed by Mexico, and across the Pacific to Hawai'i and the Philippines.

The question for the future is about what I have termed the corrosion effected by empire: Chalmers Johnson has termed it "blowback".[7] Blowback, as Johnson develops the idea in a number of books, accompanies the endless wars during which empires are frequently established, and whose techniques and justifications rebound, through habits of conquest and constant vigilance against resistance, upon their origin, the "home" country.[8] James Bryce long ago distinguished two kinds of empire.[9] In one, like the Roman and perhaps modern equivalents, an ultimately futile geographical, cultural or economic contiguity is sought. The conqueror seeks a form of assimilation important to itself and in a classical register of power tries to persuade the disempowered that what the powerful want, they want, too.[10] In another form, the British Raj, in Bryce's view, the imperial power seeks merely to rule, generally for reasons of trade and profit and abandons the effort when it perceives the cultural or commercial returns to be insufficient. Bryce

5 Arthur Cash, *John Wilkes: The Scandalous Father of Civil Liberty*, New Haven, CT, Yale University Press (2006).

6 Richard Immerman, *Empire for Liberty: A History of American Imperialism from Benjamin Franklin to Paul Wolfowitz*, Princeton, NJ, Princeton University Press (2010).

7 Chalmers Johnson, *Blowback: The Costs and Consequences of American Empire*, New York, NY, Henry Holt (2000).

8 Daniel Ross, *Violent Democracy*, Cambridge, Cambridge University Press (2004).

9 James Bryce, *The Ancient Roman Empire and the British Empire in India*, New York, NY, Elibron Classics (1914, reprinted 2005).

10 Steven Lukes, *Power: A Radical View*, London, Palgrave Macmillan, 2nd edn (2005); Daniel Beland, Review of Lukes, July/August, *Canadian Journal of Sociology On-Line* (2006).

would have been unsurprised by Great Britain's abrupt and largely unsentimental departure from the sub-continent in 1947.

The final puzzle the text explores – and here I can in part simply generalize and signal a trend to which many exceptions may be found. Whilst the Americans experimented with the new ways envisaged by Wilkes to balance the constitutional power of executive government by judicial means, English and Scottish courts became increasingly conservative and retiring.[11] Nevertheless, and this is why I should like to see the study of social ordering, including law, broadened, a new avenue was constructed by which the governed many could access and influence the manner of their governance, connected with law in its ordering effect, yet disconnected by an increasingly authoritarian and positivist notion of law. The participatory notion of coming to order as it developed in, say, the institutions of municipal government, locally directed policing and, above all, in education, had more in common with the spirit of the early modern Whigs than with either the command/sovereign conceptions of law or with the reaction to them. The tenor of the civil war debates, after all, was not that of smashing and beginning afresh, a Jacobin or Bolshevik imperative, but rather one of augmenting government and increasing participation. Radical politics by the nineteenth century saw neither revolution nor litigation, but participation, as the route toward change and they had a two-century tradition of discussion and action to guide them.

11 Although not uniformly so. Judges were indulgent to large landowners, allowing creative re-drawing of loan contracts secured on estates so as to lower interest rates if the contractually agreed rate seemed to them unreasonably high. See David Sugarman and Ronnie Warrington, Land Law, citizenship and the invention of "Englishness": the strange world of the equity of redemption, in John Brewer and Susan Staves (eds), *Early Modern Conceptions of Property*, New York, NY, Routledge (1996), ch 6. Such creativity was not generally extended to other borrowers.

Chapter 1

The themes introduced

Law, the subject, sovereignty and certainty

We live in the twentieth and twenty-first centuries in times like those which Thomas Paine described as trying men's souls.[1] Our world is one of perpetual emergency, pointless wars, invasions justified by deceptions and accompanied by imprisonment without trial and torture. The literature is large and growing. Paine was writing during the American Revolution, a period in which all political categories, law, the subject of politics and empire were undergoing the changes outlined in the preface, and the resistances to them. The categories of political, including imperial, practice, subjectivity and law were interwoven. And, to continue the spinning metaphor, important sub-threads will become apparent. The British Empire, as Paine was writing, had already entered what many historians have seen as its second, and more authoritarian phase. One inquires, historically, in a kind of dialectic. We find our object inevitably from a perspective, with particular motivations. Yet if we are narrativists of an open, but disciplinary kind rather than writers of myths and legends, the object of inquiry assumes not simply its own integrity, as well as a lesson for ourselves. In Paine's world we find much of relevance to our own, if we are looking for it.

After the end of the Seven Years' War, in 1763, the empire of Great Britain was increasingly, if unrealistically seen as one of conquest and occupation, by the inept new ministries which took office shortly after the accession of George III. There were, of course, slaves in British America, and Britain was a major, perhaps *the* major trafficker in Africans destined to labor in the Americas. But white men, at least, had permitted themselves to believe that in the Atlantic world, there existed only free-born Englishmen, loyal subjects of the Crown, but each more or less self-governing through their legislatures and courts, whether those institutions were in Britain, Massachusetts, Pennsylvania, the Caribbean or elsewhere. On the one hand, Great Britain's invincibility seemed to have been proved everywhere on the globe, from Plessey in Bengal, to Quebec in Canada. Yet this is the material from which paranoia is constructed. Success had been achieved, but as constitutional

1 Thomas Paine, The Crisis Number 1, in Bruce Kuklick (ed), *Thomas Paine: Political Writings*, Cambridge, Cambridge University Press (2000), 41.

law at that time required, the new monarchy necessitated a new government, one, of course confining the monarch, but at the same time requiring his "confidence", as it was put. Lord Chatham, Pitt the Elder, an experienced statesman who had overseen the Seven Years' War, was replaced by, for the most part, men of little experience and less acumen.

The threat from the defeated European Catholic powers, but not only them, as perceived in London by George's new ministries, seemed to require a consolidation of imperial government. India provided a model. Thanks to Sir Robert, later, Lord Clive, millions of Indians had fallen under British rule – by the East India Company, to be sure, but the Company was chartered under English law and was therefore technically subordinate to the Westminster Parliament.[2]

The environment of the free-born Englishman, heir to the liberties of person and property achieved in the seventeenth century, began to disintegrate, to appear to be a danger, again from a London perspective, a London of new ministries under the new king. Colonists and colonial subjects, American, Indian or West Indian, now began to be considered, from London, as naturally subordinate to Westminster sovereignty. Sub-continental Indians were clearly not suited to self-government, so why should Americans demand it for themselves? There was certainly emergency, as Paine wrote: London waited for resurgence of French and, to a degree, Spanish power.

The Americans, whom Paine hoped by his writing to help constitute as united, faced a bleak defeat until the successful intervention of France and Spain on their behalf. Ironically, this intervention was an outcome that had led London into its vigorous assertion of Westminster sovereignty in the first place. Another way of looking at events is to see, as a number of contemporaries did, the first empire as not really an empire at all.[3] Many Scots, English Whigs, and prominent Americans later associated with the move to independence, saw a confederation whose center of gravity would in time move to the larger land. Many British rulers after 1763, on the contrary, began to wish for a more centralized form of empire. A feature of empire proper, I shall argue, or at least empire in the European tradition, is constant paranoia. If the possession it represents – whether outright occupation or dominance in the form of economic exploitation – is not threatened with seizure from without, it is faced with disintegration from independence movements within. Only a strong sovereign can withstand the constant emergency. It is where s/he emerges from in the form of strong executive government and lack of constitutional or civic restraints. Even in the United States, where, as we shall see, Hannah Arendt considers sovereignty in the old sense to have been abolished with the repairs to the 1688 Whig constitution effected by the new Republic in the

2 See Nick Robins, *The Corporation that Changed the World: How the East India Company Shaped Modern Multinationalism*, London, Pluto Press (2007).

3 See David Armitage and Michael Braddick (eds), *The British Atlantic World 1500–1800*, London, Palgrave Macmillan (2009).

1780s, some modern commentators have warned of the dangers of overweening central executive power. The best-crafted documents have, as we know from recent memory, not protected us from executive action sanctioning war and torture in "civilized" countries, or at their behest.

White governments in many parts of the world have supported, adopted or reverted to what I have elsewhere termed meta-legal sovereignty, an office *of* the law, but somehow not *within* the law. I see this idea as bogus and implausible from a Whig/liberal position, but also, of course dangerous. A Hobbesian/Benthamite sovereign that is antecedent to the law, whose will the law is, should, I will argue, be regarded as a preposterous barbarity, a lunacy for which only a person who would buy the Eiffel Tower from a man in a pub would fall. But we saw apparently intelligent prime ministers and presidents lining up to do the precise equivalent of that prior to Gulf War II and the faltering intervention in Afghanistan. It is this time that tries men's souls in which I write. I have written in this book about the English subject – had I been Canadian, Australian, or US-American, I would no doubt have written about those subjects and perhaps much the same could have been said about any of them. The English subject, to put it in a simplistic way that I shall later qualify, exists as a culturally constituted artifact – a product, as Locke puts it, of education – and as a legal subject, a being-subject, as Bentham sees it, of the will of the sovereign. Neither constitution can be separated, but as will be clear, my view is that a pre-domination of the subject by the will of the sovereign allows least scope for participation and change. Nor does it, I believe, permit a progressive concept of legality.

On the issue of times that try men's souls, I can cite Matthew Sharpe:

> The only antidote for the increasing framing of law and politics in the vague and anxiety-ridden terms of "national security", "enemies", and "unusual and threatening circumstances" . . . will *have* to start with continuing vocal opposition to today's executive exceptionalism. But it will not end without the vigorous promotion of public education, the defense of an open, free (which means not monopolized) media and the encouragement of active participation at every level of the political process of citizens in the economic and political decisions that affect their lives.[4]

The implication, in the above quotation is that "difficult times" can, as we have seen, erode democratic political practice and associated civil liberties with alarming rapidity and completeness unless a new understanding is learned about the subject of politics and its relation to social order. Anglophone jurisdictions are familiar with "emergencies" that render what would otherwise be unacceptable

4 Matthew Sharpe, "Thinking of the extreme situation . . .": On the New Anti-Terrorism Laws, Or, Against a Recent (Theoretical) Return to Carl Schmitt (2006) 24 *Australian Feminist Law Journal* 95–123, 123.

and systematic abuses of government power apparently acceptable: in the case of the United Kingdom one thinks of Ireland, but also, over a long period of time the colonies – rebellions throughout the British Empire and in US territories such as the Philippines, or during world wars. The fond hope is that these are geographically or temporally contained, "exceptions" in their way, resiled from when the emergency is over. The burden of Sharpe's article and other writings is that citizens of so-called liberal democracies (whose colonialist practices, some would say, have invited reprisals from exploited regions, or at least made otherwise unacceptable violent responses appear justifiable to the perpetrators) must re-assess their relations with executive governments only too eager to use the vaguely-defined "war on terror" to extend their control domestically. The role of citizen, or the ordered subject of liberal democracy, is a learned role, in need of repeated rehearsal, as Sharpe suggests.

Legality and politics in "exceptional times"

What I trace in my book is a legality which has been taught not to see the exceptional times in which it exists, or the possibility of alternative careers of education and law in the production of this ordered subject. The careers of learning and legislating are entwined, although they frequently present profoundly gendered alternatives when taken to extremes – empires need a strong sovereign – the manly Westminster legislators and Viceroys of an earlier colonialism, or the stereotypical he-man US Presidents in our own era.[5] The teaching depicted in Dickens' *Hard Times* would have to figure as a stern manly institution, a lower orders' version of Dr Thomas Arnold's reformed mid-Victorian Rugby.[6] In the period referred to in my thesis, sovereign order, order by legislation, appears just as the woodcut from the first edition of *Leviathan* pictures the sovereign author of legality, the final word of what is to be obeyed as the sole condition of order, as a man, carefully bounded and composed of smaller men who have, in their various degrees, ceded to him their rights. *Learning* the arts of co-operation, a curiosity-led as well as prudential route to the management of diversity, and what I have termed "agreeable disagreement", has been an important source of social order, but one at different times characterized as effete, effeminate, and definitely hostile to the project of empire.

As Sharpe observes in the article from which the above quotation is taken, a "naïve faith in the rule of law" is not sufficient to preserve democratic politics in

5 During the 2008 competition of the two main contenders, a woman and a black man, to be nominated by the US Democratic Party, there was some speculation that, despite, or perhaps because of racist attitudes about black masculinity, a black man was seen as more suited to govern an empire than a woman. And see Frank Rich, *The Greatest Story Ever Sold: The Decline and Fall of Truth: The Real History of the Bush Administration*, New York, NY, Viking (2006).

6 Kathryn Tidrick, *Empire and the English Character: The Illusion of Authority*, London, IB Tauris (1992), ch 6 indicates the severe limitations of the reforms. Fighting, drinking and constant bullying continued.

times like the present, times that can be designated by those who control the law, exceptional. Indeed, it is the possibility of that control, vested in the practical imagining of law, that constitutes one of the problems. The "war on terror" simply intensifies what has been implicit since at least the time of Thomas Hobbes, to cite a conveniently succinct and schematic writer. Alternately demonized for recommending tyranny and lionized for promoting a template for the restoration of order, Hobbes was for the most part simply emphasizing to a largely skeptical audience, and updating the benefits of Absolutist rule. If peace, prosperity and "security" are to be made stable, then it seems that law is necessarily the primary instrument in this tradition, and the most tempting and easily understood model of law has been seen as a body of rules ultimately traceable to a primordial sovereign. This office of sovereign may be designated by, but is, according to many writers, ultimately beyond, the law.

Not all writers, I observed, have been happy with the abstract template designed by Hobbes. As Sharpe warns, it vests power in a place, in the end, uncontrolled. The template, suitably airbrushed, is, or has become, a lawyer's model, one which has come to dominate political thinking. As a consequence, in the minds of many who are skeptical of what is colloquially regarded as "spin", in other words, propaganda, "the enemy within" is not principally the infiltrated terrorist, but an executive branch of government, first unleashed to calculate the public's best interests and then to design draconian countermeasures to any threat to those interests.

I shall argue that, undeniably, laws perform invaluable technical work – in the disposition of property and populations, for example; but that their elevation to a more fundamental status on the sovereignty model of their operation is associated with empire, the government of subordinate peoples, uncontrolled and dangerous. Lawyers can, and do, argue that in modern liberal democracies, it is the people who elect legislatures, and it is elected governments who, one way or another, appoint judges. But this is not enough. We shall see the metaphysics that underlies even that most liberal of twentieth century jurisprudential writers, HLA Hart, concerning the validity of laws: the recognizing laws as valid by "officials and certain private persons". We can guess which private persons; the officials are hidden even from the elected legislators. In a recent conspiracy which might have come from a Robert Ludlum thriller, some of them led several liberal democracies into a war declared illegal by an international majority, that, while merely a catastrophe, could have been a cataclysm, and may yet provoke one.[7] The "ungovernable people" of England whom I shall refer to – Braudel writes of obdurate peasants in France, too – the crowd, whose "moral economy" governed peaceful resistance, did not believe in the authority of law; they believed in examining its substance for its moral force and its use, for them. I will later qualify Hume's remark that government authority is based on opinion, but it has enough

7 See the remarks by the UK Ambassador to *Le Canard Enchaine*, reported in a Melbourne *Age* editorial, 3 October 2008, to precisely this effect.

truth for the moment. If we opine that law is based on sovereign authority, then it *will* be, we will have made it so. Is that what we want? Perhaps some of us do. We have, on the other hand, examples of imagining subjects differently, I shall suggest, examples from the indubitably undemocratic time of post-1688 England, when its rulers sought a glue to hold the social order in place; but their solution may help promote ideas of democratic practice in the present. I shall argue that the law of the post-Benthamite lawyers, which has recently dominated legal theory, is a product of empire.

The first British Empire, as many term it, was anomalous. Like post-Revolutionary England (1688), whilst externally predatory, it became a confederation of propertied white men who gave government to themselves. Their property included African slaves and land stolen from indigenous peoples, but, like post-Revolutionary England more generally, it contained the political germ of something better. I shall explore this more fully later in relation to Great Britain. In Britain's second empire, which was not only rule over and the exploitation of brown people, but increasingly over "natives" at home – the working class, women – the doctrine of sovereignty increasingly informed discourse about law.

The twelfth century common law writ of Habeas Corpus, which many commentators have noted in connection with the ideal of "the rule of law", came a little later after the initial revolution, to give legal form and technical application to a preceding political commitment to informed adversarial processes among equals, but it was an *effect*, never that commitment itself, an inscription of the political idea behind it, which is implicit in the now-expanded idea of "the free man". The constitution, similarly an effect, whether the "balanced" Whig constitution of eighteenth century Great Britain or the document reflecting the transformation of colonies into states in America, and their subsequent relinquishing of independent status in a new union, can be the basis of laws, I suggest, to the extent that subjects work to learn who they might be under it. My focus is not North American history, but, to repeat, I suspect that behind the transition of the "free-born Englishman", the white male property-owner of the Pennsylvania colony, say, to citizen under the new constitution of the United States, was a process of learning, reflected in the advances made by the new system over its Whig model, which seemed to Americans as they re-made themselves, to have failed in the continuation of its aspiration of balancing government power. In the British case itself, I shall suggest that a great deal of learning, negotiation, and compromise underwrote the choreography of the "English" subject. If that learning project ultimately failed, with the temptations of empire and conquest, it could scarcely with equal safety to the public be replaced by that insubstantial and insecure being, the subject of law. So I will argue, differentiating between what, for shorthand purposes I have sometimes called legislation, an abrupt exercise of power; and education, which implies learning, the participation of its subjects.

But we must not – this is Sharpe's message as I read it – allow lawyers to run away with the law. However good their intentions, their model of law can literally court disaster when taken beyond its technical remit. Edmund Burke, with his disdain for abstract and universal concepts – the expression, "the rights of man" was in sights at the time of his writing – in effect divided law as he saw it in the Great Britain of the late eighteenth century, into two. One was the rules and techniques beloved of the "pettifoggers" (a term preceding Burke and not actually used by him). This resembles the model of law about whose efficacy in safeguarding freedom and democracy Sharpe has reservations and I shall say more about it in due course. The putting into effect of such a model of law is useful in the routine administration of commerce and property, the disposition of criminal cases and the like, but, if Burke's conviction of the necessary dispersal of power were to be realized, it would need to be subject to the scrutiny of his other division of legality. Here is the broader, more constitutionally contextualized landscape of changing but socially ordered being. This resembles the recommendations contained in the last part of the quotation from Sharpe. To understand them it is useful to notice Burke's insistence on the importance of the history and changing customs and expectations of particular communities. He considered that, although there had been many changes in the English and, as it became, British underpinnings to constitutional and, based on this, legal practice, a balance still existed and ought to exist, between the various operations of government. Burke was profoundly not democratic, but along with the task of blending continuity with customary expectations of change, he felt that the application of the pettifoggers' rules required mediation by a conscientious regard for the public good. This is an appeal to the possible "grandeur of law", which, he writes, cannot be left to lawyers.

The priority apparently given to "law" here must not, then, be taken to indicate its priority in the argument that follows. Law is an imperatival language practice that subjects learn. And they may reject its presumptions of ultimate authority because those subjects are also speakers of other languages, in the examples I look at, those of empire and those of Englishness. Law is a language which changes and which also brings about change. The danger to which Sharpe alludes is the belief that sovereign authority seems to subvert moral responsibility and diminish the power and purchase of ethical evaluation.

I shall claim no essential nature for any of the practices to which I have adverted, law, the subject and the empire. I have sometimes referred to them as characters, since they appear in an unfolding drama in constant dialog with each other, not reciting a given script, to be sure, but confined at any given moment within certain limitations on what it is possible to say. They each exist, for the book, as interacting, and changing with every interaction, as I shall explain. The thread that joins these shifting identities is, for my purposes,[8] the effort discernible no doubt in many societies and the subjects of them, to establish certainty. The law,

8 And, of course, nobody educated in Anglophone history can miss the irony and the irresistibility of England's having been importantly defined in the enormous Bayeux Tapestry, commissioned in the late eleventh century by a Viking-Norman mere decades after England's conquest by William I. England's wealth lay in wool; its identity would for many years be defined by a woven cloth.

unquestionably in many western conceptions, aims for certainty, albeit with the paradoxical ambition to be open to change in response to changing social circumstances.[9]

Thus, the subject, English, French, Australian, or any other, intends, by this identification, to establish itself as precisely its certain self. Freud, like David Hume before him, and many more before that, deny the subject's capacity to know itself, deny its stability. For practical purposes, it seems that there must be an I who knows. But this involves two assumptions – a knowable subject and a knowable object – both of which, as I shall suggest later, are not entirely secure. Finally, among the topics in my title, empire, the close ally of sovereignty of the strong and meta-legal kind, I shall suggest, is a changeable notion, particularly in its effects, what subjects understand it to be, and what effect it has at different times on who they are and how they consider it appropriate to act. It is worth adding, since "relativism" is a philosophical *bête noir*, that my own observation of a pervasive uncertainty does not imply the circular logic of "everything is uncertain" except the assertion that "everything is uncertain". My refuge from circularity and contradiction is in Hume's disclaimer concerning certainty: "for my part, I do not know".

Having said all that, it is necessary to provide a few initially oversimplifications as entry points into the book. The other quality, aside from certainty, sought by the communities I am concerned with, is order. How may subjects be constituted or reconstituted in such a way as to produce order? In my book, I have noticed two processes of subjectification, the making of subjects. For want of better terms, I have, as I remarked, called them "education" and "legislation". They are not, of course discrete practices, but the writers I look at prefer to emphasize one aspect of subjectification at particular moments as if they were discrete. Some jurists – I notice Jeremy Bentham and John Austin, for example – see order as depending especially on there being in a complex society, a sovereign rule-maker to whom, by subjecting ourselves and becoming law-abiding, we create and maintain a coherent and cohesive community where there would otherwise be insecurity and chaos.

Other, largely not, or not primarily juristic, writers (it is difficult to categorize writers such as the early to mid-nineteenth century writer, administrator and politician, TB Macaulay) prefer to stress the role of acculturation. If the British middle classes lifted their intellectual horizons to embrace loftier aspects of civilization than learning to be good grocers or competent commercial travelers, then according to Matthew Arnold in the later Victorian era, the "brawling" working classes could in turn learn from them about civilized behavior. The wider the right to vote spread, the more the commons seemed likely to have, not merely virtual but actual representation in the House of Commons, the more urgent their

9 See Julius Stone, *Legal System and Lawyers' Reasonings*, Sydney, Maitland Press (1964), ch 8; Julius Stone, *Social Dimensions of Law and Justice*, London, Stevens (1966), ch 14.

education appeared to many Victorian to become. The brawling that Arnold saw as endemic among the working class would cease only after appropriate civic instruction when all could aspire peacefully to "sweetness and light". The midwife at the birth of these new "Englishmen" – the wise middle class exemplar and the dutiful working class pupil – was to be the detached intellectual. But Arnold, like others, imagined a civilized peace in which constructive learning and the existence of a strong state coexist and reinforce each other. I will return to the dangers of this, but also to the potential subversion of the strong state through constructive learning.

Later, I will indicate where I have found the insights of Jacques Lacan and Michel Foucault helpful as figures of the priority of learning. Lacan, in particular, provides, for my purposes, the model of a subject who, as a symbol-using human being, seeks guarantees that will ground the validity of the symbols s/he is using. The order of symbols has many guarantors, none of which exists, but in which, to avert chaos, the subject must place its trust. Second, for Lacan as I shall read him, the subject yearns for a lost belonging, and in this search finds substitutes in a multiplicity of social institutions. Foucault's account of his early work illustrates the overlapping nature of the categories used here, education and legislation and the relations of power and truth, or knowledge. Commentators, especially in the 1980s, focused on Foucault's remarks concerning power, and particularly on his refusal to oppose truth to power – which is usefully summarized in a 1976 lecture: "my problem is this: what rules of right are implemented by the relations of power in the production of discourses of truth?"[10] As Ellen Messer-Davidow *et al* write, for Foucault, "'Truth' is not objective or socially independent, but a system of ordered procedures for the production, regulation, distribution, circulation and operation of statements".[11] Later, Foucault writes that his principal goal has been, not power *per se*, but the creation "of a history of the different modes by which, in our culture, human beings are made subjects".[12] He refers to three heuristic categories: those of "science", which in their many manifestations objectify, say, the speaking, working, or socially changing subjects of linguistics, economics or history. "Dividing practices" distinguish the sick and the healthy, the sane and the insane, "the criminals and the 'good boys'":

> Finally, I have sought to study – it is my current work – the way in which a human being turns him- or herself into a subject. For example, I have chosen

10 Colin Gordon (ed), *Michel Foucault: Power/Knowledge. Selected Interviews and Other Writings 1972–1977*, Brighton, Harvester Press (1980), 93.

11 Ellen Messer-Davidow, David Shumway and David Sylvan, Introduction: Disciplinary Ways of Knowing, in Messer-Davidow *et al* (eds), *Knowledges: Historical and Critical Studies in Disciplinarity*, Charlottesville, VA, University of Virginia Press (1993), 7.

12 Michel Foucault, The Subject and Power, in Hubert Dreyfus and Paul Rabinow (eds), *Michel Foucault: Beyond Structuralism and Hermeneutics*, Brighton, Harvester Press (1986), 208.

> the domain of sexuality – how men have learned to recognize them selves as subjects of "sexuality".[13]

Foucault is drawing attention in this last passage, obviously not to a libertarian heaven in which we can all be whomever we want, but to a more participatory realm in which knowing who I am is clearly confined within the cultural horizons of what is given as a possibility to say and do and be available, but in his example of sexuality, the discursive activity observed is not a production line from which identically unreflective artifacts emerge.

I begin the next section of this chapter with Adam Smith, because as a moral philosopher, legal theorist and, as many believe, the inspiration for the economics of free-market capitalism, he occupies an apparently contradictory site. I have seen the enterprise of empire as something which is gendered as masculine, not because sovereign-emperors are men – imperial sovereignty is, after all an office rather than a person – but because of the codes within which gender normally operates. As will become clear from other writers, the masculine represents the qualities of strength, rationality and autonomy, whilst the qualities of weakness and irrationality, the need of supervision, are coded as effeminate.[14] Toward empire, Smith is a skeptic: order is, for him, not so much a matter of the strong supervising the weak as a learned cultural project of participating agents and agencies. Commerce among those left free to engage in it is, for him more fruitful than global conquest and empire. Trade will, he thought, prosper when the desire for empire abates and, empirically, perhaps, the example of America vindicates his argument. Britain and the United States prospered more vigorously, with some blips, after the war of independence; commerce flourished in ways unpredicted under the later imperial regime. On the other hand, left completely to itself, in Smith's view, commerce would oppress and undermine the conditions of its existence – this much some of his successors learned from his work (one can scarcely fail to interject that his successors on Wall Street and the City in later centuries were not good pupils). There is, then, if we follow him, a fundamental role for a cultural politics in the achievement of order in any society of which he was aware. Hobbes' subject achieves order from potential chaos and meaninglessness only at the cost of conjuring a potential monster which is beyond restraint. Smith's subject sees itself as a more participatory figure in the process of discovering who s/he is and what

13 Foucault, *ibid*, 208.

14 Ian Duncanson, Mr. Hobbes Goes to Australia: Law, Politics and Difference (2000) 13 *International Journal for the Semiotics of Law* 279–303. I have taken gender to be the discourse in which sex, among other phenomena, is mobilized. Masculinity is rationally self-interested and independently motivated. The feminine is irrational, volatile and in need of constant supervision. See Judith Grbich, The Taxpayer's Body: Genealogies of Exertion, in Pheng Cheah, David Fraser and Judith Grbich (eds), *Thinking Through the Body of the Law*, New York, NY, NYU Press (1996); Mrinalina Sinha, *Colonial Masculinity: The "Manly" Englishman and the "Effeminate" Bengali in the Late Nineteenth Century*, Manchester, Manchester University Press (1995).

s/he must do, how s/he arrives at meanings for the social order of which s/he seems to be a part.

Legality as relational and contingent for Adam Smith

Adam Smith's lectures on jurisprudence, theories concerning how law might be understood, delivered at the University of Glasgow in the later eighteenth century, were not published during his lifetime, but reconstructed from student notes and published posthumously. This was not because either Smith or his students considered legality to be an unimportant area of study, nor because they believed law to be insignificant in the regulation of society, but because Smith did not follow the linear, even teleological, methodology adopted by his successors in which law unfolds in the matrices of policy and the protocols of an internal logic of, as one twentieth century jurist put it, "law beyond law". In other words, he did not believe that law could be grasped as an abstract structure, but only, and in this his thought resembled that of Edmund Burke, by reference to particular contexts and specific contents.

Nor was Smith concerned with the technical/professional dimension that would enable a student of law to advise or represent clients. His priorities seem clear. Like many of his fellow-Scots, as we shall see, he adopted a stadial but not a lineal theory of human social development. As a broad generalization, humans were seen to have existed socially as hunter-gatherers – modern historians render this formula as gatherer-hunters, since women in, for example, Australian and many African societies, fed their societies by sophisticated knowledge of the flora, whilst hunting for animal meat was a sporadic and often chancy male activity. People often then, for Smith, became herders, then agriculturalists and finally people of commerce. This was not, in the Scottish analysis, a progressivist or inevitabalist model. Societies did not invariably follow the stadial scheme the Scots identified, in their view. Their conviction here was later borne out by European observations of Australian Aboriginals, who were in contact with the subsistence agriculture of the Torres Straits islanders, and later with the knowledges of the fisher folk from present-day Indonesia, but found their own economy based on superb environmental knowledge more congenial.

Smith's conviction, then, one that he shared with Blackstone and a number of others was that "the rules" lawyers deem essential to their craft do not have an internal logic that can be grasped as one might grasp the workings of a clock, or perhaps in more modern times, a computer program, set to a particular time, or with a particular purpose in mind, and thereafter determined by its design. The career of legality – something we shall return to – has to be seen as contingent, Smith insisted, on economies, politics, histories and social forms. The constitution of law depends – and I have followed the Scots here – upon the logics which these forces develop, hence the reason for noticing the relevance of empire, in my text, in England and, as the polity was to be named after the two Acts of Union, with Scotland in 1707, and with Ireland in 1801, the United Kingdom of Great Britain and Ireland. I return, in this text, to a preoccupation that has informed many of my publications in the past, that "law in context", a slogan and now merely a cliché from the 1960s, is properly not "law and . . .", "Law and History", "Law and Literature" – which are, of course, good enough working titles generated by the law in context movement, as conferences and workshops began, and probably precariously, to inform academic law curricula. But law is best not understood as separate from that from which it proceeds. Conceptually better, if one wants to follow Smith's direction, is rather "law in . . .". This author qualified as a practitioner of law, "learned" from "teachers", on courses about how to be a practitioner. Stupidly, certainly irresponsibly, perhaps even on occasion mendaciously, pretending that the intellectual study of law in isolation was a coherent program with an internal logic, academic law had long lost its way. Of course, the mechanic of social technologies must learn how to wield a spanner or its equivalents – the pettifogger is indispensable. One does not expect a disquisition on legal theory from the conveyancer or tax consultant to whom one consigns one's affairs. But there is more to be said about social technology than technical proficiency.

The danger threatened by a stunted discipline of law – if one wants a practical demonstration other than the overbearing claims to executive sovereignty generated by the "war on terror" mentioned earlier, with its commitment to secret torture and extrajudicial incarcerations[15] – is notorious from the famous "Nuremburg defense", in which the Nazi leaders on trial for war crimes at the end of World War II attempted to absolve themselves of responsibility for their actions on the ground that they were complying with German law as it was according to Nazi promulgations in the period up to 1945.[16] This literalist mindset is clearer still in Arendt's account of the interrogation and trial of Eichmann in Jerusalem. Arendt's title summarizes her conviction: Eichmann's bureaucratic management of the Holocaust was an evil of the most banal kind. Eichmann was not, on her reading, a wicked or evil man. He just did his job without lifting his gaze toward the context or the consequences. Indeed, he apparently was disgusted by his brief encounter with the performance of liquidating people. But he had observed at the infamous Wannsee conference, he said, his superiors' determination to decree that "inferior" peoples should be liquidated. High status civil service, Party, government and military officers were present, most of them far out-ranking *Obersturmbanfuhrer* Adolf Eichmann. To his interrogators in Jerusalem, Eichmann described this as his "Pontius Pilate moment". Who was he, a cog in the machine, to question the direction the juggernaut was taking? Subsequently, he could apply his administrative expertise without the need to examine his conscience or examine the ethical implication of what he was doing. Tony Judt's

15 On the serendipitous nature of the publicity which US tortures in Iraq gained, see *Melbourne Age*, 28 June 2008; on the use of US Navy prison ships and aircraft and their role in delivering terrorist suspects to regimes practicing torture, see *Guardian Weekly*, 6–12 June 2008.

16 Judith Shklar, *Legalism*, Cambridge, MA, Harvard University Press (1964).

suggestion[17] that, in imputing to Eichmann a failure to think, Arendt is accusing him of stupidity, misses the point. Of course, he thought, and of course he was not stupid. What Arendt is drawing attention to is his (and others') willingness to surrender his ability to make moral choices for who knows what reasons – laziness, career opportunities, or the sheer willingness, which is perhaps more common than we would like to believe, to suspend moral judgment when there are others to assume responsibility.

This has been the effect of empire on the conceptualization and management of legality, to a greater or lesser degree, I shall argue. Colonies of quite recent memory, in British Kenya, the former Southern Rhodesia and apartheid-era South Africa, and contemporarily in Israeli-occupied Palestine simply assume the inferior nature of their subjected peoples.[18] To suggest that African black people or Palestinian and Bedouin peoples are denied human rights, is to miss the point. Rather, such peoples were, and in the case of Palestine, are, seldom denied to be human, but are denied equal political membership of the polity in which they live or seek to live. This denial of political equality, enforced by legislative policies and compliant judiciaries, is reflected in the callous disregard for the suffering and death of the oppressed, deemed necessary for successful control and the maintenance of superiority in the "master race". And, of course, it has further ramifications. Israeli soldiers, in one of Makdisi's examples, taunt Arab children with provocations, electronically amplified, in Arabic – "Where are the dogs of Younis . . . Son of a bitch . . . Son of a whore . . . Your mother's cunt" – to bring them within grenade range and then blow them up. Makdisi quotes Chris Hedges, *New York Times* reporter:

> A percussion grenade explodes. The boys, most no more than ten or eleven years old, scatter. The soldiers shoot with silencers. The bullets from M16s tumble end over and through the children's slight bodies. Later in the hospital I see the destruction: stomachs ripped out, gaping holes in limbs and torsos.[19]

The soldiers are doubtless exceeding their brief; but they have learned three things from the regime, as soldiers of colonial, or regimes of occupation often do. One is that since constitutional bureaucracies have little room for ethical niceties when it comes to colonialism or occupation, so, by implication, why should the military? They have learned that the victims were of no political consequence, second; and third that the inconsequential status of the people over whom the

17 Tony Judt, *Reappraisals: Reflections on the Forgotten Twentieth Century*, London, William Heinemann (2008), 78.

18 Saree Makdisi, *Palestine Inside Out: An Everyday Occupation*, New York, NY, WW Norton (2008). At 291, he cites Archbishop Desmond Tutu and other "veteran South African anti-apartheid campaigners" equating the situation in Israeli-occupied Palestine with that in apartheid South Africa.

19 Makdisi, *ibid*, 267.

soldiers have been given power means that there is little that they, or their relatives or other "native" supporters can secure by means of remedy in the dominant legal system by virtue of its unconstrained contempt for them. Of course, dominated peoples do fight back, with suicide bombs and the comparatively light weapons at their disposal. But Arabs had from the first, in 1948, been outgunned and outnumbered by a foe convinced that Jews should have no "inhibitions" about ejecting "a large minority" from their homeland in order to secure the new Jewish state.[20] Their resistance is *ipso facto* illegitimate: *cet animal est mechant: quand on l'attaque, il se defend.*

British legality after the second empire

In the case of the British Empire – an institution, with the United States and France, supportive of Zionist ambitions and against the Palestinian cause from the outset – it has been suggested that brutality was less entrenched once the slave trade and then Caribbean slavery itself were made illegal in the early nineteenth century. British responses to the 1857 Insurrection in India, the hangings of Afro-Caribbeans in Jamaica in 1864 at Morant Bay and General Dyer's firing into a crowd at Jalianwallah Bagh well into the last century, were, on this view isolated instances. Perhaps. There may be a place in which to compare the relative degrees of oppression, the numbers of dead from murder or starvation during Partition in 1947 maybe, the good or bad intentions of the regime of oppression, for example, but this is not that place.

Of course, there were ethical-looking justifications in British imperialist practices for the conquest and government of inferior peoples: the latter required teaching, preferably Christian teaching.[21] But if that was not practicable, as it seldom was in India, then there could be substituted the teaching of how to be as British as possible, the necessary incompleteness of whose accomplishment consigned the native to a reflexive second-rate-ness as efficiently as Christianity, for a time. A character in Vikram Seth's novel, set in post-colonial India, insists that the only place to buy children's toys is Hamley's of London. He admits, after polite questioning, that he has not actually been to London, his capital of the world, but it is his intention to do so soon. During colonialism itself, as Ashis Nandy put it, the colonized's "identification with the aggressor bound the rulers and the ruled in an unbreakable dyadic relationship".[22]

20 Makdisi, *op cit*, n 18, 249, 245.

21 At the 2008 New Worlds, New Sovereignties conference at the University of Melbourne, Gary Foley argued that Christianity had been a worse scourge of indigenous people than smallpox and tuberculosis, also brought to Australia by Europeans.

22 Ashis Nandy, *The Intimate Enemy: Loss and Recovery of Self under Colonialism*, Delhi, Oxford University Press (1983), 7.

These processes coincided with the perception among Britain's rulers that British greatness and pre-eminence in the world depended on its empire. Threats to commercial, industrial and military pre-eminence from without, from Germany, the United States and Japan, and from within, from the working class and from women, could be resisted, from a governing perspective, only with firm discipline applied through firm rules. And firm rules required teaching, first of those who were to apply them, and second, of those to whom they were to apply.

In a reversal of Adam Smith, historical and anthropological concerns about how societies might be conceived to have developed, or about how and why different societies developed differently, as well as sociological inquiries anent contemporary social order "at home" were subordinated to the prescriptive needs of social ordering and the production, in maintaining social order of, precisely, subordination for the "good of the subject" – the passivity of employees in industrial relations, or security from foreign threats, for example – where this comports with the good of the dominant. This always has sinister implications and, to a significant degree, we are still subject to this pattern of thought. One has only to think of the prescriptive work which "development" does in the international sphere.[23]

Teaching, which is not the same thing as education, is indispensable in this context, law-like and rule-heavy as it is. Thus FR Leavis makes the distinction between the indispensable instructor and the academic abundantly clear:

> My aversion from the word "teach" preceded – it was only intensified by – my acquaintance with those American "notes on contributors" that tell one that X, Y or Z "teaches" Joyce or Thomas Mann or Faulkner or the Cantos at this or that college or university. If one's concern is with literature one doesn't think of oneself as "teaching". One thinks of oneself as engaged with one's students in the business of criticism – which, of its nature, is collaborative. The student on his part, ought to be able to think of himself as belonging to a collaborative community formed by the English school as a whole, undergraduates, graduate students and permanencies, and the more, let me parenthetically add, he can feel it transcends departmental frontiers the better . . .[24]

An historiography for a relational and contextual legality

In the footsteps of Smith, to some extent, Leavis, and others, the book that follows is contextual and historiographical in intention. I have tried to minimize references in this chapter, since many of the propositions made here will be encountered more fully later. The text sees the narratives we tell about ourselves, ours' and others'

23 Jennifer Beard, *The Political Economy of Desire*, London, Cavendish (2007).

24 FR Leavis, *Nor Shall My Sword Sleep in My Hand: Discourses on Pluralism, Compassion and Social Hope*, London, Chatto and Windus (1972), 108–9.

pasts, as inevitably informing not only an understanding *of* the world, but justifying certain actions and disapproving other actions *in* the world. This is a proposition that may seem obvious enough, but is, equally, overlooked sufficiently often in scholarly practice to need restating.[25] Does my emphasis on the performative work always done by conceptual activity put me in opposition to Marx's diagnosis of the inadequacy of how *he* considered philosophical scholars saw the purpose of their writing at the time of his own analyses: "the philosophers have only *interpreted* the world in various ways: the point is to *change* it"?[26] I am unsure. Perhaps, and this seems likely, it is only Feurbach's conception of his own role as a philosopher that Marx has in mind, since there is little doubt that historians, philosophers and theorists of every stripe have always had profound, if often indirect influence on social action, quite apart from the "think-tank" mercenaries nowadays hired to serve the "policy" interests of pressure groups and governments by telling them what they wish to hear.[27]

As the theme of the book implies, to repeat, I intend it to be a sign for the interaction of legality, as understood, at least, by English, but not only English common law at various times, but of the English subject as it evolved as, naturally, among other things, a subject of law, but also, and this is an important third segment, a process in which s/he is a subject involved and changed by empire. None of these dimensions of the subject, all of them, of course political, or the areas studied here can be understood separately. But I have taken the subject as such as a pivotal concept. Plainly one cannot imagine a single subjectivity in a political or social formation, but one can discover a range of positions offered to a person to act out his or her performance. This is not, as will become clear, akin to the sociological notion of *role,* in which the already-subject assumes many personae, as mother, daughter, lawyer, etc. I am assuming that there *is* no subject prior to the adoption of available languages; without that, there cannot be a subject who speaks, knows, etc.

When I turn to law, I focus mainly on English law, more particularly where it speaks of sovereignty in the context of political theory; on the English subject; and on the British Empire. I am following Edmund Burke's adjuration that one be specific, something I have adverted to and shall return to. How, for example, Burke asks in his criticism of the French Declaration of the Rights of Man and Citizen,[28]

25 Keith Jenkins, *Re-Thinking History*, London, Routledge (1991) summarizes the malleability of historical thought. Leavis, *ibid*, ch IV. Leavis was a firm believer in the performativity of scholarly work, seeing the role of the academic critic as collaborative between lecturer and student, and perspectival and changing in relation to the canon and how its context might be seen. See also Anne Samson, *FR Leavis*, Toronto, University of Toronto Press (1992), ch 4.

26 Karl Marx, Thesis Eleven, Concerning Feurbach, in Lucio Colleti (ed), *Karl Marx: Early Writings*, Harmondsworth, Penguin (1975), 423.

27 Peter Osborne, *The Triumph of the Political Class*, London, Simon and Schuster (2007).

28 The term "man" only sometimes prior to the late nineteenth century signifies both men and women, and certainly governed the meaning of "citizen", as women who claimed equality in revolutionary France discovered to their cost.

can one understand the nature of a subject as simply "a man"? It was a question which seems to have quite surprised Agamben two centuries later.[29] How could a mere Irish Whig have thought so profoundly? Burke was echoed almost a century and a half later by Hannah Arendt. One, of course, she insists, needs more specificity than the airy category of the human. The abstract human has no polity, even, as a colonial subject, a place in an oppositional polity. S/he, one might say, is not constituted politically. The slave and the woman in classical Athenian society were not principally sources of cheap labor, but rather regarded as human animals because they were not part of the city other than in the physical sense.

I have already struck a number of theoretical reefs: the English subject, English common law, the British Empire. Without at this stage encountering the Welsh or, more manifest, the Irish questions, it is evident that the United Kingdom is not a nation. Even "being British is not an ethnicity, it describes citizenship . . . cooked up by James (VI/I) . . . invented as a cultural identity corresponding to the political identity, British, only fairly recently".[30] Young finds "Britishness" emerging only in 1884, and Englishness to be, as I shall describe, a largely Scottish invention, and in post-eighteenth century usage to be used largely to describe absence and diaspora, as in Rupert Brooke's poem, where England is conjured only to refer, significantly, to burial in some "foreign field" which is as a consequence, "forever England".[31] Defoe is more trenchant and satirical about any pretense of purity or an essential English nature. He lists the multi-ethnic invasions from Roman times to his own and concludes, "A true-born Englishman's a contradiction/ In speech an irony, in fact a fiction".[32] Scotland abandoned its Parliament for nearly three centuries, but retained its Kirk and its law, and still played a large role, as mentioned, in maintaining both the English subject as it was reconstructed after the ravages of the UK/dis-UK civil war of the seventeenth century, and the balanced constitution upon which English law rested. Britain, as it becomes in 1707, in an act putting to an end the ambiguity of the dual monarchy which was an empire of Britain only in Stuart monarchy fantasies of the nature of the two countries they governed. It was essential for Scotland to be part of a British union and equally essential for the English continually to be reminded of the secrets of stability, liberty and safety of property on to which they had stumbled.

29 Giorgio Agamben, *Homo Sacer: Sovereign Power and Bare Life*, Palo Alto, CA, Stanford University Press (1998), 127.

30 Robert JC Young, *The Idea of English Ethnicity*, Oxford, Blackwell (2008), 11.

31 Rupert Brooke's War Sonnet, The Soldier, begins, "If I should die, think only this of me:/That there's some corner of a foreign field/That is forever England. There shall be/In that rich earth a richer dust concealed.

32 Daniel Defoe, The True-born Englishman, in PN Furbanks and WR Owens (eds), *The True-born Englishman and Other Essays*, London, Penguin (1997), 34, 35.

Mapping the nature of law

The second reef is the concept of law, which, as I shall say later in this chapter and again later in the book, is not stable, not merely as to substance – what it contains, whether a contract requires consideration, or a contract for future exchanges, for example, is enforceable. It was unstable over time as to its very nature. It was the outcome of custom at many levels and types of jurisdiction, varying with the relative powers of the parties composing the jurisdiction. It was certainly not the preordained outcome of centralized rationality, as some textbooks would have it and its tessellated structure remains now in the mass of tribunals, delegated systems and discretions of modern officials whose authority is often shrouded in mystery, even from themselves. Overlooking this, and forgetting their own past was, for European colonizers, quite convenient. If "non-primitive" law had certain invariable characteristics which, according to nineteenth and twentieth century legal theorists, it did, as we shall see in the writing of HLA Hart, it was easy to portray societies without particular organs with which Europeans considered themselves governed by, and had, by the early modern period become familiar, to change or implement law – legislators, professional judiciaries, "rational" bureaucracies, for example – as "simply" not possessing law and thus in need of European tutelage in order to develop, modernize and to be capable of governing themselves.

Third, in my discussion of the subject, I appreciate that I run the risk of being labeled essentialist or even determinist. I have, as I suggested, taken the subject to be a civic or political being, more than an animal that works and breeds; and the more intensely s/he is a participant in the tribe, city or state s/he inhabits, the more intense that civic or political subjectivity seems to me to be, and the further we move from the bare, or abstract, human toward the performance of something more concrete. Participation, as I have suggested, may take the form of resistance, as in the example of Sinn Fein or the other colonial resistance movements. As to essentialism, I have drawn, admittedly freely, on the writings of Foucault and Lacan to explain how we might understand how the neonate becomes a communicative social and potentially political being. At one level, of course, there is always some room within the symbolic order for reflexive change, or simply misconception. If there is a Lacan who both belongs but also "sees" the symbolic order in a certain way, then there seems implied some flexibility in "the" symbolic order(s). We are not confronted with Althusser's mechanism of interpellation, where the "Hey, you" of the Ideological State Apparatus determines the human as an entirely involuntary subject-bearer of the social order.[33]

33 Louis Althusser, *Lenin, Philosophy and Other Essays*, London, Verso (1971).

The mirror of the developmental gaze and its Lacanian theorization

I have for the most part assumed Lacan's structure, for the sake of argument, but not the almost functionalist version which apparently attracted Althusser to Lacan's work. There are delusional – from points of view generally deemed normal – orders inhabited by untreated paranoiacs or psychotics, but most subjectivity is derived from something Lacan would regard as more than a consciously-adopted convention. Belonging to a symbolic order, an order of language, is enabling, not imprisoning; but I want to leave open the possibility that there does exist a consciousness of ambiguity, a "psychic distance", as Ellie Ragland-Sullivan puts it[34] and alternative pathways of enablement.

Since the subject occupies a central position in the book as the subject of various social artifacts, law, political community and empire, it is worth saying something more at the beginning about how I am to approach the idea of its dynamics, how I am going to make use of Lacan. David Hume, the eighteenth century Scottish philosopher, considering the problem of social order at the very beginning of empire and in the shadow of the near-disintegration of order both in Europe and in Britain and Ireland, observed that the key to its understanding was opinion: the governed many believed that the governing few possessed the legitimacy to do so. They understood themselves to be subjects of a particular kind – subordinates. It was not, as Hume saw it, a one-way traffic, governors to governed, as his image of the rowers of a boat indicates. The person at the helm, the people at the oars and, perhaps, the person shouting directions and keeping the rhythm, see themselves as conducting a mutual and necessary enterprise. He attributed this, not to a deliberate contract, but to something less reflexively available, though not completely unavailable, to consciousness, to conventions, in other words, of which the subject may not be fully aware.

Roughly two centuries after Hume, Jacques Lacan explained this "convention" in psycho-analytic terms, from which a number of insights can be drawn, shedding both light and shadows on the related issues of my thesis, what can be known, and the limits of knowledge about law, the English subject and empire, and about the impossible necessity of certainty. The following is not an exposition of Lacanian theory, merely a borrowing of some ideas. In particular, Lacan explicitly denies a connection with developmental psychology. Nevertheless, his subject seems to exist in three overlapping phases, albeit phases that can be grasped only retrospectively once it has entered Lacan's world of the Symbolic, the world, that is to say, of a culture, of language in which s/he can articulate an apparent past and of a certain perceived future necessity for acting in one way rather than another. The phases explore social ordering more fully than Hume's gestural "convention".

34 Ellie Ragland-Sullivan, *Jacques Lacan and the Philosophy of Psychoanalysis*, Urbana, IL, University of Illinois Press (1987), 40.

As a neonate, the subject exists in a state of unity with its world, not distinguishing itself from its carer, generally the mother, and the source of its nurture, generally the breast and the hands and voice, from all of which a recollected security seems to have projected the subject onward. The significance of this which, for the psyche, can be only a memory recalled from a time when it is capable of articulating its past in thought, is the haunting moment of blissful oneness, of harmony, of a tranquil being-in-the-world which forever eludes the bearer of language, but nevertheless exists like myths of Shangri-La. The past is, indeed, as mythical as it is elusive since, as observations of nursing mothers indicate, the relationship is not free of authority and control, they are simply not remembered.[35] Red-faced tantrums of externally and internally imposed helplessness surface censored into adult humiliation for perceived failure to conform.

Nostalgia for lost belonging and acceptance is extremely powerful. It can never be recovered, not simply because it exists in its desired form only as a memory trace, but because it is inconsistent with the second memory trace to which Lacan draws attention – the mirror stage, which, as we shall see, seems to the subject to demand, not an organic unity, but inevitable separateness from others. The substitutes for uncomplicated belonging interrupt the atavistic urge or nostalgia for one-ness can be, as one might expect, positive and negative in social terms. For the subject, they mercifully and usually inevitably interrupt what would otherwise be a degenerative psychic passage to an early infantile perception and response to the world it inhabits. We can understand them in Lacan's terms as the *objets petits a*, little others which act to ameliorate the unbearable separation to which I refer in the next paragraph. Religion can temporarily comfort me with the thought that I am already one with the world, or that I shall be made at one and forever in the realm of an Almighty, free at last from the cursed separateness that explained the necessity for Hobbes' sovereign.

The appeal of Tolkien's *The Lord of the Rings*[36] is surely in the end the Elves. The hobbits fail to shield themselves from worldly conflict, and at the end of the trilogy are destined to fade. The dwarves for the most part perish, albeit heroically. By the end it is men who inherit a world of perpetual conflict in the shadow of a defeated but ever-threatening, evil. Immortal, the wood elves still in Middle Earth long for Elvenhome, to which they will, in the end, migrate forever: to "the distant realm beyond the Western Seas", hymning meanwhile the High Elves already in the west: "O Elbereth Gilthoniel!/We still remember, we who dwell/In this far land beneath the trees/Thy starlight on the Western Seas". But, unlike the heavens of the religions of redemption, the peaceful sanctuary of Elvenhome exists for the creatures of Middle Earth as a memory trace for those who remember the departure of the Elves and those who hear the stories and lament, elegiac.

35 I am grateful to Judith Grbich for this suggestion.

36 JRR Tolkien, *The Lord of the Rings*, 3 vols, London, Allen and Unwin (1954–5).

Sociability can be thus explained, elegiacally or in its more mundane manifestation of seeking at least a belief in a place of belonging; membership of the Party, the trade union, the race, the nation, academic collegiality for example. Theweleit studied a more sinister fantasy of loss, that of the soldiers of the German Freikorps, formed from defeated members of the Kaiser's army, on the surface of things, at least, to fight communism. The men were fiercely misogynistic. The figure of the mother, that once lost one-ness, now appeared threateningly powerful. The woman endangered the *bruderbund*, she was a fantasized communist woman, perhaps drawn from a mythologized Rosa Luxemburg, a Polish-German Bolshevik murdered, presumably by anti-communists, in 1919. Having lost their identification with the once-powerful army of the Kaiser, the only camaraderie acceptable to the Freikorps soldier was the remnants, the beerhall guardians of a purer *Reich*. The Weimar Republic, the government formed following the abdication of the Kaiser, became the effete, womanly enemy of manly courage.[37]

But sociability, I suggested, comes also from a different and contradictory direction. In 1936 and in a 1949 revision, Lacan writes of a subsequent aspect of the subject's, experience, equally with effects that transcend the instant, and this time it is a matter of an insecure self-consciousness which, Lacan remarks, non-human primates, whilst in other respects precocious by comparison with humans, do not have. A baby chimpanzee, seeing its reflection, initially regards it as another chimpanzee, but, finding it to be, presumably odorless and two-dimensional, loses interest. Lacan is writing of the "mirror phase formative of the *I* function".[38] Here, the human infant first learns to be an "I", but again, the process literally *impresses* itself, leaving only traces in the subsequent unconscious, with implications for the consciousness of the speaking "I". Whether literally in a mirror, or in the gaze of a carer, the child, from six to eighteen months on, identifies itself as something which it is not, namely a complete, competent and discrete individual. Lacan uses the metaphor, among others in relation to this individual, of a fortified camp, its walls serving as a separation from an outside and, at the same time, as a symptom of the fear of invasion and loss. At the same time as realizing his or her distinctiveness, s/he emerges from the organic connection with the world. At the same time, this independence, a source, so Lacan says, of initial "jubilation", is actually dependent on the other.

37 Klaus Theweleit, *Male Fantasies*, 2 vols, Cambridge, Polity Press (1977–78).

38 Jacques Lacan, *Ecrits*, New York, NY, Norton (2006), 94; Ragland-Sullivan, *op cit*, n 34, ch 1. This is a tricky area. Animals reared or in constant contact with another species seem to adapt to the characteristics of other species. And I recall as a boy seeing sheep at St Mary's Loch in Scotland, aggressively muscling into tourist picnics to steal sandwiches (and their paper wrappings). An un-sheep-like behavior learned from and reinforced by, the consequent traditional sheep-like behavior of the tourists – to run away! The difference, for Lacan, would be the failure of sheep to incorporate this learning unconsciously into the psyche of a speaking subject.

Once more, the importance is less to catalog the migration of tiny person to toddler to full-size person than to try to explain the effects which the traces of these inaccessible experiences have on the adult symbol-using subject. For Roudinesco,[39] it is this vision – that the theorist Henri Wallon termed the Imaginary – that made possible the illusion that the subject was whole and coherent, to the subject, whilst separate in relation to others. Hume had never doubted the illusory, although undoubtedly necessary nature of this conviction of the discrete wholeness, intellectually and physically, of the subject, whose sanity nevertheless depended on sociability. And we shall see the importance in Smith's account of how morality is possible. For him, it is the spectator who explains to us by means of approval or disapproval of our actions and thoughts what it is appropriate to do. To begin with the spectator is external, like Lacan's mirror, or, more likely, a carer's gaze. Later the spectator is internalized – and this is, of course, from Smith, too – I disapprove of my own possibly cruel thoughts about someone who has slighted me, without an external observer being aware of them.

In Lacan, who, Roudinesco writes, never mentions the earlier writings of Wallon, it is the Imaginary phase, the world in which identity relies on Smith's spectator, with its reliance on there being an Other, which draws the subject into the Symbolic. This is the world of language culture, a world that always precedes the subject. There is no sense in which the culture to which the subject must belong in order to speak is monolithic, but if s/he is to obtain from it the necessary reassurance of his/her authenticity, then it must itself seem to her/him to have an authenticity that transcends, or is beyond or above the subject. This is not Lacanian language, but it seems to me that the subject imputes to the social world of symbol-using others a reality guaranteed by a higher level of reality which cannot actually be there. We shall return to this in the form of an ever-present desire for certainty which is always lacking. Incomplete, the subject seeks reassurance from something which s/he has to believe does not itself require reassurance. This is the Big Other of Lacan, or at least of Zizek's Lacan.

I mentioned Hume's picture of the world as, so far as he could tell, unknowable beyond the fictions necessary to negotiate the everyday, fictions that might well be disappointed in their efficacy. He included himself in that welter of uncertainty and anticipated only modest insights into himself. The psychoanalytic tradition to which I have made brief reference offers more theoretically organized reasons for suggesting a puzzling, tumultuous self and some social conclusions are possible. The traces I noticed, the yearning for organic belonging that cannot be realized and the role of the gazer – the mirror image or the carer's gaze mean that for there to be one there must be at least one other. These traces can only be partially perceived in the world of symbols into which the subject enters, because they operate at a

39 Elisabeth Roudinesco, The Mirror Stage: An Obliterated Archive, in Jean-Michel Rabate (ed), *The Cambridge Companion to Lacan*, Cambridge, Cambridge University Press (2003). I am indebted to Judith Grbich for this reference.

level different from production made possible by the fantasy of the whole and the reflection. But wholeness and coherence are the only, albeit shaky, often shaken, perceptual apparatus s/he has consciously available. These considerations alone imply a subject which is fissured and not present to itself. There is a third consideration and this is the manner, or the condition of the subject's belonging to the world of symbol users. It is equally a fantasy if its identity is ultimately guaranteed by the Big Other, something whose desire one wishes to have in order to anchor one's own, but which, if its existence is unspecifiable, must repress all but inferably acceptable identities. The Big Other, which guarantees the truth of the Symbolic Order, cannot itself be guaranteed. In the strictly non-Lacanian, strictly political terms of Whig or Jeffersonian politics, it is where a social order has given government to itself – the other is, so far as possible, oneself. It is this that requires exploration and upon this that liberty depends. And, of course, for this reason, it is what is most denied and distorted.

For Freud, as for Lacan, the split is not a conscious dilemma, resolvable, if only uncomfortably so, such as the one depicted in Kazuo Ishiguro's novel, where Slater, the butler in a between-the-wars country house, must choose whether to remain at the bedside of his dying father, or supervise the smooth running of an important conference his employer has organized at the house.[40] Slater abandons his father and takes care of the household, explaining his conduct to himself with the thought that this is what father would have wished him to do. Rather, the subject does not know him-/herself or the world, and what it is s/he should do to be at home in the world. This insecurity, or series of them, imposes a sort of police censor over the longings we have observed and, as Freud put it, this unconscious evades what represses it without the knowledge of the conscious subject in the guise of "symptoms, jokes, paraparaxes, dreams etc".[41] The symptoms in the "hysterics" of Freud's early work – strange fears or phobias, or paralyses with no physical cause – were, he became convinced, like the symbolic language of dreams, a distorted memory of something remembered, but which the conscious subject wished to repress. The task of the analyst is not to restore the analysand to a *reality*, which Lacan in any event considered not to exist, the subject belonging to a symbolic order for which no objective foundation existed, but to help to unravel the symbolic structure which produces the suffering.

It is not my intention in what follows continuously to refer historical events, decisions, intentions or effects to a psychoanalytic model of explanation as though that were a key to unlock the secrets or unravel otherwise hidden truths. The point of the foregoing is to argue that these are necessarily hidden or only partly revealed, they cannot act like a motor manual to explain the mechanisms hidden under the bonnet of a motor car or a computer hard drive. Some tendencies manifest themselves under prompting from the mysteries they confront, and some

40 Kazuo Ishiguro, *The Remains of the Day*, London, Faber and Faber (1989).

41 Dylan Evans, *Dictionary of Lacanian Psychoanalysis*, London, Routledge (1996), 218.

seem to me more benign than others. A nostalgia for a golden age of completeness in the empire of Rome, as its mythology was passed down, motivated assured political arrangements that we would learn later were unsustainable in a different era. The legions and the bureaucracy that went with them, not merely provided security, but underwrote a money economy through wages, the spending of them, and payments for bureaucrats and armaments that in a later age was impossible to organize, impossible to recognize.

But empire retained a misty ambivalence, a mythology of liberty beneath an ultimate appeal to force and authoritarianism until the 1860s, with Lord Palmerston's dispatch of a gunboat to Piraeus with the argument that, just as a Roman citizen could summon the might of empire with the utterance *civis Romanus sum*, so should a British Empire subject be able to summon the Royal Navy to the defense of his freedoms (and the oppression, in this case, of Greeks) with the invocation, *civis Britannicus sum.* And of course, much is correctly made of the current cynical profiteering made by US corporations close to the White House under the guise of whatever lies lie to hand.[42] But the process would not be convincing without the need to bolster an empire that, like Rome's *Senatus Populus qua Romanus*, insists that freedom needs to be firmly imposed if it is to make the imposer secure. In a secular and multipolar religious world, "God bless America" has limited resonance, which is why there have to be invasions, military bases, fleets and military posturings world-wide.[43]

In the years of empire's post-medieval occlusion, at least in Christendom, Absolute monarchy seemed to provide a certainty under God that was unobtainable otherwise. But if law could not be grounded in this way, then later theorists of nation or empire would find a home for it, they would render its somewhat *outré* claims, as Freud would say, *Heimlich* in the household of the sovereign of secular provenance, the sovereign of the Enlightenment. It is not within my remit to consider the European Enlightenment, except to notice in due course its unintended and perhaps shortlived – depending on whom one reads – difference from the Anglophone enlightenment, and this is where I have made my distinction between education and legislation. Learning how to be a reciprocally recognizing citizen, to effect a Jeffersonian "agreement of the people", giving government to each other, as the gentlemen and aristocracy of the English Convention of 1688 attempted, is exclusionary. The Convention of 1688 and the Declaration of 1776 launched states of extraordinary external rapacity. One looks, not for the certainty of virtue, but for the promise of a sovereign which is a cultural learning-to-be with an ethical potential, the potential, in particular, to accept the failure to ground, the failure to achieve closure and certainty.

42 See the BBC Panorama documentary on the topic re-broadcast on the Australian Broadcasting Corporation's Four Corners, 30 June 2008.

43 See, on the political trajectory which many attribute to the contemporary United States, Chalmers Johnson, *The Sorrows of Empire: Militarism, Secrets, and the End of the Republic*, London, Verso (2004).

Statecraft and historical schemas

Under the influence of the myth of an eternal quintessence of England – a rural place so important to soldiers in the Great War who had actually seldom been outside their cities – rural fantasies familiar to readers of Orwell and so influential in the sedative rhetoric of Prime Minister Stanley Baldwin in the inter-war years, England seems self-originating. Few of Baldwin's listeners would have known what a hay wain at dusk or a corn-crake at dawn were, and fewer still, of urban, often slum-dwellers would have played cricket on a village green – all continually evoked by Baldwin. Perhaps, in our own era the films of Merchant Ivory return us to this magical place, to which we have never actually been, and which probably did not exist.[44] What makes England Great Britain, in the opinion of Kazuo Ishiguro's protagonist, the butler, Stevens, is the avoidance of "unseemly demonstrativeness" in its rural landscapes, rolling dales and gentle slopes, as opposed to the wild rivers and spectacular peaks in foreign lands which he has seen only in photographs. In a similar way, English dignity emerges in the novel's fireside chats between butlers about one, unnamed, butler who, on finding a tiger beneath the dining room table in his employer's country house, goes to the drawing room, attracting the employer's attention from the company he is entertaining with a discreet cough, explains his discovery and suggests the use of a twelve-bore. Three shots are heard by the guests below and dinner proceeds on time without further inconvenience.[45] Stevens, like the imagined colonial subject, takes comfort amid loss from the solidity which the gentlemanly hub of essential Englishness seems to provide.

At an important level, the novel is perhaps about genteelly-concealed resentment and subliminally-coerced "dignity". But Stevens abandons independent judgment, and ceases to be much more than the impression made into a malleable substance by his masters. The novel exemplifies, in the hierarchies of the subordinated – man- and maidservants – the emulation of the various masters, what inspired the Subaltern Studies enterprise, for whom Indian nationalism as represented by Nehru and Gandhi and the public school, Oxford and London bar educated Congress Party cadres are little more than local replacements for colonial rule.[46] Always silent in Ishiguro's novel is Edward Said's well-known argument that it is the subordinated who make the Other possible. In Simon Gikandi's words, "Margins, boundaries, and peripheries are not muted places in which the dominated act out their resentment or even resistance; on the contrary, they are key

44 Peter Mandler, Against "Englishness": English Culture and the Limits to Rural Nostalgia (1997) 7 *Transactions of the Royal Historical Society* 6th Ser 155–75.

45 Ishiguro, *op cit*, n 40, 29, 37.

46 There is a summary of this position in Ranajit Guha, On Some Aspects of the Historiography of Colonial India, in Vinayak Chaturvedi (ed), *Mapping Subaltern Studies and the Postcolonial*, London, Verso (2000).

ingredients in the making of the implosive center itself."[47] The household of *Remains* depends upon the abjectness of Stevens and his choreography of the movement of the household staff, and who witnesses anti-Semitism and listens with impassivity to the fatuous praise of fascist virtues by his master and guests. Over the text's horizon, just postulated as over the horizon for Subaltern Studies, lies, not utopia, but the possibility of both impending horror and grassroots empowerment, the first generated by Hitler and threatened by his naïve British supporters like Slater's employer and his friends, the second a possibility of power for the people, which never really eventuated either under Nehru or the leaders of former African colonies, or under Clement Attlee after the landslide postwar Labour victory, which promised, and failed to deliver, an end to plutocracy in the United Kingdom.

In attempting to provide an historical and social context in which to understand the common law, an historical phenomenon *par excellence*, I have to a degree followed the fairly conventional narrative of English history familiar from writers like Perry Anderson.[48] As with Europe more widely for the most part, the "parcelized sovereignty" of the medieval period up to the fifteenth century was superseded by more centralized monarchies claiming exclusive ultimate sovereignty for themselves. The difference in emphasis that Anderson detects in England is the particularly precocious, post-Conquest (1066) demand from William I that the subject's loyalty to his king was always prior to that due to his immediate liege-lord – this, at least in formal terms put an end to the – to modern eyes – strange jurisdictional situation familiar enough in the Europe of the time generally, in which a landlord might claim that his tenant, a mounted knight or a foot-soldier, was bound by his allegiance to his lord, to oppose the monarch, the landlord's own lord, at the landlord's command.

In addition, paradoxically, whether by cause and effect or not, Anderson finds in England a gradually greater and earlier degree of civilian and commercial preoccupations among at least the lesser nobility, than was the case in mainland Europe. If this seems at odds with school history we learned of the almost continual warfare and turmoil which seemed to characterize relations between England and France, in particular the Hundred Years' War, we perhaps need a reminder both that feudal monarchy was not a national enterprise. And that, since the Hundred Years' War was conducted on French soil, the lesser nobility in England might well focus on matters detached from the interests of a king whose territories happened to include England. England's rulers seldom understood the

47 Simon Gikandi, *Mapping Englishness: Writing Identity in the Culture of Colonialism*, New York, NY, Columbia University Press (1996), 37.

48 Perry Anderson, *Lineages of the Absolutist State*, London, New Left Books (1974). See also John Martin, *Feudalism to Capitalism: Peasant and Landlord in English Agrarian Development*, London, Macmillan (1983); John Holton, *The Transition from Feudalism to Capitalism*, London, Macmillan (1984).

vernacular of those whom they ruled. As Norman Davies has pointed out,[49] the HMSO guide to English and later British monarchy[50] has only a certain plausibility. Early post-Conquest "English" dynasties communicated with their officials by writ in medieval Latin; they spoke a form of French, and understandably, perhaps, preferred to live in Bordeaux or Languedoc than in London – hence the demand from English-based "freemen" in Magna Carta, 1215, that litigation that required the Crown's participation be given "some certain place" in England, a court of Common Pleas to hear causes in lieu of the normal absence of the monarch.

The patriotic English lines put by Shakespeare into Henry V's mouth, which every English schoolchild learns:

> Once more into the breach, dear friends, once more
> Or close the wall up with our English dead
> . . . the game's afoot:
> Follow your spirit and upon this charge
> Cry "God for Harry, England and Saint George!"[51]

were attributed to a culturally French man born in Monmouth, Wales, a country not formally assimilated to England until the reign of Henry VIII, married to a French queen, and who died in Vincennes, France. But whilst "Plantagenet England . . . was little more than an outpost of French civilization",[52] the Tudor dynasty, of whom Henry IV was the first, did begin an England that was in many respects no longer primarily continental European. There was prior to this point no English subject, merely a European dynasty and its retainers, Europe-oriented merchants, and mostly locally-oriented subsistence cultivators living in apparently unchanging rhythm of the seasons and the tasks ordained by them.

Norman I (the Conqueror, or the Bastard, as some preferred, since he was technically illegitimate) was ancestrally a Viking whose forebears had settled in Normandy, and who owed nominal fealty to their French overlord, which may explain *his* motive in attempting to tie his English subjects to himself above their old customary, perhaps primary, allegiances to their landlords. By virtue of 1066, Anglo-Saxon lands became an India, lands occupied by foreign-based rulers for purposes of their own. And, as with British India, the trajectory, certainly the ambition, of the post-Conquest monarchy tended toward the form of sovereignty that was later, in European context, known as Absolutism. It was not an entirely effective tendency, since by the twelfth century, royal courts often relied on juries

49 Norman Davies, *The Isles: A History*, Oxford, Oxford University Press (1999).

50 Department of the Environment, *Kings and Queens of England*, London, Her Majesty's Stationery Office (1967).

51 William Shakespeare, Henry V, Act III, sc ii.

52 Davies, *op cit*, n 49, 423.

who could be selected by the sheriff of the county on the basis of which litigant bribed him the most.[53]

The apotheosis of this absolutist ambition in England, what I have called the "strong" model of sovereignty under the Stuarts, originated in a recognizably early modern form with the Tudors which existed before and after the defeat and death of Richard of York at Bosworth Field in 1485, but whose foundations began slowly to crumble. If Henry VIII represented kingly office as above the law, he nonetheless found it prudent to implement his most controversial laws through Parliament. The doctrine of royal Absolutism, above the law, was articulated most clearly in the writings of the nominee to the throne of the last Tudor, Elizabeth I, of her successor, the Scottish Stuart, James VI/I in 1603. In Scotland, the Stuarts had been dogged, by convictions from as far back as Duns Scotus (1265–1308), by a conviction that Scottish kings were *primus inter pares*, with their subjects. This post-Tudor James sought primacy in England and Scotland.

In his reign, most clearly, the legitimacy of law and government was seen in the formal terms, now familiar from our modern-day legal positivists – what was of interest in was the *source* of promulgations, not their *substance*, still less their acceptability. Incipient Absolutism, toyed with by James VI/I and his son, was arrested by the brief republican experiment of the mid-seventeenth century and brought to a more conclusive end with the 1688 revolution.[54] The seventeenth century was a period of experiment and struggle, retrospectively viewed with some horror. David Hume, as we shall see, summed up the imbrication of religion and politics, which explains both the continuing ruling classes' hostility to Catholicism and the diffidence in mainstream circles toward dissenters. "Enthusiasm", necessary to combat "superstition" (i.e. as Hume understands it, Catholicism) and safeguard property and liberty, was, after it had done its work, possibly dangerous in its multiple certainties, intolerances, and consequent internecine schisms, to political stability. The medium-sized commerce everywhere made possible by dissenting merchants, and the writing and academic work, often connecting with the definitely non-Church of England Scottish universities in the eighteenth century belied this danger, but it seems to have been a necessary myth.

It is difficult to understand sufficiently the position of law in the post-revolutionary period, I argue, without noticing that the whole apparatus of legality rested, not on a sovereign, but on something called the constitution, something so deeply a cultural product and so deliberately vague as to provoke Paine to insist at the end of the eighteenth century, that no such beast as a British constitution existed. Latitudinarianism pervaded politics and an ideologically relaxed Church

53 See, for example, the complaints aired in Paston, *The Paston Letters*, 2 vols, London, Dent (1924). See also HS Bennett, *The Pastons and Their England* (1922), Cambridge, Cambridge University Press (1970), chs I and XII on bribery and the law.

54 See John Miller, Crown, Parliament and People, in JR Jones (ed), *Liberty Secured? Britain before and After 1688*, Palo Alto, CA, Stanford University Press (1992).

of England, and permitted even the poor and unenfranchised a voice.[55] Established religion had a political face, as many historians have noticed.

The time before and after exceptionalism in statecraft

But the strength and weakness of constitutional doctrine lay, I argue, on its resting in turn on the production of an English subject – at least of the political classes, although many would say that its reach was greater – that was mannered, polite and more inclined to compromise rather than confront in the event of disagreement. This production was not solely, or even mostly, the work of the English, but of protestant Irishmen such as Hutcheson and Burke, and Scots such as Hume, Ferguson and Smith, who shared with the earlier English writers, Locke and Shaftesbury, as we shall see, an hostility to dogmatism in the wake of the disturbances of the seventeenth century. Some writers have seen the epitome of *opposition* to "enthusiasm", an opposition with which politeness could be connected, in the commitment to moderation in the Church of England, in particular the latitudinarian doctrines embodied in various Archbishops of Canterbury. Prest, for example, refers to Archbishop Herring's emphasis on "the reasonableness and simplicity of (the Church's doctrines), productive of an innocent, and useful and pious life. Human sinfulness or Christ's promise of eternal life scarcely rate a mention". Christianity of this kind "emphasized reason, scripture and the study of Nature by the experimental methods of the new science as the best means of understanding god's purposes".[56] Clerics sometimes saw in the Church the source of a moderate living and a good estate[57] and were often lampooned:

> When George in Pudding time came o'er
> And moderate men looked big sir
> My principles I changed once more
> And so became a Whig, sir.

The narrator justifies the vicar's pragmatism in trimming his doctrines according to the preferences of five different regimes:

> And this is law, I will maintain
> Unto my dying day, sir

55 See, for example, John Brewer and John Styles, *An Ungovernable People: The English and their Law in the Seventeenth Century*, New Brunswick, NJ, Rutgers University Press (1980).

56 Wilfrid Prest, *Albion Ascendant: English History 1660–1815*, Oxford, Oxford University Press (1998), 140, 138. Alexander Pope's famous "God said, 'let Newton be!' and all was light" gestures toward a church determinedly untroubled by dogmatism.

57 Prest, *ibid*, 140.

That whatsoever King may reign,
I will be the Vicar of Bray, sir.[58]

Whatever the accuracy of the satire, it does suggest an atmosphere of not taking things dangerously far, of mutual accommodation.

Post-Stuart politics became once again drawn toward doctrines of sovereignty with East India Company conquests in Bengal, Bihar and subsequently beyond, from 1756–57. Compromise and negotiation with "native" peoples, as opposed to white protestant men of the Atlantic empire, seemed less appropriate. Rule *by* law rather than government *through* law seemed more appropriate and, as I argue, this view affected not only the governance of brown people, but the British government's new approach to the thirteen American colonies, and subsequently also to working class and franchise-extension movements and, in the end to women seeking an end to the doctrine of coverture, which assimilated their property with that of their husbands on marriage, and their agitation for the vote, in the Britain of the nineteenth century. At the same time, the "civilizing mission", which saw the empire as a pedagogic exercise to enable, especially Indians, to govern themselves peacefully without the British, was advocated for Britain itself, extending the Lockean reliance on the civilizing effect of education and manners to others than potential gentlemen of the upper classes.

Utilitarianism

Utilitarianism, a "manly" response to the politeness of the earlier Whigs, derived significantly from the European Enlightenment's influence on Bentham, found its time in the struggles with revolutionary France – soon turned from liberty to draconian imperialism – and spread through Bentham's disciples, such as Chadwick, the elder Mill and Kay-Shuttleworth. Bentham's writing was circulated and discussed, but went largely unpublished. It is essentially an authoritarian belief, never entirely extinguished, by the kind of program most clearly expressed in Coleridge, of the intertwined and pacifying natures of pastoral and pedagogical care. Later in the Victorian era and into the twentieth century, there was the addition of the English discipline, often broadly conceived, as a particular form of, as Coleridge put it, drawing out, and rendering a human into a social subject.

Education and moral suasion may, of course, and did, from time to time take hypocritical, authoritarian and xenophobic forms,[59] but seem less intrinsically prone to them, despite the utilitarian Gradgrindian attempt to hijack it and teach only certainties – "the facts", than internally-directed military or paramilitary responses to discontent, than the criminal law and the prison and certain coercive types of "welfare" and industrial relations.

58 Anonymous poem from the first half of the eighteenth century, "The Vicar of Bray".

59 See Ben Wilson, *Decency and Disorder: The Age of Cant, 1789–1837*, London, Faber and Faber (2007).

Statecraft in twentieth century Britain

We witness, in the twentieth century, I argue, not a social order governed principally by or even through law, but what Toby Miller, drawing on Foucault, terms, the "technologies of power". These:

> Form subjects as a means of dominating individuals and (bring) them to define themselves in particular ways; and "technologies of the self" . . . are applied by individuals as a means of transforming their conditions into those of a more autonomous sense of happiness.[60]

There is a guarded anti-determinism here, and certainly in the more recently translated Foucault, reminiscent of Marx's remark that people make history – see and govern – themselves, although not in conditions of their own making. It is not, then, because positivist accounts of the sovereignty of law and the government of people implode when closely scrutinized, or reduce to a "because I say so" justification of rule that I reject them as insufficient accounts of Victorian and subsequent British government, even for the education of lawyers. The culture of manners and a degree of respect for difference, I shall argue, underlay the possibility of the eighteenth century constitution, and it faltered with dire results in the 1760s for much of the mainland American empire. Equally, the culture of education, of civic cultivation, underlay the constitution of nineteenth century order – of disorder, too, but was not productive of fatal disorder.

The governing classes' stress on manners in the late seventeenth century and after becomes a concern with "civilizing" a century or so later, which is necessarily a patronizing practice when applied by one culture to another, but may be less so in the communication of ideas within a heterogeneous culture which is in a transformative stage of political unity, at least in aspiration. What I mean by this is revealed, as we shall see, in the expressions of the need for the education of the working classes by various nineteenth century figures. Samuel Taylor Coleridge, originally a celebrant of the French revolution's liberating potential but, like Burke, recognized its potential for centralized Absolutism, may have been motivated principally by a humane concern about poverty, exclusion and unnecessary suffering, but he was also concerned about the extremes to which alienation caused by poverty and hopelessness might lead their sufferers. Neglect was, on the other hand, justified by, among others, Thomas Malthus who, in a kind of pre-Darwinian social Darwinist spirit expected natural causes to take care of any excess breeding among the poor. The fittest and thriftiest would survive and the others would not. Coleridge was acutely aware, if Malthus was not, of the dangers posed by social unrest, though, and of the dangers it could pose if unaddressed.

60 Toby Miller, *The Well-Tempered Self*, Baltimore, MD, The Johns Hopkins University Press (1993), xiv.

Macaulay, writing in the 1830s and 1840s, and Matthew Arnold in the 1860s were clearly aware of the approach of some form of democracy in Britain, as were all nineteenth century commentators. Repeated riots and petitions and the earnest discussion anent female suffrage made it abundantly clear that "improvement" of an auto-didactic, institutional or domestic kind[61] was likely to provoke a respectable working class and female demand for the vote, and was a vital pre-requisite of further parliamentary representation. Macaulay insisted that state assistance for the elementary education of the poor added to the legitimacy of government. For how could a magistrate punish a person for incivility without assuming the responsibility for teaching him (or her) how to act civilly? Arnold adds to this the hope that the best that has been thought and written in the world should be as widely available as possible, deploring the trade school and rote learning techniques then being proposed by the commercial middle class for their children. All three felt that the legitimacy of governing norms lay ultimately, not in forms of brute superiority and control, but in the existence of forms of learning that would facilitate informed compromise. To the chagrin of some 1970s British Marxists, embarrassed by the apparent collusion of the Victorian working class, many of them believed that, too. They wanted, not to smash the state, abolish its laws and begin afresh, but to become part of it, as many of them felt more than capable of being. Although they did not want to become part of Great Britain, Indians who embraced British culture later caused some embarrassment, just as the British Orientalists who adopted or admired Indian ways caused embarrassment to their compatriots in much of eighteenth century India.

The politics of writing theories of legality

Who are the characters in my narrative, and what are they doing there? Edmund Burke wrote, as we have seen, in response to the French assertion of the rights of man, that he could make little of such a generality. The rights of an Englishman according to his, British, constitution or of a Frenchman according to the constitution of the French, were, he considered, calculable, his remedies for wrongs done to him capable at least of argument. But, by implication, since "man" is such a vague abstraction, how might this theoretical figure's rights be asserted? Where were the procedures, what was the cultural commitment appropriate to his place and time? The abstraction from specifics, which the first (and subsequent) French Declarations signified, the rejection of the concept of constitutions crafted for a

61 Beatrice Webb, *My Apprenticeship*, London, Longmans Green (1926), esp ch VII, notes some of the contradictions, though. As a highly educated woman she felt she had a voice through her "rarity value" which was not diluted by her threateningly also having a vote. Accordingly, of course she initially aligned herself with those opposed to female suffrage, although she later recanted. JS Mill dreaded giving a legally endorsed voice to those, male laborers or women not already culturally prepared by education: JS Mill, *Autobiography* (1873), Harmondsworth, Penguin (1989), 175.

particular place and changeable over time, or of men recognized as the subjects of a specific period of history and geography, was bound to lead to extravagance and potential disaster, he felt.

Burke has often been dismissed as a reactionary, an Irishman with an ambition to instruct Englishmen about the importance of their own traditions. Whatever the man – who was, when all is said and done, a supporter of the American cause for independence – it will appear in what follows that I have taken to heart as far from conservative, the need for the specificity for which he calls. Law, in my title, is, as I have said, far from the unchanging signifier that most commentators – not only lawyers, but historians, sociologists and political scientists as well as philosophers – assume it to be. It is, wherever one finds "it", far from secure or fixed construction, but rather a negotiated appeal for legitimacy; not something conceptually permanent, traveling through time much like HG Wells' protagonist, comically pedaling away from Edwardian London in George Pal's 1960 film, *The Time Machine*, always the same in his gentleman's clothes however strange the era in the background may subsequently appear. Law is always at its most formal basic, the multiple, debatable product of "its" time. A time machine of Wells' kind cannot, wherever it visits, be anything but the product of the era of its Edwardian construction. Law is not a time machine. The English subject, too, is, as a number of recent writers have pointed out, a series of performances of production and recognition. Empire, a third component in my narrative, is also an unstable signifier,[62] changing, as I shall argue, through history (also, of course, an unstable narrative,[63] although, whilst working within it, I have no space to examine this quality specifically).

My character, the subject, to some extent introduced above, then, occupies a space, usually a fairly generously defined space, at the interstices of law, empire and subjectivity – here that of Englishness. I want to explore some aspects of each. Generosity of space for the subject's positions is, of course, bought at a price. The price, that I shall mention shortly, is uncertainty. Jeremy Paxman makes the – no doubt to some outrageous – suggestion that the unideological reformation in England (Henry VIII, the *fidiei defensor*, fid.def., of pre-decimal British coinage) wanted, not a reform of church doctrine, but rather a divorce, a fresh queen and, hopefully, a male heir which Queen Catherine of Aragon supposedly could not produce.[64] The Pope, in another dynasty's pocket would not consent to the divorce. This led to the destruction of pictorial theology in English culture.[65] The beauty (and horror) of pre- and post-renaissance representations of the Christian message

62 W Roger Louis, Introduction, in Robin Winks (ed), *Oxford History of the British Empire vol 5: Historiography*, Oxford, Oxford University Press (1997).

63 See, for example EH Carr, *What Is History?*, London, Palgrave (1961, reprinted with an introduction by Richard Evans, 2001); Keith Jenkins, Introduction: On Being Open About our Closures, in Keith Jenkins (ed), *The Postmodern History Reader*, London, Routledge (1997).

64 Garrett Mattingly, *Catherine of Aragon*, London, Jonathan Cape (1942), Part 3, Ch 1.

65 Jeremy Paxman, *The English*, London, Penguin (2007). Paxman's characterization of the Church of England's god as the "ultimate good chap", always prepared to listen to a decent argument in genial spirits, may not be far from correct.

were systematically destroyed as idolatrous, Paxman suggests, from the mid-1530s. Destruction reached a crescendo during the Civil War a century later,[66] the symbols and paintings we associate with, especially, say, counter-reformation Spain replaced by the vernacular word. It was, as Hume remarked, not initially a peaceful outcome partly in Northern Europe or England, perhaps because, in a world hitherto accustomed to certainty, a multiplicity of interpretations became a multiplicity of certainties, each generating violent offense and defense.[67]

Ironically, however, a period of increasingly clashing certainties may have produced the realization, in England, and soon after southern Scotland, that they could never be resolved. This clashing of certainties, which began as a mixture of politics and theology, is an important part of my argument. For what became at the time a somewhat stultified English tradition of painting – this is Paxman's argument – is substituted Marlowe, Shakespeare and Milton, amid a host of others and English bibles, all subject to printing press piracy, plagiarism and multiple public disputations concerning their meanings. John of Gaunt, the Shakespearean author of "this England", was a patron of Geoffrey Chaucer, an author of England *par excellence*. The play in which Gaunt uttered his lines was part of Shakespeare's project of producing a popular history of the country, a project which was to bear unwelcome fruit for the Stuarts.

By the time of the general enlightenment, Reason, which sought to occupy the niche of certainty hitherto occupied by faith, was already subverted in English by a multiplicity which could not, like heresy, be erased by Inquisition without subverting itself.[68] Unwittingly, then, Henry, in search of the dynastic certainty of a male succession, unleashed not only the Elizabethan hurricane, annihilating the Spanish armada in 1588,[69] which, after a number of repeat performances, seriously eroded Phillip II's and Spain's Catholic threat to England, to impose the certainty backed by Inquisition. The Elizabethan *via media* church in England helped bowl the certainty of Catholic dominance like a certain form of bowling in the game of cricket. Henry helped create, by setting in motion the destruction of the monasteries and richly decorated churches, a scene in which the ambiguities of prose can never be resolved. How can these be illustrated in our categories of law, the English subject and the empire?

66 See Diane Purkis, *The English Civil War: A People's History*, London, Harper (2006), esp ch VII, *et seq*, which makes the intriguing suggestion at 207, that what she terms the year "when the British press really began", 1643, initiated "the newspaper (as) a secular substitute for religious observance, its regularity, the fact that everyone reads it on the same day, makes it an experience not unlike some great saint's festival".

67 James Simpson, *Burning to Read: English Fundamentalism and its Reformation Opponents*, Cambridge, MA, Harvard University Press (2007).

68 For a slightly different but similar chronology and conclusion, see Steven Toulmin, *Cosmopolis*, Chicago, IL, University of Chicago Press (1992).

69 "the Lord blew and they scattered", according a contemporary English account of the fate of the 1588 Armada quoted in Conrad Russell, *The Crisis of Parliaments: English History 1509–1660*, Oxford, Oxford University Press (1974), 244.

As to law, we shall come again eventually to Jeremy Bentham, so important in the conceptual revival of Hobbesian ideas of sovereignty, but for the moment notice the text which is probably the leading Anglo-Australasian influence on conventional philosophical and common sense articulations of law, in the media and discussions of policy in areas such as those designated political science. The English philosopher of law, HLA Hart considered himself in the mid-twentieth century to have made a new beginning in providing certainty in a foundational concept of law.[70] His most influential text attempted to link theory with practice, avoiding the distinction which the American Legal Realists had felt necessary to make some two or three decades earlier between law in action and law in the books, between deals struck and honored by businesses, say, and the rules of contract as depicted in those traditional "sources" of law, namely statutes, court decisions and textbooks.

Hart was also conscious of the difficulties that we shall see attended formalist accounts of law, those which identified its being solely in terms of its origin – the divine will, at one time, the will of the divine's earthly delegate, at a later date and, in more secular times, its origin in the expression of the will of a sovereign whose legitimacy did not originate with the divine, but with the people. (As we learn from Arendt, even the most ruthless leaders of totalitarian states represent themselves as merely the servants of the people.) Hart – as far in sentiment as can be imagined from totalitarianism – famously wanted to retain the distinction between legality and morality, articulated by Hobbes, in the seventeenth century, Bentham in the eighteenth and John Austin in the immediately pre-Victorian era.[71] Hart rejected the American Lon Fuller's position that in order to qualify as law, normative systems must satisfy certain criteria, such as publicity, comprehensibility and a lack of excessive retrospectivity, among others.[72] Hart's position, as he explained it, was not an a-moral but a pragmatic one, namely that one has to identify a phenomenon clearly in order then to criticize it from, for example, moral or, perhaps, policy grounds.

But how to identify law? From a Victorian perspective, how was one to justify the government of the uninformed or incapable, black people overseas, the working class or women, inhabitants all, in their rulers' understanding, of the Hobbesian state of nature? From a governing perspective, the sovereign law-maker was a conceptual ideal which the reason of nature's inhabitants would eventually lead them to understand. For some writers, the independence of non-European populations was not unthinkable. This is the pedagogical dimension of empire, law and rule. As we know, JS Mill was persuaded, perhaps, by Harriet Taylor, that British women, suitably educated, should have a voice in the process of their

70 HLA Hart, *The Concept of Law*, Oxford, Oxford University Press (1961).

71 HLA Hart, Positivism and the Separation of Law and Morals, (1957) 71 *Harvard Law Review* 593.

72 Lon Fuller, Positivism and Fidelity to Law – a Reply to Professor Hart, (1958) 71 *Harvard Law Review* 630; Lon Fuller, *The Morality of Law*, New Haven, CT, Yale University Press (1964).

government[73] but he remained convinced, first that an adequate education was a pre-requisite of even the minimal participation in law-making embodied in votes for the working class. And he remained firmly convinced that "semi-barbarous" populations like those of India, as yet wanting the capacity of "higher civilization", required a "vigorous despotism".[74] For Mill, an East India Company executive of some distinction, it seemed obvious that the Company, with its long-time commitment to, as he saw it, the advancement of India to political maturity, should remain for the foreseeable future its sovereign despot. The 1857–58 Insurrection undermined the perceptions of Company competence among others in Britain and sovereignty was transferred to the UK government, at Disraeli's suggestion, to the government of his Queen-Empress, complicating matters that had, for Mill, as also to those not politically *ad idem* with Mill, such as Stephen and Bryce, been straightforward. Rule by the Company made it easier to find something like an effective sovereign, since Westminster, and the Empress, whilst allowing herself to be flattered by "Dizzy" seemed generally disinclined to interfere or even interest themselves in the minutiae of Indian government.

In *Concept* Hart recognized, as had John Austin in his later, almost voiceless years, that as an empirical matter, even the apparently most straightforward political jurisdictions presented obstacles to the theorist's location of sovereign power. The branches of government interact in different ways at different times, often paying lip service, cynically or otherwise, to the authority, wishes, or good of the people over whom they claim power, who are themselves split into those who elect and those who do not, those, perhaps a majority in some representative liberal democracies, who voted for the governing party or parties and those who did not.

An early attempt by Hart to avoid this sovereignty that what was after all the legacy of the quest for certainty in the divine right embodied, however disguised, in most formalisms, was to direct attention to linguistic usage. Words, ordinary language philosophers like "the later Wittgenstein and unequivocally (JL) Austin",[75] argued, gain their meaning from the way in which they are used. What could be more seductive, then, than to solve the form-substance divide in an area such as legality and end the fruitless search for the (holy) wholly grail of ultimate legal authority by the substitution of a reference to usage? We simply look at how words are used. The crucial question is what we mean when we use the word "law" and the answer by the ordinary language user gives us the answer. As to the interior

73 Harriet Taylor Mill, Enfranchisement of Women (1851), in Alice Rossi (ed), *Essays on Sex Equality: John Stuart Mill and Harriet Taylor Mill*, Chicago, University of Chicago Press (1970); John Stuart Mill, The Subjection of Women (1869), in Alice Rossi (ed), *Essays on Sex Equality: John Stuart Mill and Harriet Taylor Mill*, Chicago, University of Chicago Press (1970).

74 JS Mill, *Considerations on Representative Government* (1861), Buffalo, Prometheus Books (1991), 345–46.

75 Keith Graham, *JL Austin: A Critique of Ordinary Language Philosophy*, Brighton, Harvester Press (1977), 6.

of law, the substance of normative or empowering provisions, once again, whilst allowing for some temporal drift or scope for making choices, meanings would reveal themselves in the way in which people use words.

Fitzpatrick's superb critical chapter on Hart's legal philosophy[76] emphasizes the intellectual debt of *Concept* to Wittgenstein's later writing; but in what is here an introduction to the *dramatis personae* of the narrative, after all, not an exposition it is unnecessary to decide whether JL Austin or Wittgenstein made the larger philosophical contribution. Wittgenstein seems on the face of things to be a more subversive theorist than Austin, and more difficult to yoke to the cart Hart's text seeks to move, but this is a discussion for which there is insufficient space here. It is worth noting, however, that whatever the politics of Ludwig Wittgenstein the man, his later works are anti-foundational and radical. There is no comfort to be found in them for the conservative seeker of certainty and ultimate truth. On the other hand, whatever the politics of Herbert Hart the man (left-liberal, progressive and humane),[77] Fitzpatrick is surely correct to note the utterly conservative direction and foundational nature of his legal positivism, and this fits Graham's description of JL Austin's method of discerning meaning:

> Although Austin deprecated the idea of constructing new idioms from the armchair, it seems he had no objection to the adoption of that posture for the practice of his own method. Certainly, he never advocated any alternative.[78]

The dependence of the meaning – in this case, of the law – and how this is developed in the second part of *Concept*, introduces us once again to the second character in our narrative, namely the subject. Who is this "we" whose usages are to be taken to be authoritative, writers have asked since ordinary language theory arrived on the bookshelves. Candidates for the post have varied from the wryly proposed cadre of senior academics at Oxford high tables to a slightly more widely scattered set of the inhabitants of north Oxfordshire. *Concept* makes an excursion into something called "the internal point of view": an implicitly English legal subject, properly situated, interprets legal rules, since that is what he understands by them, to *obligate* him in a particular way, even when, for conscientious reasons, he declines to follow them. He has, in other words, a share in the words that govern him (or her), unlike the gangster's victim who is *obliged* by the threat imposed by the naked coercion applied.

But then the suspicion that seemed to have affected JL Austin's method of discovering meaning crept into Hart's *Concept*. Would Austin have permitted dialectal variations of meaning-formation, let alone Creole, to inform his system?

76 Peter Fizpatrick, *The Mythology of Modern Law*, London, Routledge (1992), ch 6.

77 See Nicola Lacey, *A Life of HLA Hart: The Nightmare and the Noble Dream*, Oxford, Oxford University Press (2004).

78 Graham, *op cit*, n 75, 40.

Could Hart suppose the "odiously smooth; rather a vulture beneath the skin" Julius Stone, a contemporary of his, but unlike himself – an affluent Jew – a lower class Jew with long experience of anti-semitism and a taste for socio-legalism and flashy American cars,[79] to have an equal authority over the meaning of the law with himself and the elite of Harvard and Oxford? Still less, could the unlettered be permitted the luxury of an "internal point of view" concerning their obligatedness as opposed to their being obliged? Being obliged is common to people in totalitarian states and animals coerced, in Hart's words, like sheep to the slaughter; being obligated is something which arises when one is liable to pay taxes or buy a tram ticket, even when one dodges the requirement through a trick.

We are returned to Mill's advocacy of a "vigorous despotism" for those uninformed about civic responsibility and the nature of law in the process of self-government. Toward the end of *Concept*, therefore, we reach an intellectual terminus more than somewhat at odds with the personal convictions of the well-meaning figure who convincingly emerges from the pages of Lacey's biography. The logic he develops in the second two-thirds of *Concept* leads him to a potentiality which, to his personal beliefs, was anathema. It is a logic summarized in the cliché of the "slippery slope". Law, conceived in the discrete sense recommended by the legal positivists, and practiced in legal education, if education properly describes it, exists on the continuum that Arendt recognizes, from liberal democracy through the party politics of "front-benchism" to the effectively one party state, where real choices may be denied the voter, to incipient totalitarianism. It is what the US author, Naomi Wolf – and a number of other commentators – warns of in her appraisal of the tendency of US politics.[80]

What finally gives a normative system its legitimate, that is, its institutional, legal status in *Concept* is not what ordinary people believe about it; *they* may use it or comply with it for a variety of motives, none of which can be, from its structure, in the end of concern to the text. The figures whose beliefs are of interest, whose "internal points of view" are decisive are, as we shall see, an elite. "Elite" here, means, not as in Australia under radical right-wing politics, discerning or dissenting intellectuals, but those who, by reason of class or wealth, occupy positions of power. The majority is in all legitimate possibility (and in the recent Middle East debacle, we find little to reassure us), in the words of Robert Redford's recent film, "Lions for Lambs", hostages to the possibility of authoritarian vice or imbecility disguised by wealth as Ivy League or Oxbridge wisdom. Redford's film concerns the mixture of opportunism, illogicality and sadism which underlay the invasion of Iraq and with which Seymour Hersh familiarized us.[81] Tony Blair, interviewed by a French television company shortly

79 Leonie Starr, *Julius Stone: An Intellectual Life*, Sydney, Sydney University Press (1992).

80 Naomi Wolf, *The End of America: Letter of Warning to a Young Patriot*, Melbourne, Scribe Publications (2007).

81 Seymour Hersh, *Chain of Command: The Road From 9/11 to Abu Ghraib*, London, Allen Lane (2004).

after being more or less forced to resign as British Prime Minister, justified his collusion in the invasion in lines that could only have been lifted from Norman Foster's lamentable 1955 film, *Davy Crocket, King of the Wild Frontier* – you have to do what you think is right, even when it makes you unpopular.[82]

And here the third of our characters again emerges: the empire. We met it in the form of the relationship depicted in Ishiguro's novel, which suggests that the idea of the personal being political is not a new one. No doubt the structure is much older, but the later Saxon practice of the peace – from which derive the office of the justice of the peace and the offense of a breach of the peace, and which crosses the boundaries of present-day political and private realm. Save for the outlaw, everyone in Saxon England was in the peace of someone: a woman was in her father's or her husband's peace, he in his lord's and so on until we reach the king, whose peace, in the course of a very few centuries ousts the others, although a vestige remained for a long time in the law of coverture, according to which the wife is legally infantilized on marriage, and in the action *per quod consortium et servitium amisit* – an action available to a husband for "damage" to his wife by the defendant, and the husband's resultant loss of wifely services.

We have already, in effect, met empire, if we follow Fitzpatrick's critical account of Hart's *Concept of Law*. Looming large in the later stage of Hart's enterprise is the palpably "imperial" nature of its schematic anthropology. Since law is not, for Hart, self-generating, its primordial beginnings must be social norms. Are these lost in the mists of antiquity, buried in a dreamtime traced in myths that lack a determinate author, or are they purposive, deliberate, in a word, "developed"? Societies abstractly considered seem, in *Concept* to begin at some pre-historic and pre-legal phase of their existence and to operate according to what Hart terms "primary rules", rules like those of the Decalogue or the Twelve Tables, which prohibit or require certain forms of conduct of those subjected to them. "Do not covet . . .", do not steal, murder, etc. The early Israelites and the earliest Romans were purified by a stern simplicity befitting their status.

But in the contemporary world, these accounts sound, as Fitzpatrick observes, suspiciously like the descriptions of the "native" societies "discovered" by Europeans on their civilizing missions. What societies of this kind possess in their primitive condition, is a normative form that also characterizes morality; what they lack is what Hart terms "secondary rules", that is rules that permit deliberate change, accomplished by designated officers, or "officials" in Hartian vocabulary. A developed society, then, for *Concept*, has some form of executive, legislative and adjudicative arms, rules enabling the creation and functioning of these offices whilst a primitive society must rely, presumably, on the imperceptible evolution of customary norms.

The empire that was historically the busiest and most officious in its civilizing mission was that of the British. It will later emerge much more fully, but here it is

82 Broadcast in Australia on SBS, 31 January 2008.

sufficient to allude to its enigmatic nature for historians. Not only juristically diverse, if one thinks of the European-originated differences – Quebec, a French civil law province of British North America, the Cape Colony, a Roman-Dutch jurisdiction in South Africa, originally colonized by the Dutch – and the plurality of motives that Pue and McQueen and Sugarman[83] discover in lawyers' places in nation-building (along "respectable" lines) in Canada and Australia, but wallowing in customary practices it tried to manipulate. Was the empire, observed from the metropolis, an accident, run by buffoons,[84] an earnest enterprise run by dedicated professionals,[85] a source of pride to the United Kingdom[86] or an irritant largely unnoticed until the "Empire Windrush" delivered its shipload of workers from Jamaica to balance the labor shortages of postwar Britain?[87] The nature of the subject positions we consider to be available at the intersections of legality and empire will depend upon which (amalgam) of interpretations we find most persuasive. Discussion of them in detail must wait.

The ghosts of a secular politics

There is, finally, another character in the present narrative, a ghostly presence, perhaps, whom we have already encountered. This is a quality that we need but now know we cannot have, namely the certainty which the belief in the intimacy of the divine with the secular seemed once to promise, in its endorsement of current legitimacy in government – the king was God's deputy on earth – and deferred promise of judgment, where earthly good and evil would definitively receive their deserts. Both certainty and its lack haunt the legal subject and its imaginings by virtue of their unbelievability. Marjorie Grene finds this "age-old dream of certainty" in Descartes as in Newtonian physics, in Carnap's neutral observation language and in Russell's mathematics. The conviction is that there

83 David Sugarman and W Wesley Pue, Introduction: Toward a Cultural History of Lawyers, in W Wesley Pue and David Sugarman (eds), *Lawyers and Vampires: Cultural Histories of Legal Professions*, London, Hart Publishing (2003); Rob McQueen, Together We Fall, Divided We Fall: the Victorian Legal Profession in Crisis 1890–1940, in W Wesley Pue and David Sugarman (eds), *Lawyers and Vampires: Cultural Histories of Legal Professions*, London, Hart Publishing (2003); John McLaren, Reflections on the Rule of Law: the Georgian Colonies of New South Wales and Upper Canada 1788–1837, in Diane Kirkby and Catherine Coleborne (eds), *Law, History, Colonialism: The Reach of Empire*, Manchester, Manchester University Press (2001); Helen Irving, *To Constitute a Nation: A Cultural History of Australia's Constitution*, Melbourne, Melbourne University Press (1997).

84 Piers Brendon, *The Decline and Fall of the British Empire 1781–1997*, London, Jonathan Cape (2007).

85 David Gilmour, *The Ruling Caste: Imperial Lives in the British Raj*, New York, NY, Farrar, Strauss and Giroux (2005).

86 John MacKenzie, *Propaganda and Empire: The Manipulation of British Public Opinion 1880–1960*, Manchester, Manchester University Press (1984).

87 See Stuart Hall *et al*, *Policing the Crisis: Mugging, the State, and Law and Order*, London, Macmillan (1978).

must be, in relation to any order, a place outside from which it can be measured and objectively evaluated.

Hume is, according to Grene, "brilliantly consistent" here:

> He recognizes explicitly that every theory which gives an account of human knowledge must include itself in the knowledge it legitimates; and so, meditating on the habit-forming associations of the human mind, he seeks no securer sanction for this meditation. He who is induced by habit to believe, habitually believes that he is so induced to believe.

As to the "he":

> The self, he says, is a bundle of impressions, and, though this is one of his most devastating expressions, there is, quite literally, nothing else for the self to be.[88]

Hume, without perhaps anticipating the twentieth century characterization of "relativism" as a positivism which asserts the idiotic certainty that "everything is relative", simply says that he does not know. His skepticism may be unjustified, but, he says, he has encountered nothing which will satisfactorily dispel it. Grene herself, independently of the work that the French theorists were doing, but which were not then translated, and in the wake of the advances that had been made on Cartesian certainty, and the Greek writings of Plato and Aristotle, with which she associates Newtonian physics, by Einstein, Godel and Heisenberg, insists that "our judgments of fact depend on our constitutive judgments of value and not the other way around".[89] "It is not a variety of formalisms we are looking for, but assent to a variety of formalisms".[90] There is a subtle difference. There is no Archimedean fulcrum, in other words, from which we can hope to base a movement or an understanding of the universe. The universe-ity is not – and this is Leavis's point – a striving for an objective end-point, but a perpetual dialog, the famous, "it is so, is it not?" There is, in Grene's account, and whether we are in the realms of the natural or the social "sciences", in every certainty a faith, in every end-point, a position for negotiation, compromise and revision.

As to faith, in his Introduction to the arch-positivist, Bentham's, correspondence concerning the proposed panopticon, a circular structure of imprisonment in which convicts and indigents would be at all times visible from a tower containing (or not) an inspector impossible for them to see, Bozovic discusses the relevance to the understanding of this model of Bentham's fear of ghosts. This was a fear which originated in a trick played on Bentham by a servant when he was a child, a fear

88 Marjorie Grene, *The Knower and the Known*, London, Faber and Faber (1966), 95, 101, 102.
89 Grene, *ibid*, 159.
90 Grene, *op cit*, n 88, 203.

which continued during his adult life. Why were Bentham's rational arguments that ghosts do not exist of no comfort to him as an adult once the daylight had gone, the lamps extinguished? Bozovic answers that it is precisely because Bentham does *not* believe that they inspire the peculiar terror in him. At the same time, although Bozovic does not put it in this way, Bentham cannot *not* believe in the terrifying world in which ghosts have their being. They belong to an unknown and unpredictable realm whose existence he cannot disprove by virtue of its defiance of mundane reason. This is a situation that Bozovic connects with Bentham's model prison whose inmates must consider themselves under constant surveillance without knowing whether they are or not, without even knowing that the omniscient in-specter exists or is present in his tower, inscrutably watching them. If he were to appear as a woman or man like themselves, he would belong to their world, he would possess a certain degree of predictability based on their knowledge of that world and of how people behave within it.[91]

The same might be said of a reversal, of the situation of the "bare human" as s/he appears in Agamben's writing about the Nazi camps, a person abstracted from the *polis* or the *civis* with all its familiar dense cultural and political connectivity, and upon whom incomprehensible cruelty is practiced with no reason available to traditional cultural understanding. This human, stripped of anything but his animal nature, exists in a bewildering world in which anything may conceivably happen just because of its very inconceivability.[92] Like Bentham's ghost, s/he is only eerily present in the consciousness of the camp guards and the subjects of the Nazi state more generally. This nightmare situation is, of course, fostered by the totalitarian regimes in which the camps are run. As Arendt writes:

> Present totalitarian governments have developed from one-party systems; whenever these became truly totalitarian they started to operate according to a system of values so radically different from all others that none of our traditional legal, moral, or common sense utilitarian categories could any longer help us to come to terms with, or judge or predict their course of action.[93]

The camp inmates most destroyed by this situation of radical meaninglessness, to the extent that their survival was no longer important to them, were termed, for whatever reason, "mussulmen", and not expected by their fellow-inmates to survive. If the subject of my narrative exists within the interstices of several discourses, of legality, of Englishness, and of empire, informing that narrative, stalking it, and identified by many of its characters – the eighteenth century Scots

91 Miran Bozovic, Introduction, in Miran Bozovic (ed), *Jeremy Bentham: The Panopticon Writings*, London, Verso (1995), and see Letter I at 34.

92 Agamben, *op cit*, n 29.

93 Hannah Arendt, *The Origins of Totalitarianism*, San Diego, CA, Harcourt Publishing (1995), 460.

come to mind, of course – is the point articulated most recently and clearly by those who experienced World War II Europe. Arendt and others have pointed out that being human is a political construct, creating, however contingently, order out of the *unheimlich*, the spectrally unbelonging, whilst at the same time recognizing that state of contingency. The need for certainty and predictability often takes the form of sovereignty, which is, in the end, a justification for dogmatism, as we shall see, and many tragedies have formed its legacy.

That calculation requires a predictability not its to command was, at a mundane level one of the preoccupations of lawyers, and returned to especially by twentieth century legal writers in the United States, eventually returning us to conceptions of empire, the apparently ultimate guarantor of certainty. In the course of his voluminous writings on jurisprudence, the American Roscoe Pound refers repeatedly to the dilemma confronted by both the office lawyer seeking to advise a client and the legal theorist providing an exposition of his/her subject. American Legal Realism, as it became known, and of which Pound may or may not have been an exponent,[94] has particular appeal to all common law students, since they experience, both in the lecture room, and in practice, as members of the bench, the bar or the office have termed it, a discrepancy endlessly rehearsed, between the law in the books and the law in action, the world as it should be according to the canonical texts and the world as it is experienced. Recommending a safe course of action for clients seeking advice or providing a stable, comprehensible account of social norms whose fluidity was not merely inevitable but increasingly viewed in the context of the US's New Deal as fundamental to the task of re-engineering society, confronted lawyers with a dilemma, one that it seemed possible to resolve in a new canonical form, the character of the judge who, for reasons that we shall come to, occupied a more prominent role in the common law of the United States than in that of the United Kingdom after the beginning of the nineteenth century.

In the United States of the 1930s, indeed, the judge was in juristic writing the hero of American common law and the vanguard of progress, hence the enigmatic embodiment of certainty. "The prophecies of what the courts will do in fact, and nothing more pretentious, are what I mean by law", Oliver Wendell Holmes Jr had pronounced several decades earlier, establishing the basis for the judge's pivotal role and projecting the legitimacy of the office and its privileged role[95] – also, of course, setting the scene for its scapegoating by conservative commentators when reform seems to them to have taken the social order in unwelcome directions.[96] Holmes himself was not entirely the force for progress and enlightenment as he is

94 See William Twining, *Karl Llewellyn and the Realist Movement*, London, Weidenfeld and Nicolson (1973), for an explanation of the appeal of the movement of Realism, both at the time and now.

95 Oliver Wendell Holmes Jr, The Path of the Law, (1897) 10 *Harvard Law Review* 457, 460.

96 See Jonathan Raban, 'Dictatorship is the Danger' on the retiring Reagan appointee to the US Supreme Court, Sandra Day O'Connor's warning that political attacks on the US judiciary are taking the United States down the road to dictatorship, *Weekly Guardian*, 13 March 2006.

sometimes depicted – his enthusiastic endorsement from the US Supreme Court of the Virginia court's approval in *Buck v Bell* of Virginia's program of compulsory sterilization of women deemed promiscuous, or "imbeciles", legitimating similar eugenics policies in a number of other states.[97] The policy was applied, not only to "imbeciles", whatever that may mean, writes Gould, but to unmarried mothers, women (of the lower class) who had several sexual partners and others categorized by the English IQ proponent Francis Galton as inadequate.[98]

As Holmes' use of the word "prophecy" implies, a certain faith is conjured – and here we are, of course returned to Bentham's *geist* masquerading as pure rationality – into the apparently secular institution of law, and this is long before, it has to be remembered, the phraseology of the Declaration of Independence was altered on the Jefferson Memorial (in Washington, DC) completed in 1941, with FD Roosevelt's approval. Americans' pragmatically Whig "unalienable" rights as expressed in the Declaration of 1776 were replaced by the more transcendental-sounding "inalienable" rights; before the enhanced oath of allegiance under Eisenhower made the United States one nation "under God"; and before "In God we Trust" replaced "E Pluribus Unum" on some of the currency.[99] The firm commitment to a secularism within which state a multiplicity of religious practices and even political beliefs might flourish and might experience a freedom rare in eighteenth century Europe is clear from the Declaration, the Articles of Confederation and, finally, in the constitution of 1784. At the inception of the Republic, even Benjamin Franklin's suggestion that the sessions of the Continental Congress begin with a Christian prayer was rejected in this early institutional manifestation of secular Enlightenment principles. Religious difference was to be tolerated, but none enshrined.

But the liberation from the need for certainty which Jonathan Israel for one associates with the Enlightenment[100] appears recently to have abated, to the point where, as Arundhati Roy writes, a former US Attorney General can insist that "US freedoms are 'not the grant of any government or document but our endowment from God'". So, she adds, "We're confronted with a country armed with a mandate from heaven".[101] The search for an elusive certainty which has, or can be discovered will be one of the themes which will haunt this text.

Of course, and whether one is or not in prophetic mode, relying on what the courts will decide for one's definition of law, is not helpful if one is a judicial member of the court – a point made by Hart. From where is the guidance to

97 SJ Gould, *The Mismeasure of Man*, New York, NY, Norton (1981).

98 The case Holmes endorsed with so much enthusiasm was *Buck v Bell.* See Gould, *ibid.*

99 Frank Fetter, The Revision of the Declaration of Independence in 1941, (1974) 31 *The William and Mary Quarterly* 3rd Ser 133–39.

100 Jonathan Israel, *Radical Enlightenment: Philosophy and the Making of Modernity*, Oxford, Oxford University Press (2001); Jonathan Israel, *Enlightenment Contested: Philosophy, Modernity and the Emancipation of Man 1650–1752*, Oxford, Oxford University Press (2006).

101 Arundhati Roy, *An Ordinary Person's Guide to Empire*, New Delhi, Penguin (2005), 54.

emanate? Happily for our theme, the answer, according to one writer and his followers, is a subject-creating and imperial one. There are, it transpires, answers to the conundra that provoke litigation.

To begin with:

> We live in and by the law. It makes us what we are . . . we are subjects of law's empire, liegemen to its methods and ideals, bound in spirit while we debate what we must do.[102]

The retreat to the illusory certainty of the middle ages is palpable. Ronald Dworkin's ideal judge, whom he calls Hercules, a classical allusion to pantheism (but perhaps, the US part of North America attaches no significance to the differences between classical and medieval civilization), of course, but to undaunted invincibility, a model, not necessarily any more a reality than the panoptical inspector/in-specter, but a supposition dis-covering the theoretical visibility of certainty and right answers. Hercules naturally seeks the best possible solution to conflict and in this spirit draws together the totality of his jurisdiction's cultural, political and legal traditions and in them finds the correct principles governing the deployment of rules he has to apply to a specific case. Dworkin admits that the Herculean judge may be forced to compromise, and that most judges, his "princes of law's empire", are less than Herculean and prone to make mistakes. He appeals to "philosophers", the philosophers whom, I have suggested, have already, in a curious collusion, accepted the assumptions of legal positivism, to assist in redeeming these likely imperfections, to help find "law beyond law", the ghost in the machine, "purity" ministering to the process of "law working itself pure".[103] As the title of Dworkin's book indicates, Anglophone legal theory returns us to empire as the guarantor of security and certainty, and to faith, that there can be such qualities.

At some point of this opening chapter, I invoked Burke's appeal for specificity, and later on mentioned Arendt's observation that civic humanity is not a biological or zoological expression, but a political one. Neither sentiment was imagined by its utterer to be innovative, rather something mundane, but for which reminders are always timely and frequently unheeded. What I want to do now is examine, necessarily episodically, the ways in which legality, empire and Englishness intersected to make possible a certain subject position. I chose the English subject, not because everyone concerned with its production was English, or because English is somehow metonymic of the British Isles, or because the United Kingdom, the British Empire and common law approaches to sovereignty are peculiarly and uniquely worthy of study, but because they are familiar to me, and the contiguity of the three is insufficiently remarked.

102 Ronald Dworkin, *Law's Empire*, London, Collins (1986), vii.

103 These are phrases from the final chapter of *Law's Empire.*

Partly also – if one wants to address questions of motivation – I wrote out of a frustration and the growing disappointment I have expressed above and elsewhere with legal education;[104] and perhaps a certain alarm that in many parts of the Anglophone world (Australia may lead the field here) other parts of the academy seem to be following in its footsteps. Plainly, restaurateurs, travel agents and golf course managers need to be trained, but one wonders what intellectual speculation is foreclosed when the intricacies of airline ticketing or the form that gastronomic special offers in restaurants might take come to dominate the university curriculum. As Jacques Barzun puts it:

> You can forget the details of history or chemistry and have gained immense profit because by learning them you have become a different being; but forget the details of real estate management or ice cream making and you have nothing.[105]

The narrative which follows locates the authoritarian thread which makes legal positivism seem a fruitful means of understanding social order, both synchronically and diachronically, in, first, the perceived exigencies of empire, and, second, in what seemed necessary to control disorder "at home": top–down discipline. Long after the wider empire had gone, its presence haunted the decision making of Britain's ruling elites as late as the Suez affair of 1956; but more importantly for our purposes, perhaps, it lingered, providing a template for appropriate methods of keeping order among the natives "at home", women, the working class and, analogously with the Orientalists who, as later wisdom had it, "went native", middle class architects of the welfare state. In this politics of rule, an agreement of the people cannot be contemplated and the sovereign's power is constituted by the people's ignorance. They are not wise judges of their own best interest and therefore depend on an office which can step outside the agreement in order to protect that interest. Curiously, executive government has grown steadily in power in the United States to a point rivaling that of George III's ministries, which, by a consensus including British Whigs and Americans in the 1770s, "has increased, is increasing, and ought to be diminished", an evolution with an explanation that Arendt in part foresaw. At the same time, equally curiously, closer links with the European Union, supposedly, if we believe the Tories, an unresponsive bureaucracy, have strengthened a hitherto compliant judiciary to the point where they evidently feel able to dilute the sovereignty once attributed to Parliament.

In the meantime, the doctrines of legal positivism justified a narrow configuration of legal education which both Blackstone in the 1750s and 1760s, and

104 Ian Duncanson, The Ends of Legal Studies, (1997) *Web Journal of Current Legal Issues*, http://webjcli.ncl.ac.uk/1997/issue3/duncan3.html; Ian Duncanson, The Centre May not Hold (2001) 8 *International Journal of the Legal Profession* 69–85.

105 Jacques Barzun, *The American University: How it Runs, Where it is Going*, 2nd edn, Chicago, IL, University of Chicago Press (1993), 217.

Adam Smith, were trying to transform, and continue to do so in the Anglophone world with only occasional inspirations.[106] Of course, as I have conceded, and Burke himself acknowledged, the technicalities of legal practice are vitally necessary. But in their evanescent, ice cream-making, way they miss what he called the "grandeur of law"; only temporal and geographical contextuality can recognize it. Obviously I cannot emulate Adam Smith's breadth of vision and in any event do not share some of his preoccupations, but I have tried to follow his example of looking at the continuities with other areas of study of the study of legality. As the student notes of his jurisprudential lectures make clear, a priority for him was developing theories of how societies evolved, how, in each of the stages he detected, they learned and might continue to negotiate a sociable moral and economic means of polite interaction. Legality was, for him, dependent and disentangleable from these questions, and this implied that the priorities which we will see preoccupied the governors of empire were, in his work both secondary and generally unproductive. So, then, we shall explore the evolving nature about legality and empire and the implications for the English subject.

106 For an account of how these attempts are combated, see W Wesley Pue, Educating the Total Jurist?, (2006) 8 *Journal of Legal Ethics* 208–21.

Chapter 2

Making good the lack

The form of the phantom in the progress from sovereignty to civility

In Chapter 1, I introduced some themes, the subject, law and empire, and reflected upon their interactive natures. Empire as an impulse represents, I suspect, an always unsuccessful striving for certainty by the subject. How does s/he know what s/he knows, or even that s/he is? The 1999 Wachowski brothers film, *The Matrix*, in which the hero is "chosen" to release dormant humans from the illusion that is only a dream of living, is merely a modern version of the nightmare. *The Matrix* began implausibly with a plausible question – how can we know? – but quickly descended into bathos, its ill-advised sequels rendering the question apparently pointless.

Clifford Bax put it more eloquently in 1919, set appropriately hauntingly to sixteenth century music:

> Earth might be fair and all men glad and wise.
> Age after age, their tragic empires rise, built while they dream and in that dreaming weep.
> Would man but wake from out his haunted sleep,
> Earth might be fair and all men glad and wise.

The "dream" was, of course, both divine knowledge, but that secular unity on Earth, "all her people one" be achieved. It was bound, as the English colloquialism has it, "to end in tears".

De Saussure, the structural linguist from whom Lacan derived a good deal, related language to the world as the signifier, that which points, or gestures toward a worldly signified, identifying it and giving it a place in the human social world. Together the signifier and the signified produce the sign, something in the real world, and something that we may alter as we learn more about it, or which changes as society and language practices change in relation to it. His is a science designed to demystify. But language is, for Saussure, unlike Bax, grounded in something that lies beyond a dream, or revelation. The truth, in the words of a famous TV series, is out there.

Lacan, by contrast, wants to remove the signified. He wants to emphasize the impossibility of the sign. What he means by an expression he often used, "the endless play of the signifier", is that human symbol-users never arrive: their entire world exists in the language they use. Unlike the Wachowski brothers, who were, it seems compelled, ultimately to ground their illusion in the Big Other of the machines who created the illusions, Lacan settles, like Hume before him, for uncertainty.

Marxists and realists in the 1970s were apt to argue that to fall off the top of a building is not a conceptual but a physically compelling event, thus proving that a real world does exist rather painfully beyond conceptuality. What they missed, of course, is that the event does not exist in a way that is accessible to us without language, or signification. My fall is always a meaning, for me if I survive and narrate it to myself or to others; and in police reports, coronial inquiries or funeral obsequies if I do not. Why I mention this is to explain something about the subject who, once s/he is sentient, experiences a real world insofar as it can be explained – except that the last six words are made to seem redundant. We believe that there is a real world accessible to us without symbolic work. The lack of a sign is unendurable. Lack, for Lacan, forms the basis of desire, desire to disguise or fill with an imaginary substance, precisely, the lack. Sometimes – and this underlies a quip by Lacanians, "make sure you want what you desire" – we fill the lack with something we may not want, in the end, or may subsequently regret.

To return to specifics, the cruciality of which I continually stress, the English subject as it emerges is one such substitute for the lack of a sign. It is, to use a phrase of Lacan's a *point de capiton*, like the quilting points in, for example, a duvet which stop the filling from sliding everywhere; it halts, or appears to halt, the endless and chaotic play of the signifier, so that we can understand. To the politically aware Englishmen of the Tudor period, the sign was the sovereign, sanctioned ultimately by god. The confusion of the changing of the gods by the Henrician reformation of the 1530s and the brief return to Roman Catholicism under Mary, 1553–58, may explain the enormous popularity of *The Book of Martyrs*, published by John Foxe after the accession of Elizabeth in 1558. It chronicled, or purported to chronicle, the cruelties of Catholicism, identifying the English subject as necessarily protestant, under a protestant sovereign. For Henry VIII in the sixteenth, as for James VI/I in the seventeenth century, sovereignty and empire were closely related, but empire here meant mostly, independence from Roman ecclesiastical interference. What I argue below is that, whatever the attraction of empire and sovereignty may have been to the political classes under the Tudors, sovereignty as the Stuarts understood it, and attempted to practice it, began increasingly to seem irksome to England's rulers. They searched for another sign, as in order to conclude the convulsions of the seventeenth century, and found it in the notion of civility. The Scots, I argue in Chapter 3, powerfully assisted with this project.

The sovereign as the emperor

> One can hardly over-emphasize the importance for the understanding of Tudor and Stuart symbolism of the fact that the Divine Right of Kings to rule over both church and state was a derivation from the claims of Roman Emperors to be represented in the councils of the church.[1]

Chapters 3 and 4, continuing the themes opened earlier, look specifically at the suspicion which the English seem to have entertained about doctrines of sovereignty exercised outwith the political and legal processes upon which the political classes had agreed. In Chapter 3, the emphasis lies principally with the Scottish influence. Chapter 4 looks at the influence of empire, which was, to a significant extent, in the opposite direction, challenging civility with imperial authoritarianism. The Scots, in the Lowlands, at least, whilst for their most part determinedly Scottish, tied their fortunes to the English, so long as their Kirk and their law remained distinct. Whilst theologically dogmatic – a quality which mellowed in the eighteenth century – the Kirk looked skeptically at claims to political authority. Because the Scottish education system was far superior to the English, Scottish professors provided a powerful dynamic driving the claims of liberty and property, and placing the identity of law at any one time in a moral and, as we shall see, socio-historical context, something not entirely at odds with post-Revolutionary Whig principles.

In a prelude to the constitutional struggles of the seventeenth century, the English lawyer, Coke's exclamation to his king that English kings had, since medieval times, been subject not only to God (as Hobbes would argue for his Sovereign), but also to the law, and that, no, James I could not adjudicate in the courts that sat in his name. Courts sat *Per Curiam*, the King was within, not outwith or above the law. Coke was not noted for his tact and, perhaps he was unduly abrupt, but perhaps not controversial. The Scots were familiar with the idea that principle had to be weighed against authority and might prevail. James' fear that a similar doctrine was developing in his new realm was no doubt alarming to a monarch wishing to establish absolutist government. Deference among the commons[2] was one thing, since it existed within a framework of local customary expectations, even if they were frequently disappointed, but abjection and despair seems not to have been considered. Writing of Henry VIII's reign, Loades says:

> In theory, every aspect of a man's life was tightly controlled by the king, the Church, or his local trade guild, but in practice the inefficiency of all these

1 Frances Yates, *Astraea: The Imperial Theme in the Sixteenth Century*, Harmondsworth, Penguin (1975), 41.

2 It is probably worth making the terminological point that the commons were the people who were not aristocrats; the (House of) Commons was where they were taken to be represented, a few directly by voting, most "virtually", in Burke's terms, or via petition, increasingly vocal behavior at elections, and occasionally by riot.

> agencies left most men a good deal of freedom, especially if the community was indulgent, as it often was.[3]

There was a surprisingly high level of male literacy, even in England, and a surprisingly high level of political awareness and engagement among both men and women, though less so in England than Scotland. The Scots entertained a certain nervousness, which I think it is as well to bear in mind: could the English be trusted to maintain the accomplishments of the post-Revolutionary settlements, a balanced constitution and a divided sovereignty and the integrity of law, however corrupted and compromised it might on many occasions be? A strange alliance between the still-stern Calvinist Kirk of Scotland and the somewhat languid Latitudinarian Church of England after the 1707 Union of the countries seems to have resulted in an internally, relatively mild regime, hedged about with restrictions; and a viciously aggressive external state. Adam Smith, as we saw, never published his works on law, but significantly began his writing with discussions on moral sentiments. They were the basis, he had clearly learned from Locke and Shaftesbury, upon which law rested. The English called this their constitution. Yet the ghost of the sovereign and its certainty, whether resented or a comfort, lay heavily on continental European civilization.

Yates writes that the "phantom" of empire had haunted Christendom from the time that Romulus Augustulus, the last western Roman emperor, was deposed in 475. It was a phantom that took many forms. *Dominus mundi*, the Emperor as lord of the world in Roman law, translated in feudal terms into claims of suzerainty over mere monarchs by those claiming the imperial inheritance. The Pope, for example, claimed secular superiority under the forged Donations of Constantine, in which the secular but Christian Roman emperor appeared to have ceded his worldly power to the spiritual head of the universal church. Charlemagne, crowned lord of the world by the Pope in 800, saw himself, not merely as head of the earthly city in opposition to Augustine's City of God, but as the worldly defender of the eternal. The widely accepted logic to which Yates refers, takes (the later) Filmer one step further than he might have wished to go in justifying divine right in terms of the patriarchal entitlements of the father in a family:

> As all the powers within an individual man must be under one ruler, his intellectual power; as there must be one to rule a family, the paterfamilias; one to rule a city; one to rule a kingdom; so there must be one to rule the universal world.[4]

Here is the yearning for a lost union and the desire for the desire of the Big Other, as Lacan or Zizek might phrase it. But this vision of oneness and certainty in

3 David Loades, *Henry VIII: Court, Church and Conflict*, Kew, National Archives (2007), 12.

4 Yates, *op cit*, n 1, 9.

hierarchical authority as the only precondition of world peace, was shattered by the multiplication of political authorities until briefly revived by the inheritance by Charles V of all the then Habsburg territories in Europe, from the Netherlands, through Germany to Spain and Italy; and to the Americas. His defeat of France in 1525 and the crushing of the Protestants at Muhlberg in 1547 carried the promise of a new world order informed by Catholicism under the protection of a new Roman Emperor. Ironically it was he who, through his control over Pope Clement, denied Henry VIII's application for a papal annulment of marriage to Catherine of Aragon and ensured the breach of England from Rome. Roman Emperor, *Dominus mundi*, guarantor of the certainty of the one true faith, he was not to be: he retired to the certain world of a monastery in 1555 and divided his empire.

The legacy of Yates' "phantom", though, has two important implications. Its notion of One-ness as a *sine qua non* of peace under God gave us not only Charlemagne and Charles V, but also the Crusades and other forms of Christian complicity with territorial aggression and conquest. It gave us in addition the particular ideas of imperium that would cause so much difficulty later. Post-Reformation monarchs, at least in England, were not simply secular sovereigns, but also the secular arm of God, emperors of a tiny imperium with a divine obligation, and thus divine blessing. James Simpson[5] is doubtless correct to stress that one appeal to Henry of the Evangelical movement that sprang especially from Tyndale's translation of the Bible into English was that opposition to the king was therein understood as opposition to God. He is also no doubt correct to imply that if the authority of the Catholic priesthood had not been undermined by the direct textual access permitted by the translation, the Reformation would not have been as relatively acceptable politically as it was. This was why Henry, sensing excommunication and a break with Rome if he convened a court that would annul his marriage to Catherine and subsequent marriage to Anne Boleyn, was able successfully to seek help from Parliament.

What is obscured in Simpson's text is the political dimension, hence the connection between constitutional politics, religion, and legality which was to surface more violently in the seventeenth century. Catherine of Aragon, who bore to Henry "only" a girl, Mary, was the widow of Henry's deceased brother, Arthur. So convinced was Henry that political stability depended on his leaving behind a male heir (perhaps deluded: Roman Catholic Mary was a disaster, although perhaps not: would Elizabeth have been such a success without the protestant martyrs Foxe was so eloquent in deploying? Would we have the Bloody Mary?) that he allowed himself to be persuaded that the Old Testament insistence that a marriage to a brother's widow would be childless really meant boy-less.

Appreciating that Pope Clement, dominated by his enemy, the Habsburg Emperor Charles V, would never permit Henry's curial divorce from Catherine in

5 James Simpson, *Burning to Read: English Fundamentalism and its Reformation Opponents*, Cambridge, MA, Harvard University Press (2007).

the Vatican, Henry set up his own court in England under Archbishop Cranmer, which declared an annulment of the marriage to Catherine of Aragon and he married Anne Boleyn, who was then crowned queen. But if Henry VIII's claim to be reforming a corrupt church by resiling from Rome was a brilliant propaganda coup, it had unforeseen consequences. To put it in terms that contemporaries would not have done, if Protestant communities came to require spiritual guidance and advice but not the intercession of the priest in their collective worship, the church would become an organization of administrative experts, albeit with a unique moral authority, and its head, the imperial monarch, a head of state – in other words, potentially something less than an extension of the divine. Much of Yates' later discussion is devoted to an account of the rich layers of ritual and mythology attached to the image of Elizabeth, the Virgin queen, efforts, largely successful, to maintain the monarch's unique relation to the divine; efforts that began rapidly to lose their efficacy under her successors.

In light of the above brief discussion of Yates' opening section, it comes as no surprise that, in Canny's account, "the word 'empire' was particularly favored by Henry VIII after his breach with Rome, and called to mind the relative isolation of England through the centuries rather than its dominion over foreign territories".[6] It was connected to a particular view of what was meant by sovereignty: not simply a realm not subject to authority from without, but a ruler not subject to authority within. The Act in Restraint of Appeals of 1553 was in much the same mind, although as a parliamentary measure it probably implied a more inclusive sovereignty than that of Henry.[7] But "a coterie of royal legists and rhetoricians (who) appropriate(ed) the exalted concepts associated with princely rule by court humanists in High Renaissance Italy" had made possible a "court humanism" in the context of which Henry could claim, even in 1515, two decades before the Reformation, that "kings of England have never had any superior but God himself"; and later, "we, of our absolute power, be above the law".[8] This should perhaps be qualified in a manner that will resonate with arguments later in my book, by Penry Williams' observation, quoted above, that in a relatively affluent society, government by consent was possible.[9]

6 Nicholas Canny, The Origins of Empire, in Nicholas Canny (ed), *The Oxford History of the British Empire vol 1: The Origins of Empire*, Oxford, Oxford University Press (1998), 1. As monarch of a puny monarchy, Henry had few hopes of overseas success.

7 JGA Pocock, The Union in British History, in JGA Pocock (ed), *The Discovery of Islands: Essays in British History*, Cambridge, Cambridge University Press (2005), 165.

8 Brendan Bradshaw, The Tudor Reformation and Revolution in Wales and Ireland: the Origins of the British Problem, in Brendan Bradshaw and John Morrill (eds), *The British Problem 1534–1707: State Formation in the Atlantic Archipelago*, London, Macmillan (1996), 52–53. Alan Smith, *The Emergence of a Nation State: The Commonwealth of England 1529–1660*, London, Longmans (1984), argues that Henry was considered subject to law, but surely in only a restricted sense, since even by Elizabeth's reign, he says, Parliament was not seen as the proper forum for discussion of "high matters of state".

9 Penry Williams, *The Tudor Regime*, Oxford, Oxford University Press (1979), 464. Maybe "assent" would be a better word.

The efficacy of Henry's rule had a more mundane basis than he cared to admit. And there was non-English territory there within Henry's realms. Wales, from which the Tudors claimed to originate, was one, formally assimilated to England in 1536. Henry's post-Reformation, "imperial" assertion of sovereign independence from Rome was also coeval with the continued English assertions of what can now be conceived to be a colonial imperium over Ireland, with all the incidents of imperial rule and, ultimately exogenous rule, even if contemporaries understood the relation with Ireland to be one of feudal overlordship.[10] It was not a pretty sight:

> The distinguished historian and Abolitionist, Henry Hallam (1777–1859) pointed out the racist affinity of the Spanish genocide of the Moors and the English oppression of the Irish . . . The preeminent Anglo-Irish historian William Lecky (1838–1903) noted how the people of the English Pale in Ireland came to "look upon the Irish as later colonists looked upon the Red Indians".[11]

Michael Collins, the Irish patriot, writing about the good that came from the failed rising against the British in 1916,[12] could well have been writing about the British occupation of Australia: massacres, the attempted suppression of religion, language and law, and the theft by the invaders of indigenous land.[13] Some of what was lost was irrevocably lost, some could be regained; and what above all was achieved was the assertion of self respect. Ireland was in many different ways, an early laboratory of empire, of colonialism and of resistance to it. The liberation of what became Eire has led, eventually, to the creative vitality and prosperity that the country was denied by British rule. Canada's grant of semi-autonomy to first nations people will doubtless produce a similar outcome.[14] After a decade of political somnambulance, with a federal government with a mindset familiar from the 1930s, Australia's new federal Labor government has opened the possibility for both Aboriginal equality and difference from European and Asian Australia, releasing, not xenophobic nationalism, but openness and a shared creativity.[15]

10 Perhaps we should see this as a transitional moment: the extirpation of local law and custom and evictions of Irish tenants certainly did not conform with traditional feudal ideas of "good lordship": see DM Loades, *Politics and the Nation 1450–1660*, Brighton, Harvester (1974).

11 Theodore Allen, *The Invention of the White Race vol 1: Racial Oppression and Social Control*, London, Verso (1994), 29.

12 Michael Collins, The Proof of Success: What the Rising of 1916 Did, in Michael Collins, *The Path to Freedom*, Dublin, Mercier Press (1996).

13 See Henry Reynolds, *The Law of the Land,* Melbourne, Penguin (1987).

14 See James Tully, *Strange Multiplicities: Constitutionalism in An Age of Diversity*, Cambridge, Cambridge University Press (1995).

15 See *Melbourne Age*, 15 February 2008 for the text of the then new Prime Minister's speech of apology for land-theft and attempted genocide, and the *Melbourne Age*, 16 February 2008 for commentary.

The Stuarts and the figure of the emperor

James VI of Scotland, Elizabeth I's nominated successor to the throne of England was also, like Henry, much taken with the imperial idea, referring to his post-1603 dual monarchy as "great Britainne's imperial crowne" or, the "Empire of Great Brittaine".[16] What distinguishes the Stuart monarchy is the rigorous attempt by its members to unite four peoples in two islands into one political entity[17] which then, of course, established "plantations", i.e. colonies of settlement, largely under crown charter, in North America.

The attempt failed, to the extent that relations with Ireland remained one of dominance and exploitation – and here the resemblance with the settler colonies to which Allen draws attention recur. English and Scots Protestants who settled in Ireland were looked down on by English governments as lacking cultivation whilst the settlers themselves were if anything more severe colonists than the metropolitan governments – something later echoed in Australia. Also, as is clear from the later Union debates under Anne, the last of the Stuarts, the English governing classes, whilst putting up with James' fantasies about his empire of Great Britain, had been most unwilling to share their trade and commerce with the northern part of the phantom empire, with the Scots.[18]

As to the sovereign claims which James associated with his "empire", the Jesuit, Salamonio's, conclusion, that a sovereign, whilst superior to each of his subjects individually, is inferior to them collectively, and his fellow Jesuit, Suarez's, insistence in the early seventeenth century, that there is a right of resistance to a monarch where "it becomes necessary for the preservation of the commonwealth itself"[19] "cut right across the doctrine of the divine right of kings enunciated by James VI in his *Trew Law of Free Monarchies*".[20] According to this text "Kings are not only God's lieutenants upon earth, but even by God himself are called Gods . . . Kings exercise a manner or resemblance of Divine power on earth".[21] Suarez,

16 Canny, *op cit*, n 6.

17 Jane Dawson, Anglo-Scottish Protestant Culture and Integration in Sixteenth Century Britain, in Steve Ellis and Sarah Barber (eds), *Conquest and Union: Fashioning a British State*, London, Longman (1995).

18 Michael Fry, *The Union: England, Scotland and the Treaty of Union, 1707*, Edinburgh, Birlinn (2006).

19 Quentin Skinner, *The Foundations of Modern Political Theory vol 1*, Cambridge, Cambridge University Press (1980), 178 on Suarez; 1, 63 on Bartolus and Marsiglio.

20 Michael MacGraith, The Gaelic Reaction to the Reformation, in Steve Ellis and Sarah Barber (eds), *Conquest and Union: Fashioning a British State*, London, Longman, 150.

21 Glenn Burgess, *Absolute Monarchy and the Stuart Constitution*, New Haven, CT, Yale University Press (1996) argues that the Stuarts were regarded as bound to rule according to the law, but takes the Hobbesian position that no secular remedy could be available if they did not. Only Whigs, he thinks, could see this as absolutism. But see Julian Franklin, Introduction, in Franklin (ed), *Bodin on Sovereignty*, Cambridge, Cambridge University Press (1992), xxvi, who attributes Jean Bodin's belief that a sovereign not subject to a right of resistance is nevertheless governed by law to "optimism".

a "monster", according to James, had his writings burned by royal decree in London.[22] "A lawfull good king, having received from God the burthens of office, whereof hee is accountable"[23] acts according to law "yet hee is not bound thereto but by his good will". The sovereign sits "upon God his throne on earth".[24]

In the famous episode in 1608, James' assertion that judges were mere delegates of the king was, as we have seen, challenged by Sir Edward Coke, Chief Justice of Common Pleas, who, on his own account of the encounter at least, "replied that that Bracton saith, *quod Rex non debet esse homine, sed sub Deo et lege*"[25] – in effect, the King is subject to none but God – and the law. But, of course, Coke's Bracton was not the medieval Bracton, the man of deep canon law learning and perhaps learned in whatever Roman Law was then available.[26] *That* Bracton was, Milsom suggests, at a crossroads. Bracton (whoever he actually was) proposed a university textbook in Latin which would have been based on systematic principles. It could have been a fruitful union of what Roman law was then known, and common law. English law could have become a scholarly discipline. But Oxford and Cambridge which, until the eighteenth century taught only Roman and Canon law, did not for the most part trouble themselves with common law. Common law practitioners were:

> Professional men, literate men, but men not at home in the Latin tongue and not interested in the riches to which it gave access. The common law had started its career as an alternative learning, cut off from even the legal learning of the universities . . . What centuries of learning had made so clear centuries earlier was to them alien learning; and they were starting again.[27]

It was this starting again was what enabled Coke to argue against those who understood sovereignty to be necessarily "indefeasible and illimitable", and that Stuart sovereignty moreover permitted "no appellate jurisdiction for if there were,

22 James VI, The Trew Law of Free Monarchies, and, A Remonstrance for the Right of Kings and the Independence of their Crownes Against an Oration of the Most Illustrious Card. Of Perron pronounced in the Chamber of the Third Estate, in Charles McIlwain (ed), the *Political Writings of James I*, Cambridge, MA, Harvard University Press (private edition 1918), 53 and 169 respectively. On the burning see McIlwain's Introduction, lxiv.

23 James VI/I, Basilikon Doron, in Charles McIlwain, the *Political Writings of James I*, Cambridge, MA, Harvard University Press (private edition 1918), 18.

24 *Ibid*, 54.

25 Sir William Holdsworth, *A History of English Law in Sixteen Volumes, Vol V*, London, Sweet & Maxwell (1924), 430. Bracton was a thirteenth century judge of the King's Bench and reputedly author of an early legal text, *On the Laws and Customs of the English.* According to an observer quoted by Holdsworth, at Coke's assertion, "his majesty fell into that high indignation as the like was never known in him, looking and speaking fiercely and with bended fist, offering to strike (Coke)".

26 SFC Milsom, *Historical Foundations of the Common Law*, 2nd edn, London, Butterworths (1981), 41.

27 Milsom, *ibid*, 41–42.

then that jurisdiction and not the king's would be sovereign."[28] For some common lawyers the argument seemed to be this: if the king drew his authority from the law, then he was subject to it, as Coke has Bracton say; if law took its rise from the king then it was properly subject to the king. This is the logic, but where was the empirical basis for either position? As Pocock has shown, the common lawyers were on shaky historical ground.[29] However, Skinner finds a second argument against the Royal Prerogative, and Royal claims to possess:

> the prerogative right to tax, to imprison and execute his subjects whenever he judges such actions to be in the public interest. To claim such discretionary powers, it was objected, is to leave everyone in dependence on the will of the king. But to live in such dependence is to live as a slave and to live as a slave is to be bereft of liberty.[30]

The rhetorical force of the freeman – not a slave or a villein, but, like them, a legal category nevertheless – was to have an eventful political career taking freedom into Anglophone politics in England and America. It is the birthplace of citizenship. In an early enunciation of the doctrine of the separation of powers, Coke continued: "The King in his own person cannot adjudge any case . . . betwixt party and party . . . cannot take any case out of any of his courts and give judgment upon it himself . . . judgments are always given *per curiam* and judges are sworn to execute justice according to the law and customs of England". Whatever law was to become, with Parliament, it was at this time, in Maitland's phrase "tough law" and could see off a king or two.

It is difficult to know if the violence of James' reaction was mere outrage at the blithe assertion by Coke of a public "state" beyond the patrimony of the King, or some belated recognition that England had already begun charting new courses. The latter seems more likely. James was brought up a Scottish Protestant, among his tutors being converts from Roman Catholicism like George Buchanan. Buchanan was fiercely opposed to the doctrine of divine right and in favor of resistance to tyranny. It was said that Buchanan's refusal of divine right and his insistence that kings were servants of their people provoked James' conviction that the opposite was the case.

Pre-empting parliamentary claims to participate in his divinely imposed tasks, James warns the two Houses in 1609, "doe not meddle with the main points of

28 Alfred Dufour, Natural Law and Utility, in JH Burns and Mark Goldie (eds), *The Cambridge History of Political Thought 1450–1700*, Cambridge, Cambridge University Press (1991), 596.

29 JGA Pocock, *The Ancient Constitution and the Common Law: A Study of English Historical Thought in the Seventeenth Century*, 2nd edn, Cambridge, Cambridge University Press, with Retrospect (1987).

30 Quentin Skinner, States and the Freedom of Citizens, in Quentin Skinner and Bo Strath (eds), *States and Citizens: History, Theory, Prospects*, Cambridge, Cambridge University Press (2003), 13.

government, that is my craft, I must not be taught my office".[31] In a further pre-empting, this time of judicial claims to insulation from Royal government, he re-asserts "that he was the supreme judge" – an oddly canon law position for a Protestant – "inferior judges (being) his shadows and ministers . . . and the King may if he please sit in Westminster Hall in any court there and call their judgments into question. The King being author of the law is the interpreter of the law".[32] In 1616, he instructs the justices assembled in Star Chamber that he merely delegates his power of adjudicating according to the law administered in his name, he does not relinquish it. He compares the questioning of his prerogative to blasphemy. He tells them he knows of the common lawyers' love of arcane dogma but, "if your interpretation be such as other men which have logic and common sense understand not, I will never trust such an interpretation".[33]

The narrative of the English and Scottish responses to Stuart claims is well enough known, and some of it has already been adverted to. Hume's overview is difficult to better, although, of course, his *History* has long been superseded by the work of intervening centuries, more recently by the detailed scholarship of Christopher Hill and others.[34] Superstition, which Hume associates with later Stuart Catholicism, "is an enemy to civil liberty and enthusiasm a friend . . .". On the other hand, the evangelical Protestantism which alone at the time had the capacity to resist the incursions of the monarchy, was characterized by "hope, pride, presumption, a warm imagination, together with ignorance, the true sources of ENTHUSIASM".[35] One, the Protestant evangelism noted by Simpson, had been necessary to counteract the other, superstition, but the prudent conclusion for the present, having survived that confrontation is, "moderation in all our political controversies".[36]

The response to James I, of lawyers, property owners, merchants and the artisans who were to form the radical element during the years of the debates about the nature of government may have informed Locke's conviction later in the century that people will not easily abandon their obligations to government.[37] James died of natural causes – perhaps because he was firmly opposed to both

31 Charles McIlwain (ed), the *Political Writings of James I*, Cambridge, MA, Harvard University Press (private edition 1918), 306.

32 Holdsworth, *op cit*, n 25, 428.

33 McIlwain, *op cit*, n 31, 326.

34 See Geoff Eley and William Hunt (eds), *Reviving the English Revolution: Reflections and Elaborations on the Work of Christopher Hill*, London, Verso (1988); David Underdown, *A Freeborn People: Politics and the Nation in Seventeenth Century England*, Oxford, Oxford University Press (1996). Trevor Royle, *Civil War: The Wars of the Three Kingdoms 1638–1660*, London, Abacus (2005).

35 David Hume, *Essays*, Indianapolis, IN, Liberty Collection (1985), Essay X, Of Superstition and Enthusiasm, 76, 74.

36 Hume, *ibid*, Essay VII, 53.

37 John Locke, Second Treatise, in Peter Laslett (ed), *John Locke: Two Treatises of Government*, New York, Signet (1965), para 230.

Catholicism and evangelical Protestantism – whilst Charles, his son, married to a French Catholic and with a High Church (i.e. a cleric perceived by suspicious Enthusiasts as quasi-Catholic) preference, evidenced, in their eyes, by his later attachment to Archbishop Laud, but who made not dissimilar claims to authority, was tried by a court which, he argued, with technical correctness, had no legal jurisdiction over him. Perhaps the political nation and the lawyers took some time to estimate the distance between the conception of the state that they were compelled to adopt in order to transact their day-to-day business, and that of the court. Charles was executed in 1649. But if James kept his head, this does not mean that there were not, as we have seen, moments of high drama, moments in which the logical conundrum was confronted which earlier imperial doctrines, claims to absolutist rule, were meant to resolve.

Holdsworth – who notes James VI/I's struggle with Coke over the relation between the Royal Prerogative and the independence of the judiciary, which anticipated his struggle with Coke over the independence of Parliament, Coke's other resort[38] – quotes a contemporary observer of Coke's assertion of the "public" rather than the patrimonial nature of Royal justice, to the effect that Coke's proposition rendered the courts of record, and in particular, the King's Bench, the supreme arbiters of government, leaving the king and his officers little to do. Was the King's Bench a sovereign of some kind? As an outcome, this was unlikely, for the practical reason that judges were appointed and could be dismissed by the king, whilst Parliament was a more formidable foe, since if not summoned it could, and in fact did, refuse to fund government; and if summoned, could refuse funding save on its terms, which is what happened when the Presbyterian Scots occupied Newcastle upon Tyne on what turned out to be the eve of the civil war. The Commons refused to fund an English army to challenge the Scots, provoking hostilities between themselves and the king and the defeat, trial and execution of Charles. The logic of the situation might be that the country had, in the legislature, a new sovereign. But legislatures do not by themselves make very effective governments, and the Long Parliament was purged in 1648 to render it less of a debating chamber and one more amenable to the Army leaders. Following this the Rump which remained was effectively displaced by Cromwell as Lord Protector, who governed with the aid of an expensive army. The New Model, formed out of a parliamentary counties' association, the Eastern Association, was an army, moreover, that considered itself "no mere mercenary army". Politically conscious and committed to its cause, it had been stunningly successful against Royal forces to the point of invincibility. Of more relevance here, for a time:

38 Edward White, *Sir Edward Coke and the Grievances of the Commonwealth*, Manchester, Manchester University Press (1979).

> it was the common people in uniform, closer to their views than to those of the gentry or Parliament. And the free discussion which was permitted in this unique army led to a fantastically rapid development of political thinking.[39]

By the end of the Protectorate, the army, itself having lost or been purged of many of its radicals, was doubtless much less radical, but its reputation remained. The general radicalism led some historians to see incipient communism in the air.[40] The literate and articulate heroes of the battles of Marston Moor (1644) and Naseby (1645) against royal forces notoriously failed to see why their discipline, commitment and exposure to danger should deliver them nothing more than the old society with, perhaps, some minor changes at the top. Thus the radical, John Lilburne:

> The only and sole legislative law-making power is originally inherent in the people and derivatively in their commissions chosen by themselves by common consent and no other. In which the poorest that lives has a right to vote, as well as the richest and greatest.[41]

In the (parliamentary) Army debates at Putney in 1647 and Whitehall in 1648 about the future of government, the Levelers gained some prominence in arguments about the future shape of politics and the state. Colonel Rainsborough, opposed during the debates by the conservative Ireton for seeking to subvert the special claims of the propertied to control the country's future, is worth quoting at length:

> . . . I really think that the poorest he that lives in England hath a life to live as the greatest he; and therefore, truly, sir, I think it's clear that every man that is to live under a government ought first by his own consent to put himself under that government; and I do think that the poorest man in England is not at all bound in a strict sense to a government that he has not had a voice to put himself under . . . I should doubt whether I was an Englishman . . . that I should doubt of these things.[42]

39 Christopher Hill, *The World Turned Upside Down: Radical Ideas During the English Revolution*, Harmondsworth, Penguin (1975), 25. The example of the (New Model) Ironsides' political awareness and revolutionary potential led to some reluctance on the part of Winston Churchill to agree to the Army Education Program during World War II. Given the huge sales of the Beveridge report on the future of the welfare state, the left-wing proposals for the redistribution of wealth in the hastily-suppressed "Cairo Parliament", and anecdotal evidence of private soldiers overheard discussing social justice for a future Britain whilst sheltering in foxholes from artillery barrages in Normandy in 1944, Churchill may well have been correct, from certain points of view.

40 David Petegorski, *Left Wing Democracy in the English Civil War*, London, Victor Gollancz (1940).

41 Quoted in HN Brailsford, *The Levellers and the English Revolution*, Nottingham, Spokesman Books (1976), 117.

42 From GE Aylmer (ed), *The Levellers in the English Revolution*, London, Thames and Hudson (1975).

Even before this, sentiments such as, "I hope within this year to see never a gentleman in England" had initially caused the wealthier parliamentary supporters to hesitate before advocating hostilities against the king. The wealthy, whose motives in supporting Parliament had to do with the security of their property from the monarchy now saw it equally threatened by the radicals, and welcomed the Restoration of the Stuarts in 1660. But the continued vulnerability of the courts and the cavalier approach to Parliament taken by the restored Stuarts after 1660 was not reassuring.

At the end of the seventeenth century, however, many of the better- and less well-off felt that they had stared into the abyss of social disintegration. But having glimpsed the meta-legal experiments of the Tudors and having experienced the sovereign pretensions of the Stuarts and Oliver Cromwell's Protectorate, the men of 1689 – and before, if we think of Locke and the first Earl of Shaftesbury and their opposition to a Catholic king with predictably absolutist intentions – were unlikely to find any consolation in the solution to disorder and conflict offered by Hobbes' precisely meta-legal sovereign, the figure of the emperor to whom one must surrender all but "bare life". Yet the alternatives Hobbes set out had a famously brutal logic: "men by themselves . . . outside of civil society, can have no moral science because they lack any certain standards against which virtue and vice can be judged and defined".[43] This would be denied.

The clamor of opposing, equally legitimate and therefore nugatory rights, he located in the state of nature. Men are not necessarily good judges of their best interests, nor are they naturally sociable, but they do have a rational fear of one another, each not knowing the intentions of the other. "On going to bed, men lock their doors, when going on journeys they arm themselves because they are afraid of robbers . . . Each (man) tries to probe the other's mind. The cause of men's fear of each other lies partly in their natural equality, partly in their willingness to hurt each other"[44] – and partly, of course, in their inability to read each other's minds. If Hobbes' account of disorder seemed to better-off contemporaries so resonant of recent experience, it seemed also to have no resolution except the alienation he recommended, of all rights claims, to one, or one body above the fray, who "cannot be bound to the civil laws, for this is to be bound to himself; nor to any of his citizens".[45] For the quality of his justice and the beneficence of his regime, the sovereign could be answerable only to God, for to permit secular questioning was to risk returning to the very problem of social chaos, the solution to which Leviathan was intended to be. "By the social compact, the subject has 'made away all power of judging and caring for the common good'":[46]

43 Thomas Hobbes, *Man* (1658) New York, NY, Humanities Press (B Gert, ed) (1970), 69.

44 Thomas Hobbes, *The Citizen* (1642), Cambridge, Cambridge University Press (Richard Tuck and Michael Silverthorne, eds) (1998), 25.

45 Hobbes, *ibid*, ch 6.

46 Mark Goldie, The Reception of Hobbes, in JH Burns and Mark Goldie (eds), *The Cambridge History of Modern Thought 1450–1700*, Cambridge, Cambridge University Press (1991), quoting Thomas White (1655).

> To the care of the Sovereign belongeth the making of Good laws. But what is a good law? By a good law I mean not a just law, for no law can be unjust. The law is made by the Sovereign Power, and all that is done by such a power is warranted and owned by every one of the people, and that which every man will have so, no man can say is unjust . . . a good law is that which is needful for the good of the people and withal perspicuous.[47]

I have, and will continue to draw on those writers who draw our attention to the new – to the post-classical world, medieval and immediately post-medieval – distinction between the public and the patrimonial. The difference is succinctly symbolized by Coke's disagreement with the king. The public is governed, not merely by rules, although this is where we begin, but by other forms of regulation which, as we shall see, do not produce homogeneity, but what we can call a certain concordance, the details of which will always be fluid, negotiated and specific only in the claims and counterclaims made within it. We may be misled, for example, by the claims of Parliamentary supremacy, of sovereignty, to assimilate this device of government to the Hobbesian paradigm. In actuality, this abstraction threatened more controversy among the propertied survivors of civil war than it was likely to resolve, and was never seriously accepted. Even, as I shall have occasion to repeat, the famous Westminster doctrine that a current parliament cannot bind its successors, is not the product of an obsession with supremacy, but the obverse. A temporary majority ought not to bind future constituencies, however constituted, in which power legitimately lay.

Changing the mysticism of rule

> If it be asked what has made us to differ from others, the answer is that we never lost what others are wildly and blindly trying to regain. It is because we had a preserving revolution in the seventeenth century that we have not had a destroying revolution in the nineteenth . . . because we had freedom in the midst of servitude that we have order in the midst of anarchy. For the authority of law, for the security of property, for the peace of our streets, for the happiness of our homes, our gratitude is due to the Long Parliament and . . . to William of Orange.[48]

In Whig retrospects, the British regarded themselves as having established the basis of order and good government, liberty and the safety of property, even if,

47 Thomas Hobbes, *Leviathan* (1651), Harmondsworth, Penguin (TB Macpherson, ed) (1977), 387–88. Like Kant, Hobbes did place restrictions on sovereign right, but like Kant, and unlike the Whigs, he overlooked the need for procedural safeguards lest those restrictions were not observed: see Martin Loughlin, *The Idea of Public Law*, Oxford, Oxford University Press (2004), 135.

48 TB Macaulay, *History of England to the Death of William III, vol II*, London, Heron Books (1968), 398.

ever pragmatic, as the political classes saw themselves, there remained imperfections and the uncertain perils of, one day, democracy. Since Macaulay, in the above orotund and complacent, quotation, was writing in 1848, the year of revolution in much of Europe "when the proudest capitals of Europe have streamed with civil blood", one might forgive a little of his complacency. The retrospect of the Whigs – but not only of the Whigs – was that the abstract nature of the imperial sovereign, raised above the mundane through its divine connections, had been discredited in seventeenth century England. When the Stuart Restoration, in the figures of Charles II and his Catholic successor, his brother, James VIII/II, proved as much a threat to liberty and property as their forebears, there was no question of his divinity; James had to go, representing, as he did, an obstacle to the liberty of property and the march of agrarian capitalism.

How was his departure to be accomplished? Not, it was clear by another meta-legal sovereign, whose specter would brood over the legality s/he was both of and above. William of Orange and his wife Mary, the protestant daughter of James VI/I by his first marriage, were invited to accept the thrones of England, Scotland and Ireland, but by what authority? They accepted, and James fled, but what was their constitutional position, when no constitutional king in Parliament existed? Anticipating Hume, resort was had to a *Convention* Parliament. The political classes established their authority and the site in which they would resolve their differences by convention.

Lady Mordaunt wrote to Locke, as he waited to embark from Holland to England after the departure of James:

> I have been very ill this fortnight. The beginning was what is called a disease of one's country, impatience to be there, but it ended yesterday with violence, as all great things do but with kings. Ours went out like a farthing candle and has given us by this Convention an occasion not only of mending the government, but of melting it down and making all new, which makes me wish that you were there to give them a right scheme of government, having been infected by that great man Lord Shaftesbury.[49]

In Howard Nenner's words, "when justification in law was impossible, justification 'by colour of law' assumed the necessary burden of making proposed constitutional law appear regular".[50] In other words, law rested on constitutional custom, and this in turn rested upon conventions that would be expected to change over time. It was a sentiment, as we shall see, articulated by Edmund Burke for a later period.

49 Peter Laslett, Introduction, in Peter Laslett (ed), *John Locke: Two Treatises of Government*, New York, Signet (1965), 58.

50 Howard Nenner, *By Colour of Law: Legal Culture and Constitutional Politics in England 1660–1689*, Chicago, IL, University of Chicago Press (1977), 198.

As we saw in Chapter 1, the related view of Hannah Arendt in her comparison of the American with the French Revolutions, was that the abstract sovereign above the law had never suffered the disrepute in eighteenth century France that it had undergone in seventeenth century England, and at the hands of the eighteenth century Scots writers. Hence the de-position of the absolutist Bourbon monarchy, almost a century and a half after the decapitation of Charles in England, simply resulted in the transfer of this sovereign abstraction from the monarch to the people, whose meta-legal general will had then to be represented by a more distilled figure or body – Robespierre and the Terror, or Bonaparte and a new imperium.[51]

The nineteenth century Whig position was, of course, that English pragmatism had by the seventeenth century dissolved the mysticism of rule into the practical question of how to establish procedures under which liberty and property might be made compatible with government. The separation of powers, the logical next step beyond the balanced constitution, invented by the Americans, was not a concept available to the revolutionaries of seventeenth century England. It was in any event not an urgent necessity to the extent that "balance" existed within the classes who formed the tripartite Parliament and where, even in the event of an overbalance, as Dickinson remarks, men of common sense, especially when informed by the Scots, as we shall see, would not test the full implications of parliamentary sovereignty.[52]

It is in this seventeenth century demystification that the character of the events of 1848 in England may be explained, if not entirely in Macaulay's terms. For the European bourgeois and working class, living under Absolutisms, empires and minute principalities in Germany, their inclusion in the political system required its entire overhaul in every case – revolution in the modern sense. The revolution sought by the British working class at the time of Macaulay's writing, if occasionally riotous both earlier, in 1848, and subsequently, at other times during the century did not have as its aim the overthrow of the government, but rather sought the means of occupying a place in the political process – the secret ballot, universal male suffrage, payment for MPs. If the Chartists sought a revolution, for most it would have been a lawful one – a revolution in the old sense; a return to ancient liberties, imagined, like all politics. Even had they achieved their aims, AN Wilson suggests, "it is entirely possible that a majority of Englishmen would have voted to retain Queen Victoria as head of state, and Lord John Russell or Lord Stanley as prime minister".[53] In Wilson's assessment, support for violence was low and for extended street-fighting, as opposed to the presenting petitions to Parliament and representations in Parliament, almost non-existent. For the most part, their

51 Hannah Arendt, *On Revolution*, Harmondsworth, Penguin Books (1973).

52 HT Dickinson, *Liberty and Property: Political Ideology in Eighteenth Century Britain*, London, Weidenfeld and Nicolson (1978).

53 AN Wilson, *The Victorians*, London, Arrow Books (2002), 133.

activities did not lead to barricades or bloodshed, but rather to the said petitions – evidence of their belief in the parliamentary process, and that their inclusion in it would improve their lives (something which has been dismissed as anachronistic and false consciousness[54]). The outcome of Chartist agitation for the inclusion of the working class – its own demise as a political organization – might be evidence of the strength of the Whig state, the commonsense appeal of the Whig commitment, not to the dangerous overbalance of sovereign executive power associated with the Tories, but to the balanced constitution,[55] and the theoretically unadventurous culture in which it was embedded – a source, even in the 1970s and 1980s of irritation to those who wanted to import exciting European philosophies[56] – or the absence of a real revolutionary fervor among the working class – probably all of the above.

However, Macaulay's Whiggish conjunction of an earlier revolution as a prophylactic remains at the level of description. To Parliament's opposition to, and defeat of Charles II, the dismissal of James II and his successor's cession of most remaining private Royal power to the public realm, we could add Coke's opposition to James I's constitutional and jurisdictional claims and the refusal of many subjects to accede to taxation that had not been approved by the legislature. In a recent text whose primary purpose is to oppose conventional conceptions of the state in contemporary international relations, Benno Teschke takes us closer to a structural and perhaps economically neo-Marxist explanation. Although some of his sources are not new, he puts them together interestingly.[57]

The modern state, he writes, is thought to have replaced the heterogeneous order of "city-states, city-leagues, feudal lords and other corporate actors 'dropped out' of international politics".[58] The universal claims made by the Holy Roman Empire and the single, Roman church, were, according to conventional wisdom, replaced by relations between modern states after the 1648 Treaty of Westphalia, and more or less completely established by the Treaty of Utrecht of 1713. Teschke responds in several ways which are of interest here. Of least importance is the persistence of heterogeneous political forms after Westphalia, particularly in Germany. Of greater significance is Teschke's insistence that the Westphalia signatories were not "modern" but dynastic, or patrimonial states, something he connects to a remark quoted from Justin Rosenberg: "Geopolitical systems are not constituted

54 Gareth Stedman Jones, *Languages of Class: Studies in English Working Class History 1832–1982*, Cambridge, Cambridge University Press (1983).

55 See Henry Hallam, *Constitutional History of England*, 2 vols in 1, London, Ward, Lock and Tyler (1827), 740. ". . . to a Tory, the constitution, inasmuch as it was a constitution, was an ultimate point beyond which he never looked and from which he thought impossible to swerve; whereas a Whig deemed all government subject to the public good"

56 See, for example, Perry Anderson, *English Questions*, London, Verso (1992), ch 2.

57 Benno Teschke, *The Myth of 1648: Class, Geopolitics and the Making of Modern International Relations*, London, Verso (2003).

58 Teschke, *ibid*, 3.

independently and cannot be understood in isolation from the wider structures of the production and reproduction of social life",[59] a point whose importance in this essay will emerge soon.

In Bourbon France, to make one comparison with England (which was not a party to Westphalia, having not been a participant in the Thirty Years' War of which the treaties signaled the end), every western schoolchild knows, the expression attributed to Louis XIV made perfect sense: "*L'etat, c'est moi*". England Teschke characterizes as, at the time, the only political organization resembling a modern state. I have expressed some reservations about the application of the term "state" to the government of England. "Nothing" in Europe, Schama writes, existed "like this peculiar regime in which viable government co-existed with party polemics".[60] Unlike the European dynasties, none but this "peculiar regime", he might have added, installed its own executive. And the importance, if one follows Macfarlane,[61] of both the Black Death (1348), and of primogeniture, had ensured the extinction of the extended family, the peasantry and, at an early stage, the rise of wage labor, tenancy by money rent, in short, commodity production, with wages, prices and to a degree, guild restrictions, supervised by local Justices of the Peace as amateur and as compromising, to a degree, as the coordinating parliamentary oligarchy.[62] These were, at Coke's insistence, a part of the curious, private by custom, yet public nature of common law.

Writes Teschke of the constitutional settlement that followed the accession to the throne of William and Mary in 1689, if incorrectly referring to them as "concessions", since these were generally taken to be amiable accommodations by the Convention *to* their accession, by:

> The 1689 Bill of Rights, the 1694 Triennial Act and the 1701 Act of Settlement, the capitalist aristocracy secured essential control over taxation, the army, jurisdiction, foreign policy and the right of self-convocation. In other words, Parliament became the locus of centralized state power.[63]

The public as imaginary fellowship

We could, of course, consistently with my opening remarks, see in the Enlightened despotisms Lacan's Law of the Father – the King, as father of his people, giving

59 Teschke, *op cit*, n 57, 39.

60 Simon Schama, *A History of Britain vol 3*, London, BBC (2001), 323.

61 Alan Macfarlane, *The Origins of English Individualism: Family, Property and Social Transition*, Oxford, Blackwell (1978).

62 See Rodney Hilton, *Class Conflict and the Crisis of Feudalism: Essays in Medieval History*, London, Verso (1990); Rodney Hilton (ed), *The Transition from Feudalism to Captitalism*, London, Verso (1976); also Macfarlane, *ibid*, ch 2.

63 Teschke, *op cit*, n 57, 253.

final meaning to "his" society. Catharine, Frederick, Maria Theresa, supply a symbolic structure within which their subjects can speak a language of authority. Equally, of course, we can see the attempt to revert to a certain oneness which the *objets* of imperial honors, of the Benthamite dreams we shall later notice, of reconciling the wicked and the indigent to the singular world intended. Equally, we can see in the English subject the imaginary wholeness and independent wholeness conferred by the mirror on the child whose gaze is fixated by it. Should we see in the atavism of Lacan's impulse to the Real a regrettable lapse that can, in its inability to recognize the other, generate great tragedy? Can we see in the Imaginary, instead, a determination, even a compulsion to *preserve* the other as a guarantee of oneself?

In Macaulay's narrative account of the development of constitutionalism as simple English virtue, we stand in need of Teschke's supplementation, in terms of the strange development of the English state – in particular the development of a public sphere which, from the time at least of Coke, was seen to stand apart from, and gaze at the patrimony of the court. We still require some discussion of how this was managed by the political psyche. Absolutist monarchy, Anderson writes, "reflects (the) archaic rationality" he finds in Machiavelli's advice that "war is the only art expected of a ruler".[64] Spain's military budget accounted for 80% of its revenues in the 1550s, France's 75% on the eve of the 1789 Revolution. If a country were not at war – and major wars occupied almost eight decades in the sixteenth century, nine in the seventeenth – it was because its military capacity deterred aggression. The point of most relevance here is that the huge armies – Louis XIV maintained some 300,000 troops – were not principally local volunteers or conscripts, but mercenaries – poor regions, such as Switzerland and the west of Scotland being common sources of recruitment. They were unlikely to make common cause with the local inhabitants and formed, therefore, a resource for both the internal and external security of the regime:

> In the late eighteenth century, even after the introduction of conscription into the main European countries, up to two-thirds of a given 'national' army could be composed of hired foreign soldiers. The example of Prussian Absolutism, both bidding and kidnapping manpower beyond its borders, using auction and impressments, is a reminder that there was not necessarily a clear distinction between the two.[65]

The peasantry of almost all of Europe were, in short, colonized peoples for whom oneness was found in the, to modern eyes, bizarre counter-reformation church paintings of suffering, faith and resurrection. The jibe sometimes made at the expense of the first Charles Stuart, that he aspired to share the Absolutist practices

64 Perry Anderson, *Lineages of the Absolutist State*, London, New Left Books (1974), 32.
65 Anderson, *ibid*, 30–31.

of his European contemporaries, but did not understand the means by which they acquired them, misses out on a dimension of English politics at the time. Coke, the Long Parliament, and the free- and copyholders of post- (even pre-) Stuart England would not have dreamed it possible to grant Charles the means to recruit an army even of the equivalent pro-rata size of Louis' or, later, Frederick's or Catherine the Great's. Charles' own dreams of art, his first love, were scarcely raised to a oneness above that of van Dyke's paintings of himself. One of the reasons for opposing James II was his sinister recruitment of Irish Catholic mercenaries whom, it was feared, would perform the functions of European mercenaries (and, of course, the Hessians later sent to America by the British, few of whom could have had any idea of the nature of the struggle) and subvert the constitution and endanger those two linked practices, liberty and property. The standing army of the English/British post-Revolutionary era, every bit as large as those of Oliver Cromwell, and those which, under defeated Louis in the fields of Blenheim, Ramillies, Oudenard and Malplaquet, were *national* armies that belonged to the public, quite different to the patrimonial forces of the despots: their legitimacy and internal discipline depended on the annual vote of Parliament, the Mutiny Acts. They were the mirror that reflected Great Britain and told them of their coherent wholeness, not their metaphysical oneness, either in the eyes of a Christian God or a benevolent despot.

For the entire "archaism" Anderson finds in Absolutist monarchies, there was a method, a substitution, if we follow Teschke's characterization of the Westphalian move, of a oneness and a certainty at the level of rule, containing the corrosive questioning of the Enlightenment. We find this reassurance even in Kant's essay: the anxiety of innovation at the level of the intellect is thinkable politically only when external ultimate authority has a powerful army, or where internal authority represents the conceptually necessity of the unity of the manifold.

The despots – Catherine of Russia, Maria Theresa, Frederick the Great – were, and harbored precisely, Enlightenment. In their states were managed and accommodated, with some friction, the turbulent ideas generated, say, from Copernicus through Galileo and Newton, and the religious fragmentation and scandalous writing. Is it not interesting that behind the One-ness of Absolutism lies the possibility of a certain closure? The project of the encyclopedia seems an intellectual parallel of empire in Europe. For Kant, Enlightenment was "the age of Frederick", whilst for Hume, the foe of closure and the champion of uncertainty, the idea that George III was a despot along European lines (or that the British Enlightenment could be the Age of Farmer George) was an occasion for hilarity. Whilst for Kant, living under Frederick, the mind was necessarily the "unity of the manifold", for Hume, the mind was a heterogeneous collocation, the melancholy reality of which only dinner, backgammon and some conversation and claret enjoyed with friends could dispel. The unity of the subject, of the law and of the polity, were fictions which only skill and courage, but above all, fellowship, would enable us to employ.

In the absence of Absolutism, the English, and the Englishman, and to a degree the model of the American, in part, constructed by the Scots,[66] a process for the next chapter, were compelled to find a form of unity that would contain diversity, a move to a recognition, perhaps a "psychic distance", that made self-reflection, the dependence on the other, almost conscious.

A focus on the specific seems to characterize late seventeenth and early eighteenth century Anglophone social meditation. It is true that, even if one accepts the metaphoric quality of Locke's *Second Treatise*, it seems an apparent abstraction about the origins of government and its purposes, from which he then deduced a notion of its limit and the breach of trust[67] that would justifiably provoke a right to resistance. But the trust, by the date of the *Treatises*, was not an abstract and vague matter of hope and of generalized faith in the beneficence of those in whom the government of things, or potentially people, were lodged.[68] Associated with "ingenious conveyancers such as Sir Orlando Bridgeman"[69] and Heneage Finch, later Lord Chancellor Nottingham, the trust had become a popular way of accumulating property after 1660. As a legal instrument it had clearly by Locke's time lost its moral overtone of somehow reflecting the Chancellor's function of doing equity, Lord Keeper (as he became) Bridgeman stressing the importance for property of adhering to the authority of precedent, Lord Nottingham declaring in a 1672 case "that the conscience of the Chancellor is not his natural and private conscience, but a civil and official one".[70] The trust also became a way of safeguarding a wealthy wife's property from the depredations of an unscrupulous husband,[71] thereby allowing her some freedom, so that, given Locke's expansive conception of property to include that in one's person, it is not surprising that he drew upon its attractions as a legal device to describe a model of government.

Locke stands Hobbes on his head: where Hobbes deduces, from the supposed sovereign origin of law, the sovereign's necessarily being above the law which he

66 See the partly scholarly Michael Fry, *Bold, Independent, Unconquer'd and Free: How the Scots Made America Safe for Liberty, Democracy and Capitalism*, Ayr, Fort Publishing (2003).

67 Locke, *op cit*, n 37, paras 157–73.

68 For this reason, John Dunn's discussion of "trust and political agency" in the context of Locke's writing might not always be helpful: See John Dunn, *Interpreting Political Responsibility: Essays 1981–1989*, Princeton, NJ, Princeton University Press (1990), ch 3.

69 G Rubin and D Sugarman, Introduction, Towards a New History of Law and Material Society in England, in Rubin and Sugarman (eds), *Law, Economy and Society: Essays in the History of English Law 1750–1914*, London, Abingdon Books (1984), 11, are concerned principally with later developments in which the trust and the settlement not only made the retention and accumulation of great landed estates possible (in the case of the settlement – and for an assessment of the later effects of Bridgeman's work, see Barbara English and John Saville, *Strict Settlement: A Guide for Historians*, Hull, Hull University Press (1983), 15–16), but facilitated capital accumulation after the South Sea Bubble discredited company flotations: see Malcolm Balen, *The Secret History of the South Sea Bubble*, London, Fourth Estate (2003); Rubin and Sugarman, *ibid*, section VI.

70 CFC Plucknet, *A Concise History of the Common Law*, London, Butterworth (1948), 654. The originally private jurisdiction of Crown prerogative becomes manifestly public.

71 See Susan Staves, Separate Maintenance Contracts, (1987) 11 *Eighteenth Century Life* 78–101.

gives and maintains,[72] Locke argues that "man, not having the power of his own life cannot by compact or his own consent, enslave himself to anyone", a condition that, of course includes the installation of despotic or unchallengeable power over him.[73] A beneficiary of a trust is governed by the trustees, but only within the terms of the instrument drawn up by the original donor; moreover, in spite of those terms, beneficiaries may join to break the trust and distribute its assets, a process involving the principles of deliberation and compromise that became so politically important in later decades.

But if despite that, the bare notion of a right of resistance to government of unspecified humans provides us with as little guidance and as much scope for self-serving (even if, to begin with well-meaning) responses as does the notion of human rights when it is connected only contingently with the vocabulary of citizenship – as where we confront, in Arendt's example, refugees, figures with whom we are once again familiar – Locke foreshadows more guidance, but prudential rather than messianic. We have as much experience, little of it good, about the utopian destinations of revolutionary promises, "liberations" from above – not only in the former USSR[74] – as we have about the weak appeal of bare humans to states for whose governments the abstraction of the fantasy-other who threatens the enjoyment of the Nazi or the Communist, and who inspires fear and loathing rather than compassion.

72 And, of course, this is the power of Hobbes' theory. By a series of natural law principles, men are led to recognize that in the alienation to one who is not, until that moment, the sovereign, they abandon each other's dangerous, because tempting of realization but, equally, in the end, empty, claim to all. What has, in law, been alienated cannot be recovered. The alienee has none but moral obligations to the alienor.

73 Locke, *op cit*, n 37, 23. See also A John Simmons, *On the Edge of Anarchy: Locke's Consent and the Limits of Society*, Princeton, NJ, Princeton University Press (1993), who additionally cites paras 135 and 172.

74 See *Melbourne Age*, A3, 9 November 2004, And God Created America: How the Christian Right will Re-shape the US. Two letters to the *Melbourne Age*, perhaps coincidently on Armistice Day and reflecting on the devastating US attacks on the Iraqi city of Fallujah designed to save Iraqis from themselves, may be to the point. Noting the parallels with Vietnam, Chris Gymer recalls "the famous phrase coined by a US officer in Vietnam: 'we had to destroy the town in order to save it'". Fahreena Ahmad writes that, quite properly, great courage and expense was applied to the identification and subsequent commemoration of those who died in New York on 11 September. "However", she writes, "it would seem that when determining Muslim dead, one need only be precise to the nearest thousand . . . There is no effort to assess exact numbers, let alone names". See the report syndicated from the Guardian, *Age*, 10 November 2004 by Madeleine Bunting: "The Silence of Fallujah". "This assault against innocent civilians who live in the besieged Iraqi city will go unreported . . . The silence from Fallujah marks a new and agonizing departure in the shape of 21st century warfare" – but an eerie repetition of twentieth century warfare very shortly into the new millennium.

Locke and the dissemination of the character of the Englishman in the literature of education

It bears repeating that the arts of gentlemanly grace and agreeable forms of disagreement are prerequisite to mutuality in the gift of government, of law as conversation, of diversity, of the bearability of uncertainty and the otiose nature of closure and sovereignty in this performance.

Locke and his contemporaries did not only write of the human, or "man" as an abstract being. Locke evinced in his famous aphorism, that claims of the Hobbesian kind – that absolute and unassailable sovereignty is all that stands between order and chaos, and that, therefore, prudent subjects must accept it – "is to think that Men are so foolish that they take care to avoid what mischiefs may be done to them by polecats or foxes, but are content, nay think it safety to be devoured by lions".[75] He was convinced that citizens possessed of the right to resist "will have the sence of rational creatures" when they contemplate resistance. "Busie heads" and "turbulent spirits", "the common enemy and pest of mankind" will not prevail. The examples of particular injustice or oppression, of "here and there an unfortunate man" will not move those "rational creatures" to the extremity of removing their government,[76] though the possibility of such an extremity might well transform the conduct of government.

Laslett's re-dating of the *Treatises*[77] to which reference has been made, allows some clues about the source of Locke's confidence in "the sence of rational creatures". Studying the book-buying and reading records of Locke "show that between 1679 and 1682, Locke was more interested in publications on political theory and natural law than ever before or after". But in 1676, he had also had other concerns, the Yoltons write. In that year Mrs Anne Grigg writes to Locke about her son, being educated at home until ready for boarding school, and who, she says, often mentions Locke as his friend. In 1677, Locke is thanked by one Dr Thomas for helping with his sister and her "troublesome child" the previous winter. The future Earl of Shaftesbury in 1680 expressed gratitude for Locke's assistance with his grandson, the future third Earl, part of whose intellectual inheritance from Locke was a powerful influence on the cultural preoccupations of the post-Revolutionary period. The list of Locke's interest in education goes on;[78] and in a later passage in their introduction the Yoltons remark that for him:

> Education literally humanizes the child by bringing him to reason and virtue, the defining marks of man, and of that community of mankind which was so important to Locke . . . virtue is important for a gentleman; (his concern) also

75 Locke, *op cit*, n 37, para 93.
76 Locke, *op cit*, n 37, para 230.
77 Laslett, *op cit*, n 49, 69.
78 John Yolton and Jean Yolton, Introduction, in John Yolton and Jean Yolton (eds), *John Locke: Some Thoughts Concerning Education* (1693), Oxford, Oxford University Press (1989), 6.

> had a deeper and more dynamic motive that virtue was the very fabric and basis for humanity.[79]

Locke was clearly fond of children, at least those of his own class, and they of him. In the *First Treatise*, he rejects the patriarchalist opinion that fathers, or parents, enjoy absolute authority over their children, but merely that authority which proceeds from the duty to act in their best interests.[80] His systematically articulated *Considerations* of 1692 were prompted by the advice he was requested to offer the Clarke family about the education of their children. Locke would have been familiar with the manuals on child rearing mentioned in the Yoltons' Introduction and the resemblances of his work to the thought of the north German Monarchomach, Althusius (1557–1688)[81] seems too close to be coincidental, especially given Locke's period of exile in the region during James VII/II's reign:

> According to the Monarchomachs, politics and society rest on the principle of voluntary association, of *consociato.* Althusius defines politics as 'the art of associating men for the purpose of establishing, cultivating and conserving them'.[82]

Society is conceived by Althusius and a writer in similar vein, Clemens Timpler, as a web, more especially as a web of smaller associations in which none is sovereign, governed by the practice of active co-operation and consensus, conversation and civility. Etiquette, trivialized by the English jurists of the nineteenth century is, to these writers, of the utmost importance. Indeed, Gelderen points out, Althusius, in his book, *Civilis Conversationis* "devotes a whole chapter to the art of civil eating". Sitting together throughout the entire meal, observing the conventions of table manners and gastronomic ordering, and consuming food and alcohol in moderation, were essential in forming peaceful social bonds.[83] The nineteenth century historian Jacob Burckhardt, Gelderen finds:

> . . . the roots of the values of the Enlightenment not in German or French absolutism, but in Dutch and English revolutions: 'the groundwork for this way of thinking', he argued, 'had been laid by the uprising of the Dutch in the sixteenth century and the English Revolution in the seventeenth'.[84]

79 Yolton, *ibid*, 25, 39.

80 John Locke, First Treatise, in Peter Laslett (ed), *John Locke: Two Treatises of Government*, New York, Signet (1965), paras 60 *et seq.*

81 See Thomas Hueglin, *Early Modern Concepts for a Late Modern World: Althusius on Community and Federalism*, Waterloo, Wilfrid Laurier University Press (1999).

82 Martin van Gelderen, The State and its Rivals in Early-Modern Europe, in Quentin Skinner and Bo Strath (eds), *States and Citizens: History, Theory, Prospects*, Cambridge, Cambridge University Press (2003), 86.

83 van Gelderen, *ibid*, 87.

84 van Gelderen, *op cit*, n 82, 92–93.

Locke's recommendations for the education of a gentleman conform closely with this ideal of a society of unforced civility in which accord is preserved not because everyone agrees with everyone else, but because everyone attempts to be familiar with ways of disagreeing that will cause least offense, thus least sense of shame and dishonor, thus least danger of disintegration. He has practical advice about fresh air and exercise, diet and bowel movements, about not indulging the whims of minors through fear of "crossing" them and thus appearing unloving, but unwittingly storing up selfishness and impatience with restraint – we might say forming an inability to defer gratification. The child must be trained in virtue and in a love of learning: ". . . virtue is important for the gentleman; (it) was also the very fabric and basis for humanity".[85] But learning about the world, for Locke, must be distinguished from how the world somehow is. We are, in Hume's terms, as we shall see, in the world of fictions – not of falsehoods, but of necessary assumptions; of refutability, if we want to borrow the twentieth century concept of Karl Popper, who is deeply indebted to the enlightenment of which we speak.[86] To learn is not to hold a mirror up to nature, for the classifications we use for the purpose of understanding are of human manufacture. As he writes in 1689:

> . . . all the great business of genera and species and their essences amount to no more than this, that men, making abstract ideas and settling them in their minds, with names annexed to them, do thereby enable themselves to consider things and discourse of them, as it were, in bundles, for the easier and readier improvement and communication of their knowledge . . .
>
> . . . in framing these ideas, the mind searches not its patterns in Nature, nor refers the ideas it makes to the real existence of things; but puts things together as may best serve its own purposes, without tying itself to a precise imitation of anything that really exists.[87]

Locke has much to say about habits. Thus:

> Carriage is not as it should be till it becomes natural in every part; falling, as skillful musicians' fingers do, into harmonious order without care and without thought. If in a conversation a man's mind be taken with a solicitous watchfulness about any part of his behavior, instead of being mended by it, it will be constrained, uneasie and ungraceful.[88]

85 Yolton, *op cit*, n 78, 39.

86 Karl Popper, *Conjectures and Refutations: The Growth of Scientific Knowledge*, London, Routledge & Kegan Paul (1963). Bentham's later castigation of Blackstone's "legal fictions" as legal falsehoods were, of course, a positivist misunderstanding.

87 John Locke, *An Essay Concerning Human Understanding* (1706) (PH Nidditch, ed), Oxford, Oxford University Press (1979), 420, 431.

88 John Yolton and Jean Yolton (eds), *John Locke: Some Thoughts Concerning Education* (1693), Oxford, Oxford University Press (1989), 151.

The inculcation of good habits by encouragement, "kind words", produces in later life agreeable manners that are performed naturally. *Rules* may be forgotten or deliberately flouted, but the *habit* of a sociable disposition lies below the horizon of consciousness once established.[89] Here we find the character of the Englishman, that figure who is also to fill again that void which lack has instituted.

Articulacy in conversation without dominating, wit which is not at another's expense, learning without the aim of exposing another's lack thereof, are all social lubricants of an environment in which disagreement does not lead to offense and may, indeed be productive. Locke was, after all, a scientist among his many accomplishments, and appreciated the positive contribution of disputation to the advancement of knowledge:

> I do not say this, that I think there should be no difference in conversation, nor opposition in men's discourses. This would be to take away the greatest advantage of society, and the improvements to be made by ingenious company, where the light is to be got from the arguings of men of parts . . . 'Tis not the owning ones dissent from another that I speak against, but the manner of doing it.[90]

The seemingly trifling matters of competence on the dance floor, grace in one's carriage, modest attention to one's attire and appearance all formed, too, for Locke, vital prerequisites for managing difference peacefully and constructively. Seized by an impetuous boor, the *Second Treatise* could be a social and political disaster. Such a person would read the situation he faced badly and begin his response too soon, even if his resistance to authority could ultimately be justified. Failing, by his lack of grace and appearance of good judgment, he would fail to persuade others and, finally, fail in his cause. If Locke was indeed a radical, a conclusion for which there may be sound evidence[91] his message was that tactful, modest and polite radicals produce the best results. Where political change is difficult, violence and repression may be preempted by rhetoric and refinement. The man who can make use of the right to resistance is, then, no abstract creature of nature, confronting a stereotyped opponent, but a highly specified person who has analyzed a particular situation, possessed of sufficient learning to gauge and engage with his opponent constructively.

Manners and the scene of the English gentleman

> To enlightened minds, the past was a nightmare of barbarism and bigotry . . . Enlightened opinion repudiated old militancy for modern civility. But how

89 Yolton, *ibid*, 121.

90 Yolton, *op cit*, n 88, 205.

91 See Richard Ashcraft, *Revolutionary Politics and Locke's 'Two Treatises of Government'*, Princeton, NJ, Princeton University Press (1986).

> could people adjust to each other? Sectarianism must cease . . . rudeness had to yield to refinement . . . This accent on refinement was no footling obsession with petty punctilio; it was a desperate remedy meant to heal the chronic social conflict and personal traumas stemming from civil and domestic tyranny and topsy-turvy values.[92]

Like a pleasing deportment, manners, as the Englishman, also help render the sovereign otiose. In Kate Fox's amusing observations of the English, she remarks that if someone collides with me on a busy street because she is looking another way, it is not the post-adolescent way to curse or threaten blows, but to apologize on one's own behalf for the mistake of the other.[93] Doubtless, the perpetrator will also apologize. Other cultures have similar traditions. Courtesy in road traffic or at supermarket checkouts defuses the frustration of congestion precisely because it is self-government, not required by rules. Aggressive behavior on these occasions is regarded as evidence of bad breeding.

After the above quotation, Porter goes on to quote Voltaire's observation that at the Royal Exchange in London, "the Jew, the Mahometan and the Christian transact together . . . the Presbyterian confides in the Anabaptist . . . the Churchman depends on the Quaker's word. And all are satisfied". A roseate view, of course, belonging to the tradition of Montesquieu's *Persian Letters* – a message to the French – but hopeful without being utopian or evangelical in the revolutionary or messianic sense we have once again lately learned to distrust. It draws on the Lockean conviction that human civility can be humanely inculcated, and on the view of the third Earl of Shaftesbury, Locke's protégé, that "the scene of the gentleman in polite conversation (was) a model for discursive and cultural activity and authority";[94]

> The paradigm of politeness offered an alternative to the reliance on traditional authoritative institutions for ordering the discursive world, because it sought processes within the babble, diversity and liberty of the new discursive world of the Town that would produce order and new direction.[95]

To Shaftesbury, in the urban(e) setting of the gentleman's world "gravity is of the very evidence of imposture", religious "enthusiasm" a major generator of fear, hence of strife and instability, "bloodshed, wars, persecutions and devastations". Tolerance and free criticism is as much the *sine qua non* of enlightened thought

92 Roy Porter, *The Creation of the Modern World: The Untold Story of the British Enlightenment*, New York, NY, Norton (2000), 21–22.

93 Kate Fox, *Watching the English: The Hidden Rules of English Behaviour*, London, Hodder and Stoughton (2004).

94 Lawrence Klein, *Shaftesbury and the Culture of Politeness: Moral Discourse and Cultural Politics in Early Eighteenth Century England*, Cambridge, Cambridge University Press (1994), 9.

95 Klein, ibid, 11–12.

here as many decades later it is to be for Kant: the Turk in his mosque and the "Romish . . . in the time of High Mass" are to be undisturbed, for:

> There can be no impartial and free censure of manners where and peculiar custom or national opinion is set apart and not only exempted from criticism, but even flattered with the highest art.[96]

What is more:

> It is only in a free nation such as ours that imposture has no privilege and that neither the credit of a court, the power of a nobility nor the awfulness of a church can give her protection from being arraigned in every shape and appearance.[97]

Sense and "middle temper" are to be preserved by "wit" and "freedom of raillery and humour", to which there are, of course, limits that require social negotiation. In Australian Rules football, it took some time for audiences and players to appreciate that moments of extreme tension were not defused by referring to Aboriginal players as "niggers". A recent incident in which a player, observing a fellow-player's tattoo, remarked, "I'd like to fuck her". This resulted in a physical altercation but, as Deb Waterhouse-Watson commented, the type of the breach of etiquette was misconceived. The tattoo was of the player's young daughter, who was not understood to be "fair game" for the comments, but, as Waterhouse-Watson points out, a culture of the denigration of women is a form of violence leading away from a civic basis for an equal "agreement of the people". Only equals can agree and disagree:[98]

> It is a breach of the harmony of public conversation to take things in such a key as is above the common reach, puts others to silence and robs them of their privilege of turn . . . we shall grow better reasoners by reasoning pleasantly and at our ease, taking up or laying down these subjects as we please . . . I put you in mind of the (recent) conversation . . . A great many fine schemes were destroyed, it is true, many grave reasonings overturned, but this being done without offence to the parties concerned and with improvement to the good humour of the company, it set the appetite the keener to such conversations.[99]

96 Third Earl of Shaftesbury, *Characteristics of Men, Manners, Opinions, Times* (1711), Cambridge, Cambridge University Press (Lawrence Klein, ed) (1999), 8, 7, and generally in a section entitled "A Letter Concerning Enthusiasm".

97 Shaftesbury, *ibid*.

98 Deb Waterhouse-Watson, All Women are Sluts: Australian Rules Football and Representations of the Feminine, (2007) 27 *Australian Feminist Law Journal* 155–62.

99 Shaftesbury, *op cit*, n 96, 37, 31.

In the essay, entitled "Sensus Communis: an Essay on the Freedom of Wit and Humour", Shaftesbury connects this particular common sense to politics and political action in a way that Kant was later unable to do in the context of Absolutist government. Here is the basis of a free and practicable constitution, hence the foundation of legality and the proper consideration of its student. Much later, as we shall see, such consideration came to seem marginal to the study of law based on the study of its sovereign source. "Obey promptly, but criticize freely" sounds Kantian, but was actually a Benthamite injunction and comes out of the same tradition of political *action* with which Shaftesbury was concerned to disagree. From where does the person politically motivated find her/his moral or practical criterion for criticism of what now appears to have become legitimate authority? By taking into account, Bentham was to tell us, "the greatest happiness of the greatest number". In "Sensus Communis", Shaftesbury anticipates him:

> . . . if these gentlemen who delight so much in the play on words, but are cautious how they grapple with definitions, would only tell us what self-interest was, and determine happiness and good, there would be an end of this enigmatical wit.[100]

To anticipate ourselves, to this accent on manners, Lord Kames offers another. Dedicating his *Elements of Criticism* to the new king, George III, in 1761, he reflects on the fresh dangers of discord – one to which George's ministers might well have attended more conscientiously – less from an excess of enthusiasm, but from an excess of luxury. "A flourishing commerce begets opulence; and opulence, inflaming our appetite for pleasure, is commonly vented on luxury and on every sensual gratification; selfishness rears its head . . . infecting all ranks".[101] He develops his theme later in the same volume under the heading, "Custom and Habit", where he recommends the encouragement of esthetics. Men (he is, of course addressing men, since he distinguishes the pernicious desire to enjoy a woman from that of wishing to cultivate affection for her) are naturally inclined to seek gratification. He distinguishes habits, which he associates with animal satisfactions and the possibility of intemperance, from custom which, over time may lead us to the higher "relish", for beauty.[102] "The venting (of) opulence on the Fine Arts", Kames urges George, "riches so employed, instead of encouraging vice, will excite both public and private virtue".[103]

The coffee house was the repository of both social accommodation and the kind of pedagogy that informs Kames' work. Those who did not aspire to be gentlemen

100 Shaftesbury, *op cit*, n 96, 56.
101 Lord Kames, *Elements of Criticism vol 1*, Edinburgh, Bell and Bradfute, A Constable & Co (1817), vii.
102 Kames, *ibid*, ch 14.
103 Kames, *op cit*, n 101, vii.

or important financiers doing business at Lloyd's coffee house appreciated the news, informed debate and commerce available to travelers at the "penny universities" that provided coffee, newspapers, liquor and lodging. Neither Klein nor the other recent historian of Augustan British refinement, John Brewer[104] contends that the urbane ideal of the coffee house, with its restrained conversation and mannered interaction always represented an actuality, but they stress the importance of the ideal for the shaping of the social order. And if the gentlemen's magazines in which civic sophistication was esteemed by the likes of Addison and Steele did not eliminate the rake any more than the "moral economy" detected by EP Thompson eliminated the occasional out-of-control riot, historians have found in them both the reflection and the production of greater social peace.

A taste for polite writing and the Englishman

A typical statement of the period is Addison's introduction to his *Spectator 1* as "a work which endeavours to Cultivate and Polish Human Life". In a later *Spectator* he continues:

> As the great and only End of these my Speculations is to banish Vice and Ignorance out of the Territories of Great Britain, I shal endeavour as much as possible to establish among us a Taste of Polite Writing.[105]

As Queenie Leavis observes, "he succeeded". She quotes him informing readers that three thousand copies of the magazine were distributed each day. His own informed guess was that each copy was read by twenty people, giving his project the support of 60,000 in London and Westminster. Leavis tells us that circulation rose to 20,000, perhaps 30,000 with, on Addison's evidence, 9000 copies of bound back volumes, a readership of perhaps 1 million in a (1700) population of 6 million:

> In the history of the self-educated in the eighteenth and nineteenth centuries . . . volumes of the *Tatler* and *Spectator* were observed to turn up in the homes of the respectable poor as their early reading, so numerous were their editions.[106]

In uniting a reading public to equate a knowledge of the world with virtue and gentility, Leavis argues, they were "finding an idiom for common standards of

104 John Brewer, *The Pleasures of the Imagination: English Culture in the Eighteenth Century*, London, Harper Collins (1997).

105 Addison, quoted in QD Leavis, *Fiction and the Reading Public*, London, Chatto and Windus (1932), 122.

106 Leavis, *ibid*, 123.

taste and conduct".[107] Her interest is in the way in which this early post-Revolutionary journalism, bringing together, she believes, the more courtly Aphra Behn with writers such as Defoe, Mrs Hayward and a line of novelists from Richardson "ultimately (to) Goldsmith and Austen". Readers are invited, she suggests, to focus on "the regulation of feelings rather than the regulating of property (they are nevertheless the same kind of feelings)".[108] My purposes in this instance are not very different. A common currency of taste, honor and virtue and self-restraint underwrites social order and thereby the security of property and with *that*, as contemporaries would have seen it, no doubt correctly, the constitution of (relative) liberty.

Barker-Benfield concurs in noticing the reach of the Addisonian values of taste, manners and self-restraint well into society. By the mid-eighteenth century, he writes, "clubs of apprentices and artisans marked political anniversaries by the breaking open of hogsheads of beer rather than by the breaking of heads. Feasting, entertainment and present-giving replaced rapine and violence".[109] And, most importantly, social cohesion was maintained.

There are a number of things to add to this much more figurative or esthetic reading than sovereign practice underlying the rule of law identified by Thompson in the appendix to his text on the Black Acts – or underlying the constitution, if we want to follow the vocabulary that informs, say Blackstone. The latter, we recall, locates an English sovereign in Parliament:

> This being the place where that absolute despotic power, which must in all governments, reside somewhere, is entrusted by the constitution of these kingdoms.[110]

Commonly, since the eighteenth century, the phrase "entrusted by the constitution" has been ignored, but clearly Blackstone envisages a prior authority on which the acceptance of any "absolute despotic power" depends. Much has been made by the positivists of the Septennial Act of 1716, by which Parliament extended the life of Commons elections from the three years required by the 1694 Triennial Act to seven years. Does this not prove the absolute supremacy of Parliament? The answer given by the Wilkes controversy later in the century suggests not. Here, as Burke made clear, the issue was whether the Commons had the power to decide whether the candidate with the most votes at an election should take his seat, or whether the House could substitute someone of their own choosing. It was decided in the courts that the Commons was obliged to accept

107 Leavis, *op cit*, n 105, 124.

108 Leavis, *op cit*, n 105, 12.

109 Leavis, *op cit*, n 105, 123. GJ Barker-Benfield, *The Culture of Sensibility: Sex and Society in Eighteenth Century Britain*, Chicago, IL, University of Chicago Press (1992), 90–91.

110 William Blackstone, *Commentaries on the Laws of England vol 1*, Oxford, Oxford University Press (1765), 156.

the candidate with the most votes. There was, in other words, something constitutionally underlying and restricting the power of Parliament.[111]

Blackstone's discussion of natural law – "no human laws are of any validity if contrary to this: and such of them as are valid derive all their force and all their authority, mediately or immediately from this"[112] – is often now seen as mere lip service to convention, but there seems no reason not to suppose that Blackstone saw natural law as part of the constitution that entrusted the government with this despotic power. The impression is strengthened at the end of his discussion of Locke's right of resistance to an unpopular despotic government, a doctrine still then widely held: it does not exist; "*so long . . . as the English constitution lasts*, we may venture to affirm that the power of Parliament is absolute and without control".[113] Arguably, this was Locke's point: the constitution is the trust, which, when all else seems to have failed, and with appropriate caution, the trustees may bring to an end. As we saw, Lady Mordaunt described such an event when she wrote to Locke as he waited to embark for England in 1689.

The figure of the Englishman with his civility and politeness

What I have tried to do in this chapter is trace a progress from one figure of the emperor, of a country suddenly self-conceived (by its monarch and his humanist courtiers at least) as "an empire entire unto itself", with a sovereign subject to no external or internal jurisdiction, to the threshold of another figure, the figure of the Englishman. If, for historians like Glenn Burgess, Absolutism mis-describes a regime where the king regards himself as bound by the law as a matter of his goodwill, and where no redress exists at the expiry of that good will, people of the later seventeenth century saw things differently. The century witnessed their experiments with doing politics in new ways, some of them rejected, some of them rendered more promising by the attention to the necessary polite ingredient of a successful polity. Despite its context, an oligarchy of landlords and gentlemen, elitist and by turns earnest and sincere, and corrupt and cynical, it seems to me that emergent Whiggism has much to teach the twenty-first century present.

The Scots, "Sister Peg", certainly considered that they had much to teach the English John Bull about the implications of what he had done in establishing, however precariously, the balanced constitution, displacing the overwhelming power of the monarch in the process. Neither the English nor the Scots were attracted by the Hobbesian social contract as a solution to disorder because it repeated still more vigorously the political philosophy of the Stuarts. Besides,

111 See Arthur Cash, *John Wilkes: The Scandalous Father of Civil Liberty*, New Haven, CT, Yale University Press (2006).

112 Cash, *ibid*, 41.

113 Cash, *op cit*, n 111, 157, emphasis added.

order was sought, not simply for its own sake but to safeguard property and with it liberty, which a Hobbesian regime could not do. The Lockean social contract did not lose all credibility, or Hume would not have rejected it so sharply almost a century after its formulation. Moreover, government as a trust for the benefit of the people, which they could legitimately end if there was a breach of that trust is taken seriously by Francis Hutcheson, as we shall see, and informed the politics of the Thirteen Colonies in 1776. Where there was considerable consensus, both theoretical and practical, was on Locke's insistence on the importance for constitutional stability of civility and politeness; and that it was on the foundation of civility and politeness that the constitution depended, making possible a predictable legality on which property and liberty rested. The Scots, in particular were:

> decidedly propagandistic, for they wished to proselytize their polite gospel of virtue and sentiment to a rapidly growing reading public. Finally, as critics and authors, they sought to cultivate the taste of this new, and often female, readership in the interest of social sympathy and virtue . . . They were determined to bring their educational message to a politically powerful but ethically suspect and pedagogically misguided John Bull.[114]

It is to their efforts, the reception of them and the first overseas empire of the "freeborn Englishman" that I want to turn in Chapter 3.

114 John Dwyer, A "Peculiar Blessing": Social Converse in Scotland from Hutcheson to Burns, in John Dwyer and Richard Sher (eds), *Sociability and Society in Eighteenth Century Scotland*, Edinburgh, Mercat Press (1993), 6–7.

Chapter 3

The Scottish writing of the civility of the "Englishman"

English constitutional practices had, as discussed, acquired, by European standards of the late seventeenth century, some unusual characteristics. Not only was there, by those standards, a high degree of national self-consciousness,[1] but its monarchy was chosen and constrained. It had combined the qualities of a war machine like the Absolutisms of mainland Europe, but much more efficiently, with commercial acuity and a liberty of personal freedom and the protection of property comparable with the United Provinces. England had two attractions for the Scots. Lowland Scots were, naturally, convinced of the superiority of their law, their educational organization and their Kirk. But they saw a country to their south many times larger, flourishing commercially in a way that Scotland was not. There was also, I believe, a Presbyterian perspective. Presbyterian teaching, since Buchanan, James VI/I's sometime tutor, was, for the time, remarkably egalitarian, politically, despite its authoritarian theological dimension. All men and women should be literate and all tyrants should be resisted. England had, Scots thought, stumbled on the practice of liberty, but may not, through their obsession with commerce's more philistine dimensions, have the wit to avoid stumbling into something less savory than education, literacy and civility.

This may have been an unjustifiable fear. Perhaps the Church of England was too languid for the Scottish intellectuals in the fairly homogeneous triangle of Glasgow, Saint Andrews, Aberdeen and Edinburgh, although there is little evidence of Calvinist evangelism in *their* writing. The men – and they were all men – were conscious of the Highlanders to their north and west in a way that was different from the English awareness. For the English, the Highlands nourished a threat, a bewilderingly, largely non English-speaking population which, Roman Catholic like most of the Irish, offered a French invasion route. For the Scots – and the Irish

1 Europe's ethnicities were distributed across dukedoms and principalities in which populations were simply the subjects of a dynasty: see Geoffrey Parker (ed), *The Thirty Years' War*, 2nd edn, London, Routledge (1997); Graham Robb, *The Discovery of France*, London, Picador (2007), chs 1–3 argues that it was not until the nineteenth century that even the French established a national, rather than regional identities, each region with its own patois.

Presbyterian Hutcheson, whose academic life was in Glasgow – it may be that we can see at work something like Said's "Orientalism".[2] Life in the Borders had been, and remained for many years after the 1707 Union with England, much like the Highlands.[3] Urbane Scots identified themselves against the societies whose, to them, chaotic orders prevailed through Cumberland and Dumfriesshire in the west, Northumberland and the Tweedside counties of Eastern Scotland.

But if proselytizing Presbyterianism is absent in Scottish enlightenment writing, David Hume, as we shall see, emphasized the wisdom and continuing need for toleration in England, if Great Britain were to survive, a latitudinarian balance between superstition (i.e. Roman Catholicism) and enthusiasm (i.e. evangelical Protestantism). The Scots, in the triangle I have described, are rescued from the backwardness they witness or remember. But this rescue, and the enlightenment made possible by it, relied on the solidity of England and the Union.

In this chapter, then, I look principally at the role of the Scots in the creation and maintenance of the figure of the sociable Englishman, the character for whom the capacity for agreeable disagreement in culture would permit constitutional politics, liberty and security of property.

Scotland and the invention of England by the Scots

> Smith observed that, whereas in France and England, talented scholars and writers were frequently drawn to the church, in Scotland and the other countries of Reformed Europe "the most eminent men of letters . . . have not all, indeed, but the far greater part of them been professors in universities.". The authority of professors extended beyond the ranks of students formally enrolled in classes.[4]

At risk of overloading the text with quotations, it is worth noting two other remarks. From a Scottish perspective:

> Since the "natural condition" of humans is life in society, the premise from which norms are generated must also be social. It is therefore illicit to generate those norms from some extra-social or extra-temporal perspective. We cannot meaningfully assess the legitimacy of a government by invoking such a perspective, by, so to speak, stepping outside our social selves.[5]

2 Edward Said, *Orientalism: Western Conceptions of the Orient*, London, Routledge & Kegan Paul (1978).

3 George MacDonald Fraser, *The Steel Bonnets: The Story of the Anglo-Scottish Border Rievers*, London, Pan (1979).

4 James Moore, Natural Rights in the Scottish Enlightenment, in Mark Goldie and Robert Wokler (eds), *The Cambridge History of Eighteenth Century Political Thought*, Cambridge, Cambridge University Press (2006), 292.

5 Christopher Berry, *The Social Theory of the Scottish Enlightenment*, Edinburgh, Edinburgh University Press (1997), 31, quotation marks in the original.

From an Enlightenment perspective more generally:

> If reflection has meaning only within a particular tradition, there will be limits on its ability to call this tradition into question. To suppose that it is possible to place ourselves in a position where we could reflect on the validity of that tradition is on a par with the assumption that we could somehow step outside of our language and certify that it does indeed give us a true account of the world.[6]

The third quotation takes us in a sense back to Wittgenstein and his differences from JL Austin. Austin wants us to instantiate certain amiable usages, which are not those of "us" all, whilst the later Wittgenstein invites a more heterogeneous us to question them all. As Moore makes clear, not only that, as we shall see, writing, debate and innovation through academic controversy made Scotland a vigorous and intellectual environment – the most vigorous in Europe at the time, perhaps – but that the reformed universities in Scotland were required from 1690 to engage in scholarly practice in previously forbidden spaces. Let us not forget that Locke's books were among the last to be burned in public in England as late as the 1670s, which makes the Scottish practice very few decades later a rapid change from the previous doctrines of Absolutist monarchy and the duties of passive obedience to established authority. And also, of course, consistent with the more constitutionally liberal principles established in England by the Revolution.[7] This intellectual and political commitment enhanced by the Act of Union of 1707 and cemented by the commercial motivations that led the Scots to abandon their Parliament, though not their Kirk and their law, determined the Scots to ensure that the English kept and improved their Englishness. The form of the Scottish conviction that this was where their future lay was shaped by, not only by, their, as it turned out, possibly greater commercial acumen, a thorn in the English side because it was before long so successful, but also by their combined empirical curiosity about the nature of social order and about the moral principles which ought to shape it.

In Chapter 2, I suggested that patrimonial regimes in their European manifestation of absolute monarchy seemed to serve the cause of enlightenment in two ways. Optimists, such as, perhaps Kant, and certainly Bentham, saw the enlightened despots as providing encouragement and the only stable framework within which social and intellectual innovation could be pursued. If Kant's injunction, *sapere aude* is, as James Schmidt suggests, to be read as daring to think *for* oneself, rather than daring to think *by* oneself, then perhaps the realms of the Bourbons, Catherine of Russia, Frederick the Great and Maria Theresa did provide the peaceful conditions of sociability within the state that made the culture of reason

6 James Schmidt, Introduction, in Schmidt (ed), *What is Enlightenment? Eighteenth Century Answers and Twentieth Century Questions*, Berkeley, CA, University of California Press (1996), 20.

7 Moore, *op cit*, n 4, 295.

possible. Whilst not a supporter of absolute monarchy, Burke understood its traditions as having had, until the cataclysm of 1789, the ability to contain the corrosive potential of abstract reason and therefore, presumably, of preserving certain beneficial aspects of enlightenment.

I attempt here to contrast with absolutist practices, the conditions of sociability that made enlightenment possible in eighteenth century Britain. The British elites and a considerable proportion of other subjects[8] evoked a suspicion of authoritarian government by phrases such as liberty and property and the free-born Englishman. Protestant manliness ensured a vigorous commercial spirit. Since "property is the foundation of power", it followed, for Daniel Defoe, for example, that freeholders should have the right to govern themselves and the other inhabitants of the country through representatives chosen freely as the most likely to benefit the common purpose, as well. Although Defoe does not mention it, the Revolution settlement indicated the awareness by the propertied of the need for an independent judiciary to uphold the code of property, the common law.[9] This had been secured "in an act for the further limitation of the crown, and better securing the rights and liberties of the subject", providing that "judges' commissions be made *quamdiu se bene gesserint* and their salaries ascertained and established; but upon the address of both houses of parliament it may be lawful to remove them".[10]

The Scottish experience had in the past been, in some ways, the opposite of England's, yet the best way forward for Scotland in the new union, formed in 1707, was expressed by a number of writers in remarkably similar terms to those expressed by English writers. We can summarize the similarities and notice some differences, and finally make a brief return to Edmund Burke, one of the Rockingham Whigs who opposed the American war; and a first generation Protestant who was neither English nor Scottish, but Irish, who sums up a widespread position on social order as it had developed since the Revolution and the Union, and before that position changed its hue and became more authoritarian. Social order in England and Scotland (excepting the Highlands) was seen as resting on a series of concordances – conventions, agreements, similarities of outlook and a commitment to a sociable civility that would permit the negotiation of dis-similarities. To this social view, discussed in Chapter 2, some of the Scots were concerned, as we shall see, to investigate the histories, economies and typologies of social order so as to explain why relationships among people varied across time and geographical space. This concern was not new, as Montesquieu's writings indicate but took on a greater prominence and systematicity among some of the Scots.

8 Wilfrid Prest, *Albion Ascendant: English History 1660–1815*, Oxford, Oxford University Press; Kathleen Wilson, *The Sense of the People: Politics, Culture and Imperialism in England*, Cambridge, Cambridge University Press (1992).

9 Daniel Defoe, The Original Power of the People in England, in PN Furbanks and WR Owens (eds), *Daniel Defoe: The True-Born Englishman and Other Writings*, London, Penguin (1997), 104, 109.

10 Preamble and Part III of 12 13 Will III c.2 (Act of Settlement 1701),

The elements of order in a sense condense into a constitution which expresses itself in government and laws. Popular order (although not in the modern quasi-democratic sense), the constitution, government and law were seen as interacting in complex ways that differed from the conceptions of Thomas Paine and the men of the American revolution. Locke and the men of the English revolution condemned the constitution as they found it prior to the revolution, as a threat to Protestantism, property and liberty, and justified its popular overthrow and replacement on that ground. Triennial Parliaments were widely seen as a part of the constitutional settlement. In 1716, the year after the first major Jacobite rebellion, Parliament, whose legitimacy stemmed from the constitution generated by the revolutionary settlement, found three-yearly elections to be a threat to the constitution, "very grievous and burthensome", because frequent elections were expensive and a cause of "violent and lasting heats and animosities" among subjects "at this juncture when a restless and popish faction are designing . . . to renew rebellion within this kingdom and an invasion from abroad . . . destructive to the peace and security of the government".[11] So, Parliament altered the constitution.

Finally, in the era framed by Locke and Burke, we find Burke himself telling the House of Commons in 1775, anent the conduct of American affairs that:

> Whilst *manners* remain entire, they will correct the vices of the law, and so soften it at length to their own temper. But we have to lament that in most of the late proceedings we see very few traces of that generosity, humanity and dignity of mind which formerly characterized this nation.[12]

Manners are, then, to correct the laws. As for the constitution, according to Burke, its exercise must be subjected to the customs and limitations of time and place if it is to survive. Thus, in relation to, in his examples, the prerogative of the Crown to veto legislation, and of the Westminster Parliament to legislate for the Americans, the "propriety" may be (in 1775) insisted upon, but "the exercise itself is wisely forborne".[13] The "apparent omnipotence" of the king in Parliament, he observes to his fellow parliamentarians, would not allow it to "alter the established religion of this country". The reason is that it is the purpose of the legislature "to follow, not to force the public inclination, to give a direction, a form, a technical dress and a specific sanction to the general sense of the community . . .".[14]

11 1 Geo I, stat 2, c 38 (Septennial Act 1716). Septennial elections actually proved more expensive: see JH Plumb, *The Growth of Political Stability in England 1675–1725*, Harmondsworth, Penguin (1969).

12 Edmund Burke, Speech on Moving His Resolutions for Conciliation with the Colonies, House of Commons, 22 March 1775, in Peter Stanlis (ed), *Edmund Burke: Selected Writings and Speeches*, Washington, DC, Regnery Press, 231.

13 Burke, *ibid*, 240.

14 Burke, *op cit*, n 12, 240–41.

Although they differed considerably as to when such a power might be exercised, most of the writers of the period between Locke and Burke believed that if sufficiently ill-served, a community might resist its government and substitute another. In Burke's writings this at first sight is the least clear, since, as Womersley remarks, his principal concern was with trying to render the changing constitution, particularly the position of the House of Commons in relation to the Crown, consistent with its traditions. He would not have supported the Americans had he not seen them as asserting concrete and traditionally-inspired rights; but it is difficult to interpret his remarks of 1775 as anything other than advocating a power to return, not to a stasis, but to an interrupted and definite trajectory of constitutionally progressing freedoms. Equally difficult, if one wanted to rule out entirely his view of resistance, would be his polemics on the corruption of the parliamentary process. If the *House* of Commons were to allow itself to become a rubber stamp for executive policies, would this not justify the intervention of the commons itself?[15]

The English monarchy of the seventeenth century had been too strong for the men of property to feel secure about their property. The strength of the Crown had to be opposed, and then that opposition prevented from turning into hostility toward all authority and hence into anarchy. Scottish government was for long too weak. In both cases, the solution was seen as civility, a self-policing requirement fundamental to peace and commerce, and neither before nor after Union capable of arbitration through religious consensus.

The English solution, we have seen, recognizing that, as Hume was to put it, government is based on opinion,[16] was to seek some means of coordinating that opinion, ensuring that, among the most influential at least, disagreement across a range of matters, whilst inevitable, indeed to be encouraged, could be moderate. A number of historians, I suggested in Chapter 2, find evidence that the "polite" solution to conflict extended well below the official "political nation", those who voted or held office. In a reversal of what came gradually to be believed during the Victorian era, it was etiquette, civility, sociability and politeness in the theatrical performance of public life, or life in public at many levels, which underpinned, made possible, the constitution and the laws consequent upon it, not the other way round. The script for this performance, I suggested, was provided by writers like Locke and Shaftesbury and later the pages of *The Tatler* and Mr Spectator, and aspired to and replayed in a thousand variants at many social levels. Until the 1760s, whilst not a politically tranquil, or internationally affable, society, England, Great Britain as it had become by the Act of Union with Scotland, and the Atlantic communities, avoided the earlier chaos of the civil wars and managed internal

15 Edmund Burke, Thoughts on the Present Discontents, in David Womersley (ed), *Edmund Burke, A Philosophical Enquiry into the Origins of Our Ideas of the Sublime and Beautiful and Other Pre-Revolutionary Writings*, London, Penguin (1998).

16 David Hume, *Essays*, Indianapolis, IN, Liberty Collection, 32.

differences with considerable success. This process is at the same time the reinvention of England, to a significant degree, as we shall see, by the Scots; and until later in the eighteenth century, Americans, too, understood themselves as "free-born Englishmen", and there was considerable regret in radical circles that the secession of the Americans likely meant a blow to the progressive direction that Englishness might take.

With the exception of its brief rule by Cromwellian England, Scotland had remained the only member of the four nations of the British Isles to have retained independence from England, although, since Elizabeth's death in 1603, sharing a monarch with England, first the Stuarts and then the joint monarchy of William III and Mary II. Economically depressed, in 1707, in return for the abolition of border tariffs and access to English commerce and empire, Scotland dissolved its independent Parliament and formed a union with England, to form Great Britain. It was an unusual step[17] – countries do not standardly abandon their political independence voluntarily – and it was not entirely compensated by the quite small representation of Scotland in the Westminster Parliament. On the other hand, the Act of Union contained, as we have seen, guarantees of independence for the two most significant Scottish institutions, education, Scots law and the Presbyterian Kirk.

Eventual commercial prosperity as a product of union was entirely foreseeable, particularly for ports and trades able to profit both from a bigger market and from the Atlantic traffic, increasingly, of course, in slave plantation products. Cultural efflorescence in Scotland might, when union was mooted, have seemed less likely. Scotland had traditionally been a decentralized polity, the Lowlands sharing more of the local and kin-dependent structures of government with the Highlands than they were later to do, or later like to remember. In both Highlands and Lowlands until the seventeenth century, the resolution of disputes to the possession and ownership of land, or disputes resulting from injuries, was typically some form of arbitration at the behest of the victim or the kindred of the victim or deceased person, preceded in some cases by a feud between the kin involved. Even when royal justice may have been available from the Crown in Edinburgh, speed and effectiveness made recourse to a local laird or settlement among the heads of the relevant kin the preferred option for many disputants.[18]

Jenny Wormold notices two consequences of this: the poor, or those whose families lacked the means or power to bargain or compel reparation for wrongs done, remained unsatisfied; and a considerable amount of disorder characterized government. Unlike the English gentleman, the literati of eighteenth century

17 Accomplished at a practical level by bribery and intimidation from England, its actual form unsatisfactory for many Scots who favored and its commercial advantages for a time uncertain: See PH Scott (ed), *1707: The Union of Scotland and England in Contemporary Documents*, Edinburgh, Chambers (1979).

18 Jenny Wormold, Bloodfeud, Kindred and Government in Early Modern Scotland, (1980) 87 *Past and Present* 54–97.

Scotland did not, to repeat, look back at the extravagantly strong claims to authority of a putative absolute monarchy, necessarily contested by violent and "enthusiastic" means, but with a resulting period of social chaos. Instead, the Scots both looked back at the unrest and violence occasioned by a weak monarchy dependent on the quasi-ordered instability of the feud; and they looked north and west at the same time, to the, to their minds, uncivilized and unprogressive conduct of the feud, as it persisted among the Highland clans. Later distaste from within the cultured triangle, Glasgow, St Andrews, Aberdeen and Edinburgh, for the Highlanders, perpetuating an earlier form of society until the mid-eighteenth century may, however, conceal an embarrassment about practices shared only too recently.[19]

The Scottish Reformation, three decades after the English, largely a Lowlands affair, did eventually offer a solution to the disorder identified by Wormold, but at a cost. Looking at the English Reformation from his vantage point in the mid-eighteenth century David Hume remarked on the fragile basis of rational stability. In the English seventeenth century the road to stability had led through the confrontation of what he saw as Roman Catholic superstition by evangelical, "enthusiastic" Protestantisms. Only when society was able to become neither superstitious nor enthusiastic and accept a latitudinarianism not universally shared, but from which all benefited, could the state, liberty and property enjoy security. Hume could not have said the same about Scotland where – the monarchy still weak – under John Knox, a form of theocracy attempted to displace the governing practices permitted under the Roman Catholic monarchies and did so with great Calvinist vigor until a Moderate hegemony began to prevail a century and a half later, under the influence of the likes of Francis Hutcheson and his fellow, mostly academic, literati.

The Scottish Reformation was more ideologically driven than the English Henrician reforms of the earlier sixteenth century had been, where the nascent Church of England retained many of the Roman forms of worship, even preserving for itself the designation, "Catholic" church. The change from Roman Catholicism in Scotland to a Calvinist form of Protestantism was greater and therefore more contentious than the English Reformation had been. The regent, Mary of Guise and her daughter, Mary, Queen of Scots, were both Catholic, frustrating the universality of reformation for a time[20] and while eventually "to a large extent" Knox's "mission to create the New Jerusalem in Scotland succeeded"[21] it did so as a form of harsh proto-state in conditions of political turmoil, an authoritarian

19 Wormold, *ibid*, 97. Walter Scott's *Rob Roy* provides a contrast between the commercial honor of a London businessman and a Glasgow merchant, on the one hand and the honor of the noble savage represented by Rob, on the other.

20 The two Marys and the English Elizabeth, under whom the Church of England famously adopted its *via media* policy, formed Knox's "monstrous regiment of women".

21 Arthur Herman, *The Scottish Enlightenment: The Scots' Invention of the Modern World*, London, Fourth Estate (2001), 19.

theocracy that punished moral offenses with a zeal unparalleled in England. In her studies of witchcraft persecutions in Scotland, Larner compares the inability of the weak Scottish secular state to mitigate the rigors of theocratic order to the earlier situation in Germany, where witch-hunts and witch-burnings had also been frequent.[22]

Not all the victims of religious zeal unqualified by tolerance were women, although most were. In Scotland, as late as 1696, Thomas Aikenhead, a theology student at Edinburgh was convicted of blasphemy, having allegedly decried Christian doctrines as, collectively, "a rapsodie of feigned and ill-invented nonsense".[23] He was executed in early 1697, a sign of the fragility of academic freedom, and certainly amid controversy but, nonetheless, this was not a sign of the toleration Locke had appealed for in England in 1689.[24] In light of this case, the failure of the case against Francis Hutcheson in Glasgow, a little over forty years later, in 1738, for his Moderate rejection of some of the grimmer aspects of Presbyterian doctrines on the utter depravity of humans, of the Elect, and the sole source of virtue in religious faith, is a sign of progress toward a more moderate Presbyterianism.[25]

And the Presbyterian legacy did, as I suggested earlier, after all, have a culturally positive dimension. George Buchanan, who has already been mentioned as one of James VI/I's tutors, and an early Moderator of the General Assembly of the Kirk, had published a treatise on government in 1579, *The Law of Government Among the Scots*, advocating a form of popular sovereignty, albeit within the framework of the Kirk's intrusive and inflexible refusal to recognize anything but its theological and moral doctrines. Buchanan asserted the duty of "the lowest and meanest of men" to resist tyranny to the point of killing the tyrant and conferring authority on a source capable of managing the affairs of government in the people's interests[26] – something abhorred by James, it was suggested. If this sentiment sits uneasily with the Kirk's authoritarianism in other spheres, and never, in any event, formed a serious program of political action, it gestured toward a notion of order founded, not in rules, but in informed collective opinion, one embodied in the idea of the early presbytery, which selected its own minister.

22 Christina Larner, *Enemies of God: The Witch-Hunt in Scotland*, Oxford, Blackwell (1981); Christina Larner, *Witchcraft and Religion: The Politics of Popular Belief*, Oxford, Blackwell (1984).

23 James Buchan, *Capital of the Mind: How Edinburgh Changed the World*, London, John Murray (2003), 56.

24 John Locke, *A Letter Concerning Toleration* (1689), Indianapolis, IN, Liberty Collection (James Tully, ed, 1983).

25 Thomas Mountner (ed), *Francis Hutcheson: On Human Nature – Reflections on our common systems of morality and on the social nature of man*, Cambridge, Cambridge University Press (1993), 10.

26 Herman, *op cit*, n 21, 18. Buchanan's opposition to the doctrine of the divine right of kings obviously did not appeal to the adult James VI, to whom he was tutor between 1570 and 1578. James later became James I of England and claimed to be God's representative on earth.

Moreover, in raising the issue of informed choice on the part of the "lowest and meanest", it reflected what would be for centuries a tradition of concern by the Kirk for education. After all, in order to comply with the Kirk's doctrines about religious and moral behavior, one had to be able to discover what they were. This approach to education did produce some material results as early as the mid-seventeenth century.

Ironically, in the year of Aikenhead's conviction, 1696, the Scottish Parliament passed the Schools Act, authorizing the establishment in every parish of an elementary school, the master's or "dominie's" stipend to be met by the taxation of land. Girls as well as boys were included.[27] A century later, Herman writes, Scotland would be the world's most literate society, and publishing for the consumption of its readers would become one of the major forms of national economic activity.[28] The long-established superiority of Scottish education, conceded by Macaulay in his advocacy of a more modest provision in England in 1847, is not uncontested – Colley's "Scottophobia" continues into the present among the English – but it is otherwise difficult to see how Scots not only emigrated as desperately poor hopefuls from the Highlands, but came from the Lowlands, educated in the schools and universities, disproportionately to be represented as merchants in America and India, and as military officers and administrators in the East India Company and its successor, the Raj.[29]

The work of Miller and Camic[30] suggests that from the late seventeenth century, parish and other schools, although varied in quality and the nature of the education they provided, were, in European terms – because of the Act of 1696 – unusually accessible, and included a wide social spectrum of the male and some of the female population of children. If Burns (1759–96), the plowman-philosopher-poet from Ayrshire, and James Hogg, the Ettrick Shepherd (1770–1835), from Selkirkshire, should not be taken as typical, parish school students did make their way to university, and the universities flourished, professors increasing their incomes from the fees they could charge for adding new courses to the curriculum – fees usually modest enough to attract students also from a variety of economic backgrounds; Masters students from the English dissenting academies and students from Europe, attracted by the universities' growing international reputations. Americans, it has

27 Eliga Gould, Revolution and Counter-Revolution, in David Armitage and Michael Braddick (eds), *The British Atlantic World*, London, Palgrave (2009), 203.

28 Herman, *op cit*, n 21, 22.

29 Macaulay, Speech on Education, House of Commons, 18 April 1847, in TF Ellis (ed), *The Miscellaneous Writings and Speeches of Lord Macaulay*, London, Longmans Green (1889), 734; Eric Richards, Scotland and the Uses of the Atlantic Empire, in Bernard Bailyn and Philip Morgan (eds), *Strangers in the Realm: Cultural Margins of the First British Empire,* Chapel Hill, NC, University of North Carolina Press (1991), points to the differences among historians of this positive view of Scottish education.

30 Thomas Miller, Where Did College English Studies Come From?, (1990) 9 *Rhetorical Studies* 50–69; Charles Camic, Experience and Ideas: Education for Universalism in Eighteenth Century Scotland, (1983) 25 *Comparative Studies in Society and History* 50–68.

been suggested, found more that was useful to them in Scottish than in English universities, of which there were only two semi-serious Protestant institutions. A number of Scottish academics, such as John Witherspoon, signatory to the Declaration of Independence, were attracted to work in colonial and postcolonial America. But not only was scholarship taken seriously as an institutional practice in Scotland, but the experience of mixing with a socially varied student body in both provincial town schools and in universities helped, according to Camic, to create an intellectual climate in which a tolerant form of universalism could flourish. If the Scots were, in the modern sense, less democratic than the revolutionary Americans, both embraced considerable elements of egalitarianism in their thought.

Arendt on the metaphysics of sovereignty, the impossibility of certainty

> One can conclude – as indeed our whole tradition of thought has concluded – that the essence of politics is rulership, and that the dominant political passion is the passion to rule or govern. This, I propose, is profoundly untrue. The fact that political elites have always determined the political destinies of the many and have, in most cases, exercised domination over them indicates, on the one hand, the bitter need of the few to protect themselves from the many; or rather, to protect the island of freedom against the surrounding sea of necessity, and it indicates on the other, the responsibility that falls automatically upon those who care for the fate of those who do not.[31]

> The thought that the description of political discourse in twelfth century France, metaphysics in nineteenth century Germany and painting in fifteenth century Urbino might some day flow together to create a seamless tapestry which would be our ideal *Intellectual History of Europe* is an elevating one. But it is the idea of a book written by no human hand.[32]

The first quotation above reflects the concern we have seen Arendt expressing in her work about the threat posed to political freedom by the strong notion of sovereignty that was to inform legal positivist thinking in the nineteenth century – the sovereign as sole authority for government and unique and certain source of valid law. She contrasts the American and French Revolutions, arguing that the latter, by substituting popular for Absolutist political sovereignty, missed the opportunity taken by the Americans for liberating themselves from the single sovereignty the British were belatedly trying to impose on them from Westminster.

The sovereignty of the Absolutist French monarch was not to be resisted, since he was the deputy of the Divine. The General Will was substituted by the

31 Hannah Arendt, *On Revolution*, Harmondsworth, Penguin Books (1973), 276.

32 Richard Rorty, JB Schneewind and Quentin Skinner (eds), *Philosophy in History*, Cambridge, Cambridge University Press (1984), 9.

revolution for Absolutism, but in practical terms, she remarks, it is always a person or an official who speaks for the popular and who, therefore, like the Bourbons, is not to be resisted. The Americans, in Arendt's view, had the advantage of not confronting either this legacy of political absolutism or the French "sea of necessity", the poverty of a large population faced with the inability to mobilize the resources to ameliorate that necessity. For both the French legacy of politics and the prevailing poverty, certainty of knowledge and leadership were necessary, but at the same time unattainable, like the history to which Rorty *et al* refer us in the above quotation. In a large land with apparently unlimited resources, Americans recognized the role of the compacts, negotiations and compromise in forming the basis of cultural and social order among white men. Here is Jefferson's "agreement of the people", a political phenomenon different from that of the Convention Parliament mainly in its inclusion of a larger proportion of the population.

Arendt's argument is too complex to be followed any further here, addressing as it does, not merely the question of how the apparent legitimacies of different kinds of political order are established, but a conviction that haunted her work, that social and liberal democracy, dictatorship and totalitarianism exist on a continuum such that one can slide from the first to the last category all too easily. Arriving in the United States as a wartime refugee, for example, she recognized the possibly corrosive effects in the post-World War II era of one of the reasons for the republic's early success – its affluence compared with 1789 France. Affluence in 1776 was by 1950 in danger of becoming obsessive consumerism, material goods and private display displacing citizenship and public service.[33]

She escaped totalitarianism to a liberal democracy that within a few years of her arrival survived the McCarthyist era in the United States, even if worse things were to come. We seem increasingly in "the west" to be moving from the social/liberal democracy that characterized the immediate aftermath of World War II to a crackpot authoritarianism that, confronted by timorous intellectual opposition, justifies itself in terms of economic development and the need to counter with war-like measures ever-substitutable "enemies" – communism, drug traffickers and other kinds of mafia; and now Islam and terrorism. These are wars, which conveniently cannot be won, especially since the later ones were initially financed and then provoked by the very powers that condemn them.[34] It is all part of what Furedi and others have termed "the politics of fear", the justification for increased state control of populations.[35]

33 See Tony Judt, *Ill Fares the Land*, Melbourne, Allen Lane (2010).

34 Western support for Israel is an obvious example, as are the US arming of the Taliban in order to oppose the Russian occupation of Afghanistan, and its arming of Saddam Hussein in his war with Iran.

35 Frank Furedi, *The Politics of Fear: Beyond Left and Right*, London, Continuum (2006).

Re-scripting the great chain of being

For the moment, whilst not abandoning the issue of political legitimacy and its implication with legality with which the chapter began, and which no reference to Arendt's work can ignore, I want to turn to the continuities with an earlier tradition of thought represented by aspects of the Scottish Enlightenment, but also some divergences and relations between epistemological and political challenges to authority. I can do this by juxtaposing two unlikely candidates: the great chain of being and some tendencies of the work of Immanuel Kant.

Berry's remarks, quoted earlier,[36] trace the questioning by the subject of its own subjection. As the subject gains power, as the inquiring agent through whom the regularities of the universe are known, its political power over its own regulation becomes an issue. The implication of Chapter 2, and the argument I shall develop here is that in an important sense the early modern and eighteenth century thought with which I am concerned here had not abandoned, but merely re-oriented or re-characterized the aspect of a theme apparently commonplace, if losing its credibility in its original form, in Elizabethan cosmology, one that has been termed the great chain of being.[37]

Conventionally, in the divine gaze, every particle of the universe is connected in some way with every other. The unnatural upsetting of authority represented by the murder of King Duncan by Shakespeare's Macbeth, in the tragedy of that name, for example, is famously accompanied in the play by stories among the servants of equally unnatural events in the heavens and by the revolt of beasts against their masters. When Shakespeare's King Lear unnaturally relinquishes his power and divides his realm among his daughters, two of them respond with an equally unnatural withdrawal of their love and care for the dignity and even personhood of their father, who at one point stands on a storm-blasted heath accompanied only by a perceptive fool and the Earl of Kent, blinded by Lear's daughter.[38]

In the intellectual reorganization that accompanied, as both cause and effect, the political upheavals of the seventeenth century, the discerning gaze became primarily a human one – obviously, in the case of the drama, the members of the audience – hence the aptness of Edmund's expression of skepticism before the audience at the court in 1605.[39] Intellectual emphasis had by the middle seventeenth and eighteenth centuries changed to questions about human judgment,

36 Berry, *op cit*, n 5, 30.

37 EMW Tillyard, *The Elizabethan World Picture*, London, Pimlico (1998). The contemporary, skeptical, perspective, that social custom's role in forming the subject, not the conjugation of the stars, is responsible for his actions is expressed by Edmund, objecting to the consequences of his illegitimacy, in Shakespeare's *Lear*, Act 1, Sc 2.

38 William Shakespeare, *Macbeth*, Act II, Sc iv, or *King Lear*, Act III, Sc ii and Sc iii.

39 Arguably, of course, sixteenth century drama had already positioned the audience as a more critically responsible participant than the didactic passion plays of the medieval era, for which the watchers were more of a congregation.

understanding and the form of their organization.[40] The unifying links in the great chain were now provided by the intellectual work of the human subject. Order and the unity implied by the notion of a universe became increasingly a feature imposed by the human mind, observing, in conditions of sociability, both nature and, reflexively, the observing mind itself, as part of nature. Politeness, restraint, conversation and compromise, as we saw in Chapter 2, do not operate simply to *preserve* social order, which is something now recognized as an entity having no natural basis, but rather as being something which is in need of continual cultivation. These qualities of conversation and restraint seemed to be the basis of social order and, connectedly, they were now seen as the pre-requisite of learning. Locke appreciated this, as we saw, and the Scottish Enlightenment writers were to take it very much to heart.

But there is another tradition in the realm of order and discipline, *just* sufficiently different as to make it worth contrasting briefly with the work of the Scots, namely that of Kant. We could, at risk of triteness, characterize the contrast as one between Kant's preoccupation with the morally just society and its abstract necessity, its conceptually unavoidability, even, and the Scots' contrasting preoccupation with the socio-historical pragmatics of how a more or less morally just society might be accomplished. The Scots, as we shall see, perhaps because of their old tradition of seeking education in the Netherlands before their own institutions achieved an equal intellectual status, recognized England as, with the Netherlands, the freest society in Europe. At the same time, there was, as I have mentioned, the suspicion among the Scots that English freedoms were the result of an accident which the geographical English might not be capable of sustaining because they did not really comprehend its conditions of existence. This may have been an unjustified conclusion, in the shadows of Locke and Shaftesbury, but a slightly more plausible view in light of the conflict with Americans later in the century, and the preoccupation with authority that was later to characterize both the empire and the politics of Britain in relation to Ireland.[41] The Scots may, like Arendt, have discerned the authoritarian worm in the bud of "liberty". In any event, without being over-affectionate toward the English – a sentiment more than reciprocated by the English toward the Scots – Colley's "Scottophobia"[42] – the Scots felt the need to help create an England that would continue the aims of writers like Shaftesbury. This was, as indicated at the end of Chapter 2, perceived as an urgent and practical project.

40 Classically, John Locke, *An Essay Concerning Human Understanding* (1706) (PH Nidditch, ed), Oxford, Oxford University Press (1979).

41 AN Wilson, *The Victorians*, London, Arrow Books (2002), ch 11, reflecting on the aftermath of Chartism.

42 Linda Colley, *Britons: Forging the Nation*, New Haven, CT, Yale University Press (1992). Increasingly, during the eighteenth century, the superior Scottish education system made them irritatingly indispensable to the operation of empire.

There are two reasons that might justify neglecting the work of Kant here. One is that the focus of the book as a whole is on Anglophone writers without, naturally, supposing them to be autonomous of other influences or embodying a particular virtue that eclipses all others. But boundaries have nevertheless to be drawn, as our quotation from Rorty *et al* suggests. A second reason may be that, although, as Hans Reiss writes, "Kant's impact on German legal theory was profound", eventually "shaping the notion of the *rechtstaat*, the state governed according to law" – the epistemological equivalent of the certainty of Reason. The greatest modern Kantian exponent of the Kantian *rechtstaat* was, of course, Hans Kelsen, the arch-positivist. But, Reiss argues, the nationalism and Romanticism that came to dominate Germany after Kant's death "introduced into German thought a note of irrationalism which permeated almost all areas of . . . thinking for a century and a half between the Napoleonic wars and the end of the second world war".[43] Certainty was not an evanescent necessity, politically, socially or scientifically, but an Imperative. Despite this, Kant's powerful counterblast to Humean skepticism, is one which it will be obvious that I do not find convincing, I remain wedded to Hume.

It seemed to me nevertheless to be worth noting briefly some interesting differences and similarities between the Scots and Kant, since Kant is often taken to be both the culmination and the pinnacle of the mainland European Enlightenment, and his influence on the intellectual thought of the later Coleridge and of John Austin, was clearly considerable. Kant (unlike Austin and, for most of Coleridge's life, unlike him, too) combined a belief in inalienable rights, the equality of men, the moral duty of the sovereign to respect such rights, and admiration of the American and French Revolutions despite a conviction that "whatever the status quo may be, good or bad, rebellion is never legitimate",[44] "It is in the highest degree illegitimate for the subjects to seek their rights in this way".[45] Quoting from the *Conflict of the Faculties*, which Arendt says, in the last section "shows clear evidence of his mind's deterioration", she cites his observation, "it is so sweet to plan state constitutions, a sweet dream whose consummation is not only thinkable but . . . an obligation not (however) of the citizens, but of the sovereign".[46]

How can one believe in human rights as sincerely as Kant obviously did, admire an at least initially popularly-inspired revolution in France, which he considered had accomplished them, yet deny the legitimacy of the action of their accomplishment? In the essay on Perpetual Peace, for example, we find the following passage:

43 Hans Reiss, Introduction, in Reiss (ed), *Kant: Political Writings*, Cambridge, Cambridge University Press (1991), 11, 13.

44 Hannah Arendt, *Lectures on Kant's Political Philosophy* (Ronald Beiner, ed), Chicago, IL, University of Chicago Press (1982), 47.

45 Kant, cited in Arendt, *ibid.*

46 Arendt, *op cit*, n 44, 16. See also Reiss, *op cit*, n 43, 31.

> . . . the smaller the number of ruling persons in a state and the greater their powers of representation, the more the constitution will approximate to its republican potentiality, which it may hope to realize eventually by gradual reforms. For this reason, it is more difficult in an aristocracy than in a monarchy to reach this one and only lawful kind of constitution, while it is possible in a democracy only by means of a violent revolution.

But he has already told us that, of the forms of sovereignty, monarchy, aristocracy and democracy, the latter, "in the truest sense of the word, is necessarily a despotism".[47] That a democracy may, indeed, become a "tyranny of the majority", especially in an era of commercially dominated media was neatly illustrated in George Clooney's 2005 film, *Goodnight and Good Luck*, concerned with aspects of the conflict of the famous US columnist, Ed Murrow with Senator Joe McCarthy, where Murrow was depicted as hampered in his quest to deliver "the truth" to the "people" by the need of his employer, CBS, for business sponsorship. But one wonders if this has the status of "necessity".[48]

In Kant's *Conflict*[49] philosophy is the scene of the search for the truth (and we will find echoes, conscious or not in the twentieth century writings of the legal writer, Ronald Dworkin), but is subordinated to the "higher" faculties of medicine, theology and law in terms of power in the university and the state. Power and truth occupy distinct realms in the Kantian academy, even if it is the duty of truth to inform power and the duty of power to respect and respond to truth in a struggle if, realistically never to be ended, aspiring to unite the two. "Kant . . . proposes", Foucault writes, " a sort of contract – what might be called the contract of rational despotism with free reason: the public and free use of autonomous reason will be the best guarantee of obedience, on condition . . . that the political reason that must be obeyed itself be in conformity with universal reason".[50]

No assertion appears here, of the kind that one finds in Smith: ". . . there are certain limits to the power of the sovereign, which if he exceeds, the subject may with justice make resistance".[51] "(P)romot(ing) this binary (Kant) appears to contrive a division of labor in which the philosopher confines his public language to utterances of a constative mode, and resigns to the sovereign the performative language of command".[52] In one sense, following Derrida, we could say that the

47 Immanuel Kant, Perpetual Peace, in Hans Reiss (ed) (1991), *Kant: Political Writings*, Cambridge, Cambridge University Press, 101.

48 See Peter Osborne, *The Triumph of the Political Class*, London, Simon and Schuster (2007).

49 Immanuel Kant, The Conflict of the Faculties, in Richard Rand (ed), *Logomachia: The Conflict of the Faculties*, Lincoln, NE, University of Nebraska Press (1992).

50 Michel Foucault, What is Enlightenment, in Patricia Waugh (ed), *Postmodernism: A Reader*, London, Edward Arnold (1992), 99.

51 Adam Smith, *Lectures in Jurisprudence* (22 March 1763) (R Meek, D Raphael and P Stein, eds), Indianapolis, IN, Liberty Classics (1982), 315.

52 Richard Rand, Preface, in Richard Rand (ed), *Logomachia: The Conflict of the Faculties*, Lincoln, NE, University of Nebraska Press (1992), viii.

two practices are dependent upon each other in this schema, as one leg requires the other in the activity of walking. The foundation and maintenance of a university in which the "lower" faculty of philosophy seeks the truth, cannot be an intra-university act – why not? – but must be one of sovereign power. In his essay on the European Enlightenment, Kant remarks that:

> Only a ruler who, himself enlightened, does not himself fear shadows and at the same time has at hand a large, well-disciplined army as a guarantee of peace, can say what a republic dare not: *argue as much as you want and about whatever you want, only obey!*[53]

Giving government to each other, as in the Convention Parliament, or, more broadly, an agreement of the people could scarcely be further away. Equally, of course, neither law, nor the other higher faculties, nor the state itself, can properly found themselves. "The foundation of a law is not a juridical event" any more than "the foundation of a university institution is . . . a university event". Both are, if they are to work in a participatory way, conventions.[54] A "genuine peace" among the participants in this exercise, the state and the higher faculties, which are, in a sense its extension, is possible only where philosophy is able to "purify" the reasons for the activities of the former by rendering them consistent with the requirements of reason.[55]

The explanation from Kant is that *qua* soldier, priest, teacher or other professional, subordinate to the public discipline of the calling in question, the subject has a duty to act in accordance with that discipline. Any other discipline would encourage anarchy. In his "private" capacity (in other words, acting or speaking in the role we might now paradoxically, from Kant's point of view, term a "public intellectual"), s/he must speak. So, on the other hand, whilst it is his/her duty to articulate the imprudence of the military command s/he must obey, the falsity of the religious doctrine s/he is required to preach or the injustice of the law s/he is employed to apply, it is his/her duty to obey professional imperatives. A regard for professional discipline creates the ordered conditions in which inquiry, which may lead to their transformation, is possible. Kant's injunction in the latter essay, *sapere aude*, have the courage to reason for yourself and not rely on the judgment of others, is, of course, consistent with the Scots' programs of investigation, although for Hume reason is always at the service of what he termed "passion" and cannot determine the decision – otherwise, as Derrida was later to

53 Immanuel Kant, An Answer to the Question, "What is Enlightenment?" in James Schmidt (ed), *What is Enlightenment? Eighteenth Century Answers and Twentieth Century Questions*, Berkeley, CA, University of California Press (1996), 63 (original emphasis).

54 Jacques Derrida, Mochlos, in Richard Rand (ed), *Logomachia: The Conflict of the Faculties*, Lincoln, NE, University of Nebraska Press, 30.

55 Mary Gregor, Translator's Note to Immanuel Kant, *Conflict of the Faculties* (1798), Lincoln, NE, University of Nebraska Press (1992); Rand, *op cit*, n 52, 149, 165.

remark, it would not be a decision, but merely the application of a rule. Moreover, Kant's belief that freedom of expression for the man of letters was a fundamental component of an enlightened age was something he shared with both the men of politeness and the northern literati, the two branches of Englishness.

Kant's arguments for liberty of expression and academic freedom as the *sine qua non* of enlightened thinking, sharpened by his experience of the censorship of his religious views and the later intellectual reaction and more general censorship in Prussia under Frederick William II, are, as Mary Gregor puts it, "attractive". They depend for their practical efficacy, though, "as he is obliged to admit"[56] upon the self-restraint of sovereign power, of which Frederick the Great's son seemed, in his admonitions of Kant's religious views, less possessed than his father. The lesson seems to be, as the British may have been able to predict, that when Enlightened Despotism is good, it is very very good, but when it is bad it is awful.

The metaphysics of sovereignty to which Kant gestures in his panegyric to Frederick the Great,[57] occasionally seems to have repeated the form of Absolutism and introduced into political discussion generally an intellectual obscurity and ultimately paralysis down to the present. Arendt quotes Sieyes' *Who is the Third Estate?* as an illustration of the difficulties introduced by this metaphysics, she:

> Describes how sovereignty . . . demanded in the course of the French Revolution in the form of an absolute principle capable of founding the legislative act of constituting power . . . ultimately winds up in a vicious circle.[58]

It is possible, Arendt writes, that "Kant himself did not see the destructive side of his enterprise", that he considered that "when he was through with his Critique",[59] the subversive effects were confined to undermining the intellectual authority of what had until then been conventional philosophy. In Ronald Beiner's Interpretive Essay, appended to the 1988 edition of Arendt's *Essays*, he suggests that she felt that she no longer needed to find a specifically political theory of political judgment in Kant. She abandoned the distinction between political and other forms of judgment. She:

> admits that, because of the old prejudices according to which politics was about rule or dominion, about interest, instrumentality and so on, even Kant

56 Derrida, *op cit*, n 54, 29.

57 ". . . this age is the age of enlightenment, or the century of Frederick", in James Schmidt (ed), *What is Enlightenment? Eighteenth Century Answers and Twentieth Century Questions*, Berkeley, CA, University of California Press, 62.

58 Arendt, *op cit*, n 31, quoted in Giorgio Agamben, *Homo Sacer: Sovereign Power and Bare Life*, Palo Alto, CA, Stanford University Press (1998), 41.

59 Arendt, *op cit*, n 44, 35.

> himself did not realize that *The Critique of Judgment* belonged to political philosophy. But in concerning ourselves with judgment, she holds, we break free of the old prejudices about politics: "We deal with a form of being together (shared judgment, community of taste) where no-one rules and no-one obeys. Where people persuade each other".[60]

If power, interest and rule are still in existence, it may be that sharing, persuasion and so on are the fundamental apparatus on which they are based. It is clear that this interpretation of Kant reflects Hannah Arendt's insistence upon an ethical view of politics as a form of esthetics, and this puts her, as we shall see, much closer to Shaftesbury and the Scots than to the later Anglophones of the high imperial era. Whether she is putting words on to Kant's pages in writing the political theory that she believed he would have written, had he been consciously setting one out, is perhaps of less interest than, first, how she analyzed politics and by implication legality, the discussion of which must be postponed until later chapters; and, second, the contrast between what Kant did write about politics in his shorter essays, and the work of Locke, Shaftesbury and the Scots. Like the last-named, Kant was vehement about the need for a humane and ethical politics, and did, as they did, link politics with taste. But unlike them, whilst celebrating his government – "the Age of Frederick" – he was, for the reasons suggested, not celebrative of active safeguards for the ethics he advocated, not pragmatically or, perhaps, historically and sociologically concerned with how citizenship rights had been or might be achieved or preserved, beyond the persuasive character of their basis in reason.

Hume's semi-ironic remark that the despotic potential of the House of Commons was balanced by the venality of its members in seeking offices under the Crown[61] is transformed in Kant's conviction that in Britain, since, he believed that a sovereign government and a sovereign source of valid law must exist somewhere in a state, its invisibility there must be occasioned by a conspiracy on the part of corrupt members of Parliament to disguise from the voters the reality that Royal bribery has converted Great Britain into an absolute monarchy.[62]

Questions of authority, then, appear to have been approached differently among English- than among German-speakers, at least in the period framed by the Glorious Revolution and the secession of the Thirteen Colonies and the rise of legal positivism. This seems not to have escaped some European attention. Porter, as we have seen, reminds us of the admiration from their perspectives as subjects of an absolutist monarchy in France, of Montesquieu, Voltaire and others for at least what they understood to be the essence of the British constitution – a model

60 Arendt, *op cit*, n 44, Beiner's Interpretive Essay, 141.

61 David Hume, Of the Independency of Parliament, in David Hume (ed), *Essays*, Indianapolis, IN, Liberty Collection, 42–46.

62 Kant, *op cit*, n 49, 163.

of balanced authority quite at odds with Kant's assimilation of the British to the European models of government with which he was familiar: constitutional monarchy as concealed despotism.

If power and truth are not given a conceptually necessary distinction – as they seem not to have been among the Scots – then the authority into which Kant urges the man of letters to inquire and, if he deems it appropriate, to challenge, may equally be *political* authority. The power of Frederick the Great, the enlightened despot of Kant's Prussia, may well have formed the prerequisite of the exercise of reason in free debate, but, as Kant himself remarked, Frederick's disposition to permit or deny freedom of expression was equally significant, as the reaction to the enlightenment which set in under Frederick's successor, Frederick II, indicated.

The puzzle that Kant's political thought represents for the "Englishman" whom both Scots and English (and the protestant Irish) were creating during the major part of the eighteenth century may be explained by both Reiss and a number of nineteenth century Germans themselves. Germany was, as Metternich was later to say of Italy, a "geographical expression", a hotchpotch of smaller and greater despotisms. Kant's East Prussian, perhaps Pietist world, in which intellectuals would focus exclusively on abstract topics, certainly not to the detriment of the philosophical world, could have been one some of the Scots literati would have preferred – although Hume is hard to place in this category if one pays heed to Annette Baier[63] – but they were firmly attached to liberty as they, at least, experienced it. The hustings that even the voteless – perhaps especially the voteless – attended, according to Wilson,[64] to heckle, brawl and articulate their politics and instruct their MPs and demand their ration of beer, was a phenomenon probably unimaginable to Kant, despite his penchant for travel literature. If the Scots were to explain political being in this context, to their own satisfaction, neither the people nor their power in the realm were phenomena they could afford to ignore. In the Borders burgh of Hawick, in 1777, faced with the theft of one third of the burgh commons by the Dukes of Buccleuch, the common men who customarily rode the bounds of their burgh wrote:

> Magistrates! Be faithful trustees,
> Equal poise the scales of justice,
> See our Commons rightly giudit
> Quirky lairds nae mair divide it.

When confronted with the abolition of the Hawick Common Riding in 1794 by the town council, a popular petition of artisans and others who "were of the

63 Annette Baier, *A Progress of Sentiments: Reflections on Hume's Treatise*, Cambridge, MA, Harvard University Press (1994).

64 Wilson, *op cit*, n 8.

opinion that the Common Riding should be continued" was laid before the council, which hastily backed down and restored the tradition.[65]

Not unconnectedly, before leaving the contrasts between the enlightenment scholars, Kant and the Scots, while the Scots and the English, let alone the Americans, could hardly abstain from opinions expressed by the brawling masses, Kant was, Arendt suggests, committed to the position of the non-Smithian spectator. A rebellion could seem inexcusable before, and afterwards appear acceptable in the judgment of a spectator if the consequence was an improvement on the preceding state of affairs. Such a judgment could not be made impartially by an actor in the rebellion, but only by a spectator, capable of a balanced evaluation afterwards.

For the Anglophones from Locke to Smith, the methodology of enlightenment directed inquiry into *all* authority and discipline: how it was acquired, maintained, questioned and, if unsatisfactory, how it was to be overturned and replaced. If Hume considered that the authority of the most absolute ruler depended upon opinion, Millar finds more to say about the formation of opinion in the society with which he was familiar:

> Wherever men of inferior condition are enabled to live in affluence by their own industry, and, in procuring their livelihood, have little occasion to court the favors of their superiors, there we may expect that ideas of liberty may be universally diffused.[66]

Whether any of the Scots was personally committed to some form of populism, whether they were, in the event of the revolt, pro- or anti-American independence – and clearly Hume, Smith and Witherspoon were on the side of independence – seems beside the point. It is the tendency of their texts and their analyses of the basis of society, its state and the laws, their views on the constitution of all of those, which form the focus of our interest. Again, it would be absurd to look for uniformity in their conclusions, but one does find repeated an anti-authoritarian propensity manifested in several ways.

65 Kenneth Bogle, *Scotland's Common Ridings*, Stroud, Tempus Publishing (2004), 101, quoting from the documents of the time. I am grateful to my daughter, Kirsty Duncanson, for the reference (and the book).

66 John Millar, The Powers of the Sovereign, in Alexander Broadie, *The Scottish Enlightenment: An Anthology*, Edinburgh, Cannongate Books, 545. In John Millar, The Origin of the Distinction of Ranks: Or, an Inquiry into the Circumstances Which Give Rise to Influence and Authority in Different Members of Society, 4th edn (corrected 1806) Edinburgh, Blackwood (1771), ch 5, http://socserv2.socsci.mcmaster.ca/~econ/ugcm/3113/millar/rank 88 (accessed 3 June 2007), the phrasing was altered in minor ways between 1771 and 1806, but the sentiment remains identical. See also Berry, op cit, n 5, 125.

Anti-authoritarian tendencies in Scottish thought: Hutcheson and Hume

The work of Hutcheson, an opponent of "a religiously-backed moral authoritarianism which has been a significant part of our cultural heritage", or, as Mountner later puts it, an opponent of "the moral legalism of orthodox theology",[67] sometimes seen as the founder of the Scottish Enlightenment, is a good place to begin. A Moderate Presbyterian, born in Ireland, and a professor in Glasgow for twenty-two years, Francis Hutcheson was familiar with Henry Molyneux' 1698 *Case of Ireland being bound by Acts of Parliament in England*, which argued for the co-equal authority of both legislatures. He was also friend to Henry Molesworth, who had published, in the preface to his translation of Francis Hotman's *Franco-Gallia* in 1705, an argument for an association (in other words, a confederation) of England, Scotland and Ireland "upon equal terms (for upon unequal, it would be no *union*)".[68] Robbins quotes at length a passage from one of Hutcheson's own works, *A System of Moral Philosophy*, in the course of which he began by assuming that all political unions were formed for, and must be subordinated to, the good of its members and continues, writing of colonies:

> If the plan of the mother country is changed by force, or degenerates . . . from a safe, mild and gentle limited power to a severe and absolute one; or if . . . oppressive laws are made with respect to the colonies or provinces; and any colony is so increased in numbers and strength that they are sufficient to themselves for all good ends of a political union, they are not bound in their subjection.[69]

More generally, Hutcheson sees "national love and the *dear idea* of a COUNTRY" as dependent upon our ability to take a beneficent view of the "friendships" and "humane sentiments" it encourages, and if we prefer our own country to another with which we might equally sympathize, this may simply be a matter of familiarity and happy youthful memories. But in all cases, our national love is undermined by tyrannical and unjust government, "a *Corruption of* Manners and *any thing* which occasions the Misery of the Subjects".[70] This is because, having rejected the stern and repressive moralism of orthodox theologies as the outcome of undue pessimism about human nature, Hutcheson also

67 Mountner, *op cit*, n 25, 29, 39.

68 Caroline Robbins, "When It Is That Colonies May Turn Independent": An Analysis of the Environment and Politics of Francis Hutcheson (1694–1746), (1954) 11 *The William and Mary Quarterly* 3rd Ser, 214–51, at 227. Robbins suggests that Hutcheson may have had more in common with the Anglican Latitudinarians than with the orthodox Presbyterians.

69 Francis Hutcheson, *A System of Moral Philosophy*, cited in Robbins, *ibid*, 216.

70 Francis Hutcheson, *An Inquiry into the Original of Our Ideas of Beauty and Virtue* (1725), Hildesheim, George Olms Verlag (1990), 149.

considers wrong the Epicurean belief that humans act out of self-interest for the purpose of maximizing pleasure and avoiding pain.[71] Our affection, and ultimately the political loyalty that underpins the constitution, is for him gained through public and private acts of benevolence.

Not everyone is naturally virtuous in this sense, but for Hutcheson, "we can cultivate virtue in ourselves; and through writing, teaching, conversation and social interaction, we can cultivate it in others".[72] Mountner compares religious and moral texts of this time with the modern genre of self-help, self-improvement texts:

> The right kind of moral philosophy (Hutcheson) believed, would help us to overcome the cheerless and depressed mental condition induced by a certain kind of religious and moral environment, and would help to make us more harmonious and capable of a sense of joy.[73]

There is a clear connection with Shaftesbury, which suggests a dimension in this earlier literature which is largely missing from the self-improvement manuals of modern popular psychology. The cultivation of virtue, as Hutcheson sees it, involves the recognition of actions of benevolence, actions promoting the public good, and it is a co-operative, sociable endeavor. "Feeling rather than reason is the root of moral judgement. Proper behavior must be grounded in the natural affections, suitably reinforced by social custom. Hutcheson builds an elaborate system of ethics founded upon the imperative of sociability",[74] even if, as John Bishop suggests, the stronger adherence to Stoicism in his later writings led him to emphasize the virtue of the dispassionate individual.[75]

Humean sociability

Selby-Bigge's 1893 Introduction to the *Enquiries* of David Hume, whose writing overlapped with that of Hutcheson, and who corresponded with the latter, begins by counseling "caution" in approaching Hume's "philosophic writings". The volume of his work, the differences in the expressions of his ideas in different places and the variance of the perspectives he uses and the connections he makes, Selby-Bigge suggests, all preclude finding a unity in

71 Francis Hutcheson, *An Essay on the Nature and Conduct of the Passions and Affections* (1728), Hildesheim, George Olms Verlag (1990), 13.

72 John Bishop, Moral Motivation and the Development of Francis Hutcheson's Philosophy, (1996) 57 *The Journal of the History of Ideas* 277–95.

73 Mountner, *op cit*, n 25, 49.

74 Susan Purviance, Intersubjectivity and Social Relations in the Philosophy of Francis Hutcheson, in John Dwyer and Richard Sher (eds), *Sociability and Society in Eighteenth Century Scotland*, Edinburgh, Mercat Press (1993), 23, 24.

75 Bishop, *op cit*, n 72.

the work itself.[76] Annette Baier, on the other hand, argues that "the unity of Hume's thought, not merely in the *Treatise* but in all his writings is increasingly recognized".[77] Selby-Bigge was not an entirely sympathetic editor, finding the *Treatise* "ill-proportioned, incoherent, ill-expressed"[78] and the *Enquiries*, which were intended to address the failure of the earlier work to attract much attention, at times "tiresome" and "egoistic". These differences are not irrelevant to our project. As Appleby *et al* suggest, Hume

> sought to push the empirical philosophy implicit in Newton's methods to its logical conclusion, and in doing so came to doubt the very possibility of scientific knowledge itself. In doing this he continued the Enlightenment tradition of strict avoidance of comforting metaphysical assertions, but unlike some earlier zealots, he found a useful, even necessary place in social life of the seemingly irrational world of custom and tradition.[79]

In doing this he also reflected a world view significantly similar to that of Hutcheson – stressing the sociability and conversational construction of values, and, of course, of "facts" – and those of Smith and Millar, as we shall see. He differed famously from Hutcheson's project of achieving and teaching "true" virtue by these means, seeing himself as a "moral anatomist" rather than a moral painter, an analyst rather than an ethicist, although we may suspect him here of one of his wry jokes. Did not his anticipation of the uncertainty principle recommend a certain politics, a certain morality – those of tolerance? Declining, as he saw it, the competence to advise people what to do, he contented himself with analyzing how the making of judgments about morality were made. "For my part, I know not what ought to be done . . . I can only observe what is commonly done".[80] This is not the reliance we find in Kant on the munificence of the great Frederick.

Contenting himself with the idea of knowledge as simply inferences from the coherence of perceptions, "whether they be true or false; whether they represent nature justly or be mere illusions of the senses" he was unlikely to attract agreement from Idealists or Positivists in Selby-Bigge's or TH Green's era. Our notions of cause and effect, our related and perhaps slightly Pavlovian conviction that some apodictic reliance about the present and the future may be drawn from

76 LA Selby-Bigge, Introduction to David Hume, *Enquiries Concerning the Human Understanding and the Principles of Morals*, 1777 edn (LA Selby-Bigge, ed), Oxford, Oxford University Press (1972), vii.

77 Baier, *op cit*, n 63, viii.

78 Selby-Bigge, *op cit*, n 76, x.

79 Joyce Appleby, Elizabeth Covington, David Hoyt, Michael Latham and Alison Sneider, *Knowledge and Postmodernism in Historical Perspective*, New York, NY, Routledge (1996), 73.

80 David Hume, *A Treatise of Human Nature* (1739–40), 2nd edn (LA Selby-Bigge and PH Niditch, eds), Oxford, Oxford University Press (1978), 268.

observations of the past, or that objects continue to exist when we can no longer see them, are all, for Hume, inferences necessary to the being which requires them. They are, of course, social, that is, social conventions. If their inaccessibility to reason as proof of their absolute truth becomes unbearable, relief, too is sociably and conventionally at hand:

> Nature herself suffices to that purpose and cures me of this philosophical melancholy or delirium . . . I dine, I play a game of back-gammon, I converse and am merry with my friends; and when, after three or four hours' amusement I wou'd return to these speculations, they appear so cold and strain'd and ridiculous that I cannot find it in my heart to enter into them any farther.[81]

If Arendt's Kant seems unaware of the subversiveness of his philosophy, Hume is clearly not at all unaware of the subversive nature of his own. If reason is insufficient to explain the world, it clearly will not suffice to ground claims to sovereignty. Just like claims to property, the right to exclude others from one's possessions without consent, Hume thinks that the claims to obedience made by a sovereign will have originated in force or fraud. He fails, perhaps, to give Locke credit for recognizing that the conceptual framework he used to justify the acceptance or rejection of political authority, the contract creating a trust, depended for its plausibility on the appropriate education of the political classes. Nevertheless, he rejects the social contract as the basis of authority, for the social contract assumes the sanctity of promises. It assumes that both subjects and government put themselves under a binding obligation, to govern according to certain terms, the breach of which dissolves the relation. But, Hume wants to know, why are we bound by our undertakings? "Your answer, *because we should keep our word* . . . nobody, till trained in a philosophical system can either comprehend or relish".[82] Hume favorably supports "the sentiments of the rabble to any philosophical reasoning (f)or it must be observed that the opinions of men, in this case, carry with them a peculiar authority and are, in a great measure, infallible".[83] The source of a moral obligation to concede authority is that "every one thinks so".[84] Promises are social conventions, and are kept only when it is the convention to do so.

The aim of Lockean social contractarians, Hume believes, is agreeably to justify limitations to government. However, although this was accepted by the interestingly-termed "Convention Parliament", convened to debate the terms and

81 Hume, *ibid*, 269.

82 Hume, *op cit*, n 16, Essay XII, Of the Original Contract, 481. Legality would count as a "philosophical system".

83 Hume, *op cit*, n 80, 546.

84 Hume, *op cit*, n 80, 547.

justifications for replacing James II by his son-in-law William of Orange, the idea of a social contract seems to Hume to introduce more problems than it solves. The absence of empirical evidence that a contract was made is the least of the problems, and one that Locke himself dealt with by pointing out that we seldom hear of the childhood, parents, or children of classical heroes, but are not thereby compelled to conclude that there were none. But to Hume, to invoke a contract between rulers and subjects is to write history backwards rather than forwards, to find breaches of actual or tacit undertakings that were never given rather than to focus on the construction of a better and freer future;[85] moreover, how are subjects to be taken to be bound to a contract made by their forebears? "I flatter myself that I can establish the same conclusion" about limitations "on more reasonable principles".[86] People come together in political societies, he writes, out of interest: principally that "security and protection" which would be otherwise unattainable. But if a government, through its oppressive and unjust behavior ceases to meet this interest, the subject is no longer bound to it. Rejecting the Whig doctrine of the social contract, then, does not lead Hume either to the Kantian spectator, who can judge only after the event and without participating in it, or to the Tory doctrine of passive obedience:

> . . . common sense teaches us that, as government binds us to obedience only on account of its tendency to public utility, that duty must always, in extraordinary cases, when public ruin would evidently attend obedience, yield to the primary and original obligation. *Salus populi suprema Lex.* The safety of the people is the supreme law.[87]

And how are we to understand safety in this aphorism? The human who becomes a political subject does so by *convention*, a concept to which we are returned over and again, and of the form of which, in happy times, s/he may (or may not) be perfectly unaware, but the issue becomes more visible and more fraught should times become less happy. There is a parallel here with his earlier observation that, also in the happy circumstance of a conventional fiction, s/he is unaware that the subject's continuity of identity generally, cannot be guaranteed.[88] Clearly, in Hume's account, James II's "lofty idea . . . of his legal authority . . . left his subjects little or no right to liberty but what was dependent on his sovereign

85 Hume, *op cit*, n 16, 470. In modern contract law in common law systems, of course, the "intentions of the parties" in disputed contracts are always retrospective achievements on the part of adjudicators.

86 Hume, *op cit*, n 16, 550. See also David Hume, *Enquiries Concerning the Human Understanding and the Principles of Morals*, 1777 edn (LA Selby-Bigge, ed), Oxford, Oxford University Press (1972), 306.

87 Hume, *op cit*, n 16, Essay XIII, 489.

88 Hume, *op cit*, n 16, 207.

will and pleasure",[89] and thus no interest, no safety or security in continued loyalty. Little was to be hoped for in the "expedient" offered by "some lawyers, entangled in the subtleties and forms of their profession", notably their belief that the monarch with whom both Whigs and Tories intended to replace James, William of Orange, succeeded by right of conquest. The problem here was that noticed by Arendt, in her criticism of the French Revolution, that it merely replaced one sovereign with another, that the "principles of liberty" for which the English Revolution stood, according to Hume, remained at risk.

Despite playing with the dangerous fire of social contract doctrine, England avoided "violence, tumult and disorder", and with its "singular" revolution managed to produce for its citizens "great tranquility and freedom".[90] By replacing, peacefully, one monarch with another, the subjects of a "new epoch in the constitution" gained more than liberty, and he adverts at the end of the chapter to the cultural and economic possibilities opened by the passing of the Stuarts. It may, Hume wrote:

> Be justly affirmed without any danger of exaggeration that we, in this island have since enjoyed, if not the best system of government, at least the most entire system of liberty that was ever known amongst mankind.[91]

I think this should be understood, not as chest-beating chauvinism, since what Hume was celebrating was an English achievement, while Hume was not an Englishman, nor had any desire to become one. It was a reminder to the southern neighbor of their perhaps inadvertent accomplishments, in the stability of which all Scots had an interest.

Sovereign authority in Millar and Smith

> When we contemplate the amazing diversity to be found in the laws of different countries, and even of the same country at different periods, our curiosity is naturally excited to enquire in what manner mankind have been led to embrace such different rules of conduct.[92]

Two interacting schemes of ordering are worth noticing in Millar's and Smith's writing: the ordering of the self, the possibilities of which require some interrogation of what people are like; and the ordering of society, which requires inquiry into the nature of the society in question. Thus Smith finds speculations about man

89 David Hume, *The History of England from the Invasion of Julius Caesar to the Revolution in 1688*, 6 vols (1778), Indianapolis, IN, Liberty Collection (1983), 520.
90 Hume, *ibid*, 528.
91 Hume, *op cit*, n 89, 531.
92 Millar, *op cit*, n 66, 1.

in a state of nature entirely unhelpful, since no such state exists. Equally, contract as the basis for authority seems to him a less plausible original basis for government and the acceptance of laws than the acceptance of certain claims to authority, and the utility of the laws to those who consent to be subject to them.[93] Questions of utility refer us to the well-known four-stage model of social order which Smith adapted from Pufendorf.[94] It is impossible Smith concludes, to explain the usefulness that causes adherence to laws relating to property unless we know which of the "four distinct states which mankind pass through: 1st, the Age of Hunters; 2ndly, the Age of Shepherds; 3rdly the Age of Agriculture; and 4thly the Age of Commerce". In the first "Age", rules relating to property would not be useful at all; each of the subsequent stages produces laws that correspond to its condition.

Questions of authority raised by the Scots also, for them, refer us to the stadial model insofar as it will be a specific society that provides, to invoke Lacan once again, a "mirror" in which the subject sees reflected back to itself the "propriety and impropriety of his own passions" in the approval or disapproval of fellow-subjects.[95] These responses are effective because people are naturally sympathetic to the judgments and feelings of each other. We feel sorrow at the misfortunes of others and take comfort from unburdening ourselves to others when we suffer misfortune. Sympathy is the medium in which social approbation and disapprobation are effectively communicated. In his chapter on duty, Smith writes that we learn about propriety – and to Smith's contemporaries the word "propriety" embraces the modern concept of property, so proper action is not simply a matter of rules – also from reports and the assessments made by people about the behavior of others. We learn that we can avoid actions – such as, for example, theft – and expressions, of, say boorishness or offensive remarks, that draw upon ourselves social detestation: "it is thus that the general rules of morality are formed".[96] Successful socialization is, then, possible when we learn to see ourselves through the eyes of others. Smith's "impartial spectator", that other who may be ourselves before migrates to the external world, subsequently re-migrates from the external world into ourselves,[97] and adjudicates thoughts and actions unseen by actual spectators, and overcomes the self-deceit that derives from a natural tendency to self-love. A man of "constancy and firmness . . . does not merely affect the sentiments of the impartial spectator. He really adopts them".[98] Or, as Burns was a little later to put it:

93 Smith, *op cit*, n 51, 397–98, 404.

94 Smith, *op cit*, n 51, 14 *et seq*.

95 Adam Smith, *A Theory of Moral Sentiments*, 6th edn (1790) (D Raphael and AL Macfie, eds), Indianapolis, IN, Liberty Classics (1982), 110.

96 Smith, *op cit*, n 95, 159.

97 Jacques Lacan, *Ecrits*, New York, NY, WW Norton (2006), ch 5.

98 Lacan, *ibid*, 158–59.

O wad some Power the giftie gie us
To see oursels as ithers see us.
It wad frae monie a blunder free us.[99]

Through education and discipline, albeit that people cannot become perfect, most behave with "tolerable decency". And, to repeat, "propriety" here can be given its extended meaning as both conduct deemed proper to the society and occasion and property in its modern sense of something owned, which is a proper relationship with others, non-owners to the extent that it meets the approval of the impartial spectator.[100] Propriety/property is safeguarded even when invisible to outsiders. And Smith was consistent. His opposition to empire was the pragmatic one that trade among independent countries would flourish compared with trade between colony and metropole – which proved to be the case after America seceded – but theft of others' lands was not recommended.

Smith is explaining *how* the environment in which law exists comes to be. It is "a sociological/institutional rather than (a) rationalist/individual explanation", as with the Scots generally.[101] However, there is a normative component in that the necessarily *specific* environment that most enlightenment writers insist we have to focus on in order to make sense does seem to set some limits to the operation of law. For example, England is "ever the friend to liberty", as demonstrated by the independence of the judges, the existence of the jury, and the division of the "*summa potestas*". Here, indeed "is a happy mixture of all the forms of government properly restrained and a perfect security to liberty and property".[102] If a sovereign may not have a sovereign and remain a sovereign, and if the king in Parliament occupies that site in Britain such that the limits on its power are unknown, "there are however certain abuses which no doubt make resistance in some cases lawful"; and Smith considers this must be the case "on whatever principle government be founded".[103]

As is clear from the quotation at the beginning of this section, John Millar insists on an explanation of law in terms of the specifics of the society in which it is found, not merely, for example, its economy, but the state of its arts, its size and the climate, among other factors:

99 Robert Burns, To a Louse (1784), in James Mackay, *The Complete Works of Robert Burns*, Ayr, Alloway Publishing (1986).

100 See K Haakonssen, *Natural Law and Moral Philosophy: From Grotius to the Scottish Enlightenment*, Cambridge, Cambridge University Press (1996), ch 5.

101 Christopher Berry, Sociality and Socialization, in Alexander Broadie (ed), *The Cambridge Companion to the Scottish Enlightenment*, Cambridge, Cambridge University Press (2003), 251.

102 Smith, *op cit*, n 51, 421–22, and see Wilfrid Prest, Law, Lawyers and Rational Dissent, in K Haakonssen (ed), *Enlightenment and Religion: Rational Dissent in Eighteenth Century Britain*, Cambridge, Cambridge University Press (1996), esp pp 182–89, for an account of the similar sentiments being expressed in English writing about law, particularly by Richard Price and Joseph Priestley.

103 Smith, *op cit*, n 51, 434.

> General systems of law have rarely, if ever, been formed by the prospective wisdom of legislators, but have arisen gradually, and almost insensibly, from the slow progress of human experience.[104]

Stories, then, of the great legislator who produces a system of laws manifesting a complete break with the past, are probably myths. In actuality, Millar thinks, since radical departures from previous principles are likely to be resisted, the "heroes" celebrated for their innovations are likely to have crafted their reforms in conformity with contemporary attitudes. This sounds distinctly Burkean, which may seem at odds with the reluctant disagreement with Burke that Millar expresses in a letter to Samuel Rose[105] over the French Revolution. He is clear in the letter that the American constitution sets a good example to Britain, as he was clear, in the years after the American Revolution, that the Crown was gaining too much power over the legislature in the United Kingdom, and that the only remedy was to ground the Commons' power more evidently in the popular by greatly extending the franchise. In one sense, Burke is more prescient than Millar: he sees more clearly the direction in which the revolution in France tends. But Millar is writing in 1790, before the Terror, before, therefore, the awful implications of the General Will were clear. In another sense the two are in agreement that the executive is gaining too much power over the legislature: their point of difference is about how this can be ameliorated. Burke believes that the commons are represented in "their" House, and that a conscientious awareness of the responsibilities this situation entails is the basis for legislative resistance to the executive. Millar believes that only greater actual representation through possessing the vote can ensure that the people are heard.

In *The Origin of the Distinction of Ranks*, a text drawing on wide-ranging attention to historical changes and geographical differences among people, Millar, unusually for his time, discusses the influence of changing social practices on the "condition of women", and in turn the influence of that condition on the social order. Whilst in classical civilizations, even those with democratic inclinations such as Athens, women were excluded from public life, and were therefore secluded from those in control of public life and not seen as fully people, commercial society encourages much more intermingling of the sexes. What Millar sees as the barbaric aspects of Greek culture is the consequence. Polite society reinforces itself when women, by nature or nurture "possessed of peculiar delicacy and sensibility",[106] come to influence the attitudes and actions of men.

104 Millar, quoted in Haakonssen, *op cit*, n 100, 162.
105 Quoted in Haakonssen, *op cit*, n 100, 167.
106 Millar, *op cit*, n 66, 30.

Authority, contingency and consent

The writers discussed in this section share, to a greater or lesser degree, a sense of contingency. Order, whether in the natural or social worlds, is not guaranteed but has to be sought in the kind of co-operative endeavor that can be achieved by convention, not imposition. Authority exists within a framework of consent. It is purposive. The fictions in Hume and Blackstone are not delusions or lies, the work of muddled reasoning or mendacity, but assumptions made necessary either by the failure of reason to yield certainty or by the necessity of working with materials at hand. Hobbes' sovereign is, for him, necessitated by humans' inability to see into each other's minds. We could understand the elaborate protocols recommended from Locke and Mr Spectator as providing a kind of fiction that we can read others' minds. Dancing, recommended by Locke, provides not simply a graceful and therefore pleasing person, but a sociably predictable routine. Prescription, custom or convention are, in varying degree, sources of identity – this is the essence of who we are, and therefore of who we might become if we stay true to ourselves – and forms of orientation – we accept a certain magnetic north by a convention that makes the necessary day-to-day practice of sociability possible. Innovation guided by abstraction would lead, Burke considered, to disaster, since it took no account of the habits or expectations of the people who, through habits and expectations, made a community.

The two phases of empire are revealing of what the community told itself about itself. The Atlantic empire, the empire of trade and of the spread of "free-born Englishmen" comported with the social and cultural writing with which this chapter has been concerned. Legitimate government and law had to be understood as reflecting the habits and dispositions of a particular people at a particular time. They were part of the social practice of Englishness, whether this was practiced among white male Protestants in America or in the British Isles. Civil liberty, however vaguely defined, and its alter ego, freedom of property, at least from executive interference, provided a language in which the limitations of government and law could be discussed. The sea-borne empire of trade rather than conquest seemed to be a global concretization of the conversation among polite and sociable people about the purpose and implied limits of institutional social ordering. The second phase of empire, appealing to a more overtly center-periphery model of imperial governance, seems to have grown in influence following the acquisition of tens of millions of non-English subjects, territory and potentially great wealth, in India. The authoritarian nature of this new empire, the contempt and disregard in which its subjects, their religions, languages and literature were held, even the style of their dress were held by the British, was, as we shall see, new and a product of military conquest. Whilst the East India Company remained primarily a trading company, there remained also scope for its servants to embrace aspects of largely Muslim beliefs and attire, to convert and to marry local women. When the Company took on the role of military power, conqueror and ruler on the subcontinent, contempt for local culture and beliefs replaced respect and admiration.

The new subjects were not *heard* to demand political representation or to consent to being governed, their civilization became barbarous. The "new school of thought" among East India Company administrators stressed "a powerful political concept derived from Hobbes", the sovereign basis of authority.[107] The claim was in India based upon conquest but, as a number of scholars have pointed out, imperialism and pedagogy are closely associated; and ideas and practices do not in a colonial context travel only from the metropole. Sovereignty in what I have termed the strong sense, separating law from its substance, extruding ethics and politics from legal form and judging the authenticity of that form solely in terms of its sovereign origin, seems to have gained at this time a plausibility that it retains in many circles today.

107 Ranajit Guha, *A Rule of Property for Bengal: An Essay on the Idea of Permanent Settlement*, 2nd edn, Delhi, Orient Longman (1981), 33.

Chapter 4

The government of empire and its implications for the "metropolis"

> A perennial theme running throughout Britain's imperial experience has been the relationship between the ideas about the ordering of society at home and ideas about the ordering of the empire overseas.[1]

In Chapter 1, I referred to the psychoanalytic idea, originating perhaps in Freud, and developed in Lacan's writings, of the subject's yearning for a certainty s/he has not been able to achieve. Empire, and the manifold phenomena of Absolutist rule, even the genial Trumanian "the buck stops here", exemplify this yearning in political terms. The men of the 1688 Convention decided not to pretend, as the Stuart monarchy had done, that their authority originated in some yet higher authority. There was no consensus about the legal nature of James II/VII's departure, nor any urgency about finding one. The rulers of English society, for the most part large landowners, had had experience of purely legislative government. It had ended in Cromwell, the Lord Protector, a sovereign. The landlords had stared at purported certainty and did not much care for it. The conditional invitation to William and Mary, and the subsequent parliamentary provisions for the settlement, first upon Anne, the last of the Stuarts, but Protestant and firmly circumscribed in her authority, and then on the heirs of Sophia the Electress of Hanover, were designed to constitute an executive that was, at the same time, manageable. The men of the Convention gave, I have suggested, legitimate government to each other, but in order for this to succeed, they learned that it was necessary to do so politely, and two or three generations devoted themselves to this project.

In some ways it survived. Francophone Roman Catholic Quebecois, acquired by British conquest at the conclusion of the Seven Years' War in 1763, and who were expected by the American colonists to the south to join their rebellion, preferred government by religiously unzealous people for whom, in the words of Paxman already quoted, God was the "ultimate good chap". American Protestant

1 Peter Marshall, Empire and Authority in the Later Eighteenth Century, (1987) XV *Journal of Imperial and Commonwealth History* 105–22.

zealotry which Hume had criticized when he detected it in relation to seventeenth century England remained (and perhaps remains) in the east coast colonies, would perhaps have been less uncaring about the religious beliefs in Quebec City and Montreal than the British. The East India Company was equally uncaring about the strange beliefs it found in India. But it found itself in a different position. The French were a spent power in North America not, as La Fayette was to demonstrate in his intervention on behalf of the Thirteen Colonies against Great Britain, impotent, but without territorial ambitions. India, on the other hand, was different. Only the defeat by Nelson of Napoleon's Egyptian adventure, an intended passage to India, at Aboukir Bay in 1798, prevented further French invasions there. And we are familiar from Kipling's *Kim*, published in 1901, with the later perceived threat by Russia to British India which required, therefore, strong government. India was, as the above quotation suggests, and as Eric Stokes has argued, a social laboratory for British rulers attempting to deal with social and economic change at home. Strong government, then, yes, but a strange ambivalence from the beginning of British rule, one which I will trace through Great Britain itself.

From the "temper of the people" to the comforts of the law

This chapter introduces the rival approaches to the management of both empire and metropolis during the late eighteenth and nineteenth centuries. It is not possible to maintain a strictly chronological narrative, since two approaches toward government overlap, personified, insofar as it could be by Thomas Babbington Macaulay. So far as India was concerned, British presence did not originally take the form of government at all. The East India Company developed from a trading company into an authoritarian military and legislating power somewhat parasitically within the body of the Mogul Empire, maintaining the fiction that its authority was derived from the Mogul Emperor at Delhi, even when mid-eighteenth century conquests inclined Company servants increasingly to Hobbesian ideas of sovereignty. These were ideas which, as the narrative unfolds, can be seen as increasingly characteristic of both empire and metropolis, if in slightly different ways.

Politeness and civility, as we saw, enabled the English and British governing classes of different persuasions to co-exist and even extend principles of tolerance to the governed. Tolerance and an admiration of Indian civilization characterized Anglo-Indian relations at the outset:

> In Mughal India there was extensive commodity production together with a large volume of merchant capital. Roads were relatively secure and commerce included not only manufacture . . .[2]

2 Jack Goody, *The East in the West*, Cambridge, Cambridge University Press (1996), 106–7.

Commerce also included agriculture and the transport of its surplus to the urban areas. Capital accumulation exceeded that familiar to Europeans:

> Initially, the newcomers were amazed at what they saw . . . at the extent of cloth production and the riches of the country . . . On entering Murshidabad . . . Clive wrote: "the city is as extensive, populous and rich as . . . London" . . . Similar words were used of Agra, Fatechpore, Lahore and other Indian towns.[3]

The British were seduced, not merely by the material wealth and urban organization, but by the cultural and linguistic sophistication they saw around them. Attitudes of a more authoritarian kind came with the arrival, in the wake of Clive's victories, of, mostly young men on the make whose subordination of the local population somehow justified their forcible acquisition of what they learned from Hindi to call loot. After that, the "native" in Anglophone discourse began a conceptual and practical descent into what we shall later see was increasingly rule by law rather than rule by subjects of the rule of law.

Not long after that, Pitt's mooted reform of the franchise at Westminster was abandoned by virtue of the Tory opposition, and a sterner more paternalist legality rapidly eroded into reaction, as increasing hardships in the labor market created unrest and, after five years, the Revolution broke out in France, with widespread demand for political change in Britain a consequence. The Younger Pitt, whose first, "mince pie administration", derided as unlikely to survive the Christmas recess, but which actually lasted from 1784 until 1801, mostly years of war. Soon after there was the even more reactionary Liverpool Administration, which ended in 1828. And then there were the puzzling policies of the Whigs, who passed the Reform Act of 1832, but who were clearly frightened by popular hopes for something far more radical than the Act and popular anger at the disappointment of those hopes, they fell under the utilitarian spell, implementing the workhouse legislation in England, for example in the Poor Law Amendment Act of 1834, and setting in train increasing codification of English law in India; or only feebly gesturing toward at producing loyalty through cultural assimilation. The two were seen as intimately connected. Neatly connecting law, education, class, colonialism and gender, Pennycook remarks in relation to the Straits Settlements in colonial Malaya:

> The general idea of education for men (was that it) should make them more efficient, law-abiding and so on, so education for women was seen as playing a role in making them better wives and mothers.[4]

3 Goody, *ibid*, 113.

4 Alastair Pennycook, *English and the Discourses of Colonialism*, London, Routledge (1998), 97.

The immediate reaction to the 1857 Insurrection in India was, of course, a much more vicious repression than that which attended the political and industrial unrest in England decades before, going beyond the law in order to defend meta-legal sovereignty, as at Morant Bay in 1864. It was later blended with policies that delegated more power to local rulers and additionally laid more emphasis on policies of cultural assimilation to English, although, as Robert Scholes' analysis of the etymology of the term "the canon" suggests, the difference may not always be as much as we would like. The canon was, in part of its origin, a cane, a disciplining device: "many a native in India had Shakespeare as well as other canonical texts caned into him by the curricular arm of the British Raj. The Empire was based on its cannon, its canon and its canes – to a startling degree".[5] Culture is notoriously fickle and subject to challenge, perspective and change.[6] This is, as Scholes remarks, necessary: "we need disciplines in order to think productively. We also need to challenge them in order to think creatively";[7] but subsequently I argued at the beginning that one should not imagine "the law" as wheezing through history, the unchanged representative of European rationality amid the exotic, the changing and arcane landscapes of primordium, hope and ultimately disappointment and. its demise in on the shores of the poisonous ocean depicted by HG Wells – although Zizek has some acidly amusing remarks in this respect. Some Green politics seem, he suggests, to have foregone the campaign for the demise of capitalism and its replacement by something ultimately more humane, in favor of an end-of- the-world scenario in which the workings of capitalism will survive the end of human civilization.[8]

Law's very conceptual being, too, changed. Macaulay, as we have seen, hoped to bequeath to India an empire of culture and law that would outlive the global dominance of British military might, but shared the common Victorian speculation of the New Zealander one day wandering wondering through the ruined streets of London, once the hub of empire.[9] Eternity marched through the nineteenth century, linked to the inevitability of change and decline. Think of Shelley's 1817 report "from a traveler in an antique land" whose discovery of a ruined statuary in the desert reveals beneath "a wrinkled lip, and sneer of cold command" the inscription, "'My name is Ozymandias, King of Kings; Look on my works, ye mighty and despair'".[10] Or of Kipling's Recessional, eight decades later:

5 Robert Scholes, *The Rise and Fall of English*, New Haven, CT, Yale University Press (1998), 107.

6 See Raymond Williams, *Culture*, London, Fontana (1981).

7 Scholes, *op cit*, n 5, 108.

8 Slavoj Zizek, The Specter of Ideology, in Slavoj Zizek (ed), *Mapping Ideology*, London, Verso (1994), 1.

9 Gustave Dore's The New Zealander, illustration from London: a Pilgrimage by Blanchard Jarrold (1872) is reproduced on the dust jacket of Duncan Bell, *The Idea of Greater Britain: Empire and the Future of World Order 1860–1900*, London, Palgrave (2007).

10 Ozymandias, in *The Complete Works of Percy Bysshe Shelley*, London, Oxford University Press (1927), 546.

Far-called, our navies melt away;
On dune and headland sinks the fire:
Lo, all our pomp of yesterday
Is one with Nineveh and Tyre.
Judge of the nations, spare us yet
Lest we forget – lest we forget.[11]

Gikandi[12] and others have reminded us that the solidity of empire and the ultimate unity of a progressive Britain are a nostalgic retrospect reinforced in part by World War II: Victorians sought to comfort themselves from the external catastrophes of Indian rebellion and the internal demands from a by no means unified struggle of class and gender with a mixture of illusions. One attempted comfort was rule by law, by the apparent certainty of law, its sovereign source throughout the empire, anchored in the writings of Bentham and his disciples, by John Austin, James Fitzjames Stephen and Albert Venn Dicey. The second was by cultural assimilation, the form of civility advocated so successfully for the upper and middling classes after the 1688 Revolution. Writers such as Coleridge, Macaulay and Matthew Arnold assumed that for both the lower middling and working classes both were important.

In earlier chapters it was suggested that late seventeenth and early eighteenth century social thought constituting the English subject in Britain was under a certain debt, acknowledged or not, to ideas circulating in northern Europe, at a slightly earlier date – in particular to Dutch and north German writing. These ideas were concerned, I suggested, first with limited or divided sovereignty, and with the significance of "private" forms of civility for "public" stability. Second and relatedly, they emphasized the importance of investigating the social, historical and political conditions of specific social orders for understanding their practices of sovereignty and legality.[13] This multi-faceted approach to legality, to the basis of legal authority, in its contrast with the approach adopted in the European Absolutisms,[14] and later by the legal positivist work stimulated by Hobbes, will remind modern Anglophone legal educators of the twentieth and twenty-first century pedagogical distinction made by the positivists between the emotional and the rational, the sometimes vague world of the socio-legal, and the contrasting

11 Recessional (1897), in George Orwell (ed), *The Works of Rudyard Kipling*, Ware, Wordsworth Editions (1994), 328.

12 Simon Gikandi, *Mapping Englishness: Writing Identity in the Culture of Colonialism*, New York, NY, Columbia University Press (1996).

13 See the discussions of, *inter alia*, Shaftesbury and the Scots literati in Knud Haakonssen, *Natural Law and Moral Philosophy: From Grotius to the Scottish Enlightenment*, Cambridge, Cambridge University Press (1996).

14 Montesquieu, *The Spirit of the Laws* (1748) Berkeley, CA, University of California Press (1977), was much concerned with contextual explanations, but he wrote from the position of an admirer of what he took to be the Whig constitution, with its – as he understood it – separation of powers and guarantees of liberty.

world of doctrine, where more certainty can apparently be discovered – between "soft" and "hard" law, as the distinction is often labeled by the modern positivists, with all the gendered implications of that form of binary representation.[15]

I suggested in Chapter 2 that both experience of the Stuarts and their associations with the major Catholic Absolutisms – principally France and Spain – induced in the England of the immediate post-revolutionary era, a suspicion of the practice of authoritarian sovereignty preferred by those monarchs, and by the Stuarts, whose pretensions to the English throne Spain and France continued to support whilst James III, the "Old Pretender" and his son, the "Young Pretender", "Bonnie Prince Charlie", remained in exile at St Germains, pensioners of the French monarchy or removed to Rome.

Consistently with the Whig view that largely prevailed in the years after 1688, constitutional writing concerning England/Britain was even until the nineteenth century set principally in an historical register,[16] descriptions of the growth of liberty and the protection of property, their dynamics and the conditions of their continued existence being thus preferred, for the most part to lawyers' largely technical accounts, in which Burke, for one, as we saw, had little faith. Where practical analysis met political practice, lawyers and legality were far from ignored – hence Blackstone's reference to the judges as "oracles" of law. But the significance of the common law and equity and of executive and legislative performances and interactions were evaluated by commentators as to their propriety in much wider contexts in the post-Revolutionary period. Whilst Hale was a reformer in spirit, and had more faith in legislation as a vehicle for reform than did Blackstone, the conformity of law with the habits and "temper" of the people subject to it was for him an important criterion of its quality as law. Blackstone's study of the principles of English law in 1756 led to his appointment as Vinerian professor at Oxford, where he gave the first university lectures in English law to young gentlemen, most of whom would not become professional lawyers. His attempt to set up an Oxford college devoted to the study of law on liberal principles failed, but his interest in framing legal studies in a context wider than the dry technicalities, by then the stuff of the Inns of Court, remained. His conviction, evinced in the *Commentaries*' focus on the principles relating to a particular jurisdiction after a quite hasty discussion "of laws in general" was, as we have seen, echoed in Burke's insistence that "nations are not primarily ruled

15 Margaret Thornton, Techno-Centrism in the Law School: Why the Gender and the Color of the Law Remain the Same, (1998) 36 *Osgoode Hall Law Journal* 369; Ian Duncanson, The Centre May Not Hold, (2001) 8 *International Journal of the Legal Profession* 69–85.

16 Henry Hallam, *Constitutional History of England*, 2 vols in 1, London, Ward, Lock and Tyler (1827), may have been the last of this tradition (1987), although the Victorian William Stubbs, *The Constitutional History of England* (1874–76), Chicago, IL, University of Chicago Press (1979) could also be seen in this light. See, generally JGA Pocock, *The Ancient Constitution and the Common Law: A Study of English Historical Thought in the Seventeenth Century*, 2nd edn, Cambridge, Cambridge University Press, with Retrospect (1987).

by laws: less by violence . . . the temper of the people amongst whom he presides ought therefore to be the first study of the statesman".[17]

It is impossible, of course, to provide precise dates, a cut-off point of transition from one approach to rulership, authority and law, emphasizing custom and consent, the "temper of the people" whose laws were the object of study, to another, one more concerned with the etiology of law in the will of the sovereign, with precision. Hobbes' model, as I pointed out in Chapter 1, had been comprehensively rejected by the men of the Revolution and their immediate successors. Then, in the 1770s, Jeremy Bentham "was at pains to stress that the authority of a law is not tied in any way to an assessment of its content or the ends to which it is directed",[18] although it is not clear how long that idea took to become hegemonic. (Again, as I remarked in Chapter 1, the metaphysical underpinnings of Bentham's in-specter are in marked contrast to his insistence on the possibility of objectivity.) Paine certainly believed that the authoritarian conduct of the British in India, where "the wretched inhabitants are glad to . . . purchase . . . the privilege to breathe while he, the sole lord of their fortunes and lives, disposes of either as he pleases and prepares for Europe", traveled home and infected the remainder of the empire.[19] A transition there undoubtedly was, but Whiggery of the old kind persisted; there was a good deal of overlap. Burke was firmly in the older tradition, the ground of his support for the American cause and of his opposition to the French Revolution. And even into the nineteenth century, when Benthamite ideas about sovereignty were well known and conscientiously applied by John Austin in his subsequently published lectures at University College, London, it was possible for Prime Minister Lord Melbourne to write to Charles Greville that Benthamites "were all fools and Austin a damned fool". Greville later wrote that Melbourne had read all of Austin's jurisprudence and found *The Province of Jurisprudence Determined*, a jurisprudential application of Benthamite principles, to be "the dullest book he had ever read . . .".[20] It seems equally impossible to rule out the role of empire in producing that transition, something we shall return to.

The nature of the British Empire

A central question for the mid to late eighteenth century was:

> Were the British to be part of a predominantly Atlantic empire in which they would be *primus inter pares*, or were they to rule over a polyglot worldwide empire, most of whose peoples were clearly subject peoples?[21]

17 Edmund Burke, Thoughts of the Present Discontents (1770), in Peter Stanlis (ed), *Edmund Burke: Selected Writings and Speeches*, Washington, DC, Regnery Press (1963), 121 *et seq.*

18 Gerald Postema, *Bentham and the Common Law Tradition*, Oxford, Oxford University Press (1986), 238.

19 Paine, (1775), writing about Lord Clive, quoted in John Keane, *Tom Paine: A Political Life*, New York, NY, Little, Brown (1995), 93.

20 Lotte Hamburger and Joseph Hamburger, *Troubled Lives: John and Sarah Austin*, Toronto, University of Toronto Press (1985), 224–25.

The ideological picture of the free and "seaborne empire", one incompatible with a simple notion, or practice of sovereignty, from one perspective primarily commercial, in contrast to the territorial expansions which began, roughly, with Clive's, Munro's and Eyre Coote's conquests in north-east India following the Battle of Plassey in 1757, has been quite properly questioned by later historians.[22] Did the Thirteen Colonies, after all, not represent "territorial conquests" from first nations people; did not British North America as a whole involve the coercion of, perhaps two and a half million African slaves, transported, largely by the British, during two centuries to work as slaves in the plantation economies of the Chesapeake, and of the Caribbean, where the indigenous population, the Caribs, had been largely eliminated? And what, Wilson asks, about the Irish and before them, the Welsh in the British Isles themselves?

The "cultural imperialist" enterprise I understand similarly to Phillip Darby, although we are writing of different eras and to some extent different areas.[23] Imperial procedures applied to "native" peoples overseas and to those conceptually assimilated by Britain's rulers to the natives "at home". With a great deal of reluctance, Lord Mansfield decided that there was no basis in common law for slavery in England; reluctance, since he was concerned about the implications for the law of property. James Somerset, an African, had been bought in the Americas, where slavery was legal, and was valuable. *Somerset*, often celebrated as a case marking the commitment of English common law to freedom was, Mansfield insisted, merely a case that forbad the coercive removal of a person from the realm. The case is, of course, an admission that Somerset, once in England, was a "freeborn Englishman", ironically, of course, the status White male Americans were to engage in war to secure for themselves. And in another irony, despite his caution anent Somerset, the Governor of Massachusetts was intrigued to discover an African woman, a relation of Mansfield's, at Mansfield's home, who joined the ladies for coffee and walked arm in arm with a European relative.[24]

The situation was fluid. Lawrence and Jeanne Stone have argued that English gentry and aristocracy were unusually permeable by those with means.[25] So, consistently with my argument throughout the thesis, empire was for the English/British, an enterprise of continuity. Subject positions, as they were performed by individual human beings as part of a larger social order, and as they were perceived

21 Peter Marshall, *The Making and Unmaking of Empires: Britain, India and America, c. 1750–1783*, Oxford, Oxford University Press (2005), 379.

22 David Armitage and Michael Braddick (eds), *The British Atlantic World*, London, Palgrave (2009); Kathleen Wilson, Introduction, in Kathleen Wilson (ed), *A New Imperial History: Culture, Identity, History*, Cambridge, MA, Harvard University Press (1999), 9, 10, 11 and elsewhere.

23 Phillip Darby, A Disabling Discipline, in Christian Reuss-Smit and Duncan Snidal (eds), *The Oxford Handbook of International Relations*, Oxford, Oxford University Press (2008).

24 James Oldham, *English Common Law in the Age of Mansfield*, Chapel Hill, NC, University of North Carolina Press (2004), ch 17.

25 L and J Stone, *An Open Elite? England 1540–1880*, Oxford, Oxford University Press (1984).

by spectators, changed as social tectonics changed and offered different opportunities or changed fates. Paul Gilroy wrote some time ago about the international culture consequent on slavery.[26] For the transatlantic rulers, and most of all, for the rulers of India and Great Britain, the lower orders, black, brown or white, were a source of exploitation, troublesome, but also admissible – to Eton, Oxford and Cambridge, the City and the Bar – an attitude that did not rule out vicious reprisals against those who were not admitted or did not accept the price or worth of acceptance.

Since, at least, the Elizabethan era, Africans, Afro-Caribbeans, Indians and others have lived in England, have served in the Royal Navy or the merchant marine, and have interacted culturally or more intimately with the European community of the United Kingdom. Prime Minister Liverpool was an Anglo-Indian. They were, as travelers or residents, imperial subjects very much not "out there", but "as Gretchen Gerzina has noted, they were 'a continual and very English presence from the Elizabethan settlement onward', a fundamental and constitutive part of English culture . . .".[27]

My concern is principally with the effect on the British metropole of the practices its rulers and administrators attempted with varying degrees of success in the management of its colonies, India specifically; and in particular with the changing nature of the conceptions of government, sovereignty and legality and then of empire produced there. But if one does not accept that a flourishing civilization of South Asia, its commerce, culture and ideas did not reciprocally influence English/British culture, one is missing much of the picture of cultural interaction. If the representation, "empire of the seas", the empire of trade and of the spread of freeborn Englishmen[28] and its antithesis, the autocratic government of brown people, was in part an illusion, in part a self-serving hypocrisy, it did reflect certain beliefs about government and law in Britain; and it did involve policies of restraint that benefited at least some local and colonial subjects. In the eras immediately before, and then during Victoria's reign, the ruling classes, landowners, City men and, increasingly manufacturing capitalists did not, outright, ask themselves whether the working class "at home" were like Americans, with whom political accommodation had been and could have continued to be, shared, or like brown people, but that is what they were actually debating. And when, later,

26 Paul Gilroy, *The Black Atlantic: Modernity and Double Consciousness*, London, Verso (1983); and see Tarak Barkawi and Mark Laffey, Retrieving the Imperial: Empire and International Relations, (2002) *Millennium: Journal of International Studies* 109–27.

27 Cited in Antoinette Burton (ed), Introduction, *After the Imperial Turn: Thinking with and through the nation*, Durham, NC, Duke University Press (2003), 2, 3; Glenn Jordan and Chris Weedon, *Cultural Politics: Class, Gender, Race and the Postmodern World*, Oxford, Blackwell (1995), ch 5.

28 As we have seen, the connection of maritime trade and liberty was a persistent theme: David Armitage, *The Ideological Origins of the British Empire*, Cambridge, Cambridge University Press (2000), esp ch 4; Eliga Gould, *The Persistence of Empire: British Political Culture in the Age of the American Revolution*, Chapel Hill, NC, University of North Carolina Press (2000), ch 1.

the British confronted assertive Indians, they did not ask whether these people were like the British working class; but that is, on some occasions, I suspect, what they asked themselves. The British working class resembled the Americans of the 1760s and early 1770s: the tradition of the "free-born Englishman" has deep roots. They saw themselves as loyal subjects, but not subjects fit for oppression. Indians, of at least of the upper nationalist class, saw themselves as the white male Americans of the later 1770s and later eighteenth century saw themselves: pragmatic heirs of an enlightenment culture of abstract rights and common law remedies entitled to an independent future. The difference was, of course, and we must never overlook the contingencies of history, America faced a global titan, deluded by its joyous glance into Lacan's mirror of the identity of the image with the reality of its capacity. India, by the 1940s faced a "weary titan", victorious against some oppression, but eager to abandon its commitment to the sub-continent.[29] We run ahead of ourselves.

As to restraint in eighteenth century Whig Britain, in his speeches on America, Burke was eventually to compare Westminster's claims over the American colonies with the monarch's legal right to veto legislation passed in the Houses of Commons and Lords – best left to the fantasies of those who believe that governments are based on quill and parchment. If restraint did not in the end prevail in Britain's dealings with the Americans, it *had* done so for some time; and there were constitutional lessons to be drawn from the debate over the practical and prudential qualifications which ought to be included in discussions of sovereignty, a concept which later legal writers such as Bentham, Austin and Dicey, were to see as purely technical in nature. Although, of the Scots, perhaps one of the less sympathetic to the American cause, Adam Ferguson foresaw disaster in the imperial belief "that the grandeur of a nation is to be estimated from the extent of its territory; or that the interest of any particular people consists in reducing their neighbors to servitude"[30] – in other words, the indiscriminate claim to sovereignty attempted under George III's ministries. Ferguson was, after all, a member of the belatedly conciliatory Carlisle Committee, which attempted to address the model of federal empire originally favored by the Americans. Liberty is secured, not by grand schemes but by "continued differences and oppositions of numbers", "monarchy mixed with republic" (rejected, as we shall see, by Wellesley as Governor-General of India between 1797 and 1805). Independence is associated by Ferguson with the securing to the workman of "the fruits of his labor", leaving the chief virtue of the statesman as abstaining from mischievous interference.[31]

29 I have taken the term "titan" from Aaron Freidberg, *The Weary Titan: Britain and the Experience of Relative Decline*, Princeton, NJ, Princeton University Press (1996).

30 Adam Ferguson, *An Essay on the History of Civil Society* (1767), Edinburgh, Edinburgh University Press (Duncan Forbes, ed) (1966), 154.

31 Ferguson, *ibid*, 128, 132 and 143.

Ferguson's recommendation of executive abstinence from mischievous interference is, of course part of the theme that runs throughout the writings of the Scottish *literati*, one which we find also in those who are in large measure, their predecessors, Locke and Shaftesbury, as we have already noticed. It is worth exploring the complex web from which restraint is constructed as guided by the integration of various publics with various private mores and expectations, if only partly because, from the early political economists down to the present, it has been subject to simplistic and paradoxical interpretations, sometimes with dangerous implications. The underlying assumption, which may be articulated in its most developed form in the passages from which the above quotations from Ferguson were drawn, is that social cohesion has a fragile basis. If it is not to be secured by the despotic means rejected by the Revolution, then, for the early writers down to Hutcheson, it must be secured by the learning of sociability or the moral virtue of mutual respect. Whilst suggesting quite explicit limitations on the exercise of sovereign power and the limitations of any concept of law regarded as the will of the sovereign, it did not imply the rampant individualism sometimes attributed by shallow thought to Adam Smith. Our being assured of the services of the butcher, the baker and the maker of other goods takes place within the same co-operating order of trust as the securing to the worker of the fruits of his labor so central to the thought of Millar and Ferguson. Smith's famous "hidden hand" is merely a reflection of a theme common throughout Scottish thought, that events conclude themselves behind human backs and cannot be predicted by reason. Smith's antidote to the "moral corruption" threatened by the division and consequent intensification of labor was a broad general education, an improvement not merely in one's material condition, but, as he saw it, in one's moral improvement.[32]

Smith's model of sociability relies on the subject's internalization of his spectator's Lacanian gaze, which is, of course a procedure that presupposes but also helps stabilize and reproduce society; the scientists who, in order to continue with their work, treat their laws as part of the universe, are using a provisional shorthand within a community of researchers, as are the members of Hume's community who develop and share fictions that enable them socially to negotiate the melancholy terror of uncertainty. Both are to be contrasted with Althusser's notion of Ideological State Apparatuses, which fix the subject as merely a support (*trager*) of a social technology over which they have no control.[33] When the social basis of the illusions necessary for our existence are taken too literally, absolutely, disaster is at hand because it is always necessary to be prepared to abandon them when they no longer seem useful. The shorthand account of "law as the will of the sovereign" may save us from melancholy when some immediately pressing task is at hand, but it disguises or marginalizes more complex understandings, the secession of the thirteen colonies being one of the most spectacular consequences.

32 Gauri Viswanathan, *Masks of Conquest: Literary Study and British Rule in India*, New Delhi, Oxford University Press (1998), 128.

33 Louis Althusser, *Lenin, Philosophy and Other Essays*, London, Verso (1971).

The effects of Britain's experience of the Raj

> Royal legal authority was readily appropriated and the English common law nursed anti-authoritarian views . . . ([I]t rested upon community values and was remembered and applied variously in Puritan, Quaker and Anglican colonies i.e. in America). Its seventeenth century champions had made the rights of Englishmen into a bulwark against Royal power . . . However hegemonic the legal system may have been in structure, it functioned primarily as a local vehicle of negotiated dispute settlement.[34]

The dispersals and the increasingly provisional nature of sovereign truths, dependent on sociable compromise, that I have associated with the post-Glorious Revolutionary decades, in particular with the Scots,[35] was matched by the "salutary neglect" which Steele associates with "benign Whiggery" in the empire.[36] Hume, we saw, was unmoved by the potentially tyrannical power of the House of Commons in Great Britain, since, as he observed, in practice its power was, precisely, compromised with benign effect by the desire of its members for office under the Crown. If they wanted Crown offices, they had to support Crown ministries – but only for the most part. This "old corruption" did not guarantee a government, but it worked to produce a degree of stability. Gould sees this as a mark of the liberty often claimed for the "matchless constitution". Consent that might be coerced in a despotism had to be bought under a "free constitution".[37] Sometimes the king's ministries prevailed and sometimes they failed and fell, succumbing to country (or backbench) revolts, or, occasionally extra-parliamentary pressure, a state of affairs that Hume found not at all unsatisfactory, even though he had grave reservations about anything resembling democracy. In the same way, Steele writes, imperial trade policies, far from proceeding unproblematically from an imperial center to implementation in a colonial periphery, emerged from a similar process.[38] Colonial agents from America actively recruited the support of Westminster MPs. If lobbying, or the more vigorous process of corruption and patronage of competing interests failed of reconciliation at Westminster, "a law could be passed to placate one interest and remain unenforced to placate another". At the same time, colonial assemblies in both the island and

34 Ian Steele, The Annointed, the Appointed and the Elected: Governance of the British Empire 1689–1784, in Peter Marshall (ed), *The Oxford History of the British Empire II: The Eighteenth Century*, Oxford, Oxford University Press (2001), 113.

35 See David Paxman, Aesthetics as Epistemology, Or, Knowledge Without Certainty, (1992) 26:2 *Eighteenth Century Studies* 285–306.

36 For brief accounts of the influence of the Scots on mid-century America, see Daniel Howe, Why the Scottish Enlightenment was Useful to the Framers of the American Constitution, (1989) 31:3 *Comparative Studies in Society and History* 572–87.

37 Gould, *op cit*, n 28; also JH Plumb, *The Growth of Political Stability in England 1675–1725*, Harmondsworth, Penguin (1973).

38 Steele, *op cit*, n 34.

mainland American colonies gained increasing financial control over colonial governors, whose role as vice regal officers was thereby diminished, allowing, John Shy suggests, colonial elites to enhance their own power as mediating "between London, provincial capitals and the American grassroots".[39] British merchants in India were heavily dependent on local capital.

Marshall discusses the strands connecting American elites with Britain following the Seven Years War of 1756–63: "Models of British refinement" and taste were becoming more popular as more books were imported into America from Britain, and travelers crossed the Atlantic in both directions. In particular, as we saw in Chapter 3, Scottish academics were in particular demand in America for their breadth of scholarship. Even the conservative Scot, John Witherspoon, founding member of Princeton, whilst disagreeing with many of his compatriots anent specifics, was nevertheless a Scot, sufficiently committed to scholarly principles to recommend Hutcheson and Hume, as well as Millar and Smith, as readings for his courses.[40] Americans were able to enhance their claims to represent traditions of attachment to property and liberty in political and intellectual matters generally through these cultural contacts.[41] However, the, in the end, "more pervasive view of colonies and colonists" began to prevail in Britain, that colonies were strategic and commercial resources to be subordinated to British global struggles with Spain and France. This lack of reciprocity between American beliefs concerning the legitimate forms of government over the colonies and those of the British can be explained in a number of ways that relate to our theme, that of sovereignty and, in particular, the supposed uniquely sovereign origin of law.

Briefly, one explanation is the British rulers' fear of losing British possessions, and even the Isles themselves, to the Catholic powers, principally France. This is scarcely surprising. There had been major risings in favor of the exiled Stuart dynasty in 1715 and 1745, which were encouraged by Spain and France. The Jacobite Highland army reached Derby, in the English midlands in 1745 before retreating. They were not an unformidable foe, possessed of adequate and tactically generally well-placed artillery if lacking a supply of skilled gunners, backed by the feared Highland charge.[42] But they were massacred by an outnumbering army of British regulars under the Duke of Cumberland at Culloden

39 John Shy, The American Colonies in War and Revolution, 1748–1783, in Peter Marshall (ed), *The Oxford History of the British Empire II: The Eighteenth Century*, Oxford, Oxford University Press (2001), 309.

40 Marshall, *op cit*, n 21, ch 1; Roy Branson, James Madison and the Scottish Enlightenment, (1979) *Journal of the History of Ideas* 235–50.

41 Jack Greene, Empire and Identity from the Glorious Revolution to the American Revolution, in Peter Marshall (ed), *The Oxford History of the British Empire II: The Eighteenth Century*, Oxford, Oxford University Press (2001).

42 Christopher Duffy, *The '45: Bonnie Prince Charlie and the Untold Story of the Jacobite Rising*, London, Phoenix (2007).

Moor in 1746, commemorated in one of the most poignant of British memorials to lost causes, its viciousness witness to the nervousness of the Hanoverian government. Neither the evaporation of Spanish and French support for the rebellions, nor the relative indifference of those English who might have risen to support the Young Pretender could have been predicted before the event. The burden of Lenman's and Gibson's collection is that, despite the defeat in 1746, the Jacobite threat, with overseas catholic support, could not at the time have been safely perceived as a paper tiger.[43] Peter Marshall writes of the "dismay" among political leaders as "tension rose in the early 1750s", prior to what then became the first of a half century of global war among the European powers, the comprehensive victory of Britain in which could not have been anticipated with any confidence at the beginning of the period.[44] Given this context, there was, in the view of these rulers, he suggests, no room for a loosely confederated Atlantic empire of the kind the Americans in effect favored. The example of the Dutch Republic seemed at the time relevant. "No longer a nation" but a weak "disabled company of merchants", sunk into "insignificancy" because their myopic pursuit of wealth had led them to overlook the need for centralized political authority, the United Provinces appeared to be in severe decline.[45]

The experience of domestic popular disorder during the Wilkite disturbances demonstrated the need for firm centralized government in Britain itself. John Wilkes' use of the courts to restrain the conduct of an executive that had Parliamentary support implied a more rigorous separation of powers than many contemporary rulers considered safe. His denial of the Commons' right to decide who sat in their house, despite the outcome of election implied that sovereignty might originate with the people. That many of the people, too, thought this to be the case might be deduced from their increasingly vocal criticism of the political order. Domestic uncertainties increased as the century wore on, these and the French and Spanish threats seemed to demonstrate the need for a more centralized and unified approach to empire. At least, this may have been the firm intention in the 1750s but, as Saul David observes, it was not soon to be realized outside India, and by the accession of Queen Victoria in 1837, "the empire consisted of a jumbled collection of territories acquired in bits and pieces over generations, 'an unsystematic affair, an empire in abeyance, possessing no unity of purpose or sense of whole.'".[46] It may have been for this reason that the despotic regime of

43 Bruce Lenman and John Gibson (eds), *The Jacobite Threat: Rebellion and Conspiracy 1688–1759 – England, Ireland, Scotland and France*, Edinburgh, Scottish Academic Press (1990).

44 Peter Marshall, A Nation Defined by Empire 1755–1776, in Alexander Grant and Keith Stringer (eds), *Uniting the Kingdom: The Making of British History*, London, Routledge (1995).

45 Peter Marshall, The Case for Coercing America Before the Revolution, in Fred Leventhal and Roland Quinault (eds), *Anglo-American Attitudes: From Revolution to Partnership*, Aldershot, Ashgate (2000), 13.

46 Saul David, *Victoria's Wars: The Rise of Empire*, London, Viking (2006), 3, in part quoting James Morris.

the Raj came to have such influence on the later development of empire. Even India was a jumble, but at least it was a despotic jumble, offering the possibility of unified rule.

The second reason for the new authoritarianism in British attitudes toward America indeed lay in India, in the grant by the Mughal of India to the East India Company of the diwani, the right to administer and tax Bengal, after the Company's military victories over the Nawab of Bengal, Suraj-ad-Daula, in 1757 at Plassey and the further triumph, as it was seen, at Buxar. This delivered into the Company's, hence British hands, jurisdiction over a large population of Asian subjects and the fiscal capacity vastly to increase the Company's army and potentially increase its territorial gains still further. This, perhaps more than anything else, changed the nature of empire, whose subjects were now predominantly Indian. The "benign Whiggery" of permitting wide powers to local representative assemblies of white men in the Americas was not seen to be appropriate for subjects whose political traditions were not derived from Britain. Company servants began to see themselves as developing sovereignty of a Hobbesian kind, that is a power subject to no practicable form of participation or challenge. Hobbesian doctrines made their way into the metropole in a direct challenge to Whiggish suspicions of power and government.

Third, Kathleen Wilson[47] has traced the tendency, as the eighteenth century advanced, to see the doctrines of politeness and civility associated with the toleration of diversity and difference that had preserved the state since the Revolution, as exactly the kind of effeminacy believed at the time to have led to the downfall of the Roman Empire. What was called for to rule an expanding empire was "manliness", the social vicissitudes of which concept, and its connection with sovereignty and law, we shall explore.

Effeminacy: the re-imagining of governing the empire

> James was among the last of the English officials in India who found it possible to truly cross cultures. The new ideas that (Governor-General) Wellesley imported from England . . . made it increasingly difficult for individuals to make the leap from Britain to India, from Georgian to Mughal, from Christianity to Islam. India was no longer a place to embrace and be transformed by; it was instead a place to conquer and transform.[48]

The above, James Achilles Kirkpatrick (1764–1805), was the Company Resident in Hyderabad between 1798 and 1805, notorious or famous, depending on one's

47 Kathleen Wilson, *The Sense of the People: Politics, Culture and Imperialism in England*, Cambridge, Cambridge University Press (1992).

48 William Dalrymple, *White Mughals: Love and Betrayal in Eighteenth Century India*, London, Harper Collins (2002), 454.

view of the inquiry conducted into his activities by Lord Clive, the grandson of Robert Clive and governor of Bengal in 1801, for marrying a high-ranking Muslim woman, Begum Khair-un-Nissa. The marriage was the subject of the inquiry. As confidante of the Nizam of Hyderabad, and of the Nizam's Prime Minister, Kirkpatrick was a successful diplomat to the court of one of India's most powerful kingdoms. His marriage – out of evident love – to a girl (she was fourteen when he married her) who belonged to so high a rank, his adoption of Mughal dress – a habit well-suited to the climate and long common among Europeans, as Van Dyck's famous 1620s portrait of the first Earl of Denbigh in Indian clothes suggests – and Kirkpatrick's acceptance of the Euro-Indian synthesis. It was a synthesis which, as Dalrymple makes plain, intercourse in the sophisticated and multicultural world of India took for granted, makes Kirkpatrick, like those two ironically antagonistic figures, Warren Hastings and Edmund Burke, by that time an anachronism – hence the scandal that provoked the inquiry into the appropriateness of Kirkpatrick's conduct urged on Clive. The briskly efficient Cornwallis (Governor-General of India 1786–1793, then 1804–05) and the more Martinet-like Wellesley (1793–1804) represented a new world, one in which political subordination began to be justified in terms of the innate superiority of the subordinators.[49] In the "clash of civilizations" and of classes, we still live with consequences of doctrines of innate superiority and inferiority.

There are a number of contexts into which to put both Kirkpatrick's behavior and in particular the responses to it. Jyotsna Singh, addressing a broader question, puts the matter well, remarking, first, an issue which will become more important to us later. "The (British) concern for good governance in India also exposed the growing anxieties about the attendant social and economic dislocations that were taking place within British society".[50] As Singh adds, two intersecting forces that seemed *ex facie* at odds, actually reinforced each other. If we confine ourselves to the eighteenth century, it came as something of a shock to an *English* culture whose rudimentary education system for gentlemen elevated the language and culture of classical Athens and Rome above all others, to learn from the work of Orientalists such as linguist-lawyers HT Colebrooke and Sir William Jones, that Sanskrit both preceded historically and exceeded in complexity and erudition the languages of the classical Mediterranean that underwrote British proof of European superiority. That Sanskrit itself may have been a product of a proto-Indo-European language originating in South Asia and the root of Greek and Latin, added insult to injury and prompted ludicrous stories, for example, that Alexander the Great's Indian adventures had enabled wily Brahmins to invent a language based on Macedonian Greek and pass it off as more venerable. But if this was not

49 There is a relatively early critical discussion of this in Percival Spear, *The Nabobs* (1932), Oxford, Oxford University Press (1963), ch VIII.

50 Jyotsna Singh, *Colonial Narratives: Cultural Dialogues, "Discoveries" of India in the Language of Colonialism*, New York, NY, Routledge (1996), 53.

convincing, the evidence of an Indian past of high civilization, and of linguistic and other accomplishments, could be used to measure a regression in the present requiring British dominion to reverse it to the point where Indian subjects were once again capable of governing themselves – in the future.

The contribution made to the growing problems faced by Indian society by the imposition of unfamiliar British norms associated with the doctrines of Malthus and Bentham was ignored. Populations, particularly in times of stress, required management and restraint, but not intervention. During local famines, for example:

> Any intervention in the grain market on the part of public functionaries, whether by restricting the transport of grain, by giving advantage to particular places or individuals or places in preference to others, by attempting to regulate the price, or by compelling individuals to open stores of grain and bring them to market is impolitic and objectionable.[51]

Ironically, as Sharma observes:

> British policies to centralize the economy and spread new administrative roots were creating a highly "interventionist" state which simultaneously was professing an ideology of non-interventionism, particularly to the grain market.[52]

In the context of political economy, Jones' genuine respect for Sanskrit culture could scarcely, in other minds, be unlinked from the desire of colonial administrators both to free themselves from a reliance on native pundits, fluent in the language and the laws written in it, in applying local law – with a political economy inflection – authoritatively to local people.[53] Moreover, since it was largely the work of Englishmen, proud of the procedures of their common law, the orientalists' attempts at the codification of Hindu law prefigure Weber's obsession with formal legal rationality[54] and seem inconsistently to replace a Hindu case law procedure not unlike the common law with which they were familiar and which claimed the virtues of adaptability and flexibility, with one that replaces and rigidifies it. The inconsistencies which the Orientalists sought to remedy in their translations of the Laws of Manu are attributable, according to Brian Smith, to its context-sensitivity, not to a failure of intellectual rigor.[55] Its notion of *dharma* as

51 Circular of magistrates in the divisions of Barela and Benaras, 27 January 1818, quoted in Sanjay Sharma, *Famine, Philanthropy and the Colonial State: North India in the Early Nineteenth Century*, Delhi, Oxford University Press (2001), 56.

52 Sharma, *ibid*, 73.

53 C Bayly, *Indian Society and the Making of the British Empire*, Cambridge, Cambridge University Press (1988), 113; Bernard Cohn, *Colonialism and its Forms of Knowledge: The British in India*, Princeton, NJ, Princeton University Press (1998), ch 3.

54 Max Weber, *Economy and Society*, 2 vols, Berkeley, CA, University of California Press (1978), ch VIII. See also Anthony Kronman, *Max Weber*, London, Arnold (1983).

55 Brian Smith, Introduction, in Brian Smith (ed), *The Laws of Manu*, Harmondsworth, Penguin (1991), xlvi.

encompassing appropriate behavior, religion, right and law, was not so distant from early eighteenth century British ideas about social order – and of course, those of Burke.

Kirkpatrick's and many others', in Dalrymple's account of the adaptation of the British to the enormous variety of Indian ways acquired a different complexion, under the new dispensation that was not so much critical – because uncomprehending – of Indian culture as a whole, but increasingly contemptuous, Singh suggests, among those who became increasingly authoritative, and who saw the richness of the Indian past, if they saw it at all, as a measure of its current inhabitants' fall from grace, and evidence of a need for profound rehabilitation. The "public mind . . . of India, we found debased and contracted," the "race debased by three thousand years of despotism and priestcraft . . . sunk in the lowest depths of slavery and superstition".[56]

But we must not, as suggested, forget gender in the explanation of authoritarianism, since the law *via* colonialism, becomes increasingly authoritarian. Increasingly during the eighteenth century struggles over the matter of citizenship in Britain, the proper subject of political discourse took on a particular hegemonic form that stressed, as the basis for independence and authority, "rationality", "independence", and "manliness", which were, of course, codes for white men who pretended a particular persuasion. Wahrman issues a cautionary reminder that such self-representations of those who positioned themselves rhetorically as opposed to both an "effeminate" aristocracy of the metropolitan court and the unruliness of the mob have a provenance extending at least to the seventeenth century.[57] And, indeed, the values of spiritual asceticism and disciplined hard work in a "middling sort" are clearly noted in Defoe's observations about his society,[58] shops and shop-keepers, who were often artisans, members of this social "middle", proliferated, its ideas influential.[59] Purkiss is doubtless correct in her diagnosis, which I will repeat:

56 TB Macaulay, Speech on the Government of India, House of Commons, 10th July 1833 (concerning the Charter Bill), in TF Ellis (ed), *The Miscellaneous Writings and Speeches of Lord Macaulay*, London, Longmans Green (1889), 563, 572.

57 Dror Wahrman, *Imagining the Middle Class: The Political Representation of the Middle Class in England 1780–1840*, Cambridge, Cambridge University Press (1995). In relation to India at a slightly later period than Wahrman's, see Kate Teltscher, "Maidenly and well-nigh effeminate": Constructions of Hindu Masculinity and Religion in Seventeenth-Century English Texts, (2000) 3 *Postcolonial Studies* 159–70.

58 Peter Earle, *The Making of the English Middle Class: Business, Society and Family Life in London 1660–1730*, London, Methuen (1989).

59 Fernand Braudel, *Civilization and Capitalism Vol II: The Wheels of Commerce*, London, Collins (1982), ch 1, esp pp 62 *et seq*. Markets and subsequently shops in addition, were a European phenomenon, although England began to demonstrate particular vigor in the late seventeenth century. See also Lawrence James, *The Middle Class: A History*, London, Little Brown (2006), who traces a vigorous "middle" to late Tudor times, not coincidentally the period in which Puritanism began to irritate the political establishment of Elizabeth.

> I deplore the neglect of civil war battlefields. I'd really like to see Naseby commemorated, as Bosworth is. It's incomparably more significant. Bosworth was just a change of dynasty. Naseby changed the world men and women lived in.[60]

Christopher Hill reminds us, though, that, perhaps even before the Restoration of 1660, the political ambitions of the "middle" were defeated.[61] England may have been for its ruling order, as Hill writes, but the political activity of the "middle" became chiefly that of disciplining its own members.[62] Radical values, not all of which were in the modern sense at all liberal, continued, historians have argued, as an underground tradition, surfacing now and then, in one, more liberal form, during the French Revolutionary era, and in another, in India.

Wahrman does well to emphasize the profoundly "misogynist" turn that seemed gradually to overtake Britain after the middle eighteenth century, if it is appropriate to a turn of events which had consequences well beyond essentialized relations between men and women. Gender is more and more seen, in the context of colonial history and postcolonial understandings not "as a fixed concept offering us the 'truth' about the history of the British Empire";[63] instead what this analytical tool signifies is the "multiple and contradictory meanings attached to sexual difference".[64] Kathleen Wilson amplifies the point in another essay in the same volume:

> Gender is not a synonym for women; nor is it a "fact" of the past (or present) awaiting discovery. Historians have argued that gender was both a relation of power and a way of signifying relations of power that produced and orchestrated the changing meanings of sexual difference in time, shaping social institutions, privileges, expectations and experience.[65]

Elsewhere, Wilson tells us that the empire depended upon the "public man":

> (w)hereas the "feminine" was relegated to the realm of pleasure, eroticism, artifice, sociability and particularity. Not only women, but a range of racial and ethnic "others", from Africans to Highland Scots, as well as the English

60 Diane Purkis, *The English Civil War: A People's History*, London, Harper (2006), Q&A, 4.

61 Christopher Hill, *The Experience of Defeat: Milton and Some Contemporaries*, London, Faber and Faber (1995).

62 Christopher Hill, *Reformation to Industrial Revolution*, Harmondsworth, Penguin (1967), 142 *et seq*. Christopher Hill, *Some Intellectual Consequences of the English Revolution*, Madison, WI, University of Wisconsin Press (1980).

63 Philippa Levine, Introduction: Why Gender and Empire?, in Philippa Levine (ed), *Gender and Empire. OHBE Companion Series*, Oxford, Oxford University Press (2004), 5.

64 Levine, *ibid*, 2. The quotation Levine refers us to is from Joan Wallach Scott.

65 Kathleen Wilson, Empire, Gender and Modernity in the Eighteenth Century, in Philippa Levine (ed), *Gender and Empire. OHBE Companion Series*, Oxford, Oxford University Press (2004), 14.

> lower classes were identified in much cultural and political discourse with the symbolic feminine, as dependent, irrational, sensual or emotional.[66]

In other discourses, those of practice, she might have added, as she does in her essay in the Levine collection that the feminine was specifically identified with property, exploitation, triviality, and monstrosity and, when convenient, invisibility. With her neologism, "effeminism", "the racial construction of femininity–masculinity", Krishnaswamy provides a useful term with which to capture a later eighteenth century erotics that involved an economy, not in actuality of masculinity and femininity, which slips easily into biology, but of masculinity and effeminism.[67] Like children and women, the natives of torrid climes especially were taken to lack the courage, rationality and restraint from emotion of the proper white man. A letter from TB Macaulay on his travels in India, describes an evening of "prodigious jabbering", followed, the next morning by TBM's rescuing of his servant, who had been set upon by "rascals" who had "nearly stripped him naked; I supported the poor wretch in my arms for, like most of his countrymen, he is a chicken-hearted fellow and had nearly fainted away".[68] Krishnaswamy quotes William Hodges' comparison of a group of Bengali men in conversation to an "assembly of females", their "delicate features adorned with jewelry, their silks, linen and muslin 'dresses', while yet others, mainly perhaps boatmen, were 'wholly naked'".

The letter from Macaulay is interesting for a number of reasons. The servant in this case was accused by his attackers of the legal offense of theft, about the authenticity of which Macaulay has doubts, and here we have a kind of vigilante justice on both sides, the ruffians taking revenge on the servant and Macaulay (presumably with some assistance) beating off the attackers without organizing any kind of inquiry into their grievance. It sits strangely with Macaulay's insistence on other occasions, on the crucial nature for British rule of the utmost probity and adherence to law. The incident reminds us of Harvey's response to the passage in the *Essay on Clive* in which Macaulay stresses the difference between British Company policy and the caprice of local rulers: British rule over India depended, he asserted, on the Briton's greater claim to probity than native rulers. "The Company promises only a moderate pension after a long service. But every sepoy (that is, Company-employed) knows that the promise of the Company will be kept; he knows that if he lives a hundred years, his rice and salt are as assured as the salary of the Governor General".[69] Victorian cant, Harvey says the British

66 Wilson, *op cit*, n 47, 45.

67 Revathi Krishnaswamy, *Effeminism: The Economy of Colonial Desire*, Ann Arbor, MI, University of Michigan Press (1998), 19, 21 and generally.

68 Quoted in George Otto Trevelyan, *The Life and Letters of Lord Macaulay*, 2 vols, London, Longmans Green (1878), 386.

69 Thomas Babbington Macaulay, Essay on Lord Clive (1840), in J Grieve (ed), *Thomas Babbington Macaulay: Critical and Historical Essays*, London, Dent (1907), 517.

ruled by virtue of possessing an effective mercenary army whose power was eventually overwhelming.[70] Macaulay's intervention on behalf of his servant had, ultimately, all the power of the white man behind it.

Harvey may be correct about the cant, of course, insofar as the Empire was always a confidence trick justified in terms of improvement.[71] In part, of course, it was based on the force – summarized in the late nineteenth century aphorism relating to Africa. Remember we have got/The Maxim gun and they have not – rather than legal and moral codes. But, as the previous discussion on gender suggests, the rulers had to convince *themselves* of their entitlement to rule, and convince sufficient of the locals that an association with what English culture had to offer was advantageous to them in a world increasingly dominated by the United Kingdom.

As to clothes and nakedness, one of Burke's less happy moments in *Reflections* was of Marie Antoinette, then dauphiness, as she passed him, magnificently-appareled, "glittering like the morning star", her feet seeming to Burke scarcely to touch the ground.[72] Some years later, when she had become Queen and the Revolution was under way, a mob, notoriously *bras-nues* and *sans-culottes*, broke into her bed-chamber – in itself an account, whether true or not, heavy with sexual innuendo – and chased her "nearly naked" to her husband's "bed-chamber". The beautifully and delicately dressed are, of course, "effeminized", as are those nearly, but titillatingly never completely naked. Hodges' Bengali men are gendered feminine by their finery, as was Marie Antoinette. But her finery represented authorized royalty when Burke glimpsed her, whilst that of the Bengalis was a kind of transvestitism in British eyes. The boatmen and the fleeing queen are similarly eroticized in their suggestion of openness to public view; but if we see Hodges' and Macaulay's accounts through the passages in Burke, we see, too, that clothes represent civilization and culture. Unclothed humans are but human animals, unclothed women are second-rate human animals, like unclothed Bengalis. Clothes supply, for Burke, "the pleasing illusions which made power gentle, and obedience liberal, which harmonized the different shades of life . . .",[73] "It is taste and elegance" and not mere laws supported or promulgated by an assembly which underwrite the legitimacy of a government. In the post-Revolutionary French assembly there could be no claim to legitimacy since "a majority, I believe, of the members who attended, was composed of practitioners of law", not magistrates or distinguished advocates or professors, but "obscure provincial advocates, stewards of petty local jurisdictions, country attorneys, notaries and . . . the conductors of the petty wars of village vexation . . .".[74]

70 Robert Harvey, *Clive: The Life and Death of a British Emperor*, London, Hodder & Stoughton (1998), ch 15.

71 See Tidrick, *Empire and the English Character: The Illusion of Authority*, London, IB Tauris (1992).

72 Edmund Burke, *Reflections on the Revolution in France* (1790), London, Dent (1910), 73.

73 Burke, *ibid*, 74.

74 Burke, *op cit*, n 72, 41–42.

The "taste and elegance" that Burke associates with proper rule, are dissociated from native Indians by the 1760s, who begin increasingly to seem to the British, effete. Alliances with Indian rulers, curiosity about and respect for Indian culture and laws, even assimilation to local custom, were transformed as the East India Company was transformed from a mercantile company trading in the area, into the government of tens of millions of subjects. And, increasingly, inappropriate clothes such as the muslins preferred by Kirkpatrick, were taken by the alert detectors of effeminacy to be unmanly, the product of a softness associated with an excess of the luxury once the subject of British awe. There was some apprehension that the same luxurious vice would be imported into Britain, hence the hostility to the enormous wealth of the nabobs, the earliest and most overtly unscrupulous plunderers of India, endangering the constitution by purchasing parliamentary seats:[75]

> As to the Company and the British government, if hitherto, the British Empire in India had no higher purpose than to yield profits to the shareholders of the East India Company.[76]

Subsequently, Trautmann points out, there was a "nobler purpose, the moral uplift of the Indians" from their degraded condition.[77] Robert Clive, grandfather of the governor to whom the Kirkpatrick "problem" was referred, could certainly have found what could be construed as a lack of "manliness", seen in the terms gradually permeating empire, in his encounters in India.[78] What Clive, the man, actually thought of Indian culture and people is, of course neither clear nor relevant, since "Clive" is in fact a crucial trope in the justification of conquest and rule in India. An historiography of which Macaulay's formed a part, only too convenient for the historians of the second empire, represented an India descended into political incoherence with the struggles that preceded and followed the death of the last effective Mughal emperor, Aurangzeb, in 1707. In the subsequent anarchic hiatus, in Macaulay's narrative, a great civilization sank into decadence, passivity and decay. Into this field entered the two principal European forces of south Asia,[79] France and Great Britain (represented by the East India Company), motivated (in the French case, according to nineteenth century British retrospects) by the desire for conquest and the destruction of British power. In this narrative, the embodiment of French guile and preparedness to ally with deceitful native rulers, was the "small, vigorous and disdainful" Francois Dupleix.[80]

75 HV Bowen, British India 1765–1813: The Metropolitan Context, in Peter Marshall (ed), *The Oxford History of the British Empire II: The Eighteenth Century*, Oxford, Oxford University Press (2001), 542.

76 Thomas Trautmann, *Aryans and British India*, Berkeley, CA, University of California Press (1997), 129.

77 Trautmann, *ibid.*

78 Harvey, *op cit*, n 70.

79 The Spice Islands, from which the Dutch had decisively ejected the British.

80 Harvey, *op cit*, n 70, 34.

Modern narratives notice, by contrast, the post-Aurangzeb formation of vigorous sub-states formed from the provincial organization through which the Mughals had ruled an extremely complex empire and the way in which they and the close connections between Indian creditors, Indian rulers and British merchants facilitated the growth of British domination.[81] As this increased through a form of racket in which Company troops, paid for out of local revenues, would "protect" the local ruler, the vigor of the sub-states abated. By the mid-Victorian threshold of the 1857 insurrection, this protection racket, so Bayly argues, had substituted for a nascent form of capitalism, and simply imposed another level of rentier, the Company, draining the system of wealth and reducing the capacity of native Indians to buy British goods. This situation – noticed in the nineteenth century and anticipated by Burke's comment as early as 1783 that "the principles of and economy of the Company's trade has been completely corrupted by turning it into a vehicle for tribute" [82] – is beyond our topic, although if we wished to make some small assessment of the nature of metropolitan colonialism, which was considered to be the activity of securing raw materials and selling back manufactures, the word "myopia" might spring to mind.

More germanely, we might notice that when Bayly refers to the sovereignty of the Mughal emperor, he has in mind something different from the conception that Bentham took from Hobbes. The Mughal and his regional rulers enjoyed "overlapping rights and obligations" and the Mughal's role was as final arbiter of the authority of the prophet. Bayly remarks that the early British tactic of acknowledging this form of authority facilitated acceptance of the beginning of their rule. As Marshall puts it, "no observer in 1765 could have envisaged . . . British supremacy over the whole of India". The Company, though, had by then become "Indian rulers . . . of some consequence" according to Indian political principles, dependent on traditional practices of revenue-raising in the same nominally-delegated way as the former ruler of Bengal. Marshall adds that many Indians hoped that "the British might become assimilated into an (Indian) aristocracy committed to Mughal values".[83] The grant of the *diwani* to the Company by the Mughal Shah Alam was on condition that Islam and the "law of the Empire" should be respected. "Warren Hastings, the ruler of British India from 1772 to 1785 . . . felt that the British administration should be conducted 'agreeably to the old constitution of the (Mughal) Empire'".[84]

81 Bayly, *op cit*, n 53, ch 1.

82 Quoted in Bowen, *op cit*, n 75, 547.

83 Peter Marshall, The British in Asia: Trade to Dominion, in Peter Marshall (ed), *The Oxford History of the British Empire II: The Eighteenth Century*, Oxford, Oxford University Press (2001), 505.

84 Rajat Kanta Ray, Indian Society and British Supremacy, in Peter Marshall (ed), *The Oxford History of the British Empire II: The Eighteenth Century*, Oxford, Oxford University Press (2001), 510.

Utilitarian writing and the changing character of rule in India

The irrebuttable pretense during Robert Clive's time, that Company sovereignty could be concealed behind the Mughal's apparent delegation of authority, was followed by Governor Cornwallis's restructuring, one derived from eighteenth century Whig principles, according to Stokes, namely:

> That political power is essentially corrupting and inevitably abused; that power, to be exercised with safety, must be reduced to a minimum, and even then kept divided and counterbalanced.[85]

This implied the separation of powers and the scrutiny of executive action by an independent judiciary. But Cornwallis's Whig principles were essentially English, and implied, at least for him and his British contemporaries, the Anglicization of the Bengali administration and the exclusion of Indians in the belief of the inherent superiority of the "Anglo-Saxon race" when it came to conceptions of law and government. There was an insistence that "we cannot avoid recognizing in the people of Hindostan a race of men lamentably degenerate and base . . . retaining but a feeble sense of moral obligation". The "corruption of manners", the natives' "vices" and the "misery" that this state of affairs entailed could not but require guidance by others more enlightened. Good government in such circumstances was much better than free government and very much better than consulting the natives or giving credit to their customs and expectations.

As "notions of positive law, judicial process . . ." were introduced, "for Governor-General Wellesley and his supporters it was essential that the Company and particularly the Governor General should stand forth as sovereigns" in the Hobbesian tradition in dealing with Indian powers and their own subjects:

> The Governor-general 'should have the power of summoning a privy council and should act in it as the King or the Lord-Lieutenant of Ireland'. The ancient corporate nature of the Company councils with their near-equality between members should be dispensed with, for these had 'the character of an aristocratic republic rather than a monarchy'.[86]

To Wellesley, "it was obviously necessary that the Governor General in Council should exercise the entire legislative authority (excluding) our native subjects from all participation in the legislative authority", the safeguard being an independent judiciary. The "natives" themselves were unsurprisingly by no means convinced of the satisfactory nature of a "despotism . . . without any regard for the shari'ah and for custom",[87] in increasingly broad areas of Company conquests.

85 Eric Stokes, *The English Utilitarians and India*, Oxford, Oxford University Press (1959), 5.

86 Bayly, *op cit*, n 53, 82.

87 Bayly, *op cit*, n 53, 526.

Whilst the Utilitarians were encountering some skepticism from Whigs and Whig-Liberals, even from Tories like Coleridge, and would soon meet popular opposition in the United Kingdom, the most favorable condition of existence for their social engineering projects, namely the doctrine of law as nothing more than the sovereign will was available in India – "the (European) eighteenth century despot in altered guise".[88] The Charter Act of 1833 reinvigorated the Supreme Council and authorized the setting up of a Law Commission in India to inquire "into the nature and operation of all laws whether civil or criminal, written or customary . . .".[89] It seemed to Macaulay that "India stands in need of a code (i.e. a code of laws) more than any country in the world". It was better that it was drafted by one (British) man or a few expert men than by a committee or an assembly, as would inevitably be the case in Britain. "It is a work which especially belongs to government like that of India, to an enlightened and paternal despotism".[90]

The Indian Civil Service college at Haileybury, which had Thomas Malthus, the political economist, on its faculty, already taught Benthamite principles, although their influence on students may have in the early days have been limited by the low intellectual standards of the curriculum and the poor motivation of the students. On its publication in 1817, James Mill's *History of British India* was one of the texts used by the students, informing them that Indian culture "represent(ed) the rudest and weakest state of the human mind".[91] That the author had not been to India and knew little of the culture seemed to him to render his assessment the more objective.[92] Mill was both a friend and a disciple of Bentham and centrally placed in the Company's bureaucracy in Leadenhall Street. At a farewell dinner for Bentinck prior to his departure to become Governor-General of British India in 1827 it was, according to Stokes, to the unswervingly Utilitarian James Mill to whom Bentinck addressed his famous remark, "I am going to British India, but I shall not be Governor-General. It is you that will be Governor-General".[93]

If at about the same time indigenous Australians were politically invisible to the British invaders, and their land thus *terra nullius*, the British Empire more broadly "in the nineteenth century was premised on the presumed non-existence of extant 'native' political societies".[94] Aborigines, whose existence nobody denied, were represented as irrational wanderers, Hart's pre-legal societies, noted in Chapter 1.

88 Stokes, *op cit*, n 85, 173. Naturally, as Stokes remarks (at 177), "Bentham found himself more at home with the enlightened despots than turbulent assemblies, for is not the legislator in some sense necessarily single and despotic?".

89 John Clive, *Macaulay: The Shaping of the Historian*, Cambridge, MA, Harvard University Press (1987), 427.

90 Macaulay, *op cit*, n 56, 570.

91 Cited in Uday Singh Mehta, *Liberalism and Empire: A Study in Nineteenth Century British Liberal Thought*, Chicago, IL, University of Chicago Press (1999), 90.

92 Stokes, *op cit*, n 85, 53.

93 Stokes, *op cit*, n 85, 51.

94 Mehta, *op cit*, n 91, 121, 68.

They could not own property because they had neither laws visible to Europeans nor rules and instruments for changing laws. The emptiness of *terra nullius* represents not an absence of humans, but an absence of modern, advanced people capable of governing themselves. As one Aboriginal writer put it, before the Europeans "discovered" Australia, "us mob wouldn't have known where we were". India was, the British believed, in the same predicament. It was convenient that Mill's *History* "not only designates India's inert insufficiency . . . as part of the study of Britain, (it) also designates Britain as the compensator for this insufficiency". As Bentham was to put it a decade later, Indians have lost themselves:

> . . . you may find it difficult to give them (i.e. the inhabitants of India) to themselves. If it is determined that they must have masters you will then look out for the least bad ones and . . . I question whether you would find any less bad than our English company.[95]

Later writers claimed for Britain and the Empire, the *invention* of India, according to Mehta. Before colonization there was no national unity, no "India . . . according to European ideas".[96] Hindu and Muslim laws were a "disorderly compilation of loose, vague, stupid or unintelligible propositions".[97] The void could therefore be filled with the great codes of law, prisons modeled on the Panopticon, centralized agencies for the whole country unencumbered by boards of governance, characterized by "uniformity of management and unity of authority"[98] and administering everything from telegraphs to railways to grand schemes of irrigation – which Rhada d'Souza tells us, did not work well, eliding, as they did, local knowledges.[99] Panoptical surveillance through fingerprinting was first developed by the British in India.[100] The same absence, followed by close surveillance by Europeans could be said of Australia, a continent capably managed for 40,000 to 50,000 years by Aboriginal people and in serious environmental trouble after little more than two hundred years of mainly European dominance.

As Majeed makes clear, Mill insists that only a society in which the criterion for every action was its utility could count itself as fully civilized, and only a universal legislator, a sovereign able to make comprehensive and universally applicable and

95 Quoted in Javed Majeed, *Ungoverned Imaginings: James Mill's 'The History of British India' and Orientalism*, Oxford, Oxford University Press (1992), 125.

96 Mehta, *op cit*, n 91, 149, citing the English historian, Seeley and John Strachey, a Victorian colonial administrator.

97 Quoted in Majeed, *op cit*, n 95, 132.

98 Stokes, *op cit*, n 85, 247, 251.

99 Rhada d'Souza, International Law – Recolonizing the Third World? Law and conflicts over water in the Krishna River Basin, in Diane Kirkby and Catherine Coleborne (eds), *Law, History, Colonialism: The Reach of Empire*, Manchester, Manchester University Press (1991), ch 15.

100 Chandak Sengoopta, *Imprint of the Raj: How Fingerprinting was Born in Colonial India*, London, Macmillan (2003).

comprehensible laws compatible with this criterion, could deliver this civilization. In India, only the Company, through a progressive Governor-General and a civil service drawn largely from the "middling ranks" of British society, would accomplish this. Having, in a political sense, lost a revolution, the middling ranks were to have a role. Equally clear, according to Majeed, is that Mill's *History* doubled as a criticism of Britain itself. Whilst the later Bentham and James Mill notoriously advocated democratic government for Britain,[101] they did so because they conflated politics and the market place and understood voting as the demand side of what later economics would describe as the demand–supply equation. The citizen became a consumer, either possessed of adequate knowledge to choose, or refusing to acquire it and choosing foolishly. In practice, Mill and Bentham were convinced the middling ranks had the "requisite intellectual, moral and economic qualities which would enable them to set the tone for society as a whole".[102] Democracy was, for both writers, merely a mechanism for the achievement of utility. At root, Stokes has argued, utilitarianism was an authoritarian doctrine and the enfranchised working man was to respect its principles under the tutelage of those with more capacity and vision than himself – the middle class.

But what if he did not? Thomas Babbington Macaulay, the rhetorical master player in the success of the Reform Act of 1832, which rationalized parliamentary constituencies to reflect the changing demographics of Britain and modestly extended the franchise, both indirectly supplied the answer and illustrated the political atmosphere summarized in Krishnaswamy's notion of "effeminism". As Legal Member of the Indian Supreme Council from 1835 until 1838, he began the utilitarian program of codification in India with his draft Criminal Code. But while he could see merit in many utilitarian proposals, he was not a utilitarian ideologue – and the differences between, say Bentham, James and John Stuart Mill and James Fitzjames Stephen, all utilitarians, suggest that the closer one looks, the less one finds a unified outlook among those espousing some utilitarian principles. Whilst celebrating Bentham's jurisprudence, Macaulay opposed any significant extension of the right to vote in Britain, at least in mid-century.[103] His reasons connect interestingly with what was earlier called effeminism. And the part played by his character, "Clive", will become clear.

First, though, it is helpful to notice the somewhat later conclusions of a utilitarian and Hobbesian, James Fitzjames Stephen, a member of the Supreme Council in India for two and a half years in the 1870s, and a judge in England from 1879 until 1891. In his discussion of the middle term in *Liberty, Equality,*

101 James Mill, Essay on Government (1820), in Jack Lively and John Rees (eds), *Utilitarian Logic and Politics: James Mill's "Essay on Government", Macaulay's "Critique" and the Ensuing Debate*, Oxford, Oxford University Press (1978).

102 Majeed, *op cit*, n 95, 174.

103 Jack Lively and John Rees, Introduction, in Jack Lively and John Rees (eds), *Utilitarian Logic and Politics: James Mill's "Essay on Government", Macaulay's "Critique" and the Ensuing Debate*, Oxford, Oxford University Press (1978), 49–50, and Macaulay, *op cit*, 101.

Fraternity, Stephen responds to the views of John Stuart Mill on, among other topics, the place of women in society.[104] Men are, in Stephen's view, not only physically stronger, but stronger intellectually, with additionally "greater vigor of character".[105] "Strength, in all its forms, is life and manhood. To be less strong is to be less of a man, whatever else you may be".[106] This opened the way for the intersection of gender, class and race[107] and, indeed "he thought that in India he had found a combination of effective and benevolent government that was wanting in his own country".[108] Stephen realized that democracy in Britain was a certainty, the only uncertainty being the form it would take. Perhaps the government of the weaker by the inherently stronger, in the colonies and in the home, provided a model that would mitigate the threat of rule by majority in the country at large, or at worst, offer a consolation.

Inherent superiority and inferiority were undoubtedly for him a situation that justified a division of labor governed by the obvious absurdity of, for example, men's learning to cook, sew and keep house, or of women's playing cricket, being soldiers and rowing. Since Stephen assumed women generally to be incapable of achieving an education that would provide them with an earning capacity, to be the primary child-carer, and asserted that they lost their physical attractiveness at a younger age than a man, women would be cast aside as they aged. It thus followed that, for him, equal treatment would amount to oppression. The woman required protection, not independence. Moreover, because this dependency seemed to imply marriage, marriage should remain indissoluble; the relation needed to be inescapable, since, without a husband to protect her, she would be helpless and, perhaps a prey to debasement and vice. In marriage, by analogy with a ship, or a factory, in which there must be a master and obedient recipients of commands if things are to proceed in an orderly fashion, even where the recipient is more skilled than the commander, so the wife's promise to obey her husband must be taken absolutely seriously.

There are two matters worthy of note. First, there are in this model, not only men who are stronger and women who are weaker, but also degrees of manliness, and in both cases, and whilst the weaker are entitled to the protection and kindness of the stronger, they must also defer to the stronger. Second, though, even if we were to ignore the point about degrees of manliness, the existence of strong women who engaged in heavy manual labor was widely acknowledged, not only by the surprising number of men in the early days of photography, who were obsessed by

104 James Fitzjames Stephen, *Liberty, Equality, Fraternity* (1873), Cambridge, Cambridge University Press (1967), ch V.

105 Stephen, *ibid*, 194.

106 Stephen, *op cit*, n 104, 199.

107 See Anne McLintock, *Imperial Leather: Race, Gender and Sexuality in the Imperial Contest*, New York, NY, Routledge (1995).

108 James Colaiaco, *James Fitzjames Stephen and the Crisis of Victorian Thought*, London, Macmillan (1983), 153.

them,[109] but evident to anyone with women domestic servants performing heavy labor or dedicated London pedestrians, of whom Stephen was one. There was some concern, among the male working and middle classes, about the abilities of women. It was not because they disbelieved in those abilities, but because they feared them and, among the working class, the leverage which female labor might provide employers to reduce wages, and among the middling sort for the challenge to male supremacy and the right to protect the weaker, "the sex". From male working class support for labor reforms excluding women from mines and limiting their hours of work in factories,[110] to the mathematization of economics to exclude women such as Harriet Martineau, there was a secret admission that women were not unequal to men.[111] The construction articulated by Stephen is thus not a piece of essentialism, but the manufacture of the subject-positions that were consistent with his sovereign-command model of law and government, at home and in the colonies.

It is possible now to return to Macaulay's "Clive" and manliness. Clive, the man and the eventual General and Governor of Bengal, began his Indian career as a writer (or clerk) for the East India Company in 1743, in time to witness the ignominious defeat of the British by the French, and the French occupation of the British East India Company's Presidency of Madras. Primarily commercially oriented in the mid-eighteenth century, the Company was in conventional accounts, militarily amateurish and inept, especially in comparison with its French equivalent, its troops poorly trained and badly equipped. Clive joined the Company's army in 1751 to fight the French and their allies, and by virtue of two spectacular successes, at Arcot in 1756 and Plassey, 1757 became the catalyst for a change in the Company's direction from mercantile company to the semi-private arm of British imperial power in India. He served three terms in India, the third of which was quite short. He proved to be an able administrator as well as a skilled and daring military tactician. "Till (Clive) appeared, his countrymen were despised as mere peddlers, while the French were revered as people formed for victory and command".[112] Macaulay's Clive perhaps performs more subtle functions than those of the "soldier heroes" of Graham Dawson's text where:

> The modern tradition of British adventure has furnished idealized, wish-fulfilling forms of masculinity to counter anxieties generated in a social world that is deeply divided along the fracture lines of ethnicity and nation, gender

109 Derek Hudson, *Munby: Man of Two Worlds*, London, John Murray (1972); McLintock, *op cit*, n 107.

110 See Mary Lyndon Shanley, *Feminism, Marriage and the Law in Victorian England*, Princeton, NJ, Princeton University Press (1989), 93–102.

111 See Dierdre David, *Intellectual Women and Victorian Patriarchy: Harriet Martineau, Elizabeth Barrett Browning, George Eliot*, Ithaca, NY, Cornell University Press (1987). George Eliot had been editor of the Westminster Review, a vehicle for ideas to which Stephen would have been in sympathy.

112 Richard Wilson (ed), *Macaulay's Essay on Robert Clive*, London, Dent (1920), 149.

> and class. The soldier heroes (are) ideally powerful and free from contradictions and undermining effects of anxiety. They offer the psychic reassurance of triumph over the sources of threat, promising the defeat of enemies and the recovery of that which is valued and feared lost.[113]

By the time of the *Essay*, the freebooting days of British India, in which "Bengal was a place to which Englishmen were sent only to get rich, by any means, in the shortest possible time" were over.[114] Clive the trope certainly figures in Macaulay's *Essay* as a paean to the manliness critical, if the empire and the sovereignty of law are to be maintained, but it is both cautionary and celebratory in its didacticism. The moral successes and failings of the legendary character delineate the boundaries of order and the impulse behind the *Essay* explains some of the inconsistencies, hypocrisies, even, noted by Harvey.[115] Macaulay begins what is nominally a review of a biography of Clive published by John Malcolm in 1836, by regretting that whilst "every schoolboy" knows about the Spanish conquest of South America, a conquest over a meager population of "savages without letters", armed, in his account of them, with nothing more sophisticated than spears, bows and arrows, the far greater accomplishment of the "Englishmen" who prevailed over a civilization with rich bankers and enormous armies with skilled cavalry, artillery, modern muskets and armored elephants, has been made to seem "insipid . . . positively distasteful".[116]

However, this Indian civilization at its height was "far worse governed than the worst governed parts of Europe now are" and in its disintegration from Mughal Empire to independent provinces evidences "nominal sovereigns sunk in indolence and debauchery, saunter(ing) in secluded palaces, chewing bang, fondling concubines and listening to buffoons".[117]

The Clive of the *Essay* brought qualities to India not hitherto discerned in his manly but willful youth in England: "judgment, sagacity, deference to legitimate authority", "firmness, vigilance and ability", winning loyalty from the British under his command and adoration from the sepoys at Arcot and elsewhere, Bengal was won in the terms of the *Essay*, not in an aggressive war, but as a response to the capricious and sadistic Nawab, Suraj-ad Daula (in Macaulay Surajah Dowlah), whose capture of Calcutta had resulted in the deaths of British captives in the famous "Black Hole of Calcutta". Clive's was a war against atrocity and

113 William Dawson, *Soldier Heroes: British Adventure, Empire and the Imagining of Masculinities*, London, Routledge (1994), 282.

114 Macaulay, *op cit*, n 69, 152.

115 Harvey, *op cit*, n 70.

116 Macaulay, *op cit*, n 69, 16. This seems somewhat at odds with the tropes of "degradation" and ignorant enslavement which is such an important trope in the justification of imperial rule elsewhere in Macaulay's writing, as the following paragraph suggests.

117 Macaulay, *op cit*, n 69, 28, 45, 46, 63, 81 and 83. Also, Government of India in TF Ellis (ed), *The Miscellaneous Writings and Speeches of Lord Macaulay*, London, Longmans Green (1889), 562.

oppression in a province where, writes Macaulay, citing a "Castilian . . . proverb . . . (about) Valencia . . . the earth is water and the men women", an "effeminate population" whose ruler "wanted spirit to adhere even during one day to a manly resolution". Children, servants and wives who "answer back", announcing views and purposes of their own different from the purposes assigned by their masters are, of course mutinous. They breach the natural order of things, and it was not simply that the insurrection of 1857 began among Indian Army troops at Meerut military base, with the deaths of fifty or so British officers that it became known as "mutiny". What else does one call a wholesale refusal of rule? The wholesale atrocities committed by the British regulars sent thither, against civilian villages, attest to a recognition by the British of the, to them, unacceptable rejection of the Raj by Indians. The British were not simply punishing under courts martial troops who deliberately disobeyed orders. Destroying villages, hanging or raping their inhabitants, firing men from cannons, was terror. Artillery, the Royal Navy, the repeating rifle, the telegraph, all demonstrated British might, whatever the cant.

It lends a certain irony to the cautionary element which Macaulay places in the parts of the *Essay* which relates to Clive's strategy preceding Plassey. Dealing with duplicitous orientals, he seems, according to Macaulay, to have felt it necessary to abandon the upright truthfulness with which Europeans conduct both negotiations and warfare. If Nawab Suraj-ad-Daula's wavering ally, Omichand, would not side with Clive, Clive believed his cause was lost, the opposing Indian army being so much larger than his own. But Clive also needed the allegiance of another, Mir Jaffir, deemed in the long run more important than the "artful Bengalee", Omichand. So two documents were prepared, one of which rewarded Omichand if he allied with Clive, and was shown only to him, and one of which, the one Clive intended to rely upon in his dealings with Mir Jaffir, omitted any mention of Omichand. For the deception to succeed, both documents required the signature of the officer in command of naval operations, Admiral Watson. Watson, according to Macaulay, would not sign the document promising a reward for Omichand's assistance, which was entirely false in intention "but Clive was not a man to do anything by halves. We almost blush to write it. He forged Admiral Watson's name". When the deception was revealed to Omichand after the event and his reward thus denied, "the unhappy man sank gradually into idiocy". Harvey makes the reasonable point, quoting a number of British and Indian historians of the period, that deception has always been a routine ingredient in the conduct of warfare and if, as he considers it to be the case here, it results in the saving of many lives, it is more than justified.[118]

Macaulay has a different and a morally-justifying imperial goal, one that has some support from a contemporary:

118 Harvey, *op cit*, n 70, ch 15.

> . . . the natives must either be kept down by a sense of our power, or they must willingly submit from a conviction that we are more wise, more just, more humane and more anxious to improve their condition than any other ruler they could have.[119]

In Macaulay's almost Bunyanesque narrative, Clive's conduct was misconceived not only because it fell short of proper standards of political integrity, which an empire as schoolmaster as well as governor, should teach. It was, pragmatically, a miscalculation because the nature of British rule in India at which Clive himself aimed, depended, in the *Essay*'s terms, on the perception of British probity. Once this was established, the loyalty of the sepoy army could be relied upon, and credit from Indian bankers would be available at rates lower than those loans made to princes whose unreliability necessitated higher interest. Clive, however, by his victories and the loyalty he earned from his Indian soldiers, soon and well and truly redeemed himself. "His name stands high on the roll of conquerors. But it is found in a better list, in a list of those who have done and suffered much for the happiness of mankind". Like John Churchill, later Duke of Marlborough, as he figures in Macaulay's *History*, who, as general of the existing King's army, deceived his king, James II, by defecting to William and Mary in 1688, thus preserving English Protestantism, property, order and liberty,[120] thus redeeming his treachery. So Clive's victories and reforms, despite their implication with oriental forms of deception, are represented as providing a foundation for an end to corruption and exploitation. Further reform culminated in the legal codes that guaranteed the rule of law and underwrote the great administrative structures of social engineering.

119 Minute of J Farich, 28 March 1838, quoted in Gauri Viswanathan, Currying Favor: The Politics of British Educational Policy in India 1813–1854 in Anne McLintock, Amir Mufti and Ella Sholat (eds), *Dangerous Liaisons: Gender, Nation and Postcolonial Perspectives*, Minneapolis, MN, University of Minnesota Press (1997), 113.

120 TB Macaulay, *History of England to the Death of William III, vol II*, London, Heron Books (1968), 279 *et seq.*

Chapter 5

Governing the "natives" at home in nineteenth century Britain

In this chapter I look at the strategies for confronting uncertainty which I suggested were associated with the Indian acquisitions. The essence of the Revolution Settlement was toleration. But the naturally inferior and childlike nature of women, "natives" and children were observable in the examination of nature according to scientific principles. No peaceful means existed of resolving divergences of knowledge, other than acceptance that they existed, except when they were external. The non-English might be fought and, in the case of black people, enslaved, equality was not something white landlords were prepared to concede to their wives, servants or tenants, and the differences causing uncertainty in those situations could swiftly be disposed of.

But white male rulers had to find means of getting along and, as they saw it, progressing. Searches for revolutionary utopias have to current times, been disappointing, and the Whigs were certainly not revolutionaries. However, if they fell short of their principles when they were able, the principles might have lessons that could be applied more widely. The Whigs were prepared to allow uncertainty to act as a form of certainty, negotiation and compromise to take the place of an imposition.

Pedigrees established authenticity – of what it does not matter. In fact it forestalls the substantive question "of what". The workhouse, "a place of hardship, of course fare, of degradation and humility" according to the Reverend HH Millman,[1] not only sat comfortably with the authoritarian turn in political life, but was actually part of Bentham's plan for rule. James Mill, by contrast, was convinced that, given a proper education, people might choose the kind of government they preferred through universal manhood suffrage. His son, JS Mill, came somewhere in between, initially democratically-inclined, but, with Harriet Taylor Mill, somewhat despondent both about the likelihood of significant improvements to education in face of the, as he saw it, profound ignorance, selfishness and brutality of the masses.[2]

1 AN Wilson, *The Victorians*, London, Arrow Books (2002), 12.

2 JS Mill, *Autobiography* (1873), Harmondsworth, Penguin (John Robson, ed) (1989), 94, 175.

The utilitarians and the rule of punishments

In this and the next chapters, the range of views encapsulated by the above writers concerning the issue of how civic order was to be produced and maintained in Great Britain and the Indian empire will be explored. I am, of course, not suggesting that the technology of producing subjects compatible with social order could be, or was ever believed to be, a stark choice between legislative demands accompanied by threats – commands backed by sanctions in John Austin's vocabulary – and schooling. Bentham's sovereign, after all, aims to teach – in the conditioning sense now associated with Pavlov if necessary – his subjects by the legislative construction of one form of behavior as less desirable than another: the certainty of being caught and punished for stealing teaches me to defer my gratification and save my money so as to purchase the goods honestly, or forego them. Macaulay's draft criminal code for India provided simple examples illustrating the purpose of its provisions. Schooling can certainly take a coercive path. It not only, as Arnold saw, kept naughty children off the streets. He knew that at its best, it must necessarily involve an unequal relationship. Only twentieth century neo-liberals imagine that students are somehow customers, ideally readers of consumer magazines, who are already knowledgeable about the "products" on offer and capable of dispassionate evaluation. As pedagogues of any ability have realized, this is not the case. Coleridge, as we shall see, placed enlightened education in the category of "educing", leading out and enabling the educed to realize his or her potential. Leavis's invocation of Marjorie Grene's work suggests a conviction that competent and effective educators distance themselves from propaganda and make of students partners, if unequal partners, in any given project of learning. Knowledge is not a commodity resembling good drilling in certainties. From it, the worrying but necessary concept of reason must be detached. To be helpful tools, rather than coercive weapons, reason, truth and certainty must be contextualized and negotiated. An empire in which the natives were to be imbued with the truths and certainties of European rationality was less than fertile ground for this realization.

Previous chapters have suggested that, "at home" at least, the path of religious and political certitude, among rulers and men and women with the capacity to cause disruption, was gradually abandoned as a policy – in mainland Britain, if not for some time in Ireland – even as such certainties haunted the government of empire. Haunting is, perhaps, an appropriate description, since Ireland occupied an *unheimlich* space between "at home" and not at home. Dissenting Protestantism and even Roman Catholicism had to be tolerated in the English/Welsh and Scottish parts of the British Isles, if full equality was a while coming, because the alternative was too divisive and chaotic to contemplate. This necessity was probably more acutely recognized when the new dimensions of social difference manifested themselves more clearly. The rights of man, however woolly Burke found them (and very soon after, the rights of women[3]), and however inadequate, even dangerous the concepts might be as a positive social program, were powerful slogans in the rhetorical armory of working class men, and then women.

How were the bearers of these potentially disruptive, if inchoate ideas to be accommodated into the structure of orderly society? Early in the nineteenth century, the political disabilities of Jewish and Roman Catholic men were removed. Women had to wait, although many did not wait patiently, and pushed, most unseemly. How were the inequalities implied by the invocation of the rights of man to be managed? Putative solutions cannot tidily be discerned and cataloged if the purpose is to attribute to particular writers consistent and differentially identifiable solutions, but they indicate the alternative, though overlapping, frameworks considered. John Stuart Mill invokes, in order to distance himself from James Mill's position on the ease with which a rationality recognizable as such by JS might be produced through schooling, especially the teaching of reading. James' unflattering views on the then contemporary rationality of Indian culture we have noticed. JS is less convinced, but optimistic that in the end, in Britain at least, a less imperfect education than he saw as generally available could facilitate popular political responsibility. An educated electorate could select a legislature capable of producing harmony from conflicting demands, but if voting rights were to be extended, for JS, they had to be weighted according to education.

One wonders, of course, just what "the whole population's" reading matter would, for James Mill, comprise, and what and whose reason was to influence them. Nothing, presumably, too subversive. James' son was more pessimistic about the ability of then-contemporary education. Arnold, we shall see, attempted a diagnosis of its failure to date – the mid-nineteenth century – and a possible recipe for its success, namely, educate the middle class to rise above their short-run trade-school mentality for their children so as to provide better leadership in an era in which traditional aristocratic leadership, although still empirically in operation, was morally and, for the most part intellectually bankrupt.

In Millman's view, referred to above, we have the early utilitarian ideology, which has surfaced over and again through the nineteenth, twentieth and succeeding centuries: "the secret of a stable society is to isolate and emasculate the miserable".[4] Sir Robert Peel's police, so admired by Bentham, the "Bobbies", introduced into London in 1829 as a coercive force alternative to the military, and thereafter copied in cities, towns and counties throughout England, had been designed to respond to the disorder created by enormous social change. This, and the changes to the Poor Law five years later, rendering it harsher – in effect criminalizing poverty and unemployment – as well as the manner in which the social changes occasioned by workplace disruption introduced by the early industrial revolution had been managed in the first place, signaled a contempt for

3 Mary Wollstonecraft's *Vindication of the Rights of Women* was published less than two years after Burke's *Reflections*, in 1792, in the same period as Paine's *Rights of Man*, 1791 and 1792 and they do not, arguably, fall into Burke's diagnosis of the Declarations, namely, wooly abstraction, one that did not favor *citoyennes*.

4 Wilson, *op cit*, n 1, 38.

the poor in England which mirrored that directed by the British toward Indians. The empire was striking back earlier than the text of that name suggests.[5]

It is an oversimplification, I have argued, to suggest a complete divide between two different approaches to pacifying a population – coercive utilitarian legislation on the one hand, and education on the other – especially since some utilitarians, such as the Mills, who, in different ways favored education primarily, whilst other utilitarians, the early Bentham more than the later, perhaps, and Chadwick, favored coercion. Chadwick would have welcomed Millman's observations, as would Kay-Shuttleworth and Robert Lowe, former member of the New South Wales Assembly and critic of democracy, and whose reactionary and penny-pinching educational theories antagonized Arnold. With these latter, we are not far from Malthus's famous remark in response to Thomas Paine's writing on the right of the subject to subsistence:

> A man who is born into a world already possessed, if he cannot get subsistence from his parents on whom he has a just demand, and if the society do not want his labor, has no claim of *right* to the smallest portion of food, and in fact has no right to be where he is. At nature's mighty feast, there is no cover for him. She tells him to be gone and will soon execute her orders . . .[6]

Education advocates, such as Matthew Arnold, though seeing the liberal education of the middle class as the most fruitful step toward calming what he conceived to be the excesses of working class habits, also allowed himself moments of coercive thought, recommending draconian treatment for the leaders after witnessing the Hyde Park Reform Bill riots, referred to later.

Macaulay had earlier combined both measures, legislative coercion, combined with an explanatory gloss, or exemplification of how each section of his code was meant to function, embodying a form of education in European "rationality".[7] His projected Code of criminal law, which was not enacted in his lifetime, contained, importantly, the intended education of an elite of Indians, in an attempt to turn them into brown English subjects. It was, naturally, prescriptive, as criminal codes are. But the prescriptions were accompanied with examples of situations in which the norms were intended to apply. They were not incompatible with ordering the colonized through legislation, and perhaps they were more paternalist in intention,

5 Andrew Thompson, *The Empire Strikes Back: The Impact of Imperialism from the Mid-nineteenth Century*, Harlow, Pearson Longman (2005).

6 Thomas Malthus (1803), quoted in Samuel Hollander, *The Economics of Thomas Robert Malthus*, Toronto, University of Toronto Press (1997), 896.

7 Confronted with some of Macaulay's more grandiloquent passages contrasting European and Asian learning, one is reminded of a remark by Kirsty Larner. Many of the people, she noticed, while heartily endorsing her apparent characterization as irrational, the witchcraft beliefs of early modern Scotland (she actually explained, rather than evaluated them), nevertheless espoused Mediterranean littoral conventional beliefs in immaculate conception and resurrection.

although in the end they offered more potential for dialog (Leavis's famous, "it is so, is it not?" to which we shall come). As a colonial administrator, Macaulay was proposing to impose a code of laws, drawn from the perspective of the colonial power, on a colony. His work on the criminal law did not come to fruition until much later, and the other codes emerged still later in the Victorian era.

But here was one arm of the colonial state begun in principle and to be continued. As a good legal positivist, Macaulay saw normative apparatuses such as statutes, judicial decisions and codes, from three perspectives. We will further explore later, what I referred to in Chapter 1, the first and most elementary question legal positivists ask when confronted with what is asserted to be a law is – did it emanate from or was it properly issued on behalf of, the legitimate source of law-making power within the jurisdiction? A sub-question that has troubled positivists is whether that source acted with legal propriety, and who is in a position to make a decision about that? Sovereignty is frequently a vexed issue, as we have seen, one that seemed to have taken the United States in one direction and, until the appearance of the European Court of Human Rights, and the European Union, which may have galvanized the common law judiciary from its Diceyan slumbers,[8] the United Kingdom in another, after the mid-eighteenth century. The "war on terror", which seems immeasurably to have strengthened executive power in the United States, *de facto* may or may not overbalance the separation of powers in the United States in favor of the executive in the twenty-first century.[9]

A second question recognized by legal positivists is whether particular laws are good or bad in a moral sense. For the legal positivists of the late eighteenth and early nineteenth centuries, dabbling with Hobbesian-influenced practices of sovereignty was not such a dangerous business as some – Hannah Arendt, for example – recognized it to be in the present, for although these early legal theorists distinguished law from morality, moral evaluation seemed as scientifically accessible to them as the assessment of whether a rule was or was not a valid law. Bentham's "*felicific calculus*" concerning the greatest good of the greatest number provided the observer, he believed, with an accurate tool with which to assess whether a particular act of sovereignty was beneficial or harmful, provided there was freedom of expression and a fully informed citizenry.

In retrospect, there is an obvious point of tension, even if it is not contradictory or an incompatibility between the "discipline" of the canon, education in how to be a proper English subject – giving him something intelligible say, as Macaulay saw it of natives in India – and punitive measures. The natives, like the British "populace", as Matthew Arnold was to call them, were in need of control, so far as their rulers were concerned. Was this to be accomplished coercively by law, or

8 Colin Turpin and Adam Tomkins, *British Government and the Constitution*, 6th edn, Cambridge, Cambridge University Press (2007).

9 Although see the US Supreme Court's ruling that the detention of untried people at the US base in Cuba on the ground that they may have been terrorists violates the US Constitution. *Melbourne Age*, Insight section, 5, 1 July 2006. Some of them are, of course, still there.

by teaching them how to behave? In the twentieth century, HLA Hart, whom we met in Chapter 1, was at pains to reject any definition of law as simply punitive – a command backed by a threat. Law is, he thought, enabling, for the most part. In India or in the United Kingdom, law enables me to make a binding contract or a valid will, for example, if I follow its directions – and if I can afford to mobilize it on my behalf.

But of course, within the machinery of the law, there is always ultimately coercion. Where legal rules stipulate that a particular contract or will conform with the law and that I have failed to comply with a duty to give effect to them, I will be penalized.[10] If I have not followed its directions, my transaction will be unenforceable. Opinions may vary about the fairness of a legal device, but the judge or other official will generally not be able to entertain a debate other than one that concerns the applicability of a rule. Education may also, as I have suggested, be coercive. It may amount to no more than the rote learning condemned by Arnold in the second half of the nineteenth century. However, it does contain more evidently the seeds of subversion and change, the possibility of comparing evaluations – of legal rules themselves, which, as we have seen, writers such as Locke recognized.

The early Whigs, like Locke, Shaftesbury and others, were concerned with differences of opinion among an elite and with how they could be peacefully managed. The English subject they had in mind was a gentleman or a lady[11] whose influence might spread much wider by their example – and this could, in Macaulay's opinion, be applied to natives of a "suitable class". Education of the "populace" at large was incipiently less predictable in its outcome than education for the privileged, but this was concealed whilst the truth about social order was believed to be revealed by science – the science of utilitarianism. The early positivists were insistent that citizens could be both informed about the general good and positioned to compare their situation with that good so as to take responsible steps to remedy anything unsatisfactory – their own behavior or that of others. An informed morality, in other words, could act as an effective curb on both demands for social change and exercises of sovereignty by asking the question, "does this law promote the greatest good for the greatest number?" Like ordinary language philosophy, though its bland assumption elides the question, who decides what is ordinary usage or, in this case, the greatest good?

Macaulay was more cautious when it came to the strict application of utilitarian principles, but his aspiration to educate an elite of the colonized was recognition that sovereign law-making alone was too blunt an instrument with which to govern effectively and required supplementation. He was confident that the exposure of

10 This is as the textbooks have it. They do not as a rule dwell on the consequences of disparities of economic power.

11 This is not to suggest that more conservative Whigs did not discern with some alarm the radical potential of Shaftesbury's views.

Indians to the culture behind which lay the principles of liberty and property established by the men of the Revolution was the foundation on which greater rationality responsibility and ultimately perhaps independence could be laid. People, largely but not exclusively men of the late eighteenth and nineteenth centuries, surveying the political horizon, noticed the challenge – or the threat – of democracy. For Bentham and James Mill, it was a challenge. Freedom of expression, which would be possible only when the potential electorate could make informed choices, was a *sine qua non* of real representative government as, although he did not put it in this way, it was for Macaulay. But, just as the utilitarians believed that the greatest good of the greatest number could be calculated and demonstrated irrefutably, so Macaulay believed in an objective rationality that could be taught. Free thought and free expression were neither of them dangerous since they were both subject to arbitration on objective principles.

Macaulay, JS Mill and other utilitarians, in short, believed in the "unlimited possibility of improving the moral and intellectual condition of mankind by education",[12] but JS as opposed to James, his father, as I have said, did not think that this had been accomplished by mid-century. So convinced was JS Mill by this failure of accomplishment that, although in favor of an eventual extension of the right to vote, a major criticism he makes of Disraeli's later suffrage reforms is that plural voting was tied by Disraeli's reforms to property rather than education.[13] But it is clear, I have argued, that neither Macaulay nor the Mills nor any of their followers was unaware of the normative dimension of education: normativity was, indeed, its whole point. Although they did not quite put it in this way, before the sovereignty of political and legal institutions, in fact, legitimating them, rendering those institutions something less than sovereigns, was the voice of the citizen. But s/he had first to be taught how to speak or to sing, although, as is clear from the fact that JS was advocating tentative steps toward democracy, he was taking a line not dissimilar from that of Locke two centuries earlier. In a progressive and free society, what is required is not a chorus, but an agreeable way of informedly disagreeing. It is the fine line between teaching to learn and to accept peacefully that others' learning may lead them to different conclusions, on the one hand – this is the ideal of democracy – and teaching right answers, in other words, intolerance to others' views.

As briefly alluded to in Chapter 1, legal theory in the meantime makes its jurisprudential way from the command theory which John Austin and James Fitzjames Stephen take from Bentham's writing, to the twentieth century model of law as enabling, as this is articulated in the work of HLA Hart – nothing very new here if one thinks of the political epistemology of the Whigs. Education as enlightenment takes a pedagogical course long foreshadowed by Locke and his Northern European inspirations as both enablement, but also as the name of its

12 Mill, *op cit*, n 2, 95.
13 Mill, *op cit*, n 2, 227.

components indicate, as *discipline.* If JS Mill needed reminding of this, Fred Wilson writes, he had only to recollect Coleridge.[14]

Three decades before, in 1840, Mill had explained the Coleridgean reaction to the *philosophes*' belief that the fabric of the *ancien régime* was so rotten that there was no remedy but to tear it all down and begin again. Order, citizenship and the ability and willingness to subordinate one's wishes to a negotiated conception of the common good, in short, that upon which law and ethics depend, is the product of lifelong education. As well as enabling, education, in short, was a "restraining discipline"[15] produced by and helping to maintain an ongoing social enterprise poised, if it worked properly, between the interests of permanence and progression.

Coleridge and rule by education

> There are indeed, modes of teaching which are producing youths of . . . different stamp . . . the nurselings of improved pedagogy are taught to deride; to suspect all but their own and their lecturer's wisdom and to hold nothing sacred from their contempt but their own contemptible arrogance: boy-graduates in all the technicals, and in all the dirty passions and impudence of anonymous criticism.[16]

> . . . the existence of Coleridge will show itself by no slight or ambiguous traces in the coming history of our country; for no-one has contributed more to shape the opinions of those among its younger men who can be said to have any opinions at all.[17]

In light of JS Mill's generous treatment of Coleridge's (non-economic) ideas, it may help an understanding of Macaulay's (and Trevelyan's and later) imperialist vision of education if we first turn to Coleridge's model of a state and its proper ends. He is notably wider in his vision than most others in his century, recognizing the value of pastoral, or welfare measures in achieving calm, in addition to coercive and educative policies. Although apparently inimical to the liberal conviction that, after furnishing protection to the subject, the task of the state was to leave as much scope as possible to pursue ends chosen by him or latterly herself,

14 Fred Wilson, Mill on psychology and the Moral Sciences, in John Skorupsky (ed), *The Cambridge Companion to Mill*, Cambridge, Cambridge University Press (1998), 232.

15 JS Mill, Coleridge, in FR Leavis (ed), *On Bentham and Coleridge*, Cambridge, Cambridge University Press (1950).

16 Samuel Taylor Coleridge, *Biographia Literaria* (1817), London, Penguin (N Leaske, ed) (1997), 8. He could be writing of modern university business schools, whose drones have caused much havoc to the innocent as CIA drones in Afghanistan.

17 JS Mill, Introduction, in FR Leavis (ed), *On Bentham and Coleridge*, Cambridge, Cambridge University Press (1950), 99.

the Coleridgean scheme permeated liberal politics through Matthew Arnold in the mid-Victorian era, to Leavis and the English grammar school of the mid-twentieth century. In this sense, we can see a politics of social order, of imagination in Benedict Anderson's sense, and of an order resting, as Hume would have it, on the belief of the governed. Having secured the safety of the person and the property of the subject, there remains the "positive ends" of the state:

> 1) To make the means of subsistence more easy to each individual. 2) to secure to each of its members the HOPE of bettering his own condition or that of his children. 3) the Development of those faculties which are essential to his humanity, i.e. to his rational and moral being.[18]

If these are the positive ends, Coleridge concludes uncontroversially that its negative ends are to protect itself and the lives and properties of its citizens. As the metal spring is essential to the working of a clockwork motor, so the state is essential to this very broadly conceived fulfillment of the duties and dignities of the citizen, for Coleridge. Linking, implicitly, his notion of the constitution with that of his eighteenth century predecessors, Coleridge entitles his last major work, *The Idea of the Constitution: On the Constitution of the Church and the State, According to the Idea of Each.*[19] An idea is, for Coleridge, something which "could not exist in its pure rational state in the forms of men, but it could be regulative of existing arrangements which may or may not conform with it"[20] or, as he put it elsewhere, something "known to be unapproachable as to realization, but a polar star, guiding a man's mind by approximation".[21] In its narrow function, the constitution is concerned with the state, and describes the organization of government and the coordination of interests. In England, there are two forces: permanence, that is, the landed interest, is represented in the House of Lords, and progression, the impulse to change associated with commerce and the professions, represented in the House of Commons. In the Lay Sermons, he made it clear that underlying and qualifying the law of property in both cases was the moral notion of a trust which the property owner should learn to recognize.

However, in Morrow's summary of the development of Coleridge's thought, whilst the constitution in its narrow sense could account for the state, the Coleridgean nation required for its constitution something more closely associated with cultivation and civilization. Coleridge was not the nostalgic worshipper of an imagined rustic past that Macaulay famously lampooned in his review of the

18 Samuel Taylor Coleridge, A Lay Sermon (1817), in John Morrow (ed), *Coleridge's Writings On Politics and Society*, London, Macmillan (1990), 142.

19 John Morrow (ed), *Coleridge's Writings On Politics and Society*, London, Macmillan (1990), ch 5.

20 Peter Kitson, Political Thinker, in Lucy Newlyn (ed), *The Cambridge Companion to Coleridge*, Cambridge, Cambridge University Press (2002), 167.

21 Quoted in John Morrow, *Coleridge's Political Thought: Property, Morality and the Limits of Traditional Discourse*, London, Macmillan (1990), 189, n 22.

Colloquies of Robert Southey, Coleridge's friend and one-time collaborator, "in (whose) mind . . . reason has no place at all"[22] according to Macaulay. A writer, by the early nineteenth century in sympathy with the accomplishments of commerce, science and their application to industry, Coleridge was convinced that landed wealth had in the past and could in the future be made aware of its social obligations, and that the "commercial spirit" possessed few checks to its tendency to undermine cultivated civilization, and the owners of fixed property ought to be reminded of their role in providing those checks, necessary to their fellow citizens. The man, for Coleridge, preceded the citizen and was in need of dignifying by making citizenship possible. This is, it seems to me, not incompatible with Arendt's conviction that first, we have the person, the human, but then, s/he needs to be treated as a citizen of – somewhere. Rousseau's conviction that men, everywhere in chains, had to be *forced* to be free, and which had figured in the ideology of the French Revolution, was not part of Coleridge's suggested program. With Wordsworth, he had been sufficient of a Revolutionary sympathizer in the 1790s for them both to have attracted British government surveillance. In retrospect, it is difficult to see opponents of the Revolution as it unfolded in a manner eerily foretold by Burke in 1790,[23] as *necessarily* conservative – though there is no doubt that many, perhaps most, were. It is difficult to place Coleridge entirely in this category. The state, in his expanded sense of the nation, secures property, allies itself with "trade, commerce, free industry and the arts", but "draw(s) up into the higher ranks whatever is worthiest from below and thus maintains the principle of Hope in the humblest families".[24]

Its capacity to do this rests upon the idea of a particular institution, Coleridge's national church freed from narrow "priestcraft", independent of the (narrow) parliamentary classes in its property and subsistence and thus able to mediate, through its "clerisy" among the different sources of wealth and between rich and poor. Among its objects:

> 1st . . . the maintenance of the Universities and the great liberal schools. 2ndly . . . the maintenance of a pastor and schoolmaster in every parish. 3rdly . . . the raising and repair of the churches, schools etc, and Lastly, to the maintenance of the proper, that is infirm, poor, whether from age or sickness: one of the original purposes of the national reserve being the alleviation of those evils which, in the best forms of worthy states must arise and must have been foreseen as arising from the institution of individual property and primogeniture.[25]

22 Thomas Babbington Macaulay, Southey's Colloquies (1830), in J Grieve (ed), *Thomas Babbington Macaulay: Critical and Historical Essays*, London, Dent (1907), 188.

23 And see Simon Schama, *Citizens: A Chronicle of the French Revolution*, New York, NY, Knopf (1989).

24 Morrow, *op cit*, n 19, 190.

25 Morrow, *op cit*, n 19, 188.

Such a body enables the humblest human to distinguish her/himself and peers from the beasts and forms the basis of a "sound constitution of the Body Politic".[26]

Political society is for him a contract, not an original contract such as one might find in the terms drawn up in a legal document, but an ongoing agreement creating ongoing mutual obligations without which the polity falls apart into the few organized predators and the many preyed-upon. Humanity here means the encouragement of those qualities that distinguish men from animals or "savages", precisely through this changing system of mutual obligation. Coleridge's terminology differs from much current writing, but I think he makes several points in the Lay Sermon that cast doubt on Mill's assessment of his economic conclusions, some of which we may now want to qualify, yet they seem to the point. One is that "men" are to be distinguished from animals and savages, among other qualities, in the manner of their husbandry: they cultivate as members of a social organization, or, as citizens, not as animals who merely happen to have human form. If agriculture thus depends upon the *civitas*, all those who participate in it are to be respected, to be used, as he learned from Kant, as ends and not as means, not merely those who establish legal title to their acres. A third argument scoffs somewhat at the farmers who (as the term "farmer" implies) rent their land from the large landowners. With the cessation of the French war, the farmers' hyper-profits are at an end, he argues, so they wish to reduce the rents they pay to the landlords and the tithes they pay to the church, the wages they pay to their laborers, and the contributions assessed for the parish poor law fund. Simultaneously, they wish still to charge the consumer their former prices for corn.[27]

But his case against the farmers does not end here. He notes in The Lay Sermon the wish of the farmer to occupy and (perhaps) cultivate all of the land comes under fire. In the normal practice hitherto, both farmers and laborers rented their land from the landowner. The Earl of Winchelsea reported to the Board of Agriculture in 1796 of "the dislike . . . farmers have to seeing the laborers rent any land"[28] (i.e. from the head landlord from whom the farmers rent their acres). One reason, he suspects, is that they wish to have the land for themselves; an important second is that the vegetables grown on land rented directly from the head landlord, the landlord of both the farmer and the laborer, coupled with the cow grazed on the commons to provide the children with milk, gave the laborers' families a certain independence from their employer, the farmer. "They rather wish to have the laborers more dependent on them", completely dependent on wages.[29] The farmers, as Snell argues, deeply resented the independence of the laborers, more than the loss of profit represented by the existence of cottage gardens and cow pasturage which could with enclosures be farmed by themselves. In order to

26 Morrow, *op cit*, n 19, 198.

27 Coleridge, *op cit*, n 18, 149.

28 Cited in KDM Snell, *Annals of the Labouring Poor: Social Change and Agrarian England 1660–1900*, Cambridge, Cambridge University Press (1985), 218.

29 Snell, *ibid.*

obliterate the resentment of seeing the laborer taking his horse to the race of a Monday without the *in terrorem* possibility of dismissal for his impertinence, subsequent unemployment and impoverishment, the farmer wished for more power.

Coleridge notes in 1817 the deprivation of the customary right of cow pasture, Winchelsea's further and unsuccessful submission to the Board of Agriculture, and remarks:

> The moment the farmer obtains his wish, he takes every particle of land to himself and re-lets to the laborer, who by this means is rendered miserable; the Poor Rate is increased; the value to the Estate to the landowner is diminished and the house suffered to go to decay.[30]

So Coleridge, *pace* Mill and perhaps others, is not seeking a return to what would become a pre-Raphaelite or bucolic economic idyll. He accepts the necessity and positive value of commerce – in what Morrow finds an interesting anticipation of Hirschman's argument on the socially cohesive effects of commerce in an era in which religion's capacity to sustain collective moral belief[31] – Coleridge criticized Fichte's failure sufficiently to appreciate the peculiar benefits of commercial activity and equally, to comprehend the economic statistics that demonstrated the point. What he objected to, in the Lay Sermon was not even a portion of the Gradgrindian fascination with the utility of "facts". It is true that some part of his objection to the Malthusian tradition was that he felt that Malthusian abstraction elided the ethical dimension of the human in political society, as opposed to the savage or the animal. Property, including property in the person, was vital to ensure liberty, an ethical end of the state. For this it was not necessary that property be distributed equally, but to deprive a person of property sufficient to ensure his liberty was to exclude him from the polity and give him no incentive to give his loyalty to it. It was for this reason that he supported Robert Peel's Bill which, when passed, limited the hours of juvenile labor, and mandated breaks. Opponents of the Bill failed, in Coleridge's view, to distinguish members of a polity from the beasts.[32]

But this was not Malthusian political economy's only methodological error owed to excessive abstraction. If more meat is produced it must be eaten somewhere: "What difference where, they say, what does it matter if three were fed in Manchester instead of two at Glencoe or the Trossachs?" We are correctly

30 Morrow, *op cit*, n 19, 149.

31 Morrow, *op cit*, n 21. The text Morrow has in mind is AO Hirschman, *The Passions and the Interests: Arguments for Capitalism before its Triumph*, Princeton, NJ, Princeton University Press (1977). Coleridge had no illusions, of course, and no regrets that capitalism had triumphed, although he did feel that the cohesive benefits were achieved only where agricultural and commercial or manufacturing capital were treated differently.

32 Morrow, *op cit*, n 21, 105.

told, Coleridge writes in the Sermon, that hitherto undiscovered talent, productivity and wealth have been conjured under the new economic dispensation. This increase depends on credit, but when regulation is unavailable and circumspection fails, unsound credit provokes a crash with disproportionate effects on the poor and weak:

> We shall perhaps be told . . . that the very Evils of this System, even the periodical *crash* are to be regarded but as so much superfluous steam ejected by the Escape Pipes and Safety Valves of a self-regulating machine; and . . . that in a free and trading country *all things find their level.*[33]

The Malthusians are, to put Coleridge into more recent terminology, guilty of a category mistake. Many things, such as water, find their level, "but persons are not *Things* . . . (B)e it that plenty has returned and that Trade has once more become brisk and stirring: go, ask the (Poor Law) overseer and question the parish doctor whether the workman's health and temperance with the staid and respectful manners best taught by the inward dignity of conscious self-support have found *their* level again".[34]

The farmers and the judiciary demonstrated between them the value to which they attached the "inward dignity of conscious self-support" in the events represented in Bill Douglas's 1987 film *Comrades*, about the Tolpuddle Martyrs, where rural workers, no longer forbidden to combine under the Combination Act of 1825 (i.e. to unionize and bargain collectively) in order to improve the conditions and rewards of their labor, were nevertheless convicted for taking an illegal oath of solidarity to their union, and transported to Australia. Coleridge died before the full force of utilitarian cruelty was unleashed on the poor after the Poor Law inquirers in their parliamentary committee in the 1830s were confronted with "scientific" evidence of excessive demands made by the rural poor, perfectly able to work, but unwilling to do so. However, he provided the outline of a pedagogic or intellectual, alternative to the disastrous reliance on legislation and sovereignty, prompted by the decline in earlier forms of ordering through religion.

I suggested that Coleridge sought to solve two related problems, anticipating Matthew Arnold, to a degree. One problem he perceived was that the normative effects of a religiously-based morality had become weaker and were in any event socially plural, contentious and as likely to invoke dis-harmony as cohesion. A second was that the doctrine of sovereignty, that is the office of a sovereign or sovereign body as the source of political and social legitimacy seemed to him potentially authoritarian, but in any event excessively metaphysical as *a priori* assumptions. He wants to know how anyone could be certain until after the event

33 Sermon, in John Morrow (ed), *Coleridge's Writings On Politics and Society*, London, Macmillan (1990), 136.

34 Morrow, *op cit*, n 19, 136–37.

the nature and extent of the powers reserved *from* a sovereign by the body over which it claimed sovereignty? His perspective differs from those of theorists like Bentham and the European heirs of Absolutist rule, for whom the sovereign is by definition ultimately above and outside the realm of the governed. Taken together, these difficulties posed for Coleridge the question of political and legal obligation, those of the individual and those of the state, institutions that each reciprocally produces the other. Relatedly, there was the question of social cohesion which, at one level is more theoretical, but quickly turns into something practical and of more or less urgency: when can we say that there is a community and how do we maintain it once we seem to have it? The passengers on a flight from London to Melbourne live for stretches of up to twelve hours or more between airports in a context which sociologists have described as a total community, cut off from the outside world and subject to quite significant discipline by the crew. In no way, however, do they form, nor would they consider themselves a community.

Into his mix, of course, Coleridge had added the idea of the ethical. For Coleridge, an idea, I suggested, was not something derived from an existing state of affairs, or a situation or conclusion expected to be arrived at. Rather it was the component toward which one's thoughts tended as the essence of a practice or set of practices engaged in. World peace is not expected, either by means of a breakthrough to an unexpected consensus on all issues, or by means of the police power of an authoritative world government. It is, rather, something which permeates and gives sense and meaning to international organizations, treaties, diplomatic exchanges, etc. Why the state should incorporate the idea of the ethical is, as we have seen, because it makes possible the idea of the political being, to use Arendt's terminology. The political being is a *citizen* in an *organization*, recognized as such, and with a greater or lesser say in the nature of the organization. The outlaw, the displaced person and the camp inmate are human, but not part of the idea of the state – constructed more like cats or kangaroos for whom humane treatment is a privilege of which they may be deprived without their consent.

If education was to form the basis of the idea of a state, or of state/individual relations, what were the practical implications – how could it be approached? A prior question, which arose during the discussion of the paper from which this chapter arose was, if Absolutist practices of sovereignty are to be eschewed, among other reasons, because of their authoritarian tendency, does not pedagogy suffer the same propensity? Is the teacher not an authoritarian figure? The answer is not as clear cut as one might imagine, I have suggested.

After all, in the context of an Absolutist regime, Kant believed that philosophy had a role as a kind of ethics committee, where scholars might, among themselves, apply reason to theology rather than involve themselves in the communication of discourses of religious teaching directed at the people. Conversely, the cleric derives his business of preaching, not from his reason, but from the word of the Christian Bible. The philosopher examines the justice of the operation of the law in the texts according to reason and perhaps natural law and may seek the true nature of the constitution. The lawyer does not conduct *her/his* business according to reason, but looks to the legal authorities contained in the texts accepted in her/his profession. And the doctor, in her/his professional capacity addresses the patient's ailments in light of the cures offered by the practices of the day rather than inquiring into the proper way to live, or, in a modern context, to reach theoretical conclusions about whether to prolong or terminate a life, or to decide what, according to reason, life is. Moral advice or disapprobation from a medical practitioner can be quite irritating – the major example in many Anglophone jurisdictions relates to practices like abortion, euthanasia or contraception.[35] Members of all three of the "higher faculties" may discourse philosophically when they are not "businessmen", paid officials of the state but it is the philosophical scholar whose business it is to apply reason systematically, to follow it freely – to "judge autonomously" as Kant puts it – wherever it takes him.

The "lower faculty", then, operates much like Coleridge's clerisy, as we shall see, as a source of critique of the others, necessary to ensure that the other faculties can enable government to carry out its duties and inform the government what is advantageous and what disadvantageous to it.[36] This presumably includes the securing of loyalty. The irritation that Kant supposes might be occasioned among the higher faculties – the professions of law, theology and medicine – at reasoned assessment from "below", even when unaccompanied by power such as theirs, is understandable. But the necessity of a philosophically-informed state to rise above the self-interest promoted by sectional interests within civil society foreshadows Hegel's and ultimately the welfare state's interest in justice for its citizens.

For Kant, although the Enlightenment has not arrived, it is coming. It is crucially a matter of courage, "to be resolute in using one's understanding without the guidance of another". "*Sapere Aude!* Have the courage to use your *own* understanding! Is thus the motto of enlightenment." However, just as we have seen that good government relies on the freedom of those whose business it is to seek truth by means of reason as opposed to those whose business it is to rely only on the authority of the texts, legal and Biblical, or upon the laws of nature in medicine, the necessary freedom itself depends upon the power whose legitimacy it authenticates:

> . . . only a ruler who, himself enlightened,[37] does not himself fear shadows, and at the same time has at hand a large, well-disciplined army as a guarantee of peace, can say what a republic cannot dare: *argue as much as you want, as much as you want and about whatever you want, only obey!*

35 The advocates of "private" health care, just as those of "private" education seem blind to the huge per capita allocation of public funds which makes these activities possible, and for which they should be subject to public ethical and financial audit.

36 Immanuel Kant, The Conflict of the Faculties (1798), in Richard Rand (ed), *Logomachia*, Lincoln, NE, University of Nebraska Press (1992).

37 And by whom, of course, but the lower faculties?

The coming enlightenment, "this age is the age of enlightenment, *the age of enlightenment* or the century *of Frederick*".[38]

There is a dangerous irony in Kant's "idea" of enlightenment. One comes to the realization of the truth of one's self, gains the courage to inquire into it, to live it, only in the guaranteeing gaze of the other – Lacan's Big Other, behind whose business of guaranteeing one strays at peril of losing one's capacity to reason at all.

Coleridge's "national church"

A British enlightenment dependent on military force, even one guided by a free-thinking intelligentsia seeking knowledge of the truth, would not only not have been persuasive but contrary to Coleridge's idea or essential tendency of the proper state. What structure and what strategies could reinforce the mutual obligations of subject and state so as to produce willing harmony? Not, for Coleridge at least, a Frederick. Education plays a big part in the realization of the idea. His descendant, Ernest Hartley Coleridge in 1909 published an account of ST Coleridge's views from as early as the 1813 Bristol Lectures:

> He observed that he ought, perhaps, before to have noticed the word, Education. It was to educe, to call forth; as the blossom is educed from the bud, the vital excellencies are within; the acorn is but educed from the bud. In proportion to the situation in which the individual is likely to be placed, all that is good and proper should be educed.[39]

"Education", Snyder explains, "properly adapted to the probable needs and opportunities of the individual, Coleridge held"; formed an organic unity, and habits composed of both intellectual and moral qualities. As we have seen, Coleridge substituted the ongoing contract between subject and state and the promise of both material and moral betterment for sovereignty as an explanation of political obligation. True humanity could be achieved only through the state and recognized through education.[40] Having diagnosed the causes of the social disharmony of his time – and British society was turbulent at the time, Coleridge recognized the material benefits of commerce and manufacturing, but also saw them as part of the problem. It was these practices which were eroding an earlier social/moral agreement and the authority of the peerage without replacing them. His proposed institutional solution, one combining pastoral care for the poor, and ensuring the provision and independence of education at elementary, secondary

38 An Answer, in James Schmidt (ed), *What Is Enlightenment? Eighteenth Century Answers and Twentieth Century Questions*, Berkeley, CA, University of California Press (1996), 62, 63.

39 Quoted in Alice Snyder, *Coleridge on Language and Learning*, New Haven, CT, Yale University Press (1929), 45.

40 Mill, *op cit*, n 15, 120.

and university levels. This was the national church, with its "clerisy".[41] He was not an atheist and considered that the inclusion of a Christian church within the secular church would enhance its authority. His church would be made independent of the power of both the landed and the commercial estates of the realm, exercised in their legislatures, by virtue of its separate wealth; it resembles, unsurprisingly, Kant's "lower faculty" in its commitment to learning and truth. The difference is perhaps that the Coleridgean national church is more pragmatic and less gesturally optimistic than the lower faculty. Its model is of a fiscally independent producer of both truths and arguments, and of citizens.

When we recall the longstanding commitment of the Presbyterian Church in Scotland to issues of welfare and education and the *literati* mission to assist, not only in the advancement of learning, but in the creation of an English subject dedicated to the stability and commercial prosperity of the community it made possible, Coleridge's program is not conceptually odd. It is simply more comprehensive in its ambition to maintain and expand a complex status quo by, for example, recruiting the more ambitious and able of the "humble" into the "higher ranks", which as we shall see, was precisely the ambition of the Liberals and liberal conservatives in the 1930s and 1940s in Britain. Since *Church and State* and the earlier of his writings upon which some of the ideas are canvassed temporally preceded the developments in Indian education popularly associated with Macaulay, as with the earlier work of the utilitarians, no simple connection can be made between regulatory social experiments in India and those in the metropole. However, with Macaulay, as with the "purer", less guarded utilitarians, in the Indian colony it is the concept of sovereignty, justified by the (to some, but not all administrators of the empire) improvable inferiority of the natives, that provides the vehicle in which social engineering practices can ride from a perceived periphery to a reconceived center.[42]

Coleridge, who is now associated chiefly with his poetry, literary criticism and perhaps the *Biographia Literaria*, which is hard to categorize, was also a visionary political theorist, but not, of course, a legislator or a politician in the traditional sense. He was a conservative, but as Mill remarks, not really a Tory. His blueprint was not intended to be static and, indeed, carried the Burkean Whigs' notion of balance, of a constitution as an emerging, changing device, not a template. It may or not be far-fetched to find both the triumphs and the shortcomings of the post-1945 British welfare state settlement in his – to use his term – ideas. What I want

41 The Idea of the Constitution: On the Constitution of the Church and State, According to the Idea of Each (1829), in John Morrow (ed), *Coleridge's Writings On Politics and Society*, London, Macmillan (1990), 152 *et seq*.

42 Antoinette Burton, Introduction: On the Inadequacy and the Indispensability of the Nation, in Antoinette Burton (ed), *After the Imperial Turn: Thinking with and through the nation*, Durham, NC, Duke University Press (2003), and elsewhere, doubts the straightforwardness of center-periphery thinking.

to do in the following chapters is contrast two modes of governance in ways already made familiar by the Foucauldians and the neo-Foucauldians.

An over-simplified contrast to which I have returned several times, would be that between the mode of government that regulates through the production of rules for legal subjects – that, in other words, produces legal subjects – and government that regulates for order by means of producing English (or French, or Canadian) subjects – that enables us to learn who and how we are and who and how we can be. Smith's approach prioritizes the latter over the former, as we saw in Chapter 1. That we cannot understand social order unless we first understand, for example, how, *culturally*, we align ourselves with legality, how we perform it, underlies this approach. But, naturally, we also want to have in our possession the cultural language that will suggest how we *should* align ourselves with legal rules, whether to ignore them, bend them, change them if we can, or criticize them if we cannot. Smith's spectator, and before him, the Mr Spectator of Addison and Steele, I suggested in the concluding paragraphs of the Introduction, and then in subsequent chapters, provide the tools for such a calculation.

Grene writes:

> Through submitting to certain rules of judgment and imposing them on what confronts him, the human person makes of himself with part of himself, into an impartial observer. But *he* makes himself so by imposing on himself the standard of impartiality, the value of truth. He takes on the role of detached spectator, and accepts the responsibility of living his part. He legislates into existence the *value* of *de*tachment. Far from preventing impartiality, the "intrusion" of "judgments of value" is essential to its existence. Only as the child comes to, or, better, takes it upon himself to live in a value-governed world, does he learn the discipline of objective perception, and beyond that the more sophisticated objectivities of scientific discourse.[43]

The American Legal Realist formula, that law is what the courts decide, needs modification, since what the courts decide and more broadly, what people do, require cultural explanation of how it is they come to suppose that this is who they are. But the Legal Positivist objection to Legal Realism, that what is decided constitutes the law does not guide the decision-maker as to how s/he should decide, applies in this wider field with equal force. Each person performs an ethical *should*, which s/he derives from an interpretation of the values of his/her culture. "Only by an evaluation do we call the story of Auschwitz or Belsen mass murder and so assimilate it to human history rather than to chemistry or population genetics".[44]

43 Marjorie Grene, *The Knower and the Known*, London, Faber and Faber (1966) 176.
44 Grene, *ibid*, 160.

Chapter 6

Cultural studies, education and legality

> What I would like to show is that an episode and transitory form, law itself is, rather, part of a much more general history of the techniques and technologies of practices of the subject with regards to himself, of techniques and technologies which are independent of law and have priority with regards to it.[1]

Here I want to emphasize the necessary contextuality of any meaningful study of legality, what Foucault above, terms "law itself": the way in which "law itself", is formed in specific societies. In the case of the United Kingdom, its ordering role was less limited and augmented by custom and the "moral economy" of the period studied by EP Thompson than increasingly by the slow development of education and civil administration It is clear from the above quotation from Foucault that, whilst their goals were very different, there is a certain convergence between the approaches of both Smith and Foucault toward the social place of law. Examining the place and the very form of law must, for both, await the study of a number of other social forces. Smith, like his Scottish contemporaries, was concerned first with the nature of particular kinds of society and, as we have seen, categorized these roughly into four types, from gatherer-hunter to commercial societies. His second interest was in how human beings came to be, or perform, in a manner consistent with the society of which they claimed membership, and he used the metaphor of the spectator, who is first of all external and then also internal in the formation of the subject. Only after these operations have been explored can we turn to the question of legality. Equally, Foucault sees law as effected by other governing principles, and as best understood as but one of many normative influences upon the construction of subjectivity. The word "transitory" as a qualifier of forms of law in the passage quoted suggests to me to convey fluidity rather than a temporary nature for the forms which will, at different times characterize law. There may always be law to study, but the manner and conclusions

1 Michel Foucault, *The Hermeneutics of the Subject: Lectures at the College de France 1981–2*, New York, NY, Picador (2005), 112.

of its study must come after other study – this is the message from Smith and Foucault. Law in Aboriginal societies, for example, was discernible only when some knowledge of the societies in question was gained by Europeans.

This may seem obvious enough but, as I suggested in Chapter 1, and will return to, a powerful conviction arose after the mid-eighteenth century conquests in India that the ultimate cement of any particular social order is the law, constituted by its sovereign. In Chapter 1, we noticed the vicious circularity in which the sovereign, through which law must be identified in this model, can be identified only in terms of its unique capacity to authorize law. Australian courts were forced to confront the issue in relation to Aboriginal land rights. Enclaves remain, but for the most part, the people who had inhabited and managed their land for perhaps 50 millennia, found themselves stripped of entitlement to their country. The logic was that the British invaders had acquired political sovereignty and thus the legal right to redistribute property. The reasoning behind the logic, expressed in earlier legal reasoning, that Aboriginal people were rude and ignorant savages without government or institutions of property, was denied by judges of Australia's highest federal court.[2]

The Australian judges were anxious to be humane and charitable (courts since have been equally polite, but have for the most part found one reason or another for rejecting Aboriginal land claims), but refused to answer the obvious question: on what basis, satisfactory to the present, could the British and their Australian successors have claimed sovereignty? Leave aside rudeness and savagery, which satisfied nineteenth century courts as justification, and was rejected as false by courts close to the twenty-first century, what now remains by way of justification of sovereign acquisition and subsequently land-theft, immiseration of indigenous people and self-righteous explanations of genocidal retaliations after Aboriginal defense of their land? In other words, serious cultural questions need to be asked before we come to the English common law. Fortunately for themselves, the judges did not need to ask those questions. Since the highest court in the land owed its existence to sovereign creation and endorsement, it could not, it felt, question the basis of its legitimacy.[3] "Native title" – echoes of empire, of course – would have to be put into conformity with the law of the unquestionable sovereign without inquiring into the question of how that sovereignty came to claim Aboriginal subjects as its own. The usual mix of metaphors of expediency surfaced in Australian judgments, which generally affirmed Aboriginal title in the abstract, whilst rejecting its application in the case before them. The sovereignty that lay behind the highest Australian court was the "skeleton" upon which the state hung. Nothing but an amoeba or a jellyfish could, by implication, exist effectively without one and retain coherence. There was no going behind it, to discover the

2 *Mabo v Queensland (No 2)* (1992) 175 CLR 1; *Wik Peoples v Queensland* (1996) 187 CLR 1.

3 Tony Blackshield and John Williams (eds), *Australian Constitutional Law and Theory: Commentary and Materials*, Sydney, Federation Press (1998), ch 4.

original government and property regimes on the continent. Or, Aboriginal claims had been washed away by the tides of history. Europeans, still less lawyers could no more influence tides than King Cnut. Nature here provided the "Pontius Pilate moments" with which we are familiar from Arendt's reporting of the Eichmann case; nobody at Wannsee was responsible, save for the (absent) Jews, who owed their fate to their "natural" sub-humanity.

Putting lawyers' law back into culture

But how does one locate an appropriate context for "law itself" in order to decide what "itself" is? My theme has been that, as Burke put it, lawyers' law misses law's potential "grandeur" with politically unfortunate results, and to the extent that lawyers' law prescribes legal theory, or jurisprudence, the "wisdom" of law, the prescription produces a crabbed, instrumentalist and exclusivist discipline. We can put an alternative, a contemporary search for context in a way not inconsistent with Adam Smith and Foucault by considering "cultural studies" as it has developed since the second half of the twentieth century. Munns and Rajan open their Introduction to a collection of essays on cultural studies with a quotation from a 1986 lecture by Raymond Williams, entitled "The Future of Cultural Studies", in which he says, "you cannot understand an intellectual or artistic project without also understanding its formation; that the relation between a project and a formation is always decisive and . . . the emphasis of Cultural Studies is precisely that it engages with both".[4] If the Scots of the enlightenment did not describe their work in quite this way, it is nevertheless what they were doing. Contextualization, although they would have abhorred the word, opening out their beloved English school to and toward other disciplines with humane hope, was what the Leavises were doing in the twentieth century, as we shall see.

In their Introduction, Greenblatt and Gunn define the interdisciplinarity of cultural studies thus:

> It is tempting to believe that every time borders are crossed at the level of disciplines one automatically enters the domain of the interdisciplinary, but this assumption confuses the desire to see from different sides of the same border with the desire to reconceive the relation between various borders. The disciplinary gives way to the interdisciplinary only when changes in interpretive frames actually manage to produce changes in what can be seen with their assistance and only when reconceptions of the question also change what can be represented as an answer.[5]

4 Jessica Munns and Gita Rajan, Introduction, in Munn and Rajan (eds), *A Cultural Studies Reader: History, Theory, Practice*, London, Longman (1995), 1–2.

5 Stephen Greenblatt and Giles Gunn, Introduction, in Greenblatt and Gunn (eds), *Redrawing the Boundaries: The Transformation of English and American Literary Studies*, New York, NY, Modern Languages Association (1992), 4–5.

In Greenblatt and Gunn's view, this new notion of literary studies results from three changes in higher education, each leading to the others. Greater access to universities has brought a greater mix of students (and faculty) in terms of "ethnic, racial, social, cultural and religious" backgrounds. They have sought answers to different questions than those posed by an earlier and more homogenous elite. Their search, of course, draws more texts into the purview of literary studies and since the act of searching is a form of demand for greater breadth of textual study by readers, forces more attention on to the reader as an active agent engaging with texts.[6] Again, as we have seen, there was evidence of some of these changes in Presbyterian schooling and Scottish universities from early in the eighteenth century, developments that crossed the Atlantic but were somewhat delayed in crossing the Tweed. The liberating nature of cultural studies thus conceived – and I would add, its sympathy for a democratic politics – is noticed in yet another introduction. Quoting John Frowe, Greenblatt and Gunn argue that "the social order constrains and oppresses people, but at the same time offers them resources to fight those constraints". Quoting Stuart Hall, they add that "*culture* means 'the actual, grounded terrain of cultural practices, representations, languages and customs of any particular society'",[7] terrain which can always be contested. Theoretical awareness of these cultural tools, their provenance, effects and potential is what Frowe regards as the resources necessary to use them and overcome their oppressive dimensions. The study of how law is, in "itself" must, in my argument include an awareness of these resources.

Purged of its cultural studies content, jurisprudence loses its implication of "wisdom" concerning law and becomes a dry catalog of the desiccated technicality given it by legal practice. (Much the same can be said of all vocational instruction masquerading as academic activity.[8]) We must return to Burke, in the last decades of the eighteenth century. He was undoubtedly sympathetic toward both Americans and Bengalis and what he saw as their outrageous treatment by British governments following the Seven Years' War of 1756–63. But the principal apprehension he expressed was associated with the missed "grandeur"; if law was not understood as based in a constitution in turn grounded in the habits and expectations of a people, it was simply a tool available for oppression. And oppression in one part of the empire would inevitably, in Burke's opinion, return home to inform the practices of its authors there. Empire and pettifogging[9] legal

6 Greenblatt and Gunn, *ibid*, 3.

7 Lawrence Grossberg, Cary Nelson and Paula Treichler, Introduction, in Lawrence Grossberg, Cary Nelson and Paula Treichler (eds), *Cultural Studies*, New York, NY, Routledge (1992), 5.

8 Thus see the comparison of critical sociology with the cheery advertizing brochure language of "Business Studies" in Ian Reid, *Higher Education or Education for Hire? Language and Values in Australian Universities*, Rockhampton, University of Central Queensland Press (1996), ch 5.

9 The term comes from CW Brooks, *"Vipers and Pettifoggers of the Commonwealth": The Lower Branch of the Legal Profession in Early Modern England*, Cambridge, Cambridge University Press (1986). Brooks focused on "the lower branch", but W Pue, in Lawyers and Political

theory, narrowing horizons, corroding responsibility for decisions taken, and ultimately hostile to inclusivist, democratic politics, were close cousins. Burke was not himself democratically inclined, but he was firmly of the view that it was the duty of Parliament to put the good of the people, commons included, before its own interests, or those of its members.

Removing local culture in India from British administration

It was never clear whether the British rule over India was to be force backed by pedagogy or pedagogy backed by force. Semantically and practically, the two practices are often not dissimilar. Schoolteachers until recently carried canes to beat, as they saw them, recalcitrant children. I remember. Professors fail students, which is a kind of violence. With the best of intentions, academics can hope to follow Leavis's injunction to work with students in a mutual learning process. But, as the British lost respect for Indian scholarship, and, viewing the poverty they had contributed to, although not created, authoritarianism took hold.

Cornwallis and Wellesley could, as Burke feared, in the India of the end of the eighteenth century, justify schemes for controlling Indian natives on the grounds of Indian incompetence and British sovereign authority to act as conquerors. Indians, not being proper English subjects, were not entitled to participate officially or effectively in their fate. Similarly, then it came to seem natural to centralize the administrative control of the English poor three decades later. If natives overseas were not entitled to participate in their government, was it not anomalous that indigent Englishmen should have a participatory role in the organization of poor relief, as was sometimes the case under the old Poor Law? Did not the British government, in the understanding and misunderstanding that had prompted the American war, exercise sovereignty over the English poor as well as over Indians? Cornwallis's Anglicization of administration in British India, his exclusion of local inhabitants, has a direct parallel in the transfer of Poor Law administration from the parish vestry, in which the poor themselves were often involved in one way or another[10] to the "Three Kings of Somerset House" in London by the Poor Law Amendment Act of 1834. Local cultures of mutual obligation, where they existed, were plainly rejected amid hysteria about the apparently rising cost to the privileged of maintaining the poor.

Liberalism in 18th and 19th Century England, in Terence Halliday and Lucien Karpik (eds), *Lawyers and the Rise of Western Political Liberalism: Lawyers and the Constitution of Modern Politics*, Oxford, Oxford University Press (1997) makes clear that progressive thought and breadth of vision were not attributes of the English bar.

10 See KDM Snell, *Annals of the Laboring Poor: Social Change and Agrarian England 1660–1900*, Cambridge, Cambridge University Press (1985).

It was indeed, according to a recent study,[11] the political economy of Thomas Malthus, lecturer to (British) Indian Civil Service students at Haileybury College, which informed the gradually forming new doctrines about the poor, rationalized the hysteria about the growing cost of the poor law to landowners, and justified the national imposition of workhouses (some poor law unions of parishes had through the eighteenth century constructed their own). The governing principle of the new poor law was "less eligibility", a phrase associated with the 1834 Act, the doctrine that forced the poor who had no means of earning, largely because they had been made unemployed by the very people who would, in effect, punish them, "indoors", into the workhouse. There they were to be physically separated from spouses and children in circumstances in which they were all to be subject to living conditions deliberately made harsher than conditions outside, had there been remunerative work for the poor to do. The poor were to be forced to pay for their immiseration by the better off, whose poor rates would be reduced. From the point of view of the better off, the poor were henceforth to take responsibility for themselves, ultimately to become "good" English subjects or accept their exclusion from the positive consciousness of the polity. If we think of Malthus's observations in 1803, quoted above, that the poor had no place "at nature's mighty feast", they should be grateful of the opportunity to make do with gruel in the workhouse, to display, in the Reverend Milman's words, humility and the acceptance of degradation. The law, like the schoolmaster with his cane, was to reject even the slight allowance made to the customs and participation of the governed.

Macaulay's purpose in rejecting the legacy of local, in this case, Indian, culture and substituting that of the British had some resemblance to this, Malthusian, project save, importantly, that it had a positive goal. It had the same justification as that of the Malthusians, that of controlling populations, the same refusal to recognize the equal subjectivity of those over whom it is possible to exercise power unless they either conform with the expectations of their English masters or learn their abject inferiority. But it offers, however paternalistically, a way forward that does not have the possible destruction of subjects, rather, their re-creation, as its alternative. This is clear from his speech to the Commons on the Charter Act in 1833, before Macaulay went to India and the year before the Poor Law Amendment Act. It is worth quoting a crucial passage:

> To have found a great people sunk in the lowest depths of slavery and superstition, to have so ruled them as to have made them desirous of all the privileges of citizens, would indeed be a title to glory all our own. The scepter may pass from us. Unforeseen accidents may derange our most profound schemes of policy. Victory may be inconstant to our arms. But there are

11 Mitchell Dean, *The Constitution of Poverty: Toward a Genealogy of Liberal Governance*, London, Routledge (1991), esp 96 *et seq*. JD Marshall, *The Making of the New Poor Law 1795–1834*, London, Macmillan (1968); Anthony Brundage, *The Making of the New Poor Law 1832–1839*, London, Hutchinson (1978).

> victories which are followed by no reverse. There is an empire exempt from all causes of decay. Those triumphs are the pacific triumphs of reason over barbarism; that empire is the imperishable empire of our arts and our morals, our literature and our laws.[12]

Macaulay's background was that of Christian evangelism, (not to be confused with twentieth and twenty-first century Christian evangelism in the United States) of Wilberforce and Zachary Macaulay. Wilberforce's English subject could not accept the slave trade, but it is far from clear that he would have accepted the implications of the inscription on Wedgwood's ceramic ware during the campaign to abolish the slave trade, the famous depiction of a chained African man, appealing to his masters, "Am I not a man and a brother?", Macaulay's mission was not particularly Christian, but his sense of Englishness, which is clear from his *History*, and his evangelism on behalf of this version of Englishness, was clear from *Clive*. It is clear from his 1833 speech, quoted, in part, above. There is, I have argued throughout some similarity of purpose between the two lines of thought about control, that required by the Benthamite/political economy-inspired legislation and that implied by Macaulay's 1835 Education Minute. It was, after all, under the utilitarian, Governor-General Bentinck, that Macaulay's educational proposals for "a suitable class of Indians", to render them English subjects with brown skins, were accepted. Because of the near-convergence of Macaulay and the utilitarians on this issue, John Clive has observed that the decisiveness of Macaulay's intervention in 1835 is not quite as straightforward as it is sometimes made to appear. The victory of English language schooling advocates over those who favored an educational policy pursued through local languages, which was signaled in the famous Minute to the Supreme Council of India, had been all but won before Macaulay wrote and then addressed the Council.

The policy of teaching Indians in the English language, inevitably importing and inculcating values from Britain, had indeed been proposed from the late eighteenth century as a means of undermining "the Hindu fabric of error" and eventually propagating Christianity. Charles Grant, later East India Company Chairman, had written in 1797, "the English language . . . is a key which will open to them (Hindus, but also Muslims) a world of new ideas, and policy alone might have impelled us long since to put it into their hands".[13] His aim was to spread the benign influence of Englishness – and to enhance commercial relations with the Company. By 1823, John Clive suggests, a number of trends were indeed coming together. A wealthy middle class of Hindu merchants who traded with the British favored both British rule and the teaching of English language and culture; and,

12 TB Macaulay, Government of India, House of Commons, 10 July 1833, in TF Ellis, *The Miscellaneous Writings and Speeches of Lord Macaulay*, London, Longmans Green (1889), 572.

13 Quoted in Alastair Pennycook, *English and the Discourses of Colonialism*, London, Routledge (1998), 67.

given the impossibility of educating the mass of Indians within British India into the belief, shared by British administrators and Hindu merchants, in the inherent superiority of British culture, a process of downward diffusion to the "mass" from the colonial rulers and native elite was the generally agreed course of action by men like Charles Trevelyan, Macaulay's future brother in law, and William Bentinck, Governor of Madras earlier in the century, where both had been energetic proponents of English language education. As Governor-General of all British India from 1827, Bentinck was in thorough agreement with James Mill's view that Hindu and Muslim literature was "mischievous" and largely useless,[14] and with Trevelyan, that only in English, a language surely at the apogee of European rationality, was a "tolerable education" to be obtained.

Company servants were now well-paid (and, therefore, expensive) – one of Macaulay's motives in becoming a member of the Supreme Council was to finance a subsequent life of politics and letters in England. The reason for paying generous salaries was to remove the temptation for the private looting of local wealth associated with the Company's reign in the late eighteenth century. Some years after Cornwallis's Anglicization of the administration of India, Bentinck was now charged with the task of reducing Company costs. British employees were expensive and enabling Indians fluent in the English language to perform low-ranking administrative tasks which would otherwise have to be undertaken by the higher-paid British, would, it was hoped, assist in the endeavor to retrench Company expenditure.

Macaulay looked beyond the Indian elite with an aim, one now widely shared by the colonizers:

> to do our best to form a class who may be interpreters between us and the millions whom we govern; a class of persons, Indian in blood and colour, but English in taste, in opinions, in morals and in intellect.[15]

Stokes, in the 1950s and a number of more recent writers such as Pennycook and Viswanathan have remarked that India provided a social laboratory from which, by virtue of the sovereignty exercised there, experiments could be attempted whose results might then find their way home. This educational invitation to collude in apparently universal values was a principal attempt. For Bentham and James Mill, law reform and codification were to be the primary tools in the civilizing mission. For Trevelyan and, to an increasing extent, Macaulay, beneath law and a condition of its acceptability and regular application – hence the security of liberty and property – lay culture and its ability to draw a society otherwise diverse and

14 Mill was, based on his observations of Ireland, unconvinced that learning English would make of Indians loyal British subjects, according to John Clive.

15 Quoted in John Clive, *Macaulay: The Shaping of the Historian*, Cambridge, MA, Harvard University Press (1987), 376.

unequal, together.[16] But here we find a tension noticed by several authors (and of course one embodied in Macaulay himself). On the one hand, GO Trevelyan, Macaulay's nephew and biographer, remarks that Macaulay's intervention, in marking the defeat of the Orientalists and commencing the diffusion or "filtration" of Englishness downward, was "the turning point of (India's) intellectual progress".[17]

Somewhat earlier, we find the administrator quoted earlier, directly linking education and the utility to efficient government that would, he considered, be served by imparting English culture. He is worth re-quoting in order to draw attention to the fine line between the several uses of the practice of discipline:

> . . . the natives must either be kept down by a sense of our power, or they must willingly submit from a conviction that we are more wise, more just more humane and more anxious to improve their condition than any ruler they could have.[18]

Since the moral authority of an established Christian church was not likely to be generally accepted in India, even after Christian missionary activity was permitted in 1813, the greater wisdom of the colonizers was to be the heritage transmitted in English literature. Bearing in mind Pennycook's comment that "colonialism needs to be seen as a primary site of cultural production whose products have flowed back through the imperial system",[19] we notice in this emphasis on the pacifying effects of education an anticipation of Matthew Arnold's emphasis on producing governability among the "brawling" masses of the English working class by spreading the "sweetness and light" of culture. Here he is, of course, echoing Coleridge, but missing Coleridge's insistence that a person not merely be taught the manner of his customary circumstances, but taught to bring about the best in himself, which might be much more than conformity, and takes us back to the Putney Debates, of which Coleridge would have been unaware.

But here is one of the tensions noticed by Viswanathan's chapter, "The Failure of English".[20] A previous chapter in her book gives us Nobinchunder Dass and

16 See Gauri Viswanathan, *Masks of Conquest: Literary Study and British Rule in India*, Delhi, Oxford University Press (1998), 91 and elsewhere. Eric Stokes, *The English Utilitarians in India*, Oxford, Oxford University Press (1959), 253, quotes Evidence given in 1853 to a parliamentary committee concerning the importance of a "progressive education" in "attaching" the natives to their colonizers.

17 George Otto Trevelyan, *The Life and Letters of Lord Macaulay, vol 1*, London, Longmans (1876), 486.

18 Minute of JT Farich, 23 March 1838, quoted in Gauri Viswanathan, Currying Favor: The Politics of British Educational and Cultural Policy in India, 1813–1854, in Anne McLintock, Amir Mufti and Ella Shohat (eds), *Dangerous Liaisons: Gender, Nation and Postcolonial Perspectives*, Minneapolis, MN, University of Minnesota Press (1997), 113.

19 Pennycook, *op cit*, n 13, 35, 132.

20 Viswanathan, *op cit*, n 16, ch 5.

Mahendra Lal Basak, two students so "attached" to the colonizer that the first can see his fellow Indians in British terms, as "natives"; and the second is convinced that "the British government (of India) was a fair one promoting national prosperity and justice" which Indians, "still sleeping the sleep of death" could not themselves achieve.[21] The "failure of English" is later explained by Viswanathan as one of the "conflict between producing greater equality through the diffusion of western culture and western ideas and western knowledge and reproducing inequality through the occupational structure".[22] The ambition contained in the project to create brown Englishmen was continually thwarted. I quoted Hume's remark, that government must be by opinion. When that opinion is culturally solicited, it invites cultural refusal in this kind of context, or at least provides the tools for such refusal.

The second tension concerned the law. I suggested a divergence, or at the very least a significant difference in emphasis, between those who sought to govern principally by cultural assimilation through education – and Viswanathan elsewhere repeats the argument that this had some successes until it collapsed under the weight of its own contradictions – and those for whom the law, as, if not a command, then a demand – was the predominant tool. In this essay in the collection edited by Anne McLintock *et al*, Viswanathan writes of the attempt, ultimately unsuccessful, to use the British identity revealed in selected literature to dissociate the rapacious conqueror from the best European minds, to provide "a surrogate Englishman in his highest and most perfect state".[23] This anticipates the Arnoldian solution for the social ills caused by his "brawling" and smashing working class, namely the re-education of the middle class. It is from them that "sweetness and light" might be downwardly transmitted, allowing, presumably, a more peaceful context for the continued economic exploitation of the working class, even if Arnold did not put it thus. Elsewhere, Viswanathan remarks on other problems with the rule-by-pedagogy policy in part being embraced. One was that whilst Indian literature was closely associated with, for the most part, either Muslim or Hindu spirituality, the neutral note sounded in British education could seem disrespectful, or unmindful of religious values.

But, on the contrary, there was a danger already referred to, and certainly not foreseen by Macaulay, that, armed with the skills of that rationalism, Indians could re-write and re-create their own myths of origin in opposition to that of the colonial power. This was understood by Sir Henry Maine as the "insurrectionary power of German Romanticism", the insurrectionary power of Whig Romanticism plainly now forgotten. The child's reflection in the mirror conceals a rather different actuality; what *seems* just to be the case substitutes for experience, and one might say the same of the Whigs' view of the world, which came to stand for the world

21 Viswanathan, *op cit*, n 16, 141.
22 Viswanathan, *op cit*, n 16, 165.
23 Viswanathan, *op cit*, n 18, 128.

itself. Lurking behind Maine's remark, too, is the perhaps unrecognized suspicion that rationality was not the simple projection of a single line of European thought, with its apotheosis in the English subject. Finally, there was the purely practical difficulty noted above, that there were insufficient jobs for educated Indians in the world of British colonialism. If the recipients of a more advanced education in Europe were intended to live the lives of gentlemen, as well as to pursue careers, similar spaces were greatly outnumbered by the candidates for such outcomes in India. And if education, moreover, held out the promise, or at least the possibility, of equality, Viswanathan argues, its failure to do so in the context of a colonial economy linked to world capitalism exposed, she argues:

> the moral pretensions of British colonialism. At one level, education as part of the state is complicit with the reproduction of an economic and cultural order. But because education is also expected to provide opportunities for advancement, it becomes an arena of social conflict, and this tension ultimately reduced the British administration to a position of acute vulnerability and paralysis.[24]

We shall later on see in the fears of rulers in some parts of the Anglophone world paralleling this anxiety about the paralysis and loss of traditional moral authority in the culture wars, where we find protagonists occupying positions we would not always have predicted. The Leavisites, whom we could not characterize otherwise than as "elitists", occupying a terrain of the necessary criticism or opposition to any government in order, as it were, to defend pluralism, were nothing but the cultural studies precursors of those whom twentieth and twentieth-first century Euro-American governments see as impediments to a new imperialism.[25] Here is the origin of the "culture wars", still, so unhappily waged in the United States.

That nineteenth century colonial legalist and culturalist policies of assimilation were not completely divided is again illustrated by the pedagogical overtones in this statement from James Fitzjames Stephen, for two years and a half law officer on the Supreme Council of India:

> . . . our law is, in fact, the sum and substance of what we have to teach them. It is, so to speak, the gospel of the English, and it is a compulsory gospel which admits of no dissent and no disobedience.[26]

24 Viswanathan, *op cit*, n 16, 164, and ch 6 generally.

25 See, for example, Allen Bloom, *The Closing of the American Mind*, New York, NY, Touchstone Books (1987) and, *contra*, Lawrence Levine, *The Opening of the American Mind: Canons, Culture and History*, Boston, MA, Beacon Books (1996).

26 RC Cocks, *Sir Henry Maine: A Study in Victorian Jurisprudence*, Cambridge, Cambridge University Press (1988), 87.

Stokes' remark, that Bentham and his followers were more interested in authority than liberty, is nevertheless, quite obviously illustrated by James Fitzjames Stephen.[27] Stephen was a Hobbesian positivist, a utilitarian, as opposed to Indian self-rule as he was to democracy in Britain on the ground that the English subject (which must have for him excluded women and the working class in Britain) belonged to a "superior" and "belligerent" race, and like an Englishman in his own home, had obtained sovereignty in India by right of conquest.[28] Colonialism and marriage were clearly, in his view, similar. As a lawyer, however, he was committed to notions of impartiality and fair hearing. The white husband should presumably give all parties, natives, wife, children and servants, an opportunity to present their cases before he gave judgment.

The tension generated by the stress on law as the basis of government was becoming evident in mid-century as the numbers of Indian students reading law in India increased. It is a point made about white settlement in New South Wales. Englishness, however rudimentarily grasped by convicts in NSW, meant the protection of property and a certain degree of liberty. In the absence of a Parliament as the arena for political expression, politics takes where it can be taken, to courts.[29] What we learn if we take understanding law in the broad sense, is that law, in this sense, forms part of a cultural terrain on which struggle can take place. It took legal positivism in the nineteenth and twentieth centuries to blinker understanding to an unimaginative focus on rules. Perhaps Indians were more creative, again, in the absence of a Parliament in which political struggle takes place directly.

Naturally, Maine saw things differently, as if, almost in a mirror of what may have been happening. In 1866, he expressed concern about the attraction of the "native bar" to the "young educated native". The bar offered both independence and a lucrative living, but carried also the danger of appealing to the Indian students' ability, delight, even, in "developing a grasp of fine detail and a remarkable capacity for subtle argument", without appreciating the breadth necessary for mature and rounded legal argument.[30] Now, there were pockets of "rounded legal argument" in the British Empire, but by the time Maine was complaining, they were hard to find.[31] This is, as we would expect, little more than a prejudice arising from cultural antagonism and a resentment that, from presumed "racial" inferiors, should emerge litigators of ingenuity and effectiveness, taking on the English at their own game and often winning. Also, Maine was reluctant or unable to see what was happening as a political-cultural struggle. Quite clearly, articulate and intellectually and financially independent Indian professionals were

27 Stokes, *op cit*, n 16, 234.

28 Stokes, *op cit*, n 16, 288.

29 See David Neal, *The Rule of Law in a Penal Colony: Law and Power in Early New South Wales*, Cambridge, Cambridge University Press (1991).

30 Cocks, *op cit*, n 26, 90.

31 Ian Duncanson, Equity and Obligations, (1976) 39 *Modern Law Review* 268–86.

able to use both the courts and the publicity they attracted to develop the cause of national independence. "Law was", as Cocks writes, "an obvious instrument of colonial politics",[32] a situation not necessarily avoided by encouraging those Indians who could afford it to attend an Inn of Court in London instead of Calcutta or Cape Town, as the later example of Mohandas Gandhi was to demonstrate.

The separation of local culture from administration "back home"

If we bear in mind Pennycook's point about imperial practices of government returning "home", we notice also that Charles Trevelyan – convinced of the connection quoted above, from Farish, the East India Company official – and Sir Stafford Northcote, were charged in 1853 by WE Gladstone, then Chancellor of the Exchequer in the Aberdeen Administration, with recommending the more rapid and systematic advancement of British civil service reforms. The Indian Civil Service was the paradigm, for many enthusiasts for change. One objective was bureaucratic efficiency. As a former Indian civil servant, an organization that for long excluded those "served" from its ranks – although an administrator of the Irish famine crisis "noted more for his logic than humanity"[33] – Trevelyan, the senior figure, had a background in the paternal practices of the "servant's" setting agendas for both political masters and the public ostensibly – no doubt conscientiously – being served.[34]

Gladstone's goal was that of "strengthening and multiplying the ties between the higher classes and the possession of administrative power",[35] in an era of threatening democracy. This directly parallels the hope that Indian elites might be used to redirect any ambitions they might entertain for independence into British cultural practices, and, after 1858, into the administration of the masses, subject to British supervision. In Britain, Robert Lowe, who, we saw, claimed, that he had learned of the perils of democracy during his membership of the Assembly in New South Wales, urged the new British service when it finally appeared some two decades later "to develop the kind of freemasonry that developed between the old boys of the great public schools and Oxbridge".[36] Something like this, although less tactlessly made public, was Gladstone's intention. Rule *by* law, which is implied by the utilitarian sovereign required some agenda-setting qualification in

32 Cocks, *op cit*, n 26, 89.

33 Roy Jenkins, *Gladstone*, London, Macmillan (1995), 165. Close to the Liberal Gladstone, Northcote later became a Conservative under Disraeli and joint leader in the Commons under Salisbury.

34 Ted Benton, Realism, Power and Objective Interests, in Keith Graham (ed), *Contemporary Political Philosophy: Radical Studies*, Cambridge, Cambridge University Press (1982).

35 Gladstone, quoted in EJ Feuchtwanger, *Gladstone*, London, Allen Lane (1975), 92.

36 Peter Cowan, The Origins of the Administrative Elite, (1987) 162 *New Left Review* (old series) 4, 32.

case the power of making law fell into the wrong hands in consequence of extensions to the right to vote. Among progressive rulers a deft strategy was evident. The new civil service would provide "responsible" advice to a potentially radical government elected by working class voters. The most responsible advice about what was possible and what would be ruinous would emerge from the service's senior branch, the Treasury, closely connected to the financial heart of the capitalist economy, the City. At more or less the same time a "suitable (i.e. the middle) class", if we follow Arnold, would learn how to be English subjects of the Shaftesburian kind, and teach the "brawling" masses how to exercise their vote when they gained it. The civil service changes were partially, but not fully implemented until Orders in Council were passed with Gladstone as Prime Minister in 1872 because mid-century Whigs and Whig-Liberals objected to what they correctly termed a paternalist "mandarinate".

The new civil service was strictly hierarchical, with no possible promotion from the lower grades to the highest. The latter were initially accessible by examination in subjects – ancient Greek, classical Latin – available in the great public schools and Oxford and Cambridge.[37] The class agenda behind meritocracy is often not hard to find. Benjamin Jowett, Master of Trinity, underwrote the administration of home and imperial law by his immense influence of placing his graduates in authority across a quarter of the globe, eventually providing an impetus to English literary studies by encouraging its importance in the Indian civil service curriculum to spread to Oxford and Cambridge. But we get ahead of ourselves and must return to Matthew Arnold, noticing, on the way TB Macaulay's change of heart on education in England.

Macaulay, whom we noticed advocating education in English for Indians in 1833–35, as a means of securing loyalty to their rulers, asked of those who were opposed to a Bill proposing government funding for elementary education for the English poor, in effect, if the same logic did not apply in England. Who would doubt that the primary purpose of government is to secure the defense of the realm, and the personal security of its members and their property?:

> This being admitted, can it be denied that the education of the common people is a most effectual means of securing our persons and our property? Let Adam Smith answer that question for me. His authority is entitled to peculiar respect because he extremely disliked busy, prying, interfering governments . . . But he has expressly told us that a distinction is to be made between the education of the poor and the education of the rich. The education of the poor, he says, is a matter of deep concern to the commonwealth.[38]

37 Cowan, *ibid.*

38 TB Macaulay, Speech to the House of Commons, 18 April 1847, in TF Ellis, *The Miscellaneous Writings and Speeches of Lord Macaulay*, London, Longmans Green (1889), 734 at 736.

A magistrate, Macaulay says, must intervene to prevent the spread of contagious diseases. What greater "distemper" exists than an ignorant multitude? He paints a vivid picture of mob violence, a besieged Parliament, fleeing bishops, prisons opened, fires begun, "beautiful and costly machinery broken", crops burned; and then the consequences: "the wretches who were shot, who were hanged, who drank themselves to death in the rivers of gin which ran down Holburn Hill". Conflations of the 1780s Gordon Riot, Reform Bill riots and the imagined cataclysm for the ruling classes of Chartism were a familiar trope in nineteenth century imaginings. The "Indian Mutiny" would later be added to the list. The reasons for the disorder: "the ignorance of a population which had been suffered . . . to grow up as rude and stupid as any tribe of tattooed cannibals in New Zealand" – English workers as colonial natives. The only alternative to the pacification of the population by weapons and grim punishments after the event is education. "To me it seems quite clear that whoever has a right to hang has a right to educate".[39] Posing the question this way, Macaulay positions his opponents – the churches who wanted to retain their near-monopoly on education for the poor, for the most part – as seeing the state as simply "a great hangman".[40]

Two decades after, Matthew Arnold, poet, literary and social critic, schools inspector and later professor of poetry at Oxford, summarized the problem as he saw it, dividing British social order into the "barbarians" (the aristocracy), the middle class Philistines, and the "populace", the latter of which, in its "sterner self . . . likes brawling, hustling and smashing; the lighter self, beer".[41] The aristocracy, in his view, appropriate rulers in an earlier era, Arnold sees as approaching the end of their power. They have given us, in their time, "staunch individualism" and the passion for asserting personal liberty. From what we have written, this claim may be shaky, or at least dependent on a view of the bourgeoisification of the earlier aristocracy. Looking back, if vaguely, into the issues dealt with in my Chapter 1, Arnold notices not only chivalry, but the accomplishments of the "politeness . . . outward gifts and graces" without which the achievement of a peaceful social order would have been impossible, as well as the "courage, high spirit and self confidence" without which the maintenance of that order would have been impossible[42] – undoubtedly both accomplishments as most historians concur, of the bourgeois-aristocracy of the Revolution and pre-Revolutionary period. But let us follow Arnold with his own Victorian version of the past. Looking forward, Arnold sees the middle class liberal dream of a joining together of the respectable working and middle classes from whose energy, as he wrote, the immense mercantile and unprecedented industrial wealth of the country, sprang.

39 Macaulay, *ibid*, 737.

40 Macaulay, *op cit*, n 38, 739.

41 Samuel Lipman (ed), *Matthew Arnold: Culture and Anarchy* (1869), New Haven, CT, Yale University Press (1994), 72.

42 Lipman, *ibid*, 69.

What is missing, he thinks, where this force for progress is apt to go awry, is implied by the outdated nature of the constitution: "there is no adequate centre of authority – that is, as our culture teaches us to conceive of authority, of light".[43] In other words there is an absence of a strong state, like the Prussian, both informing, disciplining. Yet again, one notices the priority of culture in his thought, despite its sometimes authoritarian tone. The nature of an appropriate constitution is to be gauged on qualitative, not formal grounds, as in the Benthamite tradition. We are reminded in some ways of Burke: the constitution on which law depends, is in turn reliant upon the changing customs and expectations of the people. People, Burke's "commons", now expect a greater degree of participation, and, for Arnold, this can be accommodated without catastrophe only with certain cultural constraints. Again, perhaps we are reminded of the Scots: stability, liberty and property can practically be secured only when an appropriate Englishness is accomplished.

The outdatedness of aristocratic rule is nowhere so clearly evidenced, for Arnold, than in his "wondering whether there is anything so unintelligent, so unapt to perceive how the world is really going, as an ordinary young Englishman of our upper class". His natural disapprobation of European despotism is mitigated, not by what Arnold so admires, education and the other state cultural apparatuses supported by, especially, Prussia, but by despotism's firm dealings with the "multitudes".[44] At the same time, the middle class has failed to appreciate that, with the historical demise of a social order in which each knew and most accepted his or her place, all that remains for the existing British Constitution to rest upon is "our system of checks and balances and our notion of its being the great right of the Englishman to do as far as possible what he likes"[45] – although (and this is a criticism) in his imperial domains, things are different: "we can have no scruple at all about abridging, if necessary, a non-Englishman's assertion of personal liberty".[46] In effect, then, disintegration can be avoided only by importing imperial practices into the domestic sphere. In his imperial role, there seems less uncertainty. For John Stuart Mill:

> There are . . . conditions of society in which a vigorous despotism is in itself the best mode of government for training the people in what is specifically wanting to render them capable of a higher civilization.[47]

But for both Mill and, for the most part, Arnold, something less drastic, although in Arnold's case some qualification of this stringency was called for – was he blind to the tendency of the Prussian state? – in Britain. Whilst in Europe there is some

43 Lipman, *op cit*, n 41, 63.
44 Lipman, *op cit*, n 41, 57.
45 Lipman, *op cit*, n 41, 50.
46 Lipman, *op cit*, n 41, 54.
47 JS Mill, *Considerations on Representative Government*, Buffalo, Prometheus Press (1991), 345–46.

realization that government can ultimately succeed only by accepting a duty to draw "the ordinary man's ordinary self" to a higher sense of right reason, according to Arnold, the English (middle class) Philistine dangerously does not appreciate that for the feudal order of the self's knowing its place there needs to be substituted a procedure for producing the best self that one can be. The first step is for the Philistine's ceasing to be a Philistine and setting an appropriate model of behavior to the Populace. If middle class licensed victuallers or commercial travelers were left to their ideal of education, there would be little scope for social improvement and a real danger of an enfranchised working class bringing their disorder into government. Should the middle class of his day entertain an ideal of education, Arnold suggests, it would probably be of schools for licensed grocers or traveling salesmen, although:

> Right reason would suggest that to have a sheer school for Licensed Victuallers' children or a sheer school for commercial travellers' children and to bring them up, not only at home, but at school, too, in a kind of odour of licensed victualism or bagmanism is not a wise training to give these children. And in Germany, I have said, the action of national guides or governors is to suggest and provide a better.[48]

This has urgently to change. In *Friendship's Garland* (1871), Arnold's narrative takes on a more dramatic character, when the narrator confronts an imaginary Prussian professor, Dr Arminius, with an account of the education of one "Businessman Bottles, a Radical of the first water; quite one of the Manchester school". Since the English state leaves not only the provision but the quality and purpose of education entirely to the market, Mr Bottles' parents, on the narrator's account, were able to secure for the young Bottles instruction of a kind perfectly focused on his future avocation in the hands of one Dr Silverpump in an academy in Peckham. His educational philosophy "as I have heard his pupil Bottles put it in his expansive moments after dinner: 'original man, Silverpump. Fine mind! Fine system! None of your antiquated rubbish – all practical work – latest discoveries in science – mind constantly excited – lots of interesting experiments – lights of all colours – fizz! Fizz! Bang! Bang! That's what I call forming a man'".[49] Bottles made, the narrator explains, a large fortune, but as to the kind of man or the kind of mind, he hesitates, at which point Arminius interjects, "you need not go on; I know what that man's mind is well enough".

What, then was to be done? The populace, now that the barbarians' power was rapidly waning, were at the gate and after the violence of the Reform Bill riots in Hyde Park, Arnold was convinced that more than mere mediocrity was threatened, but civilized order itself. Baldick quotes Arnold's initial reaction to these from the first edition of *Culture and Anarchy*:

48 Lipman, *op cit*, n 41, 80.

49 Quoted in Herbert Paul, *Matthew Arnold*, London, Macmillan (1902), 128–29.

> As for rioting, the old Roman way of dealing with *that* is always the right one; flog the rank and file and fling the ringleaders from the Tarpeian Rock! And this opinion we can never forsake, however our Liberal friends may think a little rioting, and what they call popular demonstrations, useful sometimes to their own interests.

"This indiscretion", a return to government *by* punitive law rather than a preparation for popular government – the Prussian influence? – *through* law by an educated and thus self-policing populace, Baldick writes, "was suppressed after the first edition".[50] The "indiscretion" looks like a return to a social theory, labeled by Arnold, "Hebraic", a reliance on the authority and rules in contrast to his "Hellenic" reliance on informed reason and dialogic argument. In more discreet moments, what Arnold and contemporary and later proponents of education for adults as well as children, expected, was an agency for producing harmony out of apparently irreconcilable difference. In the tradition of which it forms part, the subject of English literature would assimilate the classes, women and Indians and, by then other native peoples, and induct children. Its example, its demonstration of the national heritage, would guide its pupils toward their best selves as English subjects.[51] But if this is the vehicle, who is qualified to drive it? There are, according to Arnold, outside the turmoil of barbarians, philistines and populace, notably, "aliens", "persons who are mainly led, not by their class spirit, but by a general *humane* spirit, by the love of human perfection".[52] They provide "a source of authority" facilitating the production of "our best self".[53] He is clearer in other texts, declaring that the "middle classes" have the power in the mid-Victorian era of working class male enfranchisement, "to make the condition that this government shall be one their own adoption, one that they can trust".[54]

The idea of curiosity as a virtue, Arnold believes, needs to be recovered for English culture in order that here, too, we should strive "to know the best that is known and thought in the world, irrespective of practice, politics and everything of the kind".[55] Elsewhere, Arnold sees "the critical spirit", armed with "a knowledge of Greek, Roman and Eastern antiquity" and the appreciation of "Europe as being for intellectual and spiritual purposes one great confederation" (this is the rationality to be conferred by the reforms of Macaulay and others, upon the native overseas) beckoning the population as a whole to a "promised land", one nourished by cultural creativity in life and literature. The dreams of Charlemagne and Pope Gregory are never far away. This cultural vision of social

50 Chris Baldick, *The Social Mission of English Criticism*, Oxford, Oxford University Press (1983), 107.

51 Baldick, *ibid*, 82.

52 Lipman, *op cit*, n 41, 73.

53 Lipman, *op cit*, n 41, 74.

54 Matthew Arnold, *Mixed Essays*, London, Smith Elder (1879), 41.

55 Matthew Arnold, *Essays in Criticism, First Series* (1865), London, Macmillan (1921), 16.

engineering, which Arnold sometimes refers to as "Hellenism" is contrasted, we again notice, with what he terms the "Hebraic" approach,[56] the reliance upon rules to produce and maintain social change, an approach which resembles FR Leavis's "technologico-Benthamism". Happiness is not the adherence to good laws, those which seek to enable us to be happy, but the desire to become perfect, a Coleridgean idea, if you will, which we shall never achieve; we shall "die in the wilderness",[57] but, having recognized perfection, we can make a claim to progress and the "esteem of posterity".

What I have tried to indicate very schematically in this chapter expands upon Foucault's remarks quoted at the beginning of the chapter in an English context. "Law itself is . . . part of a much more general history of the techniques of ordering". Norbert Elias long ago reminded us of the utmost significance of the "civilizing process", internally to Europe.[58] (It was not to stop the slaughter of non-Europeans, Armenians, Jews and Roma, but perhaps it led to the eventual recognition of the unacceptability of this. In 1946, it was more possible for people in the "west" to believe this than now, but unsafe to be convinced of it.)

I have looked at the non-mutually exclusive social techniques adopted by successive British governments for the production and maintenance of order in an empire that, in practice, saw "natives" everywhere. I have characterized these techniques as, on the one hand "cultural", whether in the form of compromise and convention, or attempted assimilation. And on the other hand, I have noted a reversion that psycho-analysts might, in relation to an individual analysand, term compulsive-obsessive, or repetition compulsion[59] to insistences on political sovereignty as embodied in a particular approach to legality and its attributes. Neither is self-explanatory, and needs to be set in context, which is what I tried to do in referring the anxieties that seems to have led to the necessity for a sudden imagining of the Atlantic empire as a unitary state under Westminster in the 1760s. It is important, whilst schematizing, not to oversimplify. Even law-and-order Tories like Castlereagh and Wellington had looked with some distaste and not a little superiority at the doctrines of their former allies in the French wars, the "Holy Alliance" of the Czar and the emperors of Prussia and Austria. Stephen, in a sense a reformer, based on his observations of unreformed social conditions in London, was appalled by the popular response to a brutal reactionary like Haynau, who helped repress the moderate reformers in Europe in 1848. A paradox.[60]

The situation is complicated by the authoritarian positions taken by advocates of cultural assimilationism in the nineteenth century, by the Gradgrinds of

56 Lipman, *op cit*, n 41, 86 *et seq*.

57 Arnold, *op cit*, n 55, 41.

58 Norbert Elias, *The History of Manners*, Oxford, Blackwell (1982); Norbert Elias, *The Civilizing Process: State Formation and Civilization* (1978), Oxford, Blackwell.

59 J Laplanche and J-B Pontalis, *The Language of Psychoanalysis*, New York, NY, Norton (1973), 78, 281.

60 RJ Evans, *The Victorian Age 1815–1914*, London, Arnold (1948), 132.

Dickensian fiction or the Robert Lowes of parliamentary politics, as well as the more liberal positions of Coleridge or Arnold. But I still wish to stress the important differences between the social theories that follow a path traced by Bentham, Austin, Stephen and their successors, and those of the paternalist reformers, sometimes compatible, sometimes not, such as Leavis and the educational and welfare reformers like Beveridge, Butler, Keynes and others. The reason of my argument is, I hope clearer now that I have considered the implications, especially of a legal pedagogy that worships at the altar of the meta-sovereign. This is the office, or the figure whom some theorists have identified as the inevitable body who stands beyond the law and decides upon its boundaries and the terrain of the exception, where it does not apply by virtue of the very authority of the power it confers upon the sovereign that decides its limits. The work of the English, the Scots and the Americans, I have argued, following Hannah Arendt's work, demonstrates that He (and Hobbes' "mortall god" is very much positioned as a He, as Stephen recognizes) is dispensable in the production of order, and produces, contrary to Hobbesian hopes, a murderously, ultimately suicidal, potential for humanity. To ignore the dangers of a political formation that aspires to world leadership by virtue of its having the ultimate answer, the plan for a utopia, is a fatal mistake. My message is that, of course, some order must be imposed, but plurally, transiently and tolerantly. I will continue with the argument that, at least for Anglophones, the cultural analysis of authority avoids many of the dangers inspired by legal positivist obsessions with sovereignty, which I have associated, in the Anglophone world and doubtless wider, with empire.

The frequently-expressed view of Victorian conservatives and rulers was that the alternative to strong sovereignty and firm government was most likely to be anarchy, something proceeding from unrealistic, even utopic notions of human nature. Laws, according to conservatives, would be unnecessary were humans spontaneously good and capable of peaceful sociability without supervision. Since we can see the necessity of laws, we must conclude that human nature is not spontaneously perfect. There were writers, on the other hand who, far from utopic, and for whom the alternative to conceiving a social community's political dimension as being a matter of rules, rules requiring, forbidding or enabling, originating from, and implying an ultimately meta-legal source, is not an optimistic belief in human perfectibility and eventual consensus and unity, but rather something like Jefferson's "agreement of the people", the mutual giving of government to each other, as happened, I mentioned, among the ruling classes of the Revolutionary era in England in 1688 and was subsequently maintained with a good deal of hard work, not least by the Scots after the Union of 1707. See, for example, those mentioned in Chapter 3. Consensus and unity, actually, carry the sinister overtones of "*ein Reich, ein volk, ein Fuehrer*" of the Nazi era, or its Stalinist manifestation in the cult of the leader.

Mutual respect and restraint, which as Locke wrote, has to be learned, is something different from rule-making and rule-following. South Africa, post-apartheid has provided a good example of this point, not of consensus, certainly, but agreement politics. Israel/Palestine and Zimbabwe have not. On the day on which I first wrote this, 13 February 2008, Australia, under its new federal government, took a major step of agreement and inclusion, apologizing to indigenous Australians for the whites' long and barbarous practice of taking fair-skinned Aboriginal children from their parents, for adoption by Europeans or into institutional care, to be trained for cheap domestic servitude. There may be regret that more has not been done, but, as the old saw has it, every journey, however long, begins with a first step.

Education cannot be relied upon to trickle downwards in an entirely predictable manner, domestically any more than in an overseas imperial context. Yet social policing, as Donajgrodzki uses the term[61] in its broad Scottish sense of learning one's rights, duties and position anent the polis – Coleridge, we have seen, although he did not use the term "police", had this similar idea in mind – involved education. Of course, Coleridge had assimilationist intentions, although not as unalloyedly as those obvious in Macaulay's Minute to the Supreme Council of India of 1835, noted earlier. Natives capable of fluency in the culture of their rulers would in the short run be more loyal and might in the long run aspire to participation in their own rule, but, as we have seen, they were able to use their new skills in ways not intended by those who made them available.

The intention of policing in the wider sense, as Donajgrodzki's text demonstrates, was social control. As with social control through immiseration, coercion, or threatened coercion by means of rules, social control through education does risk getting out of control. The successful operation of a system of law which – in the British domestic case, at least – claims to offer equality of treatment to all of its subjects, requires an educated population, if one follows the reasoning of the Scottish Kirk, which sought to dispense with the minister as the gatekeeper to biblical knowledge. If the legal boat is to float, in other words, it needs first an educational pond, however small, in which to do so; but the nature of the pond is always likely to be contested, and it is this contest that legal positivism, with its sovereign and its need for finality, seeks to preempt. Traditionally, the English populace had been aware of customary entitlements, as we know from the works of EP Thompson, Brewer and Styles and others,[62] and well able to negotiate. But, as Thompson and Harold Perkin indicate, the system of local negotiation and local knowledges were under pressure from increased urbanization and the formalism it brought in its wake.

61 AP Donajgrodzki (ed), *Social Control in Nineteenth Century Britain*, London, Croom Helm (1977). Also, Richard Johnson, Educating the Educators: "Experts" and the State 1833–9, in Donajgrodzki, *ibid*.

62 See, for example, EP Thompson, *Customs in Common*, London, Merlin (1991), chs IV and V; John Bohstedt, *Riots and Community Politics in England and Wales 1790–1810*, Cambridge, MA, Harvard University Press (1983); Harold Perkin, *The Structured Crowd*, Brighton, Harvester Press (1983); John Brewer and John Styles, *An Ungovernable People: The English and their Law in the Seventeenth Century*, New Brunswick, NJ, Rutgers University Press (1980).

Pressure for more formal education for the working classes existed from at least the time of Lord Brougham in the early nineteenth century. It was slow in coming, as Arnold's complaints in the 1860s demonstrate, partly because class politics remained unsettled. As FB Smith remarks, the Reform Act of 1832 had not significantly empowered the middle class.[63] Wahrman writes:

> . . . whether historians stress continuity or change, there seems to be overall agreement . . . that the (1832 Reform) Act did not hand over power to the middle classes because it was not intended to.[64]

Perkin quoted Matthew Arnold acknowledging as late as 1879, that "the government is composed of a string of aristocratical persons, with one or two men from the professional class who are engaged with them".[65] It was not what he had recommended, and the situation still left open the possible continuation of rampant Philistinism and the failure of middle class capacities to spread "sweetness and light". Or, if middle class tutelage, mediated by Arnold's "alien", detached, intellectuals failed, there remained the possibility that learning might lead in unexpected directions.

Until the rise of Chartism, it was not all clear that "commercial men", particularly of the "lower" kind, and especially outside London, would not identify with "the populace" and undermine or threaten the educated elite whom Gladstone and others were anxious to associate with such of the aristocracy as were progressive and politically active. Mining, agriculture, railways and urban development, as well as banking, insurance and shipping were all highly profitable, enabling this class configuration to dominate, so far, parliamentary politics. But just as there was insecurity about empire at a time when it seemed to be flourishing, so there was a concern about the security of the ruling classes, especially if confronted by an articulate opposition from below.

William Lovett and John Collins demonstrate that many of the Chartists assume an identity of the working and middle classes in providing themselves both with a "just and liberal system of education, lest the power of educating their children be taken from them by the arbitrary act of a corrupt and exclusive government".[66] Their motive is clear: a liberal education would underlie radical alterations to the constitution, ultimately to the universal suffrage of an enlightened population. The process had, in their view, already begun, the two Chartists wrote in 1840:

63 FB Smith, *The Making of the Second Reform Bill*, Melbourne, Melbourne University Press (1966); AN Wilson, *The Victorians*, London, Arrow Books (2002), 39; Perry Anderson, *English Questions*, London, Verso (1992), 145.

64 Dror Wahrman, *Imagining the Middle Class: The Political Representation of the Middle Class in England 1780–1840*, Cambridge, Cambridge University Press (1995), 331.

65 Harold Perkin, *The Origins of Modern English Society 1780–1880*, London, Routledge & Kegan Paul (1969).

66 William Lovett and John Collins, Chartism: A New Organization of the People 1840, in Antoinette Burton (ed), *Politics and Empire in Victorian Britain*, London, Palgrave (2001), 55.

> It would be well if those who taunt the industrious classes with their "political ignorance" had first reviewed their struggles during the last ten or twelve years. If they had considered their efforts to establish the rights of free discussion, to open mechanics institutes, establish reading rooms and libraries, forming working men's associations and others of alike character, and above all, their sufferings and difficulties in establishing a cheap press by which millions of cheap periodicals are weekly diffusing the enlightened influences through the empire; and then if those scoffers at the ignorance of the millions had considered their present efforts to obtain their rights, we think they would have reserved their taunts for others than the working class.[67]

There was here a clear challenge to the views of education held by the governing classes, to Brougham, Macaulay, Mill, Arnold and later members of the country's intellectual elite. There was, in modern terms a "culture war". Lovett, according to Lloyd and Thomas was important not only as Chartism's "foremost . . . theoretician of education" but as the foremost representative of the view that apparent membership of the polity through the vote was not the primary education required, but that a good, free education was the basis on which real and effective membership of the polity rested.[68] The "elite" response, from men like Brougham and Kay-Shuttleworth, was that education was, for the employer, "analogous to the use of profit to ensure against capital loss". It entailed "teaching the poor man his political position in society and the moral and religious duties attendant on it".[69] Capitalism required something like the existing configuration of cultural relations.

"True education" *pace* Lovett, *et al*, according to Brougham and Kay-Shuttleworth, could not be judged as appropriate or not by working class men or artisans. The latter, and most certainly the former, were "decadent" and unruly. For Gladstone and for Benjamin Jowett, the task in hand was to link firmly together the intellectual and professional elites with Britain's traditional rulers. The motivation was derived from considerations of social control of the masses, or, populace, especially if many of them looked like acquiring the vote. They must be "civilized", like the natives in the empire outside Britain. But in a highly de-centralized country, which was certainly not one nation, but four, with an exceedingly politically engaged working class, provincial police under elected watch committees, and law monitored by amateur gentlemen justices of the peace, social control by rules was never going to achieve the goals for which the "experts" hoped; and there were rebels for whom education was destined to become a force for change, among subjects and for the polity as a whole.

Brougham's and Kay-Shuttleworth's difference from Matthew Arnold, what made him more far-sighted in the social control enterprise, whether he intended to

67 Antoinette Burton (ed), *Politics and Empire in Victorian Britain*, London, Palgrave (2001), 56.
68 David Lloyd and Paul Thomas, *Culture and the State*, London, Routledge (1998).
69 Lloyd, *ibid*, 99, the latter being a quotation from Kay's Minutes on education.

be or not, is that he anticipated considerable future change which would require a wider group of pedagogic governors than envisaged by those elite writers and politicians we have discussed in this chapter. Most of them foresaw and dreaded a much wider suffrage than even the 1867 Reform Act delivered, for the reasons articulated by Macaulay – and one finds it reflected in Dickens' portrayal of the demagogic and deceitful union leader in *Hard Times*, a novel which, of course preceded the Act. There is some truth in it, as I shall conclude the present chapter by suggesting, but it does not confute Lovett's ambitions for a critical, working class, education. The difference between the reformer and the utilitarian is this; that an ignorant and discontented population possessing the vote may well be swayed by self-interested demagoguery into the destruction of themselves and others. Lovett's conviction was that some part at least, of the working class had "improved" themselves by their own efforts, and could continue to with state assistance, continue to improve themselves in terms of knowledge, judgment and order. Lovett and others were seeking an educational route to equality for the working class, beyond the anarchic dangers threatened by demagogues.

But we must not misunderstand Arnold. He is not seeking equality, only harmony among the classes, a re-constituted order in which learning would have a central function in smoothing social relations, allowing each to accept his or her place. As Baldick writes:

> Arnold and many of the theorists of adult education had looked to the study of English literature as an agent of social harmony, capable of binding class to class; and this social project molded the forms of literary education as they applied variously to the teaching of workers, school-children, women and Indians.[70]

As an inspector of government schools, enduring exhausting railway journeys around the country, Arnold was familiar with the pupils, teachers and the approach to instruction that dominated current middle class thinking about early education.[71] He appreciated, as others did not, that more than a conjunction of the intellectual and professional elites with traditional rulers would do to maintain order. We have noted his disdain for the upper classes of his era. "He shuddered", Dover Wilson wrote:

> as he noted how uncivilized the (middle class) English were, lacking in the foundations of culture, self-satisfied and provincial, how utterly unprepared for the readjustment which the time demanded.[72]

70 Baldick, *op cit*, n 50, 82. The conjunction of recipients of this wisdom is, of course routine and entirely predictable.

71 John Dover Wilson, Introduction, in John Dover Wilson (ed), *Matthew Arnold: Culture and Anarchy*, Cambridge, Cambridge University Press (1932), xv.

72 Dover Wilson, *ibid*, xvii.

The middle classes had a crucial role in Arnold's obsessions about order and stability, about "sweetness and light", Wilson notes, in "urging an organized system of secondary schools", and no other class would be able to accomplish it; yet, first, they required some enlightenment themselves.

Not only did the existing British constitution – in Arnold's words, "a colossal machine for the manufacture of philistines"[73] – xenophobically exclude other subjects of British rule from its commitment to allowing the Englishman to do what he likes, but it withheld from the uneducated subject the capacity of sound judgment, even the aspiration to achieve the best, the "sweetness and light" available to mankind.[74] How was this to be avoided for the future? Some years after *Culture and Anarchy* (1869), having written of his doubt there that those Philistines, the middle classes, wanted nothing for their children but the trades schools which would reproduce their banal selves, he writes that "the middle classes have the right, in admitting the action of government, to make the condition that this government shall be one of their adoption, one that they can trust. To do this is now in their power".[75] To whom should they refer in order to exercise this power wisely? He has already given the answer: someone, the critic, not their enemy "but someone absolutely independent of them". In an echo of Kant's and Coleridge's work, for Arnold, the critic must "by remaining collected and refusing to lend himself to the point of view of the practical man . . . do the practical man any service".[76] Only in this way can the middle classes be prepared to act as "the natural educators" of the working class, and fuse "'all the upper and middle classes into one powerful whole'".[77]

Arnold's is a program, at one level, a proposal of academic freedom of thought and expression, a necessary but independent component of the state, but also an important guide and word in the ear of the state, so Arnold believes. The critic is not a servant of policy agendas originated by another arm of the state, but itself a distanced and originating intellectual force. At the same time, as I have argued, Arnold is in the social control business, too. Arnold's belief in the possibility of a neutral critic, the position he sees himself as occupying, and urges others to emulate, derives from his conviction that knowledge is found rather than made. Objectivity is therefore possible, and the critic is wise to remain aside from the immediacy of the political fray. But by analogy with the state's duty, not only to reform the convicted criminal, but to imprison him in order to protect society:

> So, too, in schools, the state has another interest besides the encouragement of reading, writing and arithmetic – *the protection of society*. It has an interest in them so far as it keeps the children off the streets.[78]

73 Arnold, *op cit*, n 55, 26.
74 Lipman, *op cit*, n 41.
75 Arnold, *op cit*, n 54, 40.
76 Arnold, *op cit*, n 55, 20, 25.
77 Baldick, *op cit*, n 50, 34, quoting Arnold.
78 Baldick, *op cit*, n 50, quoting Arnold from 1862.

The critic, then, as an independent intellectual, provides an apparatus which may or may not be accepted, but acts as a kind of polar star. Rules, moral and legal, had a part to play, but to be effective in the end, they had to be accepted as part of a common culture, and it is in helping to provide this that the critic has his function. Arnold is here amplifying a theme that had informed various reports on colonial government, on beliefs circulating, as we have seen, even before Macaulay's Minute to the Supreme Council of India. An 1855 report had concluded that the moral integrity and liberty which characterized British rule in India had been spread with the replacement of cruel and superstitious native beliefs by the more humane and distanced values inherent in British culture. This is the idea, already current, and to characterize educational ideals in Britain for another century, that behind the rules, certainly behind the law, guiding the evolution of the constitution on which the law itself rests, is a cultural lodestar which it is the duty of the critic to discern.

In the immediacy of equipping the Indian civil servant for his role, and, as we shall see in a later context, enabling the grammar school master to teach and eventually the Leavisite English students to learn the cultural studies of his evolving heritage in Britain, to learn local languages and customs, was therefore not a necessity – in this case for the British administrators who formed the Indian Civil Service. There is something here which is perfectly consistent with the substitution of contempt for native traditions for an earlier admiration for sub-continental culture, which perhaps has a less harsh dimension when we find the priority of learning Englishness prescribed for the grammar school and the English department. Candidates for Indian Civil Service positions could, it was believed, learn enough of the language (and acceptable) customs, to communicate with those whom they were to govern, on the run, or, more properly, perhaps, *en voyage.* In 1884, the Indian Civil Service was arguing for a particular role for the traditional universities in England – Scottish universities were not mentioned. Charitably, this may have been because they were already proving themselves; less charitably, it may have been because Indian Civil Service mandarins were acutely aware of Scottish candidates' skills and aware of a need to awaken Oxbridge from those of its slumbers that remained.

The 1884 recommendation was that in view of the apparently "civilizing" effect of the spread of British culture in India and possible parallels in England, given the then-current classically-oriented nature of Oxford and Cambridge educations, English studies, including especially literature, should form an important part of higher education – as it had, of course, in the extension courses, the teachers' colleges and the mechanics' institutes. It echoed the words of the 1855 report:

> We think we can hardly be mistaken in believing that the introduction of that system (i.e. of a serious study of British culture and customs) will be an event scarcely less important for this country than to India . . . We are inclined to think that the examinations for situations in the Civil Service of the East India Company will be felt in every seat of learning throughout the realm.[79]

79 Baldick, *op cit*, n 50, 71.

Later writers would assert that the 1855 and 1884 Reports *were* indeed mistaken. Nineteenth century utilitarians were, of course, convinced of the Gradgrindian view of "useful" knowledge – "the facts", as opposed to the less certain, less measurable things with which unruly theory or less material progress than down-to-earth manufacturing might be concerned. Some twentieth century retrospectives demonstrate a surprising similarity with the Gradgrinds in their diagnosis of social and economic failure in Britain. One can cite at random Martin Weiner, Williams, Williams and Thomas, and Newton and Porter,[80] and a large number of others – I shall briefly consider Perry Anderson – who have commented on the industrial decline of the United Kingdom since the 1870s compared with Germany and the United States. The Treasury–City alliance and the emphasis on banking and finance have been blamed for the failure of manufacturing industry: massive overseas investment, rather than investment in modernization at home, with maintaining sterling at high levels, etc. The Treasury–City alliance is, of course, an alliance of humanities-educated gentlemen rather than the technocrats, the latter of whom, it is assumed, governed the "successful" states of Germany and the United States.

There may, of course, be other ways of looking at "success". British success, its global dominion after the American debacle, was one in which authoritarianism was, I have suggested, in the ascendant. German success can scarcely be separated from its association with the empire of Bismarck's construction and with Nazism, from whose legacy the country has, it seems to me, rather heroically liberated itself. But German authoritarianism grew not out of some ethnic propensity for evil, but, as Arendt has remarked, from a failure to encourage technical proficiency to reflect on its ethical dimension – Eichmann's "Pontius Pilate moment", his, as she puts it, inability to think. The machinery was all at once set in motion by a higher authority. And who could doubt, watching the iconic technocrat of the US war in Vietnam, Robert S McNamara, precisely, *thinking* about past events in Errol Morris's film, *Fog of War*, or witnessing the apparently easy submission of technical proficiency to buffoonery and greed in late twentieth and early twenty-first century US Middle Eastern foreign adventures, that success seems always to mean a price paid with a great deal of someone's blood. One holds one's breath that the European Union might give success a new meaning consistent with our quotidian lives.

In relation to the United Kingdom, Cain and Hopkins,[81] among others began an alternative historiography in which British leadership in manufacturing and the devastating empire it made possible, had always been a side-effect of City financial

80 Martin Weiner, *English Culture and the Decline in the Industrial Spirit 1850–1980*, Cambridge, Cambridge University Press (1981); Karel Williams, John Williams and Dennis Thomas, *Why Are the British Bad at Manufacturing?*, London, Routledge & Kegan Paul (1983); Scott Newton and Dilwyn Porter, *Modernization Frustrated: The Politics of Industrial Decline in Britain Since 1900*, London, Unwin Hyman (1988).

81 PJ Cain and AG Hopkins, *British Imperialism 1688–1990*, 2 vols, London, Longmans (1993).

power and the culture of the amateur and the humanities, a leadership bound to cede place to larger national economies as British capital created first an informal empire and then, with the agricultural downturns of the later nineteenth century and the Lloyd-George financial re-distributions to begin a welfare state in the twentieth, a decentered, international financial empire visible occasionally in tax havens and other manifestations, a post-modern empire *avant la letter*. Perhaps Hardt and Negri were a little late in discovering it. On this view, it is possible to characterize industrialization as the Victorian writers did, after Macaulay's firm belief in progress died with him, as a generator of disorder in which the working class gathered, like Indians in their crowded cities, and plotted politics or riots.

One solution to this danger was, rather than to dominate with coercive powers, to steer society in more genteel directions, gradually inducting more of the "respectable" working class into cultural examples to their less respectable counterparts. This was Arnold's aim; he was more impressed by Prussian *Kultur* than its technical education prowess, and this is the direction much writing took after him. As we shall see, to the criticisms of Weiner and others about the overwhelming and deleterious effects of Britain's commitment, above all, to the service economy, was added an apparent aversion in its educational apparatuses from the purely vocational, the, in his day, schools for grocers and commercial travelers, in ours, university departments devoted to the management of golf courses and hotels. Even to stress English rather than physics and chemistry, to stress "pure" rather than applied disciplines, seems yet, to some commentators, to have and to continue an effete gentility.

One danger to the status quo here, as we have noticed, is that antagonists are not always assimilated, however energetically their masters' logics are institutionally affirmed. Robert Lowe's ironic comment after the franchise extension of 1867, "we must educate our masters", might not achieve practical realization as a return to everyone's knowing their place. The tone of the remark suggests that Lowe himself, like Lord Derby, whose characterization of Disraeli's Reform Act as "a leap in the dark", summed up his unease about the inevitable, was uncertain. Lowe's proposed solution to the problem of the working class vote was, then, uncertainly, education. To confront working class organization by subverting its economic base and using state violence, was not ruled out, but until the twentieth century this was not generally seen as anything but a short term solution in Britain.

The British plan for the institutionalization of "culture" in Britain

If the Reform Act 1867, while conferring the vote on the more affluent, therefore presumably "respectable" working class, recent historians have insisted, did not significantly alter the political status quo, it nevertheless indicated a trend, and, to the traditional governors, the administrative grade of the civil service, with its links to the Treasury and the City, as well as the political aristocracy, a threat. The secret ballot was to come in 1872, and yet more of the working class was enfranchised in 1884. Coverture, whereby a wife's property became her husband's upon marriage, was dealt a significant blow by the Married Woman's Property Acts of 1870 and 1882, and another by the abolition of the husband's right to demand that his wife return to him if she left, in 1884. Mill, whose views on the correctness of despotic, sovereign, British rule in India were reliably solid, had co-written, with Harriet Taylor, a feminist essay on marriage and divorce in 1832, Harriet published an article on votes for women in 1851, and JS Mill on the subjection of women in 1869.[82] Worse was to come, in the form, for example, of Indian men and even women, traveling to England to seek medical and legal educations, both having become available to Indians in India some time before, at least for men.[83]

The picture is, of course, a complicated one, as hegemony always is. Domination, through strong forms of sovereignty, as in India, is easier to explain, if in the final analysis, more difficult to maintain. Parliamentary elites were able to make common cause with "respectable" working men over the "protection" of women from heavy labor and long hours, in part because it removed from working men the competition of lower-paid female workers and delivered to them more certain free household services.[84] Feminists often, although not always[85] felt it necessary to demonstrate their political responsibility in Britain by supporting the imperial cause.[86] John MacKenzie makes the case that, for the most part, far from seeing their own lot as indicating a common cause with the overseas colonized, the British working class identified enthusiastically, he suggests, with the power suggested by the red painted across one fifth of the world and exotic spectacles like those of the Great Exhibition.[87] They were certainly not in favor, for other races, of what they sought for themselves, namely the vote and some say in the manner of their government. What the white working classes got, partly through the institutionalization of culture, was a subordinated position in a system of hegemony: what Indians had to make do with well into the Edwardian period, was largely what Guha has termed, "dominance without hegemony"[88] – although many of the quotations and examples above suggest considerable British hegemony among some Indians.

82 Alice Rossi (ed), *Essays in Sexual Equality: John Stuart Mill and Harriet Taylor Mill*, Chicago, IL, University of Chicago Press (1970).

83 Antoinette Burton, *At the Heart of Empire: Indians and the Colonial Encounter in Late Victorian Britain*, Berkeley, CA, University of California Press (1998).

84 Mary Lyndon Shanley, *Feminism, Marriage and the Law in Victorian England*, Princeton, NJ, Princeton University Press (1989), 99–102.

85 Kumari Jayawardena, *The White Woman's Other Burden: Western Women and South Asia During British Rule*, London, Routledge (1995) examines the role of reformers and anti-colonial western women during the nineteenth century.

86 Antoinette Burton, *Burdens of History: British Feminists, Indian Women and Imperial Culture 1865–1915*, Chapel Hill, NC, University of North Carolina Press (1994).

87 John MacKenzie, *Propaganda and Empire: The Manipulation of British Public Opinion 1880–1960*, Manchester, Manchester University Press (1984).

88 Ranajit Guha, *Domination without Hegemony: History and Power in Colonial India*, Cambridge, MA, Harvard University Press (1997).

Education became more institutionalized in Britain, in schools and university extension courses. School teachers, women and men, were drawn from necessarily increasing numbers of people who were not themselves educated in the manner of the elite, in classics. Nor, of course, was the university extension program aimed at the classically educated. If "extended", indeed, school education, was designed with the object of meeting what was seen as ordinary people's "need (of) political culture, instruction, that is to say, in what pertains to their relation to the state, to their duties as citizens", they also needed "to be impressed sentimentally by having the presentation in legend and history, of heroic and patriotic example, brought vividly and attractively before them".[89] The author, JC Collins, taught English literature. Thirty years before, in what one might regard as almost an aside to Macaulay's Indian Minute, teaching English was seen as making "vulgar minds" aware of their uncultivated state, "hobnailed", a clown "in a lady's boudoir".[90] Just as the Indian, who was to be made to understand that his entire literary heritage – of which many ordinary Indians were no doubt ignorant – was not worth a shelf of European rationality, so the domestic working class was to be made aware of its deficiencies. With an eye, perhaps, to the middle class, the upper reaches of which aspired to the two ancient English universities rather than the university colleges or the University of London, Benjamin Jowett, so adept at placing his students, *inter alia*, in the Indian Civil Service, oversaw the introduction of English into establishment English education at Oxford in the later Victorian years.

The educational, especially its cultural dimension, was undoubtedly xenophobic and reactionary to begin with. Xenophobic: by 1914, it was considered by many that the Germans had to be defeated in the academy as well as in the field, in part by replacing philology – an area in which George Elliot, in *Middlemarch*, had deployed the repugnant Casaubon to demonstrate the English woeful inferiority to the nineteenth century Germans – with English poetry, which Germans, because of the shape of the vocal cords their language demanded, were incapable of pronouncing correctly! Some panic was probably justified. The Germans and Austro-Hungarians had made war not only against most of Europe, but also against an enormous empire – the British – with a global naval supremacy not to be exceeded until the US Navy rapidly outgrew the Royal Navy after 1935, and incomparable resources and manpower. How had they succeeded to the extent that they had? One obvious solution was naturally overlooked: the South African war had not produced much evidence of British military genius in the field, despite of overwhelming military superiority. And, with the possible exception of General Edmund Allenby, the evidence of incompetence was repeated after 1914. And if Lloyd-George was a charismatic civilian leader, in World War I, he did not have Churchill's acumen and ruthlessness to dismiss high subordinates, civilian and

89 Baldick, *op cit*, n 50, 64, quoting JC Collins, an extension lecturer, in 1891.

90 Baldick, *op cit*, n 50, 66, quoting another extension lecturer from 1860.

military, until he found the ones most effective – oddly, since Churchill was the one responsible for the Dardanelles debacle in 1915.

Kitchener was no strategist, and Haig was a general generally consigned as someone of limited military ability, a man of "trade", in Joan Littlewood's grim stage satire of the war, somewhat mutilated in Attenborough's 1969 film of the same name.[91] But, no, the official line was that it was the quality of the people and the failure of the middle class to have provided them with education and effective leadership beforehand. Although some improvements had been made since Arnold's dire predictions about the lure of short-term practicality for the bourgeois, in 1868 and its likely consequences – the ignorance of the "populace", not enough had been accomplished:

> The most formidable institution we had to fight in Germany was not the arsenals of the Krupps or the yards in which they turned out their submarines, but the schools of Germany. They were our foremost competitors in business and our most terrible opponents in war. An educated man is a better worker, a more formidable warrior and a better citizen. That was only half-comprehended before the war.[92]

Reactionary, therefore: missions – an evocative, colonizers', term: McLintock has made us aware of the appeal and repulsion of the black whites of the northern working class[93] – had been sent to the East End and to the smoky northern cities. But there was a recollection, Wilson tells us of Arnold's observation prior to the 1866 Taunton Commission, that 2% of Prussian recruits were illiterate, compared with 54% of those recruited into the British army. Whether or not that made a difference to the course of the war, many luminaries thought it did. And they had another anxiety: Bolshevism in Russia and the formation of the British Communist Party. The solution – at least one of them: the English department, as recommended by the Newbolt Report, the result of one of several inquiries appointed by the UK government to answer questions about how to keep Britain, hence the empire, safe and pure.[94]

Wordsworth, the Report noted (it might have noted the similar observations of Locke and Adam Smith), had remarked that whilst scientists had for some time known that one cannot understand the world merely by uninstructed common sense. And whilst the teaching of science (the subject of another report) was vital, historians, poets and philosophers had much to teach the common man, and the Report felt able to give some cautious support for the greater political freedom which a knowledge of literature might confer. But I want to examine further the

91 Joan Littlewood, Oh, What A Lovely War.

92 David Lloyd-George in 1918, quoted in Baldick, *op cit*, n 50, 93.

93 Anne McLintock, *Imperial Leather: Race, Gender and Sexuality in the Imperial Contest*, New York, NY, Routledge (1995).

94 *The Teaching of English in England*, London, Her Majesty's Stationery Office (1919).

assertions anent the failure of the English subject, crafted in ways that I have described, to move into the modern world successfully by virtue of the retreat to the ethic of gentility, of Locke and Shaftesbury, of Hume and Smith, to the Whiggism of Burke. Although emanating from unimpeachably, admirably intellectual sources, it seems to me that the assertions have anti-intellectual implications. From Corelli Barnett on the right,[95] through the "decline" writers to whom reference has been made, to Perry Anderson on the left, a preoccupation with effete humanities appears to have corroded manly resolve in Britain, a resolve that would have ensured the success of ship-building and steel-making. The bourgeois "philistines" failed, for Arnold, because they so embodied businessman Bottles and could not rise above him to usher in sweetness, light and social harmony. Writers in the following century ticked off the bourgeoisie as failures for being insufficiently businessmen Bottles, so as to usher in muscular industry.

Social orders keep themselves together (or fail to) by imagining themselves in different ways and sometimes polemicists fail to notice the methods of their doing so, and the perhaps important differences. Nobody can doubt that the British Empire was a brutal affair, from its origins in land theft from first peoples and slavery, to its "post-colonial" creation of debt and financial exploitation. In its imaginary – and this is significant because it has guided imperial and more recently domestic policies, and it lies (sometimes in both senses of the term) deeply buried beneath, constituting and forming law and behavior. Locke and Shaftesbury and their contemporaries, we saw, aimed to create a world of tolerant gentlemen – this was the Englishness project, if we may so call it, furthered by others in the eighteenth century. Macaulay and Arnold in the nineteenth century began a project of incorporating colonial and working class subjects into that world. Mine is not, of course, an empirical inquiry. Whether Locke and Shaftesbury, Coleridge, Macaulay and Arnold, were "successful" is not unimportant, and I will essay a curate's egg sort of answer in my conclusion. For the present, the question relates to how those who exercised authority saw themselves, and how that influenced the directions in which they took their authority.

Since Hannah Arendt cautiously reasoned that the American legatees of Whig beliefs rescued Whig doctrines from Tory backsliding in the 1760s, it is interesting to compare the subsequent imaginaries of the two countries, while lacking space or time to investigate where these respective imaginaries have led. Critics of the United States have from the outset seen the "agreement of the people" as a sham. The new republic's democratic credentials were, in modern terms, shaky, if more firm than those of Great Britain and elsewhere.[96] Some critics of the (at the time of writing, current) Bush administration argue that they are still shaky, dependent

95 Corelli Barnett, *The Audit of War: The Illusion and Reality of Britain as a Great Nation*, London, Macmillan (1986).

96 Howard Zinn, *A People's History of the United States*, New York, NY, Harper and Row (1980); Howard Zinn, *Declarations of Independence: Cross-Examining American Ideology*, New York, Harper Collins (1990).

on corporate interests and leading a somewhat disenfranchised populace down a nationally disastrous foreign policy path.[97] Britain and Australia, of course followed the same path in invading Iraq. My point is, however, how, beneath the surface of the law – Bush, for example, is accused of not merely breaching international law, but the US constitution, and the same would have to be said of the United Kingdom (Australia does not have a constitution in the modern sense of entrenching citizen rights) – rulers imagined themselves, and successfully led those subjecting themselves by willing to share that imaginary. In Britain, the focus of my study, the proper subject was a gentleman. In the United States, the proper subject is a competent, assertive carrier of a particular manifest, that of popular democracy.

Two films make my point clear. In Michael Anderson's 1954 film, *Dam Busters*, about a RAF raid on a German industrial complex in World War II, the leader of 617 Squadron, Guy Gibson, played by Richard Todd, is a matter-of-fact, dog-loving hero, compassionate and concerned about his "chaps" and the honing of their skills. The scientist who developed the "bouncing bomb" unique to the task, Barnes Wallace, played by Michael Redgrave, is represented as an eccentric, inept at dealing with a skeptical Air Ministry bureaucracy. Asked why the RAF should allow him to use a Wellington bomber to experiment with his "bouncing bomb", he asks, diffidently, if it would help his request to mention that he had designed the Wellington bomber. This is how the Englishman of whom I have written was invited to imagine him or herself (Wallace's Home Counties family is an important component in the representation of the character) in the Lacanian mirror.

The 1986 film by Tony Scott, *Top Gun*, on the other hand, also about air war, is quite different. It is replete with video-game aerial battles and histrionic dialog from cardboard patriots. The heroes are callow technicians – an imaginary that tells us little about the inhabitants of the United States, but a little about how they are invited to see *them*selves. Their defenders are not of them. One film remembers a sentimental, mellow place from which the carnage of the Ruhr attack is planned, as a defense. The other invokes a commitment to technology, competition and self-assertion, including sexual self-assertion, as grounding values underneath the formal processes of law and order. My task was to examine the processes that enabled Anderson's *Dam Busters* to seem plausible. But it seemed appropriate to contrast the processes, which Arendt identified as beginning from a similar political place, into a very different narrative.

97 Chalmers Johnson, *Nemesis: The Last Days of the American Republic*, New York, NY, Henry Holt (2006).

Chapter 7

The "problem" of the English discipline and the rise and possible fall of legal positivism

Dispersing the culture of the rabble from the comforts of rule

The theme of Chapter 2, foreshadowed in Chapter 1, was that the rulers of England, faced with a series of crises, dangerously uncontrolled monarchs, bitter religious differences and powerful overseas enemies, had to construct authority out of consent. Sovereign authority – that of the Stuart monarchy – and colliding certainties – those of the Protestant sects that proliferated during the civil war period – were what had brought them to the brink of disaster, courting political disintegration and tyranny or possible foreign conquest, both last of which might have amounted to the same outcome. Civility, politeness and agreeable disagreement, I suggested, provided for some time a way out of the crisis. This, to a degree broke down less than a century later. Then, for more than a century the Benthamite, pedigree-view of law as merely the will of the sovereign rather than the bearer of a content, gained a great deal of persuasive power, in my argument. This was what literary theorists might term a shift to the authorial text, where meaning is restricted to what the writer intended (or what someone authorized *declares* the author to have intended). The alternative is a readerly text, where meaning is importantly connected with the context of its reception – the time, the place, the reader, etc. In 1763, the Seven Years' War produced global power for a Britain about to encounter class and eventually gender challenges within. It was the "*Annus Mirabilis*" of 1759, with victories seemingly everywhere, that, whatever the inclinations of Prime Minister Lord Chatham, persuaded his successors of British invincibility, convincing them soon after that they could not only crush the American rebellion in the 1770s, but simultaneously sustain a conflict with almost all of Europe. The lack of success here was, unfortunately, insufficient to discredit the authoritarian tendencies in government.

Despite what may have been the early reform intentions of the younger Pitt (Chatham's son, although a Tory), "(d)espite the humiliation of the Treaty of Versailles", the surrender to the colonies, "nothing better reveals the might of Britain" than "as Michel Besnier put it, she lost the war but immediately afterwards won the peace. She could in fact hardly fail to win, since she had all the trump cards".[1] Allowing for Braudel's exaggeration, there may be some truth in the assessment. But, if we are making connections between empire, the authoritarianism encouraged by it, and the drawbacks I have associated with lawyers' law, the conception of law without Burke's "grandeur", this development was not necessarily, as Sellar and Yeatman might have put it in *1066 and All That*, a good thing.[2] Nevertheless, the Eden Treaty of 1786 dictated the terms of trade for Europe and, despite his later embargo on the import of British goods to French-occupied Europe, it is said that Napoleon's troops marched into Russia with buttons made in Birmingham. Great Britain was, for internal purposes an empire in a new way at the end of the century.

I have emphasized, no doubt too starkly in order to make the point, that the externally aggressive state that emerged from the 1688 Revolution and the 1707 Act of Union was, compared with other European dynastic agglomerations (the United Provinces were another exception), internally unusual. As early as the 1640s, Colonel Rainsborough could celebrate his liberties and political equality with the conclusion that to doubt their (nevertheless contested) truth would be to doubt if one were English. The sentiment would be repeated in mid-eighteenth century America. White male Americans, at least, and no doubt many women, constructed themselves as "American" just as Englishmen seemed to have constructed themselves at quite an early date, as "English". It was not until very much later, according to Robb, that ordinary people in France developed a sense of Frenchness.[3] It matters less, of course, that there should have been a consensus than that it should have been an issue at all. Coke, Ireton, Lilburne and the members of the Convention Parliament would all have had different reasons to doubt whether the views expressed by another justified doubt about his (usually his) Englishness, but doubt of this kind was an important component in the formations of cultural and political identity, perhaps more in the Anglophone world at this time than elsewhere. The English subject in the Lacanian mirror was, naturally, multiple and contested, but it was, from the early seventeenth century imagined vigorously and with energetic collusion from the Scots and the Protestant Irish. The nineteenth and twentieth centuries were crucial to how the ambiguous inheritance of this past was to be received. One was, not coincidentally, I have suggested, the simultaneous authoritarianism and closure enacted by Jeremy Bentham and the Westminster sovereigntists of George III's ministries. The other legacy, in the 1750s denounced as effeminate, was the civility recommended by Locke and others, yet both remain like viruses which, once caught, remain in the body.

The subsequent tensions play out in unexpected fields, but with results that may in the twenty-first century, yield grounds for optimism. A strong commitment to

1 Fernand Braudel, *Civilization and Capitalism 15th–18th Century Vol III: The Perspective of the World*, London, Collins (1984), 179.

2 WC Sellar and RJ Yeatman, *1066 and All That*, London, Dent (1931).

3 Graham Robb, *The Discovery of France*, London, Picador (2007).

a polite politics, even, as many historians have shown, in riotous situations, may finally, strengthened by the connection with the new Europe, have civilized, or rendered shorter-lived the harsh "there is no alternative" of the Thatcher years. We shall encounter equally harsh opposition to "effete" culturalism from unexpected sources, but for the moment it will suffice to notice a recent commentator:

> It is no accident that Europe, one of the most powerful regions and certainly the most peaceful and prosperous in the world, comprises a community of states with a shared commitment to the European Convention on Human Rights . . . Both . . . Labour and the Conservatives are discussing the development of a British bill of rights to build on existing protections under the UK Human Rights Act and the EU Convention . . .[4]

The Victorian era in Britain is in some ways undecipherable largely, it seems to me, because its observers want answers which are, for our purposes, at least, unavailable. Strange alliances, no doubt unintended, emerge. For the Victorians, the question was one of how best to manage a bewilderingly polyglot population, not merely overseas, but also, as was recognized in a way it had not been earlier, at home. In a sense, indeed, people had suddenly become not at home, and the uncertain uncanniness generated by two waves of industrial and agricultural change and by associated demands for political change left large questions about order unanswered. The Victorians' solution was, as we saw, neatly embodied in Macaulay: education and legislation in no particular order. Repression, if left to men like Lord Liverpool (a humane man by reputation, but who acquiesced in the infamously repressive Six Acts of 1819 in response to the peaceful protests in favor of parliamentary reform in St Peter's Field, Manchester) or James Fitzjames Stephen with his famously reactionary views; educing the best a person could be, or "sweetness and light", for Coleridge and Arnold; or something banally in between for men like Robert Lowe, whose "revised code" of education, following the Royal Commission report of 1861, may deserve some comment.

I have written of both the "missionary" impulses of the middle classes in England and their parallel ambitions overseas, and of the autodidactic "improving" motives of the formally uneducated themselves, in the educational area. From before the time of John Bunyan, a contemporary of Lilburne's, in the seventeenth century, and from a mixture of motives in harsh conditions, men and sometimes women who regarded themselves as humble, energetically sought solace and understanding in their own critical grasp of what we might call high culture. Because of the influence of the Kirk on literacy and learning in Scotland it was, in my youth at least, common to find a Scottish mill-hand or collier who would quote

4 Phillip Lynch, *Melbourne Age*, 8 July 2008, "Australia should now become a human rights leader". It is worth noting that Lynch is not speaking of the human as the bare human, but in the context of the membership of intersecting but coordinated polities.

from Burns, or Scott's *The Lady of the Lake*. Children who left school at fourteen would know the dates and significance of Bannockburn and Flodden for the reflections, the imaginary of their identity as Scots as opposed to "English".

The autodidacts and the self-improvers who labored by candlelight after a day's heavy laboring elsewhere, aside (but not too much aside), it was the missionaries, as they saw their largely secular selves, and the ever-latitudinarian Christian socialists who stood in for the Kirk in England. We can find countless examples of unfortunate expressions. Is it really necessary to shame the hobnailed working man into politeness by comparing him to a clown in a boudoir? A glance at the letters of Lord Chesterfield to his son about clownish aristocrats whose behavior the son must avoid if Great Britain is to cohere reveal a similar (necessary?) cruelty. My own grammar school headmaster, explicitly renouncing any "missionary" role in favor of social work, writes, risking the patronizing tone of an institutionally accepted "improved" working class boy, but also reminiscently of Smith, holding the mirror up to the "English", that curiosity means the tolerance of uncertainty, resistance to the "insolence of office" that would instruct otherwise. He opens, and I quote him at length:

> The position of the grammar school in modern society is a crucial one. It stands at the meeting point of the elite and the popular cultures. Young men and women who wish for a higher education will normally pass through its sixth form. Increasing numbers of children, whose families have had no experience of the grammar school and little of the cultural standards which they will be expected to assimilate there, are crowding into its courses. Many of these come from that large area of society which is occupied by what used to be called lower middle and upper working classes, though it is doubtful if such terms are helpful under modern conditions, and it is certain that accurate descriptions of class characteristics becomes increasingly impossible. It is to children from homes like these that the school must transmit our cultural heritage . . .[5]

To return to Lowe: his legislation was almost exactly a century before the publication of Davies' book, and implemented the recommendations of the Newcastle Royal Commission's report on the education of the working class and the proper role of the government in that task. We know that he, along with the rest of the government, wanted cheapness. Whilst the debacle of the Crimean War in the 1850s had cost £78 million, an annual impost of £723,000 in educating the poor seemed to them outrageous. It had to be, and was, reduced. We can only speculate on Lowe's other political motives, although his fierce antagonism to democracy may provide a clue. Knowledgeable and articulate people denied participation in their society to would be troublemakers, as he learned from his

5 Harry Davies, *Culture and the Grammar School*, London, Routledge & Kegan Paul (1965), 2.

experience in the Assembly of New South Wales. Schools that were already government-funded were, of course to be made cheaper. The regime was to be one of cramming and regurgitation, not of comprehension or inquiry. Teachers were to be paid (and assessed) by managers according to the rote learning of children examined annually by inspectors. How important was it that the working class be discouraged or distracted from, in Arendt's sense, *thought*? Quite important, I believe. It is a mindset with which we are becoming, unfortunately, increasingly familiar in the present:

> Since getting as many children as possible to pass a mechanical examination of a mechanical knowledge of the three Rs was the government's main requirement from teachers, there was really very little need to ensure that they received a broad liberal education . . . there was little financial incentive to help the clever child realize his full capacities.[6]

Of course, as Rapple points out, Lowe's policy was mean-spirited and dismal. It applied a utilitarian logic that demonstrated that knowledge was potentially certain, applying Newtonian science to the universe and utilitarianism to social issues. The poor deserved their poverty, for the most part, because they were unintelligent. Lowe knew from Australia what chaos could result from the multitude's being given a political voice. In England, at least, there was certainty, threatened but saved from questioning. In a few decades, a great deal would change, no thanks to Lowe, but drawing on the inheritance of the Scots, and of Coleridge and Arnold. They were and are all, of course, criticized, which is precisely what they wished for and encouraged.

Legal positivism as a plan to institutionalize authoritarian culture

With the cultural phenomenon, legal positivism, and its gradual acceptance after Bentham's *Fragment* in 1776 and the Indian conquests, we are returned to the gravitational field of certainty, perhaps unsurprisingly. Victorian novels and law reports are replete with accounts of financial insecurity, fraud, bankruptcy and ruin. With Conan Doyle we can map the cultural oscillation perfectly.[7] Sherlock Holmes epitomizes the scientific pursuit of achievable certainty, in contrast to his bumbling foil, Watson, a medical doctor. Like Watson, Doyle was a medical doctor, no doubt as aware as his character of the uncertainties of diagnosis. Holmes

6 Brendan Rapple, Payment by Results: An Example of Assessment in Elementary Education from Nineteenth Century Britain, (1994) 2:1 *Education Policy Analysis Archives*, http://epaa.asu.edu/epaa/vol2n1.html. Matthew Arnold, The Twice-Revised Code, (1862) 65 *Fraser's Magazine* 347–65.

7 And see, of course, Walter Bagehot, *Physics and Politics* (1872), Boston, MA, Beacon Press (1956).

was, perhaps, a comfort. Doyle's later character, Professor Challenger, on the other hand, with his discovery of the earth as a living creature, and Doyle's own later spiritualism could have provoked only contempt from the character, Holmes. For our purposes, then, the Victorian legacy repeats a phenomenon already encountered: a yearning for certainty, haunting the imaginary, but with the uneasy suspicion of its unattainability.

The demise of Absolutist government in Germany, Austria-Hungary and Russia after World War I, economic, social and national instabilities, the rise of totalitarian "solutions" to those problems and the response by mediocre politicians to continuing social disorder "at home", perhaps prolonged the life of constitutional and other dogmatisms.[8] "Government . . . by bores . . . by men who were barely equipped to deal with the two great issues of the time: poverty at home and the rise of fascism overseas",[9] coupled with World War II, delayed what I see as a return to something like the sentiment of liberal Whiggism in the late twentieth century with the maturing of the European Union. This return had to await the slow revolution – in the non-millenarian 1688 sense; a return to the past, or, better, to the past as it might have been – generated by Britain's very gradual association with the new, postwar Europe, the domestic adoption of the European Bill of Rights and the resurgence of the common law. The priority of defending an obsolete imperial order at home and overseas was until recently reflected in governments' and theorists' approaches to law.

I remarked earlier on Arendt's distinction between the American and French revolutions. The balance of powers in the new American Constitution, designedly an improvement of the "balanced" constitution of early eighteenth century Whig Britain, she contrasts with the French substitution, some decades later, of the general will for Bourbon Absolutism, leading the way to Robespierre, the Terror and Napoleon. The Whig constitution, resolved in the years following the English revolution was, I suggested, under threat during the emergencies, real or imagined, at the turn of the nineteenth century, when the example of how to govern India, as the British saw it, seemed a useful one for governing the unruly at home. Because

8 Several cultural uncertainties or contradictions seemed to converge, though whether they were widely noticed is hard to determine. The British Empire expanded to include territories mandated by the League of Nations, whilst British political and economic power had been severely undermined in preceding decades. Its obvious successor, the United States, was reluctant to fill the increasingly evident vacuum. In science, the demonstrations by Godel and Heisenberg that, in perceptions of the universe, there were logically unbreachable limits to theoretical certainty were the culmination of theoretical challenges to the certainties of physics: Einstein could not be accommodated in the Newtonian universe. The discovery of Brownian movement by a Scottish scientist in 1828 was little noticed, but had already suggested that the movement of particles, even pedestrians on a crowded pavement, cannot be predicted mathematically, *contra* LaPlace who, in the French Revolutionary years, contended that, with sufficient information one might predict the future with complete accuracy. See Jacob Bronowski, *The Common Sense of Science*, New York, NY, Vintage Books (1959).

9 AN Wilson, *After the Victorians*, London, Hutchinson (2005), 323.

the emergencies only intermittently went away, class and gender antagonism grumbling throughout the Victorian era and beyond, into the eras of world wars, the temptation to invoke, in Britain, the strong leadership deemed appropriate in the empire remained; and strong leaders are tempted to legislate before they negotiate, so AN Wilson writes in his sweeping histories of the Victorian and post-Victorian periods.[10]

Authoritarianism in Britain never approached the enormities of twentieth century European totalitarianisms, although, as I pointed out in Chapter 1, one government's oppressive behavior cannot be excused on the grounds of its killing fewer people than the government of somewhere else. At least, it seems to me pointless. And whilst "human (i.e. political) rights" curbs on British executive governments have become more practically effective under the influence of a reformed Europe and the devolution of much government from Westminster to Wales – more still to Scotland – the "war on terror" appears to have enhanced executive power in the United States. This has had predictable consequences: the "extraordinary rendition" of untried prisoners to foreign countries where they can be tortured with impunity, and the creation of an "Alsatia" like Guantanamo, a place belonging to, and run by the United States by reason of a treaty imposed upon Cuba, but in which no constitutional protection from torture is available. By a bare majority of the US Supreme Court, Guantanamo prisoners' rights to due process were recently affirmed, but the court now seems a feeble obstacle to executive power.[11] The executive branch of government in the United States, from Roosevelt through Bush Junior, has had aggregated to it enormous powers, whilst a resurgent common law in New Zealand and more so in the United Kingdom, seems prepared to challenge the executive in ways that were once familiar in the United States in the years of the Warren and Burger courts.

Obviously, my book is concerned with the vicissitudes of the English subject at the interstices of legality and empire – and I have assumed the temporally contingent nature of the last two, as well as the first. A brief glance at current events in the United States – the increasingly religiously-refracted understanding of the polity has been noted – is justified to reinforce the point about the effects of empire in strengthening the executive to the extent that it takes on the character of a sovereign where it may not, as in Arendt's assessment, have possessed it before. The powers assumed by Roosevelt in implementing the New Deal, condemned by conservatives as unconstitutional, can be seen as a benign response to a major economic catastrophe, even as necessary measures to avert more serious social disorder.

Looking at later events, however, some commentators have wondered to what extent the apparent closeness of corporate power speaking the language of

10 AN Wilson, *The Victorians*, London, Arrow Books (2002).

11 Suzanne Goldberg, Bush's sole triumph: a conservative Supreme Court for decades to come, *Guardian Weekly*, 4 July 2008; Philippe Sands, *Torture Team: Deception, Cruelty and the Compromise of Law*, London, Allen Lane (2008).

Protestant evangelism to government lends weight to executive claims to act almost unilaterally, to enable the United States to pursue what it sees as, not merely human, but as God's work.[12] But God's work is even more imbricated with this new empire than it was with the British. It seems clear that Bush the second's administration is seen in some circles, at least, as an imperial one. Blumenthal quotes a White House aide's explanation to Ron Suskind of the *New York Times Magazine.* Writes Suskind, "the aide said that guys like me were in 'what we call the reality-based community (believing) that solutions emerge from . . . judicious study of discernible reality'". But, the "faith-based school of political thought" meant that "that's not how the world really works any more. We're an empire now, and when we act we create our own reality".[13] A less sanguine view of empire was taken by one of Michael Moore's correspondents in the military, serving in Iraq. He begins by defining the role of the US military as upholding and defending the Constitution of the United States. But:

> This war has nothing to do with upholding and defending that constitution. The military is for defending the republic; it is not for overthrowing dictators, building "democracy" or making the world a better place for everyone else. While these may, at times, be noble goals, it cannot be the business of a free and democratic society, or else it will cease to be a republic and become an empire.[14]

Whilst US government officials were either defending the use of torture, redefining it to exclude conduct they endorsed, or withdrawing it to extra-jurisdictional sites, in Britain one finds among the judiciary statements that almost return us to the balanced constitution, a constitution which Arendt – correctly when she wrote it – the United States had drawn from and improved. According to Cooke, J, "some common law rights (such as that against torture) presumably lie so deep that even Parliament could not override them".[15] Turpin and Tomkins cite the English Master of the Rolls, Lord Woolf, arguing that judges might either find "an irrebuttable presumption" that Parliament could not have *intended* (a circumlocution to save yet avoid the Diceyan doctrine of parliamentary sovereignty) to ouster judicial review of its legislation, or they might assert that there were limits on parliamentary sovereignty. Legislative insistence upon its supremacy would quickly cause an irresistible political demand for an entrenched bill of rights. Macaulay, reflecting on the Reform Act 1832, had long before predicted

12 Sidney Blumenthal, *How Bush Rules: Chronicles of a Radical Regime*, Princeton, NJ, Princeton University Press (2006), 108–9.

13 Blumenthal, *ibid*, 17–18.

14 Quoted in Michael Moore, *Will They Ever Trust Us Again? Letters from a War Zone*, Melbourne, Penguin (2004), 12.

15 Cooke, J, as he then was, quoted in Colin Turpin and Adam Tomkins, *British Government and the Constitution*, 6th edn, Cambridge, Cambridge University Press (2007), 67.

that, whilst Parliament had, for some moments *been* the House of (some) people, the time would come when it would have more definitively to become so. His prescience about the role of the judiciary in the process was less acute, but that may reflect the poor and subservient or compliant caliber of most English judges throughout the nineteenth and twentieth centuries.

The doctrine of *stare decisis*[16] established a self imposed rule that the House of Lords could not reverse its earlier decisions. The sacrosanctity of parliamentary sovereignty and the Dickensian Judicature Act 1873–75 established so many tiers of juridical appeal that no ordinary mortal would live to travel it. The case on which *Bleak House*'s *Jarndyce v Jarndyce* was based was reputed to have taken more than a century to conclude. In the more enlightened late 1990s, under the influence of the European Union, judges in England seem to have found more connection with citizens. Lords Steyn and Hope of Craighead discovered simply the limitations on legislative supremacy, depending on an examination of the merits of its content, citing the consequences of the divided sovereignty implied by the Scotland Act 1998 and the incorporation, the same year, of the European Convention on Human Rights into law in Britain by the Human Rights Act 1998: "the English principle of the absolute sovereignty of Parliament . . . is being qualified"[17] – as, I suggested, it always was. We are, in a sense, nearly en route back to a landscape that would have been familiar in general terms to Burke: the constitution changes gradually according to the customs and expectations of its subjects. A proper understanding of law and a broader understanding of its content requires, in a sense, a return to Adam Smith's and Blackstone's concerns about broadening education in law.

Meanwhile, government by legislation that cannot be challenged in terms of its qualities required something like legal positivism to explain and justify it, to render wider, contextual issues of history and ethics peripheral. It also required the kind of subservient philosophy that reassures the Gradgrindian "facts" men and lends them respectability. Fortunately for a more humane view, like the medical professions who have rejected the proposition that patients are machines with symptoms in need of repair, lawyers have recognized that there is more to their subject than was dreamed of in their (hitherto) philosophy.

The central tenets of the erstwhile dominant, and by no means yet dead, legal positivism have become familiar during the course of this book. They are that it is the pedigree of the norm that determines whether it is a legitimate component of the legal system: did the rule originate with the sovereign, or was it promulgated under the delegation of the sovereign? In the empire – in particular in India – this was, as James Fitzjames Stephen put it, "the gospel of the law",[18] which,

16 See Rupert Cross, *Precedent in English Law*, 2nd edn, Oxford, Oxford University Press (1968).

17 Turpin and Tomkins, *op cit*, n 15, 67–72.

18 James Fitzjames Stephen, *Liberty, Equality, Fraternity*, Cambridge, Cambridge University Press (1967), 175.

significantly, it was the duty of the British to "teach" the natives. Politics, administration, the proper organization of government itself, depended for its coherence on the sovereignty of the Governor-General, later Viceroy, who, whilst nominally subject to control from the Queen-Empress or Parliament in London, was effectively seen as the basis of authority.

In its cultural dimension, legal positivism required and still requires, we have seen, a rigid distinction between the worlds of the moral and the legal. The standard justifications for this are, first, that (by the 1960s in the UK) many areas of predominantly, but not only, sexual morality were seen, in a phrase much used at the time, as not the law's business. This was the premise of the Wolfenden Committee report[19] which recommended that male homosexual acts committed in private should not be illegal, and nor should privately conducted acts of prostitution. The sovereign's place in the bedroom was properly to be a limited one, in the view of the Committee. In an apparently liberal era following Wolfenden, suicide ceased to be an offense and abortion ceased to be illegal, subject to certain conditions.

However, the detachment of legality from morality – hence the elevation of sovereignty in the understanding of law – was not unchallenged. Patrick Devlin, a Law Lord, published a defense of the position that law was and ought to be a custodian of public morals. His alarm that even the kind of mild liberty of private action supported by Hart and others could be a prelude to the breakdown of ordered rationality and the encouragement of anarchy, was prompted by his reading of Stephen's trenchant beliefs on the subject. Wherever one looks at that time, the empire gazed back.[20] Devlin was not, therefore, an opponent of the sovereignty doctrine, but rather of the view that what he took to be the moral sovereignty of his class – its aspirations at least – should form a part of the law. The man on the Clapham omnibus, the man in the jury-box, the man of some property (since there was a property qualification for jury service when Devlin wrote), could be appealed to as a distinctly male-gendered believer in such of his betters' morality that Devlin himself believed in. It was this comfortable moral deference to an imagined upper class that the Angry Young Men, the Australian Oz collective and the 1960s radicals responded to.[21] If "free love", one of the subversive elements of sixties radicalism, was the expected exploitation of

19 Report of the Committee on Homosexual Offences and Prostitution, Cmd 247, London, Her Majesty's Stationery Office (1957).

20 Called to the bar in 1929, when the empire was augmented by League of Nations mandates, Devlin's views seem to reflect those of the conventional Edwardian middle class.

21 One thinks of the somewhat pioneering rebel character of Jimmy Porter in John Osborne's 1956 play, *Look Back in Anger*. The editors of *Oz Magazine* were on appeal acquitted of a conspiracy to corrupt public morals in 1971. Their "Schoolkids' Issue", actually written by secondary school students featured a sexualized "Rupert Bare". See Tony Palmer, *The Trials of Oz*, Harmondsworth, Penguin (1971). The trial judge was shocked that such illustrations commonly circulated in school classrooms.

women, it stimulated feminism. The man on the Clapham omnibus is no longer hermaphrodite or governed in his thinking by homosocial priorities.

Stephen, writing in the 1860s, although a strict legal positivist, a proponent of Westminster sovereignty, "was convinced that the criminal court is a school of morality, the 'organ of the moral indignation of mankind'". (This was his inspiration for Devlin.) India was, for Fitzjames Stephen, the lesson for Britain: good codes of law based on European morals and firm but benevolent administration. In Britain was "being erected a tyrannical democracy which will change the whole face of society . . . destroy(ing) all that I love and respect in our institutions".[22] Liberty, on the other hand, we recall, was for Stephen, a "system which embodies . . . all the bitterness and resentment that can possibly be stored in the hearts of the most disappointed, envious and ferociously revengeful members of the human race" against those whom they regard as their oppressors.[23]

If it was the legislative will that private homosexual acts were within the law, although Devlin did not use this example, something like it was raised by a celebrated case a few years after Wolfenden: what about the flaunting of homosexual relations, its advocacy, for example, or men holding hands or kissing in public places?[24] Where was the line between law and morality in sexual matters to be drawn? And where if the line could not be drawn here, was the boundary between efficient administration and the apocalypse to be defended?

Devlin was no doubt encouraged in a minor key to a questioning of the possibility of drawing firm lines between law and morality by a perhaps unforeseen loophole in the Street Offences Act 1959, which restricted the illegality of prostitution, like that of male homosexuality, to its public manifestation – if that could be defined; in the case of prostitution, in the form of public solicitation of clients by sex workers. In the case of *Shaw v DPP*,[25] no women approaching men on the street offering sexual services were involved. However, Shaw had produced a publication detailing the private services that were available from identifiable women, *The Ladies' Directory*. Prosecutors, as they sometimes will, resorted to the doctrine that a conspiracy to commit a lawful act can, if needs must, be a criminal offense. We are familiar with this from the famous incident of the Tolpuddle martyrs in the 1830s, where, although trade unions themselves were legal, the necessary steps of forming the union in question – affirming loyalty, etc – were deemed a criminal conspiracy, since they derogated from the legal subject's primary oath of allegiance to the Crown.

22 James Colaiaco, *James Fitzjames Stephen and the Crisis of Victorian Thought*, London, Macmillan (1983), ch 9.

23 Stephen, *op cit*, n 18, 175; Patrick Devlin, *The Enforcement of Morals*, Oxford, Oxford University Press (1965), ch VII.

24 Devlin, *ibid*.

25 (1962) AC 223.

The House of Lords in *Shaw*, in nostalgic mood, found in the eighteenth century authority for the view that the royal courts had a duty to preserve public morality, to prohibit whatever was *contra bonos mores et decorum*,[26] and they convicted Shaw of, among other things, a conspiracy to corrupt public morals. But 1960s Britain was, as we have seen, the age of satire, and the Edwardian-flavor of the prosecution in the Lady Chatterley trial had little chance of being persuasive.[27]

There are some curious epicycles which there is no space to pursue here beyond noticing them. For example, Coke's quarrel with James I involved the assertion, or, as Coke would have it, the *re*assertion of the existence of a public sphere: if the king was subject to the law, there must exist a political regime apart from the dynasty and the royal will. In the eighteenth and nineteenth centuries, rioters, parliamentary reformers and trades unionists insisted that there were legitimate collectivities, call them, if you will, civil society, outside this designated public sphere – a sphere asserted by the political classes as legal sovereignty – that the reformers, trades unionists and others, suspected was actually a mask for the advancement of private interests. In an age of civil liberty now, perhaps, endangered, diminished in some parts of the Anglophone world, slowly growing in others, Hart and his colleagues articulated a general feeling that beyond the public and beyond the collective organization of civil society, there was a personal sphere in which activities, however disapproved of by others, should not be subject to scrutiny.

However, there is another element in the narrative of the law/morals separation if one thinks of the distinction made by Hart between pre-legal, or primitive normative orders and those with more sophistication. Legal systems have three levels of operation. First, those who "recognize" rules as legal rather than rules of another kind – somewhat mystically since, as we have seen, they are private persons prior to any regime that permits a public/private distinction, and officials prior to the possibility of any criteria of officialdom. They are, of course, the Viceroy and the Indian Civil Service, together with the merchants who control the economy using the codes. Second, there are legislatures and councils whose job it is to direct change. Third, those who function to enforce the norms legitimated at the other two levels.

The apparatus operates in a way analogously to the indigenous land rights issue in Australia in two ways. The colonizers did not have to pretend that human life did not exist on the continent, since there was indisputable evidence of it. They simply noted its "primitive" nature: no princes or kings; no legislatures or other agencies of deliberate change to the law as it was traced back to the absurd myths of the Dreamtime – in no way comparable, in whites' view, to the redemption religions of the Mediterranean littoral; no bureaucracies. But after massive land theft came the moral outrage of the Australian High Court decision of 1992, *Mabo*

26 HLA Hart, *Law, Liberty, and Morality* (1963), Oxford, Oxford University Press, (1968), 7.

27 CH Rolph, *The Trial of Lady Chatterley: R. v Penguin Books*, Harmondsworth, Penguin (1961).

v Queensland,[28] which has all the tragi-comedy of a popular greetings card of the 1980s, depicting a mid-forties woman, her hand to her mouth, exclaiming, "Oh God, I forgot to have a baby". When there was so much evidence of relationship to land among Aboriginal people, so much respect for each nation's attachment to country and the need to seek permission to cross another's country, could the common law courts have "forgotten" about it? Oh God, yes.

The answer lawyers once seemed satisfied with was, in effect, indeed, "yes", but that was then. But when it remembered – and the courts did not remember for very long, if we think of the endless refusals to recognize, in the present, indigenous claims to a continuous connection with their land, as required by the colonists' law – *how* did it remember? It remembered by assimilation: the unfortunately-termed "native" title, which predated white arrivals by, at a conservative estimate 40 millennia, does not exist unless "recognized", a term so endearing to Hart and Hart scholars, by white officials – which means, not often.[29] In the same way, morality makes its feeble and primitive way through Hart's texts. It is a "soft" critical force, like land rights, negotiating its steps and relying on the "hard" realism of law for its existence. Courts may be executors of morality for writers and judges like Stephen, but the only morality "recognized" is that which enforces nature's orderings, men clearly superior to women, the middle class to others, and Europeans to "natives"; it is through this "gospel of law", the English gift to the colonies, that these hierarchies are made manifest and, crucially, enforced. Liberty, the aporia of law, was, as we have seen, to conservatives such as Stephen, a bitter slogan threatening death to the wealthy.

So, having examined the earlier, Whig, assumptions, what is the nature of the common law and the constitution which the legal positivists are so anxious to assert? The somewhat if inadvertent teleology one finds in nineteenth century historians like Maitland,[30] that central, royal, common law was always coming – an incipiently unified, logically coherent system within which, though dispute took place, resolution could be asserted through the application of its institutional authority – has been neatly undermined by Milsom,[31] who points out that, unlike early Roman Law, Common and local court records have been meticulously preserved, although his own central preoccupation was with the growth of royal law. From the records, we discover that, far from being procedurally and formally

28 *Mabo v Queensland (No 2)* (1992) 175 CLR 1.

29 An early doctrinal account is Richard Bartlett, *Native Title in Australia*, Melbourne, Butterworths (2000).

30 Sir F Pollock and FW Maitland, *The History of English Law Before the Time of Edward I*, 2 vols, Cambridge, Cambridge University Press (1895). There is a partial defense of Maitland's approach in Norman Cantor, *Inventing the Middle Ages: The Lives, Works and Ideas of the Great Medievalists of the Twentieth Century*, New York, NY, William Morrow (1992), ch 2.

31 SFC Milsom, *Historical Foundations of the Common Law*, 2nd edn, London, Butterworths (1981), Preface and Introduction; more recently, SFC Milsom, *A Natural History of the Common Law*, New York, NY, Columbia University Press (2003).

ordered apparatuses tending to centralized regulation, courts at all levels began as administrative centers in which those within the jurisdiction were technically bound to attend and attest to the local customs to which the reeve (the lord's reeve, or, in the case of royal courts, the Shire Reeve or Sheriff).[32] It was the task of courts to establish and maintain the peace of the holder of jurisdiction. Courts of Requests to settle small claims, mostly debts were replaced under protest from small businesses by royal county courts in 1846, courts leet continued to "view the frankpledge" in places until 1922 and borough, hundred and mayoral courts persisted in London, Liverpool, Salford and Derby until well into the twentieth century. Local courts, then, and courts of specialized jurisdiction persisted in a confusing mosaic of conflict and contradiction until well beyond the nineteenth century.[33]

Legal positivism as the return of the Emperor

My argument in this book is that, far from being the modernizing, rationalizing cleansing, "discovery", which is how Bentham and later John Austin and the British governors of India represented it to be, the doctrine of sovereignty on which legal positivism depends so heavily in its description of law was actually, in British and imperial contexts at least, a relic resurrected from the preoccupations and illusions of an earlier time, from an era of struggle between centralized monarchy and the jurisdictional counterclaims derived from custom and embodying an obstacle to the formation of dynastic supremacy. The doctrine of strong internal sovereignty was a necessary vehicle for the direct subjection of populations to much larger-scale rulers than hitherto, bypassing the loyalty of those populations and often their principal obligations to pay taxes to local overlords. It was also a way in which monarchs like Louis XIV could imagine themselves and try, with mixed success to put their imaginary to symbolic use. The necessity for *this* was not merely an overweening personal ambition on the part of monarchs. Once one such dynastic absolutism had acquired the capacity to mobilize large quantities of money to pay comparatively large numbers of troops – and by the end of the 1490s, this was occurring, with Castilian Spain taking a leading role and others compelled to follow suit or be conquered. Each dynasty became a war machine.

The domination of this aspirational and only ever partially realized[34] model was not overthrown for centuries until the discovery by the political classes of the

32 See Alan Harding, *The Law Courts of Medieval England*, London, Allen and Unwin (1973); Robert Palmer, *The County Courts of Medieval England 1150–1350*, Princeton, NJ, Princeton University Press (1982), ch 3.

33 Harry Arthurs, *Administrative Justice and Legal Pluralism in Nineteenth Century England*, Toronto, University of Toronto Press (1985). And see Jeremy Webber, Legal Pluralism and Human Agency, (2006) 44 *Osgoode Hall Law Journal* 167–99.

34 As Braudel puts it, "the peasant community was in perpetual conflict with its oppressors: the state, the landlord, external circumstances, hard times, armed troops and anything that threatened or

secret of how to tax *themselves* (and it has to be said those whom they ruled) through the medium of a bureaucratic apparatus, known in England as the Revenue Service, now Revenue and Customs. This process, which amounts, not to receiving government from an "outside", but of giving government to oneself and each other, has profound implications for the imagining of government. It can imply, if does not by itself produce, democracy. But it was not a process which spread easily, if at all to the government of subject peoples. In the British case, the obvious example of this is India.

Certainty and the fears inspired by its always elusive nature, plays, to repeat, a central part in the evolution and operation of legal positivism in Britain, as with other positivisms elsewhere. As Yates writes, there is a long tradition in European thought which one finds in Kant's "unity of the manifold" of perception in the imperative of assuming the individual to be one rather, than, as Hume suggests, something of an accidental aggregation that may not entirely hang together. I suggested before, and it has been a theme of this thesis, that imperialist practices have always been an enemy of democracy, just as democracy must always be the enemy of imperialism, because they are the products of systems of thought that are quite at odds. Imperialism, the bringer of rationality to the native lost in superstition, is in the end the product of the quest for certainty and in its extreme form, finality and represents a symptom of a much wider insecurity among its practitioners that I have written about here and elsewhere.[35] There is nothing that is particularly new here, if we think of Frances Yates's comments, quoted earlier.[36] For the medievals, the ultimate certainty was to be found only in the City of God, a non-secular place, a place outside time. In the secular world, the world in time and thus, of course, subject to decay, the Christian church provided the route to eternity and considerable nostalgia seems to have been invested in its political agency, the post-Constantine Roman Empire.

Whatever the "reality" of classical and imperial Rome may have been – it was an agglomeration under a veneer of Roman citizenship, not a unified system; and it was far from consistently humane, de Ste Croix writes.[37] But whatever the nature of its geographical limits in global terms, classical and post-classical civilization was remembered in the medieval European world as a golden age encompassing the "known" world. It was the earthly apogee of humane and above all unified cultural achievement that, as we have seen, haunted the western imaginary and conceptually possible only within a unified political regime.[38] This imaginary

even impeded the village community that was the condition of its existence. And in peasant eyes, all these foes were combined", Fernand Braudel, *Civilization and Capitalism 15th–18th Century Vol II: The Wheels of Commerce*, London, Collins (1982), 495.

35 See Ian Duncanson, Sovereignty: Some Considerations, (2008) 12 *Law/Text/Culture* 129–53.

36 Frances Yates, *Astraea: The Imperial Theme in the Sixteenth Century*, Harmondsworth, Penguin (1975).

37 Geoffrey de Ste Croix, *Class Struggle in the Ancient Greek World*, London, Duckworth (1983).

38 See Peter Bondanalla, *The Eternal City: Roman Images in the Modern World*, Chapel Hill, NC, University of North Carolina Press (1987), chs 1–4.

connected with another contemporary but with hindsight, incompatible priority, as Perry Anderson and Marc Bloch have shown: Europe as a unity was a noble (or ignoble, bearing in mind its predatory ambitions toward the rest of the world, which were simply to grow) dream. On the other hand, given the primitive institutional infrastructures and the rivalries and ambitions of regional dynasts, some form of state or city-state seemed more practicable in each region. Communication, so vital in an imperial setting, was in decay; the bureaucratic and fiscal apparatuses so vital for the maintenance of the legions[39] and, much later, the sepoys of the British Raj, were in woeful disarray.[40]

And, to repeat earlier remarks in Chapter 1, just as Europe seemed to have resurrected itself as a western Roman Empire under Charlemagne in 800, it became a place first besieged by pagan Scandinavian Vikings and then by militant Islam, which penetrated surprising distances into Europe's "core" areas, the French coast and the Alps. Muslims, Magyars and Scandinavians seemed to demonstrate Europe's fragility. These threats were resisted by dilution – the Magyars were defeated at Lechfeld by Otto the Great in 955 and became Christian; the Scandinavians were converted in a variety of places to Christianity. Much of Europe outside Iberia avoided Islamic conquest. It is in this context that Berman writes of a second attempted revival of the myth of one-ness in the eleventh century attempt, associated with Pope Gregory, to create a church militant, a Christendom led by the Pope[41] and unified by both a Christianized Roman law and the ambition of driving back Islam and reclaiming the Christian (actually Jewish) Holy Land.

If a Christendom of a kind envisaged in the Gregorian reform project was never realized except in the attempted alliances of Absolutist dynasties, the purging of Jews and Muslims from Iberia by Ferdinand and Isabella in the 1490s, the early atrocities of the Conquistadores in America and the establishment of a legal canon of Roman-based ecclesiastical law began to establish not only the apparent possibility of new certainties anent the dramatic superiority of European arms and, as they saw it, European rationality. That most of the early basis for this rationality in classical civilization was made possible by the careful preservatory work of Muslim scholars was conveniently forgotten. The sting in the tail in this very early modern period is, of course, in the plural – namely certainties. Absolutism was not only about establishing the possibility of centralized taxation within boundaries, however contested and confused early frontiers might have been, and about creating the logistical possibility of full-time professional armies. It was also, I have

39 See Francesco Adorno *et al*, *The World of Renaissance Florence*, Firenze, Giunti Gruppo Editoriale (1999), 214.

40 Marc Bloch, *Feudal Society*, 2 vols, London, Routledge & Kegan Paul (1965), esp the summary in chs 1 and 2 of vol 1; Perry Anderson, *Passages From Antiquity to Feudalism*, London, New Left Books (1974), ch 2.

41 Harold Berman, *Law and Revolution: The Formation of the Western Legal Tradition*, Cambridge, MA, Harvard University Press (1983).

suggested, about post-feudal dynasts, who might subdue the baronies, the "over-mighty subjects" within their boundaries, yet not able subdue their neighboring dynasts. This failure might take religious as well as other forms – hence the thirty years' war and the other schisms that followed the publications of Luther, Calvin and others. In fact, since their writing, religion was a principal vector of conflict, and since Catholics and Protestants of various persuasions were all prepared to murder each other in the name of faith and to enlist the aid of secular rulers to this end, the certainty promised by Absolutism was a chaotic and unstable one.[42]

This is what Hobbes perceived and what frightened him. In a period of *sensus communis* which the one true church was meant to provide through the medium of the hierarchies of the priesthood, or, in one that replaced it, of Reason mediated by the *philosophes*, my disability from seeing your innermost thoughts may not be a problem. Although it always was – hence the endless medieval heresies, the Inquisition and the Protestant secession. During a time of dislocation, rational prudence dictates a new possibility, that in a new and unpredictable context of unshared values I have to accept that you may intend me harm. When the threat is embodied, as it must be, in a person or body of persons, what is invoked is the search for some kind of antidote to the Yeatsian "the center cannot hold", addressing as it does a supposed dichotomy in social life: order or anarchy; prosperous, if coerced, co-operation, or the impoverishing claim of all to all. The stress of uncertainty gives way to a yearning for a strong master, a father above and beyond the control of his children, to assume responsibility. And what, therefore, as Arendt was to write of Adolf Eichmann, renders one freer than a strong master?

There were two antidotes to this stress which the Scots suggested, the first of which I discussed in Chapter 2. This first is to be cheerfully comfortable with the ultimate incomprehensibility of the universe, but to accept that we have to live and make our way in it and thus make the best sense of it that we can, adjusting this sense when it seems appropriate. Smith's essay on astronomy, remarking that the "laws" used by scientists to understand the world will not be found *in* the world, may have been written in anticipation or after Cook's observations of the transit of Venus (it is undated and published posthumously) when changes to astronomic theory were contemplated. Hume, as might be expected, gave homelier examples and noted the folly of assuming that the stairs to our apartment disappeared with the closure of our study door, but noted that we cannot from our desk prove that they have not.

The second antidote to the stress of uncertainty is, of course, related very closely to the first. Hume's stairs, invisible through the closed door, may be as logically problematic as Hobbes' subjects' inability to see inside others' minds, but, for Hume, our lives must and may successfully "go on". To brood on logical suspicions that the unseen stairs may have vanished is unconstructive and unhelpful.

42 See Geoffrey Parker (ed), *The Thirty Years' War*, 2nd edn, London, Routledge (1997).

We must assume the stairs, until the moment at which we discover undeniably, like young Davie Balfour in Robert Louis Stevenson's *Kidnapped*, that they really *have* disappeared, give ourselves rules, government, trust, Jefferson's "agreement of the people", and abandon the illusory certainty of sovereignty and certainty. Hume's fear was in fact very different from that of Hobbes. It was precisely that Hobbes might, in a misguided quest for certainty, realize his wish. Hume, though personally more conservative than some of the American revolutionaries, believed that government and the validity of laws rested on human convention, nothing more, something which was necessarily precarious. To break that convention too easily was to risk the rise of a tyrant, outside the mutual gift of government and law.

Like Marjorie Grene,[43] we observed Stephen Toulmin remarking on the political implications of the tolerance of uncertainty and its opposite, the rationalists' grim pursuit of truth, which comes with the assurance that one has it or is at least on a better track to reach it than one's opponents. Such assurance provides the motivation, or at least the justification, for governing "native" peoples. He is worth quoting at a little length:

> To understand why the rationalist's . . . dream proved a dream, indeed, we may recall some maxims that capture the central contrasts. No formalism can interpret itself; no theory can exemplify itself; no system can validate itself; no formal language can predetermine its own meaning; no science can forecast just what technology will prove of human value. In facing problems about the use of new knowledge for human good, we may ignore the ideal of intellectual exactitude, with its idololization of geometrical proof and certainty. Instead we must try to recapture the practical modesty of the humanists, which let them live free of anxiety, despite uncertainty, ambiguity and pluralism.[44]

Maitland puts this sentiment in what we would now consider legal terms, whilst noticing that the thirteenth century men he is discussing did not draw sharp distinctions between the legal, the moral and the religious duties with which people operate. They had not, he writes "conceived that in every state there must be some man or . . . body of men above all law", and would have been deeply shocked by the idea had they done so. The monarch would quickly have embodied for them that horror of all later Whigs, the tyrant of Hobbesian dreams of common-wealth.[45] Hobbes may or may not have shocked later writers, as Maitland considered he had, as opposed to provoking resistance to ideas already familiar enough from, for

43 Marjorie Grene, *The Knower and the Known*, London, Faber and Faber (1966).

44 Stephen Toulmin, *Cosmopolis*, Chicago, IL, University of Chicago Press (1992), 105.

45 FW Maitland, *The Constitutional History of England* (HAL Fisher, ed), Cambridge, Cambridge University Press (1909), 101.

example, Bodin, but he was much inspired by the certainties of Euclidean geometry and the examples it offered to the proper understanding of social order.[46] The twentieth century proposition that in all fields of inquiry, the perspectives of the inquirer, even her/his presence, will inevitably affect the objects of inquiry, organic or inorganic, would not have appealed to Hobbes. The geometer familiar to Hobbes, stands beyond the object, applying universal tools of measurement. Of course: he is the sovereign, measuring the boundaries, in the end, from without.

Bentham's dream of the separation of law, religion and morality and of a sovereign above and beyond the society governed, was equally shocking to *his* contemporaries.[47] Why his ideas were not submerged in obscurity, as the language in which they were expressed invited, is that, unlike Hobbes' successors, the rulers of nineteenth century Britain were less self-confident. Like the empire, manufacturing industry grew, and with it British global dominance; but in both cases the attendant problems grew, too: Chartism and the workers' and later feminist movements, the New Zealand wars, the Indian Insurrection and the Morant Bay rebellion in Jamaica. Even the usually docile white Australians staged a small protest against officious policies on the Victorian goldfields at Eureka.

The keys to the preservation of the United Kingdom seemed to lie in divergent, but I will argue ultimately convergent, directions. We begin with a brief return to HLA Hart, whom we noticed earlier. His concept of law is notoriously incoherent, but the point here is not that his legal theory remains dominant among practicing office and court lawyers. Recent surveys of the area of jurisprudence, whilst healthily at odds, reveal that it is no longer so persuasive there.[48] The point, though, is that the thinking that inhabits *Concept* still dominates the language of legal practice and political commentary. And lambs still go to the slaughter. They are, proven guilty or not, certainly not tried, "rendered" in the US euphemism for sending people to regimes known routinely to torture whomever they are instructed to torture by the United States.

Hart and legal positivism as the savior of the authoritarians

Law's legitimacy, once we follow Fiztpatrick's dismissal of the ordinary language discussion with which *The Concept of Law* opens, rests, for the remainder of Hart's narrative, on the recognition of ultimate rules by "officials", although where

46 See Norberto Bobbio, *Thomas Hobbes and the Natural Law Tradition*, Chicago, IL, University of Chicago Press (1993), 90–91.

47 Gerald Postema, *Bentham and the Common Law Tradition*, Oxford, Oxford University Press (1986), chs 3 and 4.

48 Thus see, for example, Christopher Norris's entry on the Philosophy of Law, in Michael Payne (ed), *A Dictionary of Cultural and Critical Theory*, Oxford, Blackwell (1996); Peter Goodrich, Law, in William Outhwaite and Tom Bottomore (eds), *The Blackwell Dictionary of Twentieth Century Social Thought*, Oxford, Blackwell (1993), or the compilation Dennis Patterson, *A Companion to Philosophy of Law and Legal Theory*, Oxford, Blackwell (1996).

officialdom originates prior to legitimate law is not clear. The circularity *is* clear enough, as I have observed elsewhere. Its second leg of legitimacy rests upon the perspicuity of "certain private persons" and here we become closer to Fitzpatrick's implied question referred to in Chapter 1, namely which certain private persons; and to my own query three decades ago of how in any event do private and public persons[49] come to be distinguished in the absence of an already-existing legal system?

The apparent divergence is evident enough if we consider, not only Foucault's perspicuous specific analyses of the Enlightenment social control literature of which the Benthams, the Malthusians, the Chadwicks and the Kay-Shuttleworths, are taken to be the English embodiment, but the trajectory of their work. The central character, whom we have met in the Panopticon's phantom in-specter, is the legislator, the all-seeing sovereign, above and outside the community s/he or they rule. This is the Benthamite paradigm: surveillance, control and in the end the self-subjectification and abjection before the sovereign. Worse than this, in a work which is still taken as the definitive, if arcane foundation on which Anglo-Australia and New Zealand rested, through which it was to be understood, it may be morally regrettable, as Fitzpatrick remarks, if its subjects are led like lambs to the slaughter; but the logic of the law remains untouched. Its bayonets may remain sheathed (for the moment, although Pue[50] and others and the example of Iraq have demonstrated the length and consequences of this momentariness) but things may legitimately change.

What I find disturbing about this – something that returns us to the concerns I expressed toward the end of Chapter 1 is the symptomatic, missing element from the *Concept*'s promise to be an essay in descriptive sociology.[51] It misses, if we may put a modern gloss on Burke's remark, the sense in which lawyers miss the law constitutionally understood. The text, *The Concept of Law* provides a philosophical justification, not only, as Fitzpatrick amply demonstrates, for the western deployment of the primitive/developed dichotomy as a justification for imperialism, pre- or post-colonial, it provides a philosophical justification for what Leavis termed "technologico-Benthamism". The sheer incoherence, as I suggested, of invoking "officials" prior to law in order somehow to define the topic; the distinction of "public" and "private" before any regime is posited – in order to posit in – within which such a distinction could be made, are breathtaking – eccentricities, oversights, we might say. But the effect is, in a foundational text, to elide any discussion of whom the "certain private persons" are who might lead certain other private persons like lambs to the slaughter. The text is, whatever the author's intentions, the legal technician's "Pontius Pilate moment" in the terms

49 Ian Duncanson, The Strange World of English Jurisprudence, (1979) 30 *Northern Ireland Legal Quarterly* 207–24; also, Ian Duncanson, Hermeneutics and Persistent Questions in Hart's Jurisprudence, (1987) *The Juridical Review* 113–30.

50 W Wesley Pue (ed), *Pepper in Our Eyes: The APEC Affair*, Vancouver, UBC Press (2000).

51 *Concept, op cit*, Preface.

Arendt quotes from Eichmann's interrogation. The author no longer has responsibility. It is precisely what Burke had in mind when criticizing the education of lawyers in the eighteenth century.

In the essay referred to earlier, Donajgrodzki[52] pointed out the importance of noticing the alternative to the production and ordering of the subject by legislative means. It can be argued that Hart himself, social activist and advocate of moral reform, was aware of the alternatives, but morality remains, in the Hartian schema, a "primitive" social artifact akin to the primary rules of early societies: do's and don'ts which can be changed only through the secondary rule mechanisms available through an officialdom as mystical as the Panoptical in-specter, and "certain private persons" who can only be those members of a social order of a certain class, like Mill's East India Company officials or those in whom "the multitude" must have "unlimited confidence".[53]

It is academically legitimate to notice the shortcomings, as one sees it, of arguments other than one's own, but my concern is that, whilst Hart's text is now half a century old, its forms of thought remain central to lawyers' understandings and lawyers' teaching of students. *Law's Empire* is in many ways an appropriate heir to *Concept*, directing the gaze away from the malign effects of what Leavis termed "technologico-Benthamism", acknowledging the role of ethics – whose ethics? – but only as the heroic judge interprets them. Law and lawyers are to be the center and arbiter of their society's entire culture in the Herculean fantasy. In Leavis's design of the university, the centrality of the English department leads out by argument, dissent and consent and compromise, to further and never-ending argument in ever-expanding textual horizons.

The Leavisite pre-emption of the authoritarians

I suggested earlier that the creation of agreeable means of disagreement, civility and politeness, albeit imperfectly achieved, promised something more politically congenial than the politics of fear, to which Benthamite or Stephenite recommendations ultimately lead. Besides which, the latter are even more utopian in the chilling way of Nazism and Stalinism than one might at first sight take them for. *If* the deviant were certain that his civil or criminal disregard for the rules would lead to a measured form of disadvantage to him, s/he might become a conformist. As with all Utopias, as Orwell's *Animal Farm* observed so well, one question is who gets to design the criteria to whom all must conform, and what will they look like? Men or pigs, or something in between? Is disagreement to be tolerated? Bentham assumed a free press which is, in light of the remarks of Matthew Sharpe

52 AP Donajgrodzki, Social Police and the Bureaucratic Elite: A Vision of Order in the Age of reform, in AP Donajgrodzki (ed), *Social Control in Nineteenth Century Britain*, London, Croom Helm (1977).

53 JS Mill, Democracy and Government (1835), in Geraint Williams (ed), *John Stuart Mill on Politics and Society*, New York, NY, International Publication Service (1976), 184.

with which we began, resembles the economists' assumption anent the can opener. A struggle to achieve a free press challenging the status quo in an age of commodified "news" would surely provoke a response like that of Lord Liverpool to the peaceful St Peter's Field rally for parliamentary reform and the extension of the franchise in 1819. In the Scotland of my youth, "No Popery" was a regular expression on public buildings of disapproval of the Anti-Christ of Rome, but physical violence was confined to football matches between the Catholic Celtic and the Protestant Rangers, and one assumes that punches were fueled by beer rather than fine differences in theological doctrine. By contrast, during celebrations of the Pope's visit to Sydney in 2008, slogans, tee-shirt messages, banners, badges and other forms of "annoying" objections to the Roman church's policies on sexual matters were criminalized by a cowed New South Wales legislature. Neither this nor Bentham's curious conviction that legal rule-breakers would be or would imagine themselves inevitably to suffer the consequences of their actions inspires any confidence in his design for social order.

What I have been arguing throughout is not that one abandons law as a technical instrument of social ordering, or the systematic study of how that is to be accomplished. Rather, I have insisted that law and its study be seen as embedded in a much wider culture of how to "be", the traditions and forward projections of civility, a modern version of the lessons of Smith and Burke. Arnold, whose views we have already visited, offers interesting insights into the cultural direction his own country and educational apparatus might take. By the time Arnold was writing about English education, and culture, as *he* saw it more generally, past mid-century and beyond, his travels in Europe had convinced him that Prussia had a vastly more sophisticated apparatus for educating its youth than England, and that France, too, at least in Arnold's opinion, was also ahead of England in both education and the care of its heritage. One's caution in approaching Arnold is not the wisdom of his educational suggestions (or his caustic response to Robert Lowe) but his, in a sense reversal of the above proposals in this thesis. Arnold is impressed by Prussia in particular, and the explanation is, I think, that its undoubtedly formidable cultural advances were embedded in its strong, controlling constitution. Arnold's own authoritarian impatience with the "populace", we have noticed.

Elitism of the Coleridgean or Leavisite kind, for all its drawbacks, promises a better and more open future. In FR Leavis's Introduction to Mill's texts, we find some evidence of where Leavis considered the educational project at its apogee had been and should properly have been going. Consistent with Coleridge's aligning the duty of the secular church with that of both "educing", drawing the subject's potential out through dialog and improving the circumstances of the subject of his or her children, Leavis sees the task of the university as one of leading the lower institutions, the elementary and the grammar schools to a certain goal, one not as "wizened" or parochial as Perry Anderson later asserted. The English school, Leavis felt, could lead to the kind of mannered, agreeable disagreement desired by Locke and essential to the survival of civilization. How should we understand the political implications of Leavis's work, and Anderson's response? To anticipate, Leavis's elitism seems to point in a more flexible and openly inquiring direction than Anderson's "scientific" Marxism.[54] It may be the stridency of Anderson's denunciatory prose in this area – in others I am a great admirer of his works of synthesis and breadth – but I find his dismissal of what I see as the achievement of Englishness inadequate. For Leavis:

> In a university English school as it should be, literary studies would lead outside themselves into other fields and other disciplines.[55]

Cambridge University English seemed likely to carry the Newbolt banner into the darkest of places, as seen from the banks of the Cam. The Report for which his name is a shorthand, recommended a "liberal" education, spread as widely as possible. Professors of English from the old universities, the new colleges and the extension programs were to be the "ambassadors" who would deliver the cultural heritage *alias* civilization in its broadest term to the inhabitants of grim northern cities. From whom were these domestic missionaries to learn and discuss the substance of their mission? The critic was a vital component in the exercise. There are several contradictions here.

Leavis, perhaps the best-known Anglophone literary critic of his era, and advocate of the liberal education to which he believed close readings of texts could lead, suffered personally as a member of non-combatant medical crews in World War I, many of whom, it is thought perhaps Leavis himself, in addition to witnessing and risking the horrors of injury, absorbed from soldiers' uniforms the residues of poison gas. He "returned to Cambridge in a stunned condition. His digestion had gone in 1915", he suffered insomnia and a temporary speech defect.[56]

However, as MacKillop's and others' biographies make clear, he did not want to talk about his experiences, formative as they may well have been, "he did not wish to tell war stories", and felt that Owen and Sassoon, who did want to tell war stories "had merit", but had not, in their poetry, transcended the pre-war Edwardian culture. But, Leavis, like many of his generation, *did* in fact tell war stories. Anne Samson writes that there was an air of "cultural pessimism" among the generation, one with a number of causes. There was an "abomination of war", unprecedented in a European context in which European civilization had nearly collapsed, the political, economic and cultural chaos in what remained; and the rise of Bolshevism.[57] Some of the cultural pessimism about the loss of certainties might have originated in the changes to the English intellectual landscape that may have

54 Perry Anderson, *English Questions*, London, Verso (1992).

55 FR Leavis, Introduction, in FR Leavis (ed), *On Bentham and Coleridge*, Cambridge, Cambridge University Press (1950), 26.

56 Ian MacKillop, *FR Leavis: A Life in Criticism*, London, Penguin (1995), 44.

57 Anne Samson, *FR Leavis*, Toronto, University of Toronto Press (1992), 18.

been coincidental, if not caused by the war. Mulhern argues that the improved opportunities for lower middle class and even some working class children, broke the monopoly that a few, often interrelated, families had exercised in Victorian and early Edwardian England.[58] Ironically, Leavis's main point in the interview after which, as an aside, he wished to distance himself from telling war stories, related to his lifelong unshakeable belief that cultural standards were rapidly falling, not merely in the period with which his wife had been concerned, since Bunyan, or, at least Austen, but more recently. Quality newspapers could no longer assume that their apparently educated audiences would comprehend a phrase in Greek or Latin, even French or German. (It seems unlikely that FR's father, a skilled but not classically educated piano dealer, would have been fluent in classical or even modern languages other than his own.)

A second contradiction is one that can be seen in Arnold, although he *did* belong to the charmed circle so lampooned by Lytton Strachey (one of Strachey's targets was Arnold's father, Thomas, the reformer of Rugby, though the architect of its restriction to entry from other than the upper classes),[59] namely that the critic who is politically an "alien" in Arnold's term, or politically unaffiliated, are likely to be unappreciated and not very honored by those whom s/he criticizes. Cambridge's treatment of neither Leavis, QD nor FR, does it much credit, given that what was, for the most part, their journal, *Scrutiny*, was one of the most influential in the English discipline, and that FR was himself, partly with his wife, for decades perhaps the most influential writer in the discipline; but it seems to me that very few institutions would have behaved differently. A frequently-expressed conviction of his was that minorities can, in the long run, make a difference, he embodied this belief throughout his life, and perhaps the threat to much conservative thought of the discipline we now think of as cultural studies has proved him to be correct.

Finally, there are aspects of Leavis' work that justify Samson's remark that "falling standards" and the loss of the organic community of Queenies's beloved Bunyan and his associates are a lament for a type of political order – which seems, she says, "to amount to little more than the acceptance by the ruled of the importance of the rulers".[60] This is, we have seen, the essence of colonialism, understood broadly. But there is something else to be said, which may in substantive terms surface later. In the meantime, what is perhaps clearer now, is the importance of appreciating that Leavis consciously positioned himself within the university, not the university as he experienced it in Cambridge, nor yet in the Jerusalem which is in twenty-first century idiom, "mission accomplished". Missions, as we saw, were originally seen as accomplishable expeditions to dark places with savage

58 Francis Mulhern, *The Moment of Scrutiny*, London, New Left Books (1979), ch 1.

59 Lytton Strachey, *Eminent Victorians: Cardinal Manning, Florence Nightingale, Dr. Arnold and General Gordon*, London, Chatto and Windus (1918).

60 Samson, *op cit*, n 57, 59.

populations, whether they lived in New Guinea, New Zealand, Salford, Newcastle on Tyne or Africa, to save souls and reorient simple or depraved subjects to hear the Christian message – or one of them – whether or not they had accessible to them a potentially satisfactory form of culture.

There is no sign that Leavis was interested in accomplishable missions, or "jerusalems". But what is clearer from a late twentieth or early twenty-first century perspective, is the substance of his message about "the university", and also the implications of the concept of the "organic community". In the Anglophone world, at least, universities have lately been conceptually assimilated to the model of the capitalist corporation. They must be "accountable" – to whom is not clear; accountants perhaps, but the Enron farce, and there have been many since, give us little confidence about the soundness of the basis recommended here. And, just as citizens seem to have been transformed into consumers before many of them realized that they were, indeed, citizens, so students have become customers, a species which, in the economists' fantasy – assume we have a can opener – has full knowledge and capacity to choose among various educational options (in which case, education and the academic seem *otiose*). Both universities and students, then, must have "missions" and they are not the civilizing missions of the past, but distinctly un-Leavisite ambitions to "teach" – another Leavisite anathema – the managers of pubs and golf courses, noble aims as they may be, but not the aim of the Leavisite university.

The first thing to note – and this is what is particularly in need of emphasizing today – is that one takes up a text, whether, in a trivial example, a manual about how one's mobile telephone or camera works, or, more seriously, the text that forms a course in which one enrolls, as someone in need of guidance. In the first example, and why it is trivial, and why it forms a beguiling normative narrative for business and authoritative government, there is no dialog. Whether the designer and manufacturer have explained themselves adequately, or the user has managed to understand, or not, there is little room for discussion. Moreover, the assumption that it is the user's fault if things take an unexpected turn, is more or less irrefutable. A second example is the one I think Leavis had in mind. His appeal to the organic community was not a Pre-Raphaelite move to lament a lost golden age, although it often took on that appearance. Rather, it was a reminder of the importance of dialog. FR's famous "it is so, is it not?" is, as he himself said on numerous occasions, not an adjuration that the audience agree, but envisages as perfectly within the dialog, the response, "perhaps, but . . .". It is the model we noticed in looking at the immediate response to the cataclysms of civil war in England; and the failure of its application to the political disagreement between Great Britain and the thirteen colonies.

There is no sense in which Leavis' (or, for that matter, of Matthew Arnold's) writing which implied that the purpose of English studies was to produce literary critics per se, still less authors. Both Leavis, and before him Arnold, in the Coleridgian tradition, rather stress the crucial social function of "critical intelligence" to be found in the practice of arguing over texts and contexts.

Nevertheless, that the English discipline could be *seen* as the starting point of an intellectual rejuvenation and a national education (even if it was not actually the starting point), prior to "other disciplines", dismayed Perry Anderson in a wide-ranging mid-twentieth century retrospect, and it was for him symptomatic of the limitations of English thought that, first, serious sociological and later Marxist theory should have been so eclipsed as a result. My position is that it was not. There is something deeply social-theoretical about Coleridge's political writing; and Arnold, JS Mill and Leavis had distinct political agendas that were not all that different from those of Pareto and Weber. And Marx? Is the Marxist, Brecht, so far from Leavis' famous "this is so, is it not?" in the scripted discussion that begins and concludes *The Caucasian Chalk Circle*?

The lament for lost disciplines and lost certainties

If Anderson were correct about the backwardness of England (by which he means the United Kingdom) in relation to European theory, there would be a certain irony insofar as the Englishness of which Anderson is so dismissive was, as we saw in Chapter 2, in part the work of the Scots, whose unsentimental commercialism and intensive contacts with European theoretical frameworks earned them widespread admiration in mainland Europe – Hutcheson, Ferguson, "le bon David" (Hume, as he was affectionately referred to in French intellectual circles) and Adam Smith. They were, as we have seen, frequently understood as inventing what we now see as an early sociology of a fairly adventurous kind, and who were, moreover, influential in the development of the work Anderson considers part of the "absent center" of English thought, namely that of Hegel and Marx. It seems to me that, despite the enormous erudition of Anderson's texts, there are a few serious misunderstandings. One relates to disciplinary boundaries. Anderson clearly considers that in missing "sociology", British culture as a consequence missed the opportunity for serious social and political thought, too, although, as we shall see, "English studies", intrinsically broadly conceived and leading outward in the way both Leavises assumed they did, did embrace political and social analysis, some of it serious, even if some of it is irritatingly self-congratulatory, if one thinks of Bagehot or Freeman[61] – but then it was not unique if one thinks of the nationalist and anti-Semitic polemics of European origin at the time.

Discussing Pugin, Ruskin and William Morris, perhaps not the best examples for our theme,[62] although they do indicate the conclusion reached Raymond Williams:

61 EA Freeman, *The Growth of the English Constitution from the Earliest Times* (1872), London, Macmillan (1876); Bagehot, op cit, n 7.

62 See Rosemary Hill, *God's Architect: Pugin and the Building of Romantic Britain*, London, Allen Lane (2007).

> An essential hypothesis in the development of culture is that the art of a period is closely and necessarily related to the generally prevalent 'way of life', and further that, in consequence, esthetic, moral and social judgments are closely related.[63]

"Prevalent" may be the key term here. That a shrewd operator like Benjamin Jowett, Master of Trinity, should have supported English Studies in the last decades of Queen Victoria, suggests the pertinence of Chris Baldick's title, *The Social Mission of English Criticism*.[64] If the status quo were to be preserved, then those parvenus, natives, women and the working class, knocking at the educational and ultimately political gate, had better learn to revere what lay within, not learn to resent the inaccessibility to them of Cicero or Plutarch. But we get ahead of ourselves.

What clearly motivated Anderson's polemics of the 1960s was that the center of self-consciously "progressive" thought at that time in the United Kingdom meant French structuralism; and for writing in the 1970s the center meant continental European grand theory in general.[65] Both of these and social theory of many kinds, some of it prompted by Anderson, have emerged in translation since he wrote the essays to which I referred, as the retrospect in his Foreword observes. We owe him and his colleagues for that a great deal although also, as a not completely paradoxical consequence, since then we have gained more reservations about earlier totalizing models and the present dystopian consequences they have had (some of them clearly cynical, as in the case of the claim that the Iraq war is an exercise in bringing democracy to the Middle East – from bases in, for example, the democratic, gender-equal Saudi Arabia!) in the twenty-first century.

To return to the days of the earlier totalitarian revolution, the ideals they generated and the disappointments they delivered, it is hard not to see in Coleridge's later political writing anything but both a reaction to its unfavorable incarnation – his later rejection of Jacobinism – and a cautious and pragmatic blueprint of a grand theory and perhaps again some cautious utopianism that might avoid the catastrophe that the French Revolution entailed. Coleridge's critics and later writers, though concerned with social analysis, were for the most part more piecemeal in their recommendations. Coleridge is closer to Franklin than Robespierre or Lenin and expresses a humane disquiet about the effects of the early nineteenth and early twentieth century zeal which the latter exhibit about the effects of their reforms on the economic circumstances on the working class.

In Coleridge's case his expanded vision is not derived from some nostalgic wish for a return to Merrie England, nor from a hostility to commerce and manufacturing, but from a conviction that economic change need not necessarily

63 Raymond Williams, *Culture and Society 1750–1950*, Harmondsworth, Penguin (1961), 137. See also Raymond Williams, *Keywords*, London, Fontana (1976), 247, "Sociology".

64 Chris Baldick, *The Social Mission of English Criticism*, Oxford, Oxford University Press (1983).

65 EP Thompson, *The Poverty of Theory and Other Essays*, London, Merlin (1978).

accompany brutality. Indeed, as we saw, he foreshadows many of the features of the British welfare state as a possible cure for the ills he acutely diagnosed, a strategy for establishing a loyalty based on sharing, not equally, to be sure, in the developing wealth of the economy. Macaulay, Arnold and Mill also had social visions, if not so sweeping as those of Coleridge, but equally concerned by the consequences for social cohesion of unbridled and uncaring dispossession in the pursuit of modernism. It is a mistake to overlook or devalue their work as not "really" social analysis.

For Anderson, because the industrial revolution (in the scheme of things as grandly radical and totalitarian as it appears in Malthus' works as in the political schemas of Rousseau or the practices of Robespierre) – or modernism, however one likes to put it – in Britain had developed imperceptibly and apparently "naturally", "the English bourgeoisie had never been outstanding for its devotion to technological or scientific education"[66] – and he evidently includes the study of social technology. Pragmatism and "experience" may have carried more weight, although both Arnold and Leavis derided those when they seemed to them to foreclose a wider inquiry into, precisely, social technologies. Again, for Anderson, because industrial capitalism – he does not mention the financial or commercial capitalism which, with Dutch help after 1688 began the tendency he is analyzing – was so integrated into the agrarian capitalism which preceded it, that there was no bourgeois revolution, hence there was no accompanying conception of the puzzling new society thus created, as a whole, as it is to be found in European or North American sociology. The aristocracy had long practiced agrarian capitalism[67] and economic relations among men of commerce and industry have been characterized as "gentlemanly capitalism".[68] Dorothy Ross puts it slightly differently:

> In contrast (to America and Germany, where social science acknowledged as such flourished), the intellectual class in England, more secure in its national identity and having accommodated to industrialization over the course of a century, could easily imagine modernity as a transformation within an ongoing stream of historical continuity and more easily stay within the boundaries of the neoclassical paradigm.[69]

One might enter several caveats here. One is that, while Anderson acknowledges the largely conservative and social-integrative aspirations of the European sociologists, he seems to find their work more intellectually sound than when he

66 Anderson, *op cit*, n 54, Foreword, and 45.

67 Christopher Hill, *Society and Puritanism in Pre-Revolutionary England*, London, Panther (1969); David Cannadine, *Aspects of Aristocracy*, New Haven, CT, Yale University Press (1994), ch 1.

68 PJ Cain and AG Hopkins, *British Imperialism 1688–1900*, 2 vols, London, Longmans (1993).

69 Dorothy Ross, *The Origins of American Social Science*, Cambridge, Cambridge University Press (1991), 218.

finds similar impulses in Tory, Whig or Liberal writers in Britain who stray, like their Scottish antecedents, with apparent indifference across literary, economic, philosophical, cultural and political studies, aspiring and to a degree, achieving the same end of socio-cultural integration. Englishness is anathema to the Anderson of the 1960s. It may be that he has taken Macaulay's critique of what Macaulay sees as Southey's preference for an idyllic, pre-industrial England for the manifestation of something more widespread,[70] equating the cult of the gentleman with the rejection of business and technological progress.[71]

To the extent that Englishness connoted, in the speeches of Stanley Baldwin, as we have seen, in the 1920s, the smell of woodsmoke, the thwack of the squire's willow against his tenant's leather cricket ball on the village green, or the vision of a haywain at an autumn's dusk, "the sounds of England, the tinkle of the hammer on the anvil in the country smithy, the corncrake on a dewy morning, the sound of a whetstone and the sight of a plowteam coming across the brow of a hill . . . for centuries the one eternal sight of England",[72] one must accede. But they were speeches on which, as subjectifying performatives, the more Churchillian "We shall meet them on the beaches; we shall meet them on the landing grounds and in the hills; we shall never surrender", were based. That the first significant defeats of the supposedly technologically superior Nazi state were inflicted by Britain does imply that one should not read too much into Baldwin's sentimental expression about haywains and woodsmoke. The Merlin engines of Spitfires and in Lancasters, whatever their name implies, did not grow organically from the mists of Cornwall or Sherwood Forest.

We may seem here to have strayed too far from our topic, but the relevance is that what I describe in this chapter as a major instrument of hegemony, namely education and specifically to begin with the English discipline cannot realistically be characterized as either a sign of effeteness or illiteracy in the area of social technology. By 1940, Britain was the most totally mobilized of any of the countries involved in World War II.[73] Under threat, the British knew how to be English subjects. Under extreme threat, they knew how to be extreme subjects.[74]

70 TB Macaulay, Southey, *Edinburgh Review*, January 1830.

71 See MJ Weiner, *English Culture and the Decline in the Industrial Spirit 1850–1950*, Cambridge, Cambridge University Press (1981); Corelli Barnett, *The Audit of War: The Illusion and Reality of Britain as a Great Nation*, London, Macmillan (1986).

72 This forms part of the sedative rhetoric of Stanley Baldwin, Tory son of an ironworks factory owner, speaking to the world's most urbanized population over the world's first public broadcaster, the BBC, http://news.bbc.co.uk/1/hi/special_report/1997; see also, Earl Baldwin of Bewdley, *The Torch of Freedom*, London, Hodder and Stoughton (1937). And *contra*, Peter Mandler, Against "Englishness": English Culture and the Limits to Rural Nostalgia, (1997) 7 *Transactions of the Royal Historical Society* 6th Ser 155–75.

73 Sydney Ratner, untitled review of Keith Hancock, *History of the Second World War*, (1959) 64:4 *American Historical Review* 398–400.

74 See David Kynaston, *Austerity Britain 1945–51*, London, Bloomsbury Press (2007).

Churchill's was, of course, masterly rhetoric, which his loss of the 1945 election demonstrates the people understood: it was morally uplifting, but dispensable for the future they aspired to when that particular kind of struggle was over:

> At the summit (of the Battle of Britain) the stamina and valor of our fighter pilots remained unconquerable and supreme. Thus Britain was saved. Well might I say in the House of Commons: "never in the field of human conflict was so much owed by so many to so few".[75]

As wartime oratory, then, this was a fine piece of morale boosting. "The few", not to be demeaned, are expertly amateurish, ordinary people like us. More than just heroic for themselves or on others' behalf, they symbolize still, the "Englishman" whether in England, Scotland, Wales or Ireland. The Hurricane and Spitfire pilots did not manufacture their airplanes or the ordnance they used, as did not the Wellington or Lancaster crews who helped destroy German cities, for good or ill. They came from city factories, from the thousands of munitions workers who died or had their lives shortened by air raids or in those munitions factories to support "the few". One is sometimes drawn, but after the event, and as a reaction to Churchillian oratory – splendid in wartime – to Brecht's verses:

> The young Alexander conquered India.
> Was he alone?
> Caesar beat the Gauls.
> Did he not have even a cook with him?
> Philip of Spain wept when his armada
> Went down. Was he the only one to weep?
> Every page a victory.
> Who cooked the feast for the victors?
> Every ten years a great man.
> Who paid the bill?[76]

As Angus Calder points out the subject-ed, subject is aware of this. The same always contains its *differend*, in Derridean terms, or, in terms from Foucault's College de France lectures, which I find more accessible, the subject which comes to know changes in its coming-to-know in a plurality of ways. The British state's slogan of 1940, "Your courage, *Your* cheerfulness, Your resolution Will bring *Us* victory" provoked the question, who were the "us" whose position "your" valiance

75 Winston Churchill, *The Second World War, vol 2: Their Finest Hour*, London, Cassell (1951). The volume is subtitled "Alone". Churchill's speeches read histrionically, but the cadences of the recorded performances interestingly belie this, falling modestly at the end of the sentences like Slater's "undemonstrative" English countryside.

76 Brecht quoted in Anthony Arblaster, *The Rise and Decline of Western Liberalism*, Oxford, Blackwell (1984), 49.

would ensure?[77] Education, wartime education quite powerfully, and the Butler Education Act 1944, enabled a population to make critical choices, although within fairly severe boundaries. A postwar Labour government, elected by a landslide majority in favor of social reform was confronted with a political situation similar to that of India, granted independence from Great Britain shortly after. Both countries, India and Great Britain, were exhausted by war, of course. Subaltern Studies has identified the shortcomings of Indian nationalism and its role in the production of independence, in relation to ordinary people. The post-independence government of India was an elitist paternalism, as the British had taught it to be. The government of the Eton-educated Atlee was similarly well-intentioned, and similarly paternalist. Was this, in both cases, like the Whig revolutions, the constitutional basis for a progressive social democracy? We do not, and this is the final message of my book, need utopians, the builders of a new Jerusalem (no doubt without planning permission); we do need enthusiastic and progressive subjects, and I have traced the vicissitudes of their coming-to-be.

77 Angus Calder, *The People's War: Britain 1939–1945*, London, Granada (1971), 71.

Conclusion

The spy novels, at least of Anglophone provenance, refer to the skills which their protagonists learn, picking locks and recognizing disguised spies on the other side, following without being detected, and so on, as "tradecraft". The woman protagonist of Kate Atkinson's recent post-Gulf War thriller, *When Will There be Good News?*[1] accepts that there will always be tradecraft, lies, bluffing, even killing, but ends the novel with the thought that some of it, she has in mind torture, will always be wrong: not merely open to criticism from another discipline, that of moral philosophy, but inherently, ethically, wrong. She rejects all the familiar arguments about the urgent need to discover from the detainee which mall s/he may have planted the bomb in, the exceptions that justify inhumanity. For her, tradecraft is a cloak, each thread of which forms a politics in need of constant evaluation.

Empire, I have suggested in my thesis, always looks back to a kind of Lacanian Real, the political one-ness that was believed to be Rome, and always looks into the future with paranoia. Backwards, with nostalgia: think of the statues of eighteenth and nineteenth century monarchs, nobles and politicians depicted, not in the clothes of their time, but in masonry draperies of classical Rome. Forward with paranoia: did the British not, since the beginnings of the second empire, peer into the future and see nothing but fear of loss? To Spain, France, Russia, Germany? And the gaze was returned. Empire is, I have argued, statecraft, one inherited from nostalgia for Rome, repeated many times, under the Carolingians, the post-Gregorian Popes and the Absolutists who continued the grand tradition of attempted genocide in the so-termed New World. Now it has returned, in a kind of matricide, to threaten chaos in the land once considered the matrix of Euro-American civilization in the name of ending tyranny, as if Euro-America ever scrupled about doing business with tyrants. But statecraft here is a cloak, like that of tradecraft, whose every thread requires careful scrutiny. One of those threads is law. Early legal positivism, having learned its ways from European Absolutists, conjured the sovereign, a ghost like that of Hamlet's father, summoned by God, the General Will, the Volk or Bentham's in-specter, was outdated in the era in

1 Kate Atkinson, *When Will There Be Good News*, New York, NY, Doubleday (2008).

which the colonial was being transformed into the post-colonial. How was rule now to be justified – not by the heathenish or cannibalistic tendencies of the natives. So how?

In Anglo-Australian terms, at least, we saw, by an equally spectral figure, bringing law to the benighted: law, defined as based on the recognition by officials (prior to the existence of the officialdom conferring the power to legitimate anything) and certain private persons (before a private/public division had been made possible). Enter Legal Positivism's savior, HLA Hart. Pre-legal peoples did not have the blessings of these phantoms and required instruction, occasionally, as we learn from Hamlet's ghost, cursing. Amitav Ghosh's Mr Burnham sees the African in *ante-bellum* Carolina as freed from the ignorant brutalities of Africa, and the coolies as equally freed from primitive Asian states by their transportation to various parts of the empire, where legislatures, judiciaries and, above all, sovereignty guaranteed the rule of law.[2] Freedom meant also, of course, the illegitimacy of the Chinese Emperor's interdict on the importation of Indian opium.

The problem with law, as I have tried to indicate in my book, relates not to its substance, which may be as we wish or otherwise. It relates to its apparent necessity as a thread of statecraft. Order there must be, regulation is necessary, but its origin in the ghostly authority whom nobody can identify is of concern. Each strand must be questioned as closely as the motives of the politicians whose instrument it is. As fifteen hundred years of empire-yearning have informed us, it is part of politics, often, part of the politics of human suffering.

We can conclude with yet another ghost, that of the democracy permitting citizen choice. In a poll published on 7 September 2008, 60% of US citizens aged 18–24 did not know and could not name the three branches of government, fewer than 50% had heard of Karl Marx, the anti-Christ of US politics, and fewer than half had heard of the Battle of Bunker Hill. This is in the country that went to war to defend the values of free choice and democracy.[3] My argument has been that, so far as England and Scotland and some of their colonial heirs were concerned, subjectification through learning rather than through law, offered more discriminating and critical choices for public activity. Hence, as I argued, the importance to those who preferred the ghost of democratic choice to something more tangible and vibrant, of the "culture wars", and the "vocational education" recommended by Businesman Bottles, whose acumen is evident at the time of writing (the recession of late 2008).

2 Amitav Ghosh, *Sea of Poppies*, London, John Murray (2008).

3 *The Washington Post*, 7 September 2008. I owe the reference to Professor W Wesley Pue.

Bibliography

Adorno, Francesco *et al* (1999), *The World of Renaissance Florence*, Firenze, Giunti Gruppo Editoriale.

Agamben, Giorgio (1998), *Homo Sacer: Sovereign Power and Bare Life*, Palo Alto, CA, Stanford University Press.

Allen, Theodore (1994), *The Invention of the White Race vol 1: Racial Oppression and Social Control*, London, Verso.

Althusser, Louis (1971), *Lenin, Philosophy and Other Essays*, London, Verso.

Anderson, Perry (1974), *Lineages of the Absolutist State*, London, New Left Books.

Anderson, Perry (1974), *Passages From Antiquity to Feudalism*, London, New Left Books.

Anderson, Perry (1992), *English Questions*, London, Verso.

Appleby, Joyce, Covington, Elizabeth, Hoyt, David, Latham, Michael and Sneider, Alison (eds) (1996), *Knowledge and Postmodernism in Historical Perspective*, New York, NY, Routledge.

Arblaster, Anthony (1984), *The Rise and Decline of Western Liberalism*, Oxford, Blackwell.

Arendt, Hannah (1973), *On Revolution*, Harmondsworth, Penguin Books.

Arendt, Hannah (1982), *Lectures on Kant's Political Philosophy* (Ronal Beinre, ed), Chicago, IL, University of Chicago Press.

Arendt, Hannah (1995), *The Origins of Totalitarianism*, San Diego, CA, Harcourt Publishing.

Armitage, David (2000), *The Ideological Origins of the British Empire*, Cambridge, Cambridge University Press.

Armitage, David and Michael Braddick (eds) (2009), *The British Atlantic World*, London, Palgrave.

Arnold, Matthew (1862), The Twice-Revised Code, 65 *Fraser's Magazine* 347–65.

Arnold, Matthew (1879), *Mixed Essays*, London, Smith Elder.

Arnold, Matthew (1896), *Essays in Criticism*, London, Macmillan.

Arnold, Matthew (1921), *Essays in Criticism, First Series*, London, Macmillan.

Arthurs, Harry (1985), *Administrative Justice and Legal Pluralism in Nineteenth Century England*, Toronto, University of Toronto Press.

Ashcraft, Richard (1986), *Revolutionary Politics and Locke's 'Two Treatises of Government'*, Princeton, NJ, Princeton University Press.

Atkinson, Kate (2008), *When Will There Be Good News?*, New York, NY, Doubleday.

Aylmer, GE (ed) (1975), *The Levellers in the English Revolution*, London, Thames and Hudson.

Bagehot, Walter (1956), *Physics and Politics*, Boston, MA, Beacon Press.

Baier, Annette (1994), *A Progress of Sentiments: Reflections on Hume's Treatise*, Cambridge, MA, Harvard University Press.

Bailyn, Bernard and Philip Morgan (eds) (1991), *Strangers in the Realm: Cultural Margins of the First British Empire*, Chapel Hill, NC, University of North Carolina Press.

Baldick, Chris (1983), *The Social Mission of English Criticism*, Oxford, Oxford University Press.

Baldwin, Stanley, Earl Baldwin of Bewdley (1937), *The Torch of Freedom*, London, Hodder and Stoughton.

Baldwin, Stanley (1997), http://news.bbc.co.uk/1/hi/special_report/1997 (accessed July 2007).

Balen, Malcolm (2003), *The Secret History of the South Sea Bubble*, London, Fourth Estate.

Barkawi, Tarak and Mark Laffey (2002), Retrieving the Imperial: Empire and International Relations, *Millennium Journal of International Studies* 109–27.

Barker-Benfield, GJ (1992), *The Culture of Sensibility: Sex and Society in Eighteenth Century England*, Chicago, IL, University of Chicago Press.

Barnett, Corelli (1986), *The Audit of War: The Illusion and Reality of Britain as a Great Nation*, London, Macmillan.

Bartlett, Richard (2000), *Native Title in Australia*, Melbourne, Butterworths.

Barzun, Jacques (1993), *The American University: How it Runs, Where it is Going*, 2nd edn, Chicago, IL, University of Chicago Press.

Bayly, C (1988), *Indian Society and the Making of the British Empire*, Cambridge, Cambridge University Press.

Beard, Jennifer (2007), *The Political Economy of Desire*, London, Cavendish.

Beiner, Ronald (1982), Interpretive Essay, in Hannah Arendt, *Lectures on Kant's Political Philosophy* (Hans Reiss, ed), Chicago, IL, University of Chicago Press.

Bell, Duncan (2007), *The Idea of a Greater Britain: Empire and the Future of the World Order 1860–1900*, London, Palgrave.

Bennett, HS (1922, reissued 1970), *The Pastons and Their England*, Cambridge, Cambridge University Press.

Benton, Ted (1982), Realism, Power and Objective Interests, in Keith Graham (ed), *Contemporary Political Philosophy: Radical Issues*, Cambridge, Cambridge University Press.

Berman, Harold (1983), *Law and Revolution: The Formation of the Western Legal Tradition*, Cambridge, MA, Harvard University Press.

Berry, Christopher (1997), *The Social Theory of the Scottish Enlightenment*, Edinburgh, Edinburgh University Press.

Berry, Christopher (2003), Sociality and Socialization, in Alexander Broadie (ed), *The Cambridge Companion to the Scottish Enlightenment*, Cambridge, Cambridge University Press.

Bishop, John (1996), Moral Motivation and the Development of Francis Hutcheson's Philosophy, 57 *The Journal of the History of Ideas* 277–95.

Blackshield, Tony and John Williams (1998), *Australian Constitutional Law and Theory: Commentary and Materials*, Sydney, Federation Press.

Blackstone, Sir William (1775), *Commentaries on the Laws of England vol 1*, Oxford, Oxford University Press.

Bloch, Marc (1965), *Feudal Society*, 2 vols, London, Routledge & Kegan Paul.

Bloom, Allen (1987), *The Closing of the American Mind*, New York, NY, Touchstone Books.

Blumenthal, Sydney (2006), *How Bush Rules: Chronicles of a Radical Regime*, Princeton, NJ, Princeton University Press.

Bobbio, Noberto (1993), *Thomas Hobbes and the Natural Law Tradition*, Chicago, IL, University of Chicago Press.

Bogle, Kenneth (2004), *Scotland's Common Ridings*, Stroud, Tempus Publishing.

Bohstedt, John (1983), *Riots and Community Politics in England 1790–1810*, Cambridge, MA, Harvard University Press.

Bondanalla, Peter (1987), *The Eternal City: Roman Images in the Modern World*, Chapel Hill, NC, University of North Carolina Press.

Bowen, HV (2001), British India 1765–1813: The Metropolitan Context, in Peter Marshall (ed), *The Oxford History of the British Empire II: The Eighteenth Century*, Oxford, Oxford University Press.

Bozovic, Miran (1995), Introduction, in Miran Bozovic (ed), *Jeremy Bentham: The Panopticon Writings*, London, Verso.

Bozovic, Miran (ed) (1995), *Jeremy Bentham: The Panopticon Writings*, London, Verso.

Bradshaw, Brendan (1996), The Tudor Reformation and Revolution in Wales and Ireland: The Origins of the British Problem, in Brendan Bradshaw and John Morrill (eds), *The British Problem 1534–1707: State Formation in the Atlantic Archipelago*, London, Macmillan.

Brailsford, HN (1976), *The Levellers and the English Revolution*, Nottingham, Spokesman Books.

Branson, Roy (1979), James Madison and the Scottish Enlightenment, *Journal of the History of Ideas* 235–50.

Braudel, Fernand (1982), *Civilization and Capitalism Vol II: The Wheels of Commerce*, London, Collins.

Braudel, Fernand (1984), *Civilization and Capitalism Vol III: The Perspective of the World*, London, Collins.

Brendon, Piers (2007), *The Decline and Fall of the British Empire 1781–1997*, London, Jonathan Cape.

Brewer, John (1989), *The Sinews of Power: War, Money and the English State 1688–1783*, London, Unwin Hyman.

Brewer, John (1997), *The Pleasures of the Imagination: English Culture in the Eighteenth Century*, London, Harper Collins.

Brewer, John and John Styles (1980), *An Ungovernable People: The English and their Law in the Seventeenth Century*, New Brunswick, NJ, Rutgers University Press.

Broadie, Alexander (ed) (1997), *The Scottish Enlightenment: An Anthology*, Edinburgh, Cannongate Books.

Bronowski, Jacob (1959), *The Common Sense of Science*, New York, NY, Vintage Books.

Brooks, CW (1986), *"Vipers and Pettifoggers of the Commonwealth": The Lower Branch of the Legal Profession in Early Modern England*, Cambridge, Cambridge University Press.

Brundage, Anthony (1978), *The Making of the New Poor Law 1832–1839*, London, Hutchinson.

Bryce, James (1914, reprinted 2005), *The Ancient Roman Empire and the British Empire in India*, New York, NY, Elibron Classics.

Buchan, James (2003), *Capital of the Mind: How Edinburgh Changed the World*, London, John Murray.

Burke, Edmund (1910), *Reflections on the Revolution in France*, London, Dent.

Burke, Edmund (1963), Speech on Moving His Resolutions for Conciliation with the Colonies, House of Commons, 22 March 1775, in Peter Stanlis (ed), *Edmund Burke: Selected Writings and Speeches*, Washington, DC, Regnery Press.

Burke, Edmund (1998), Thoughts on the Present Discontents, in David Womersley (ed), *Edmund Burke: A Philosophical Enquiry into the Origins of Our Ideas of the Sublime and the Beautiful and Other Pre-Revolutionary Writings*, London, Penguin.

Burgess, Glenn (1996), *Absolute Monarchy and the Stuart Constitution*, New Haven, CT, Yale University Press.

Burton, Antoinette (1994), *Burdens of History: British Feminists, Indian Women and Imperial Culture 1865–1915*, Chapel Hill, NC, University of North Carolina Press.

Burton, Antoinette (1998), *At the Heart of Empire: Indians and the Colonial Encounter in Late Victorian Britain*, Berkeley, CA, University of California Press.

Burton, Antoinette (ed) (2001), *Politics and Empire in Victorian Britain*, London, Palgrave.

Burton, Antoinette (ed) (2003), *After the Imperial Turn: Thinking with and through the nation*, Durham, NC, Duke University Press.

Cain, PJ and AG Hopkins (1993), *British Imperialism 1688–1900*, 2 vols, London, Longmans.

Calder, Angus (1971), *The People's War: Britain 1939–45*, London, Granada.

Camic, Charles (1983), Experience and Ideas: Education for Universalism in Eighteenth Century Scotland, 25 *Comparative Studies in Society and History* 50–68.

Cannadine, David (1994), *Aspects of Aristocracy*, New Haven, CT, Yale University Press.

Canny, Nicholas (1998), The Origins of Empire, in Nicholas Canny (ed), *The Oxford History of the British Empire vol 1: The Origins of Empire*, Oxford, Oxford University Press.

Cantor, Norman (1992), *Inventing the Middle Ages: The Lives, Works and Ideas of the Great Medievalists of the Twentieth Century*, New York, NY, William Morrow.

Carr, EH (2001), *What Is History?*, London, Palgrave.

Cash, Arthur (2006), *John Wilkes: The Scandalous Father of Civil Liberty*, New Haven, CT, Yale University Press.

Churchill, Winston (1951), *The Second World War, vol 2: Their Finest Hour*, London, Cassell.

Clive, John (1987), *Macaulay: The Shaping of the Historian*, Cambridge, MA, Harvard University Press.

Cocks, RC (1988), *Sir Henry Maine: A Study in Victorian Jurisprudence*, Cambridge, Cambridge University Press.

Cohn, Bernard (1998), *Colonialism and its Forms of Knowledge: The British in India,* Princeton, NJ, Princeton University Press.

Colaiaco, James (1983), *James Fitzjames Stephen and the Crisis of Victorian Thought*, London, Macmillan.

Coleridge, Samuel Taylor (1990), A Lay Sermon, in John Morow (ed), *Coleridge's Writings on Politics and Society*, London, Macmillan.

Coleridge, Samuel Taylor (1997), *Biographia Literaria*, London, Penguin.

Colley, Linda (1992), *Britons: Forging the Nation*, New Haven, CT, Yale University Press.

Collins, Michael (1996), The Proof of Success: What the Rising of 1916 Did, in Michael Collins (ed), *The Path to Freedom*, Dublin, Mercier Press.

Cowan, Peter (1987), The Origins of the Administrative Elite, 162 *New Left Review* (old series) 4.

Cross, Rupert (1968), *Precedent in English Law*, 2nd edn, Oxford, Oxford University Press.

Dalrymple, William (2002), *White Mughals: Love and Betrayal in Eighteenth Century India*, London, Harper Collins.

Darby, Phillip (2008), A Disabling Discipline, in Christian Reuss-Smit and Duncan Snidel (eds), *The Oxford Handbook of International Relations*, Oxford, Oxford University Press.

David, Dierdre (1987), *Intellectual Women and Victorian Patriarchy: Harriet Martineau, Elizabeth Barrett Browning, George Eliot*, Ithaca, NY, Cornell University Press.

David, Saul (2006), *Victoria's Wars: The Rise of Empire*, London, Viking.

Davies, Harry (1965), *Culture and the Grammar School*, London, Routledge & Kegan Paul.

Davies, Norman (1996), *Europe*, Oxford, Oxford University Press.

Davies, Norman (1999), *The Isles: A History*, Oxford, Oxford University Press.

Dawson, Jane (1995), Anglo-Protestant Culture and Integration in Sixteenth Century Britain, in Steve Ellis and Sarah Barber (eds), *Conquest and Union: Fashioning a British State*, London, Longmans.

Dawson, William (1994), *Soldier Heroes: British Adventure, Empire and the Imagining of Masculinities*, London, Routledge.

Dean, Mitchell (1991), *The Constitution of Poverty: Toward a Genealogy of Liberal Governance*, London, Routledge.

Defoe, Daniel (1997), The Original Power of the People in England, in PN Furbanks and WR Owens (eds), *Daniel Defoe: The True-Born Englishman and Other Essays*, London, Penguin.

Defoe, Daniel (1997), The True-Born Englishman, in PN Furbanks and WR Owens (eds), *Daniel Defoe: The True-Born Englishman and Other Essays*, London, Penguin.

Department of the Environment (1967), *Kings and Queens of England*, London, Her Majesty's Stationery Office.

Derrida, Jacques (1992), Mochols; or, The Conflict of the Faculties, in Richard Rand (ed), *Logomachia: The Conflict of the Faculties*, Lincoln, NE, University of Nebraska Press.

De Ste Croix, Geoffrey (1983), *Class Struggle in the Ancient Greek World*, London, Duckworth.

Devlin, Patrick (1965), *The Enforcement of Morals*, Oxford, Oxford University Press.

Dickinson, HT (1978), *Liberty and Property: Political Ideology in Eighteenth Century Britain*, London, Weidenfeld and Nicolson.

Donajgrodzki, AP (ed) (1977), *Social Control in Nineteenth Century Britain*, London, Croom Helm.

Dover Wilson, John (1932), *Matthew Arnold: Culture and Anarchy*, Cambridge, Cambridge University Press.

D'Souza, Rhada (1991), International Law – Recolonizing the Third World? Law and Conflicts over Water in the Krishna River Basin, in Diane Kirkby and Catherine Coleborne (eds), *Law, History, Colonialism: The Reach of Empire*, Manchester, Manchester University Press.

Duffy, Christopher (2007), *The '45: Bonnie Prince Charlie and the Untold Story of the Jacobite Rising*, London, Phoenix.

Dufour, Alfred (1991), Natural Law and Utility, in JH Burns and Mark Goldie (eds), *The Cambridge History of Political Thought 1450–1700*, Cambridge, Cambridge University Press.

Duncanson, Ian (1976), Equity and Obligations, 39 *Modern Law Review* 268–86

Duncanson, Ian (1979), The Strange World of English Jurisprudence, 30 *Northern Ireland Legal Quarterly* 207–24.

Duncanson, Ian (1987), Hermeneutics and Persistent Questions in Hart's Jurisprudence, *The Juridical Review* 113–30.

Duncanson, Ian (1997), The Ends of Legal Studies, *Web Journal of Current Legal Issues*, http://webjcli.ncl.ac.uk/1997/issue3/duncan3.html (accessed July 2006).

Duncanson, Ian (2000), Mr. Hobbes Goes to Australia: Law, Politics and Difference, 13 *International Journal for the Semiotics of Law* 279–303.

Duncanson, Ian (2001), The Center May Not Hold, 8 *International Journal of the Legal Profession* 69–85.

Duncanson, Ian (2008), Sovereignty: Some Considerations, 12 *Law/Text/Culture* 129–53.

Dunn, John (1990), *Interpreting Political Responsibility: Essays 1981–1989*, Princeton, NJ, Princeton University Press.

Dworkin, Ronald (1986), *Law's Empire*, London, Collins.

Dwyer, John (1993), A "Peculiar Blessing": Social Converse in Scotland from Hutcheson to Burns, in John Dwyer and Richard Sher (eds), *Sociability and Society in Eighteenth Century Scotland*, Edinburgh, Mercat Press.

Earle, Peter (1989), *The Making of the English Middle Class: Business, Society and Family Life in London 1660–1730*, London, Methuen.

Eley, Geof and William Hunt (eds) (1988), *Reviving the English Revolution: Reflections and Elaborations on the Work of Christopher Hill*, London, Verso.

Elias, Norbert (1978), *The Civilizing Process: State Formation and Civilization*, Oxford, Blackwell.

Elias, Norbert (1982), *The History of Manners*, Oxford, Blackwell.

Ellis, TF (ed) (1889), *The Miscellaneous Writings and Speeches of Lord Macaulay*, London, Longmans Green.

Ellis, Steve and Sarah Barber (eds) (1995), *Conquest and Union: Fashioning a British State*, London, Longmans.

English, Barbara and John Saville (1983), *Strict Settlement: A Guide for Historians*, Hull, Hull University Press.

Evans, Dylan (1996), *Dictionary of Lacanian Psychoanalysis*, London, Routledge.

Evans, RJ (1948), *The Victorian Age, 1815–1914*, London, Arnold.

Ferguson Adam (1966), *An Essay on the History of Civil Society* (Duncan Forbes, ed), Edinburgh, Edinburgh University Press.

Fetter, F (1974), The Revision of the Declaration of Independence in 1941, 31 *The William and Mary Quarterly* 3rd Ser 133–39.

Feuchtwanger, EJ (1975), *Gladstone*, London, Allen Lane.

Fitzpatrick, Peter (1992), *The Mythology of Modern Law*, London, Routledge.

Foucault, Michel (1986), The Subject and Power, in Hubert Dreyfus and Paul Rabinow (eds), *Michel Foucault: Beyond Structuralism and Hermeneutics*, Brighton, Harvester Press.

Foucault, Michel (1992), What is Enlightenment?, in Patricia Waugh (ed), *Postmodernism: A Reader*, London, Edward Arnold.

Foucault, Michel (2005), *The Hermeneutics of the Subject: Lectures at the College de France 1981–2*, New York, NY, Picador.

Fox, Kate (2004), *Watching the English: The Hidden Rules of English Behaviour*, London, Hodder and Stoughton.

Franklin, Julian (1992), Introduction, in Julian Franklin (ed), *Bodin on Sovereignty*, Cambridge, Cambridge University Press.

Franklin, Julian (ed) (1996), *Bodin on Sovereignty*, Cambridge, Cambridge University Press.

Fraser, George MacDonald (1979), *The Steel Bonnets: The Story of the Border Anglo-Scottish Reivers*, London, Pan.

Freeman, EA (1876), *The Growth of the English Constitution from the Earliest Times*, London, Macmillan.

Freidberg, Aaron (1996), *The Weary Titan: Britain and the Experience of Relative Decline*, Princeton, NJ, Princeton University Press.

Fry, Michael (2003), *Bold, Independent, Unconquer'd and Free: How the Scots made America Safe for Liberty, Democracy and Capitalism*, Ayr, Fort Publishing.

Fry, Michael (2006), *The Union: England, Scotland and the Treaty of Union, 1707*, Edinburgh, Birlinn.

Fuller, Lon (1958), Positivism and Fidelity to Law – A Reply to Professor Hart, 71 *Harvard Law Review* 630.

Fuller, Lon (1964), *The Morality of Law*, New Haven, CT, Yale University Press.

Furedi, Frank (2006), *The Politics of Fear: Beyond Left and Right*, London, Continuum.

Gelderen, Martin van (2003), The State and its Rivals in Early-Modern Europe, in Quentin Skinner and Bo Strath (eds), *States and Citizens: History, Theory, Prospects*, Cambridge, Cambridge University Press.

Ghosh, Amitav (2008), *Sea of Poppies*, London, John Murray.

Gikandi, Simon (1996), *Mapping Englishness: Writing Identity in the Culture of Colonialism*, New York, NY, Columbia University Press.

Gilmour, David (2005), *The Ruling Caste: Imperial Lives in the British Raj*, New York, NY, Farrar, Strauss and Giroux.

Gilroy, Paul (1983), *The Black Atlantic: Modernity and Double Consciousness*, London, Verso.

Goldie, Mark (1991), The Reception of Hobbes, in JH Burns and Mark Goldie (eds), *The Cambridge History of Modern Thought 1450–1700*, Cambridge, Cambridge University Press.

Goodrich, Peter (1993), *Law*, in William Outhwaite and Tom Bottomore (eds), *The Blackwell Dictionary of Twentieth Century Social Thought*, Oxford, Blackwell.

Goody, Jack (1996), *The East in the West*, Cambridge, Cambridge University Press.

Gordon, Colin (ed) (1980), *Michel Foucault: Power/Knowledge, Selected Interviews and Other Writings 1972–1977*, Brighton, Harvester Press.

Gould, Eliga (2000), *The Persistence of Empire: British Political Culture in the Age of the American Revolution*, Chapel Hill, NC, University of North Carolina Press.

Gould, Eliga (2009), Revolution and Counter-Revolution, in David Armitage and Michael Braddick (eds) (2009), *The British Atlantic World*, London, Palgrave.

Gould, SJ (1981), *The Mismeasure of Man*, New York, NY, Norton.

Graham, Keith (1977), *JL Austin: A Critique of Ordinary Language Philosophy*, Brighton, Harvester Press.

Grbich, Judith (1996), The Taxpayer's Body: Genealogies of Exertion, in Pheng Cheah, David Fraser and Judith Grbich (eds), *Thinking Through the Body of the Law*, New York, NY, NYU Press.

Greenblatt, Stephen and Giles Gunn (eds) (1992), *Redrawing the Boundaries: The Transformation of English and American Literary Studies*, New York, NY, Modern Languages Association.

Greene, Jack (2001), Empire and Identity from the Glorious Revolution to the American Revolution, in Peter Marshall (ed), *The Oxford History of the British Empire II: The Eighteenth Century*, Oxford, Oxford University Press.

Grene, Marjorie (1966), *The Knower and the Known*, London, Faber and Faber.

Grossberg, Lawrence, Cary Nelson and Paula Treichler (eds) (1992), *Cultural Studies*, New York, NY, Routledge.

Guha, Ranajit (1981), *A Rule of Property for Bengal: An Essay on the Idea of Permanent Settlement*, 2nd edn, Delhi, Orient Longman.

Guha, Ranajit (1997), *Domination without Hegemony: History and Power in Colonial India*, Cambridge, MA, Harvard University Press.

Guha, Ranajit (2000), On Some Aspects of the Historiography of Colonial India, in Vinayak Chaturvedi (ed), *Mapping Subaltern Studies and the Postcolonial*, London, Verso.

Haakonssen, Knud (ed) (1996), *Enlightenment and Religion: Rational Dissent in Eighteenth Century Britain*, Cambridge, Cambridge University Press.

Haakonssen, Knud (1996), *Natural Law and Moral Philosophy: From Grotius to the Scottish Enlightenment*, Cambridge, Cambridge University Press.

Hall, Stuart *et al* (1978), *Policing the Crisis: Mugging, the State and Law and Order*, London, Macmillan.

Hallam, Henry (1827), *Constitutional History of England*, 2 vols in 1, London, Ward, Lock and Tyler.

Hamburger, Lotte and Joseph Hamburger (1985), *Troubled Lives: John and Sarah Austin*, Toronto, Toronto University Press.

Harding, Alan (1973), *The Law Courts of Medieval England*, London, Allen and Unwin.

Hart, HLA (1957), Positivism and the Separation of Law and Morals, 71 *Harvard Law Review* 593.

Hart, HLA (1961), *The Concept of Law*, Oxford, Oxford University Press.

Hart, HLA (1963), *Law, Liberty and Morality*, Oxford, Oxford University Press.

Harvey, Robert (1998), *Clive: The Life and Death of a British Emperor*, London, Hodder & Stoughton.

Herbert, Paul (1902), *Matthew Arnold*, London, Macmillan.

Herman, Arthur (2001), *The Scottish Enlightenment: The Scots' Invention of the Modern World*, London, Fourth Estate.

Hersh, Seymour (2004), *Chain of Command: The Road from 9/11 to Abu Ghraib*, London, Allen Lane.

Hill, Christopher (1967), *Reformation to Industrial Revolution*, Harmondsworth, Penguin.

Hill, Christopher (1969), *Society and Puritanism in Pre-Revolutionary England*, London, Panther.

Hill, Christopher (1975), *The World Turned Upside Down: Radical Ideas During the English Revolution*, Harmondsworth, Penguin.

Hill, Christopher (1980), *Some Intellectual Consequences of the English Revolution*, Madison, WI, University of Wisconsin Press.

Hill, Christopher (1995), *The Experience of Defeat: Milton and Some Contemporaries*, London, Faber and Faber.

Hill, Rosemary (2007), *God's Architect: Pugin and the Building of Romantic Britain*, London, Allen Lane

Hilton, Rodney (1976) (ed), *The Transition from Feudalism to Capitalism*, London, Verso.

Hilton, Rodney (1990), *Class Conflict and the Crisis of Feudalism: Essays in Medieval History*, London, Verso.

Hirschman, AO (1977), *The Passions and the Interests: Arguments for Capitalism before its Triumph*, Princeton, NJ, Princeton University Press.

Hobbes, Thomas (1970), *Man* (B Gert, ed), New York, NY, Humanities Press.

Hobbes, Thomas (1977), *Leviathan* (CP Macpherson, ed), Harmondsworth, Penguin.

Hobbes, Thomas (1998), *The Citizen* (Richard Tuck and Michael Silverthorne, eds), Cambridge, Cambridge University Press.

Holdsworth, Sir William (1924), *A History of English Law in Sixteen Volumes, Vol V*, London, Sweet and Maxwell.

Hollander, Samuel (1997), *The Economics of Thomas Robert Malthus*, Toronto, University of Toronto Press.

Holmes, Oliver Wendell Jr (1897), The Path of the Law, 10 *Harvard Law Review* 457.

Holton, John (1984), *The Transition from Feudalism to Capitalism*, London, Macmillan.

Howe, Daniel (1989), Why the Scottish Enlightenment was Useful to the Framers of the American Constitution, 31(3) *Comparative Studies in Society and History* 572–87.

Hudson, Derek (1972), *Munby: Man of Two Worlds*, London, John Murray.

Hueglin, Thomas (1999), *Early Modern Concepts for a Late Modern World: Althusius on Community and Federalism*, Waterloo, Wilfrid Laurier University Press.

Hume, David (1972), *Enquiries Concerning the Human Understanding and the Principles of Morals*, 1777 edn (LA Selby-Bigge, ed), Oxford, Oxford University Press.

Hume, David (1978), *A Treatise of Human Nature* (1739–40), 2nd edn (LA Selby-Bigge and PH Niditch, eds), Oxford, Oxford University Press.

Hume, David (1983), *The History of England from the Invasion of Julius Caesar to the Revolution in 1688*, 6 vols (1778), Indianapolis, IN, Liberty Collection.

Hume, David (ed) (1985), *Essays*, Indianapolis, IN, Liberty Collection.

Hume, David (1985), Of the Independency of Parliament, in David Hume (ed), *Essays*, Indianapolis, IN, Liberty Collection.

Hutcheson, Francis (1990), *An Essay on the Nature and Conduct of the Passions and Affections* (1728), Hildesheim, George Olms Verlag.

Hutcheson, Francis (1990), *An Inquiry into the Origin of Our Ideas of Beauty and Virtue* (1725), Hildesheim, George Olms Verlag.

Immerman, Richard (2010), *Empire for Liberty: A History of American Imperialism from Benjamin Franklin to Paul Wolfowitz*, Princeton, NJ, Princeton University Press.

Irving, Helen (1997), *To Constitute a Nation: A Cultural History of Australia's Constitution*, Melbourne, Melbourne University Press.

Ishiguro, Kazuo (1989), *The Remains of the Day*, London, Faber and Faber.

Israel, Jonathan (2001), *Radical Enlightenment: Philosophy and the Making of Modernity*, Oxford, Oxford University Press.

Israel, Jonathan (2006), *Enlightenment Contested: Philosophy, Modernity and the Emancipation of Man 1650–1752*, Oxford, Oxford University Press.

James, Lawrence (2006), *The Middle Class: A History*, London, Little, Brown.

Jayawardena, Kumari (1995), *The White Woman's Other Burden: Western Women and South Asia During British Rule*, London, Routledge.

Jenkins, Keith (1991), *Re-Thinking History*, London, Routledge.

Jenkins, Keith (1997), Introduction: On Being Open about our Closures, in Keith Jenkins (ed), *The Postmodern History Reader*, London, Routledge.

Jenkins, Roy (1995), *Gladstone*, London, Macmillan.

Johnson, Chalmers (2000), *Blowback: The Causes and Consequences of American Empire*, New York, NY, Henry Holt.

Johnson, Chalmers (2004), *The Sorrows of Empire: Militarism, Secrets, and the End of the Republic*, London, Verso.

Johnson, Chalmers (2006), *Nemesis: The Last Days of the American Republic*, New York, NY, Henry Holt.

Johnson, Richard (1977), Educating the Educators: "Experts" and the State, in AP Donajgrodzki (ed), *Social Control in Nineteenth Century Britain*, London, Croom Helm.

Jones, Gareth Stedman (1983), *Languages of Class: Studies in English Working Class History 1832–1982*, Cambridge, Cambridge University Press.

Jordan, Glenn and Chris Weedon (1995), *Cultural Politics: Class, Race, Gender and the Postmodern World*, Oxford, Blackwell.

Judt, Tony (2008), *Reappraisals: Reflections on the Forgotten Twentieth Century*, London, William Heinemann.

Judt, Tony (2010), *Ill Fares the Land*, Melbourne, Allen Lane.

Kames, Lord (1817), *Elements of Criticism, vol 1*, Edinburgh, Bell and Bradfute, A Constable & Co.

Kant, Immanuel (1991), Perpetual Peace, in Hans Reiss (ed) (1991), *Kant: Political Writings*, Cambridge, Cambridge University Press.

Kant, Immanuel (1992), The Conflict of the Faculties, in Richard Rand (ed), *Logomachia*, Lincoln, NE, University of Nebraska Press.

Kant, Immanuel (1996), An Answer to the Question, "What is Enlightenment", in James Schmidt (ed) (1996), *What Is Enlightenment? Eighteenth Century Answers and Twentieth Century Questions*, Berkeley, CA, University of California Press.

Keane, John (1995), *Tom Paine: A Political Life*, New York, NY, Little, Brown.

Kitson, Peter (2002), Political Thinker, in Lucy Newlyn (ed), *The Cambridge Companion to Coleridge*, Cambridge, Cambridge University Press.

Klein, Lawrence (1994), *Shaftesbury and the Culture of Politeness: Moral Discourse and Cultural Politics in Early Eighteenth Century England*, Cambridge, Cambridge University Press.

Krishnaswamy, Revathi (1998), *Effeminism: The Economy of Colonial Desire*, Ann Arbor, MI, University of Michigan Press.

Kronman, A. (1983), *Max Weber*, London, Arnold.

Kuhn, Thomas (1970), *The Structure of Scientific Revolutions*, 2nd edn, Chicago, IL, Chicago University Press.

Kynaston, David (2007), *Austerity Britain 1945–51*, London, Bloomsbury Press.

Lacan, Jacques (2006), *Ecrits*, New York, NY, WW Norton.

Lacey, Nicola (2004), *A Life of HLA Hart: The Nightmare and the Noble Dream*, Oxford, Oxford University Press.

Laplanche, J and J-B Portalis (1973), *The Language of Psychoanalysis*, New York, NY, Norton.

Larner, Christina (1981), *Enemies of God: The Witch-Hunt in Scotland*, Oxford, Blackwell.

Larner, Christina (1984), *Witchcraft and Religion: The Politics of Popular Belief*, Oxford, Blackwell.

Laslett, Peter (ed) (1965), *John Locke: Two Treatises of Government*, New York, NY, Signet.

Leavis, FR (ed) (1950) *On Bentham and Coleridge*, Cambridge, Cambridge University Press.

Leavis, FR (1972), *Nor Shall My Sword Sleep in My Hand: Discourses on Pluralism, Compassion and Social Hope*, London, Chatto and Windus.

Leavis, QD (1932), *Fiction and the Reading Public*, London, Chatto and Windus.

Lenman, Bruce and John Gibson (eds) (1990), *The Jacobite Threat: Rebellion and Conspiracy 1688–1759 – England, Ireland, Scotland and France*, Edinburgh, Scottish Academic Press.

Levine, Lawrence (1996), *The Opening of the American Mind: Canons, Culture and History*, Boston, MA, Beacon Books.

Levine, Philippa (2004), Why Gender and Empire?, in Philippa Levine (ed), *Gender and Empire. OHBE Companion Series*, Oxford, Oxford University Press.

Lipman, Samuel (ed) (1994), *Matthew Arnold: Culture and Anarchy*, New Haven, CT, Yale University Press.

Lively, Jack, and John Rees (eds) (1978), *Utilitarian Logic and Politics: James Mill's "Essay on Government", Macaulay's "Critique" and the Ensuing Debate*, Oxford, Oxford University Press.

Lloyd, David and Paul Thomas (1998), *Culture and the State*, London, Routledge.

Loades, David (1974), *Politics and the Nation 1450–1660*, Brighton, Harvester Press.

Loades, David (2007), *Henry VIII: Court, Church and Conflict*, Kew, National Archives.

Locke, John (1965), Second Treatise, in Peter Laslett (ed), *John Locke: Two Treatises of Government*, New York, NY, Signet.

Locke, John (1979), *An Essay Concerning Human Understanding* (1706) (PH Niddith, ed), Oxford, Oxford University Press.

Locke, John (1983), *A Letter Concerning Toleration* (James Tully, ed), Indianapolis, IN, Liberty Collection.

Locke, John (1989), *Some Thoughts Concerning Education* (JW Yolton and JS Yolton, eds), Oxford, Oxford University Press.

Loughlin, Martin (2004), *The Idea of Public Law*, Oxford, Oxford University Press.

Louis, W Roger (1997), Introduction, in Robin Winks (ed), *Oxford History of the British Empire vol 5: Historiography*, Oxford, Oxford University Press.

Lovett, William and John Collins (2001), Chartism: A New Organization of the People 1840, in Antoinette Burton (ed), *Politics and Empire in Victorian Britain*, London, Palgrave.

Lukes, Steven (2005), *Power: A Radical View*, 2nd edn, London, Palgrave Macmillan.

Mabo v Queensland (No 2) (1992) 175 CLR 1.

Macaulay, TB (1968), *History of England to the Death of William III, vol II*, London, Heron Books.

Macaulay, Thomas Babbington (1907), Essay on Lord Clive, in J Grieve (ed), *Thomas Babbington Macaulay: Critical and Historical Essays*, London, Dent.

Macaulay, Thomas Babbington (1907), Southey's Colloquies, in J Grieve (ed), *Thomas Babbington Macaulay: Critical and Historical Essays*, London, Dent.

Macfarlane, Alan (1978), *The Origins of English Individualism: Family, Property and Social Transition*, Oxford, Blackwell.

MacGraith, Michael (1995), The Gaelic Reaction to the Reformation, in Steve Ellis and Sarah Barber (eds), *Conquest and Union: Fashioning a British State*, London, Longmans.

Mackay, James (1986), *Complete Works of Robert Burns*, Ayr, Alloway Publishing.

MacKenzie, John (1984), *Propaganda and Empire: The Manipulation of British Public Opinion 1880–1960*, Manchester, Manchester University Press.

MacKillop, Ian (1995), *FR Leavis: A Life in Criticism*, London, Penguin.

Maitland, FW (1909), *The Constitutional History of England* (HAL Fisher, ed), Cambridge, Cambridge University Press.

Majeed, Javed (1992), *Ungoverned Imaginings: James Mill's "History of British India" and Orientalism*, Oxford, Oxford University Press.

Makdisi, Saree (2008), *Palestine Inside and Out: An Everyday Occupation*, New York, NY, WW Norton.

Mandler, Peter (1997), Against "Englishness": English Culture and the Limits to Rural Nostalgia, 7 *Transactions of the Royal Historical Society* 6th Ser 155–75.

Marshall, JD (1968), *The Making of the New Poor Law 1795–1834*, London, Macmillan.

Marshall, Peter (1987), Empire and Authority in the Later Eighteenth Century, XV *Journal of Imperial and Commonwealth History* 105–22.

Marshall, Peter (1995), A Nation Defined by Empire 1755–1776, in Alexander Grant and Keith Sringer (eds), *Uniting the Kingdom: The Making of British History*, London, Routledge.

Marshall, Peter (2000), The Case for Coercing America Before the Revolution, in Fred Leventhal and Roland Quinault (eds), *Anglo-American Attitudes: From Revolution to Partnership*, Aldershot, Ashgate.

Marshall, Peter (2001), The British in Asia: Trade to Dominion, in Peter Marshall (ed), *The Oxford History of the British Empire II: The Eighteenth Century*, Oxford, Oxford University Press.

Marshall, Peter (2005), *The Making and Unmaking of Empires: Britain, India and America c. 1750–1783*, Oxford, Oxford University Press.

Martin, John (1983), *Feudalism to Capitalism: Peasant and Landlord in English Agrarian Development*, London, Macmillan.

Marx, Karl (1975), Thesis Eleven, Concerning Feurbach, in Lucio Colleti (ed), *Karl Marx: Early Writings*, Harmondsworth, Penguin.

Mattingly, Garrett (1942), *Catherine of Aragon*, London, Jonathan Cape.

McIlwain, Charles (ed) (1918), *The Political Writings of James I*, Cambridge, MA, Harvard University Press (private edition).

McLaren, John (2001), Reflections on the Rule of Law: the Georgian Colonies of New South Wales and Upper Canada 1788–1837, in Diane Kirkby and Catherine Coleborne (eds), *Law, History, Colonialism: The Reach of Empire*, Manchester, Manchester University Press.

McLintock, Anne (1995), *Imperial Leather: Race, Gender and Sexuality in the Imperial Contest*, New York, NY, Routledge.

McQueen, Rob (2003), Together We Fall, Divided We Fall: the Victorian Legal Profession in Crisis 1890–1940, in W Wesley Pue and David Sugarman (eds), *Lawyers and Vampires: Cultural Histories of Legal Professions*, London, Hart Publishing.

Mehta, Uday Singh (1999), *Liberalism and Empire: A Study in Nineteenth Century British Liberal Thought*, Chicago, IL, University of Chicago Press.

Messer-Davidow, Ellen, David Shumway and David Sylvan (eds) (1993), *Knowledges: Historical and Critical Studies in Disciplinarity*, Charlottesville, VA, University of Virginia Press.

Mill, Harriet Taylor (1970), Enfranchisement of Women, in Alice Rossi (ed), *Essays in Sex Equality: John Stuart Mill and Harriet Taylor Mill*, Chicago, IL, University of Chicago Press.

Mill, JS (1950), Coleridge, in FR Leavis (ed), *On Bentham and Coleridge*, Cambridge, Cambridge University Press.

Mill, JS (1970), The Subjection of Women, in Alice Rossi (ed), *Essays in Sex Equality: John Stuart Mill and Harriet Taylor Mill*, Chicago, IL, University of Chicago Press.

Mill, JS (1976), Democracy and Government, in Geraint Williams (ed), *John Stuart Mill on Politics and Society*, New York, NY, International Publication Service.

Mill JS (1989), *Autobiography* (John Robson, ed), Harmondsworth, Penguin.

Mill, JS (1991), *Considerations on Representative Government*, Buffalo, Prometheus Press.

Millar, John (1771), *The Origin of the Distinction of Ranks: Or, an Inquiry into the Circumstances Which Give Rise to Influence and Authority in Different Members of Society*, 4th edn (corrected, 1806), Edinburgh, Blackwood), http://socserv2.socsci.mcmaster.ca/~econ/ugcm/3113/millar/rank (accessed 3 June 2007).

Millar, John (1997), The Powers of the Sovereign, in Alexander Broadie (ed) (1997), *The Scottish Enlightenment: An Anthology*, Edinburgh, Cannongate Books.

Miller, John (1992), Crown, Parliament and People, in JR Jones (ed), *Liberty Secured? Britain Before and After 1688*, Palo Alto, CA, Stanford University Press.

Miller, Thomas (1990), Where Did College English Studies Come From?, 9 *Rhetorical Studies* 50–69.

Miller, Toby (1993), *The Well-Tempered Self*, Baltimore, MD, The Johns Hopkins University Press.

Milsom, SFC (1981), *Historical Foundations of the Common Law*, 2nd edn, London, Butterworths.

Milsom, SFC (2003), *A Natural History of the Common Law*, New York, NY, Columbia University Press.

Montequieu, Baron (1977), *The Spirit of the Laws*, Berkeley, CA, University of California Press.

Moore, James (2006), Natural Rights in the Scottish Enlightenment, in Mark Goldie and Robert Wokler (eds), *The Cambridge History of Eighteenth Century Political Thought*, Cambridge, Cambridge University Press.

Moore, Michael (2004), *Will They Ever Trust Us Again: Letters from a War Zone*, Melbourne, Penguin.

Morrow, John (1990), *Coleridge's Political Thought: Property, Morality and the Limits of Traditional Discourse*, London, Macmillan.

Morrow, John (ed) (1990), *Coleridge's Writings On Politics and Society*, London, Macmillan.

Mountner, Thomas (ed) (1993), *Francis Hutcheson: On Human Nature – Reflections on our common systems of morality and on the social nature of man*, Cambridge, Cambridge University Press.

Mulhern, Francis (1979), *The Moment of Scrutiny*, London, New Left Books.

Munns, Jessica and Gita Rajan (1995), *A Cultural Studies Reader: History, Theory, Practice*, London, Longman.

Nandy, Ashis (1983), *The Intimate Enemy: Loss and Recovery of Self under Colonialism*, Delhi, Oxford University Press.

Neal, David, (1991), *The Rule of Law in a Penal Colony: Law and Power in Early New South Wales*, Cambridge, Cambridge University Press.

Nenner, Howard (1977), *By Colour of Law: Legal Culture and Constitutional Politics in England 1660–1689*, Chicago, IL, University of Chicago Press.

Newbolt Report (1919), *The Teaching of English in England*, London, Her Majesty's Stationery Office.

Newton, Scott and Dilwyn Porter (1988), *Modernization Frustrated: The Politics of Industrial Decline in Britain Since 1900*, London, Unwin Hyman.

Norris, Christopher (1996), entry on the Philosophy of Law, in Michael Payne (ed), *A Dictionary of Cultural and Critical Theory*, Oxford, Blackwell.

Oldham, James (2004), *English Common Law in the Age of Mansfield*, Chapel Hill, NC, University of North Carolina Press.

Orwell, George (ed) (1994), *The Works of Rudyard Kipling*, Ware, Wordsworth Editions.

Osborne, Peter (2007), *The Triumph of the Political Class*, London, Simon and Schuster.

Paine, Thomas (2000), The Crisis Number 1, in Bruce Kuklick (ed), *Thomas Paine: Political Writings*, Cambridge, Cambridge University Press.

Palmer, Robert (1982), *The County Courts of Medieval England 1150–1350*, Princeton, NJ, Princeton University Press.

Palmer, Tony (1971), *The Trials of Oz*, Harmondsworth, Penguin.

Parker, Geoffrey (ed) (1997), *The Thirty Years' War*, 2nd edn, London, Routledge.

Paston (1924), *The Paston Letters*, 2 vols, London, Dent.

Patterson, Dennis (1996), *A Companion to Philosophy of Law and Legal Theory*, Oxford, Blackwell.

Paul, Herbert (1902), *Matthew Arnold*, London, Macmillan.

Paxman, David (1992), Aesthetics as Epistemology, Or, Knowledge Without Certainty, 26(2) *Eighteenth Century Studies* 285–306.

Paxman, Jeremy (2007), *The English*, London, Penguin.

Pennycook, Alastair (1998), *English and the Discourses of Colonialism*, London, Routledge.

Perkin, Harold (1969), *The Origins of Modern English Society 1780–1880*, London, Routledge & Kegan Paul.

Perkin, Harold (1983), *The Structured Crowd*, Brighton, Harvester Press.

Petegorski, David (1940), *Left Wing Democracy in the English Civil War*, London, Victor Gollancz.

Plucknet, CFC (1948), *A Concise History of the Common Law*, London, Butterworth.

Plumb, JH (1969), *The Growth of Political Stability in England 1675–1725*, Harmondsworth, Penguin.

Pocock, JGA (1987), *The Ancient Constitution and the Common Law: A Study of English Historical Thought in the Seventeenth Century*, 2nd edn, Cambridge, Cambridge University Press, with Retrospect.

Pocock, JGA (2005), The Union in British History, in JGA Pocock (ed), *The Discovery of Islands: Essays in British History*, Cambridge, Cambridge University Press.

Pollock, Sir F, and FW Maitland (1895), *The History of English Law Before the Time of Edward I*, 2 vols, Cambridge, Cambridge University Press.

Popper, Karl, (1963), *Conjectures and Refutations: The Growth of Scientific Knowledge*, London, Routledge & Kegan Paul.

Porter, Roy (2000), *The Creation of the Modern World: The Untold Story of the British Enlightenment*, New York, NY, Norton.

Postema, Gerald (1986), *Bentham and the Common Law Tradition*, Oxford, Oxford University Press.

Prest, Wilfrid (1996), Law, Lawyers and Rational Dissent, in Knud Haakonssen (ed) (1996), *Enlightenment and Religion: Rational Dissent in Eighteenth Century Britain*, Cambridge, Cambridge University Press.

Prest, Wilfrid (1998), *Albion Ascendant: English History 1660–1815*, Oxford, Oxford University Press.

Pue, W Wesley (1997), Lawyers and Political Liberalism in 18th and 19th Century England, in Terence Halliday and Lucien Karpik (eds), *Lawyers and the Rise of Western Political Liberalism: Lawyers and the Constitution of Modern Politics*, Oxford, Oxford University Press.

Pue, W Wesley (ed) (2000), *Pepper in Our Eyes: The APEC Affair*, Vancouver, UBC Press.

Pue, Wesley (2006), Educating the Total Jurist?, 8 *Journal of Legal Ethics* 208–21.

Purkis, Diane (2006), *The English Civil War: A People's History*, London, Harper.

Purviance, Susan (1993), Intersubjectivity and Social Relations in the Philosophy of Francis Hutcheson, in John Dwyer and Richard Sher (eds), *Sociability and Society in Eighteenth Century Scotland*, Edinburgh, Mercat Press.

Raban, Jonathan (2006), Dictatorship is the Danger, *Weekly Guardian*, 13 March 2006.

Rabate, Jean-Michel (ed) (2003), *The Cambridge Companion to Lacan*, Cambridge, Cambridge University Press.

Ragland-Sullivan, Ellie (1987), *Jacques Lacan and the Philosophy of Psychoanalysis*, Urbana, IL, University of Illinois Press.

Rand, Richard (ed) (1992) *Logomachia: The Conflict of the Faculties*, Lincoln, NE, University of Nebraska Press.

Rand, Richard (1992), Preface, in Richard Rand (ed), *Logomachia: The Conflict of the Faculties*, Lincoln, NE, University of Nebraska Press.

Rapple, Brendan (1994), Payment by Results: An Example of Assessment in Elementary Education from Nineteenth Century Britain, 2(1) *Education Policy Analysis Archives*, http://epaa.asu.edu/epaa/vol2n1.html (accessed July 2007).

Ratner, Sydney (1959), untitled review of Keith Hancock, *History of the Second World War*, 64(4) *American Historical Review* 398–400.

Ray, Rajat Kanta (2001), Indian Society and British Supremacy, in Peter Marshall (ed), *The Oxford History of the British Empire II: The Eighteenth Century*, Oxford, Oxford University Press.

Reid, Ian (1996), *Higher Education or Education for Hire*, Rockhampton, University of Central Queensland Press.

Reiss, Hans (1991), Introduction, in Hans Reiss (ed), *Kant: Political Writings*, Cambridge, Cambridge University Press.

Reiss, Hans (ed) (1991), *Kant: Political Writings*, Cambridge, Cambridge University Press.

Reynolds, Henry (1987), *The Law of the Land*, Melbourne, Penguin.

Rhys, Edmund (ed) (1924), *The Paston Letters*, 2 vols, London, Dent.

Rich, Frank (2006), *The Greatest Story Ever Sold: The Decline and Fall of the Truth, The Real History of the Bush Administration*, New York, NY, Viking.

Robb, Graham (2007), *The Discovery of France*, London, Picador.

Robbins, Caroline (1954), "When Is It That Colonies May Turn Independent?": An Analysis of the Environment and Politics of Francis Hutcheson (1694–1746), 11 *The William and Mary Quarterly* 3rd Ser 214–51.
Rolph, CH (1961), *The Trial of Lady Chatterley: R. v Penguin Books*, Harmondsworth, Penguin.
Rorty, Richard, JB Schneewind and Quentin Skinner (eds) (1984), *Philosophy in History*, Cambridge, Cambridge University Press.
Ross, Daniel (2004), *Violent Democracy*, Cambridge, Cambridge University Press.
Ross, Dorothy (1991), *The Origins of American Social Science*, Cambridge, Cambridge University Press.
Rossi, Alice (ed) (1970), *Essays on Sexual Equality: John Stuart Mill and Harriet Taylor Mill*, Chicago, IL, University of Chicago Press.
Roudinesco, Elisabeth (2003), The Mirror Stage: An Obliterated Archive, in Jean-Michel Rabate (ed), *The Cambridge Companion to Lacan*, Cambridge, Cambridge University Press.
Roy, Arundhati (2005), *An Ordinary Person's Guide to Empire*, New Delhi, Penguin.
Royle, Trevor (2005), *Civil War: The Wars of the Three Kingdoms 1638–1660*, London, Abacus.
Rubin, G and D Sugarman (1984), Introduction, Towards a New History of Law and Material Society in England, in G Rubin and D Sugarman (eds), *Law, Economy and Society: Essays in the History of English Law 1750–1914*, London, Abingdon Books.
Russell, Conrad (1974), *The Crisis of Parliaments: English History 1509–1660*, Oxford, Oxford University Press.
Said, Edward (1978), *Orientalism: Western Conceptions of the Orient*, London, Routledge & Kegan Paul.
Samson, Anne (1992), *FR Leavis*, Toronto, University of Toronto Press.
Sands, Philippe (2008), *Torture Team: Deception, Cruelty and the Compromise of Law*, London, Allen Lane.
Schama, Simon (1989), *Citizens: A Chronicle of the French Revolution*, New York, NY, Knopf.
Schama, Simon (2001), *A History of Britain vol 3*, London, BBC.
Schmidt, James (1996), Introduction, in James Schmidt (ed), *What Is Enlightenment? Eighteenth Century Answers and Twentieth Century Questions*, Berkeley, CA, University of California Press.
Schmidt, James (ed) (1996), *What Is Enlightenment? Eighteenth Century Answers and Twentieth Century Questions*, Berkeley, CA, University of California Press.
Scholes, Robert (1998), *The Rise and Fall of English*, New Haven, CT, Yale University Press.
Scott, PH (ed) (1979), *1707: The Union of Scotland and England in Contemporary Documents*, Edinburgh, Chambers.
Selby-Bigge, LA (1972), Introduction, in David Hume (1972), *Enquiries Concerning the Human Understanding and the Principles of Morals*, 1777 edn (LA Selby-Bigge, ed), Oxford, Oxford University Press.
Sellar, WC and RJ Yeatman (1931), *1066 and All That*, London, Dent.
Sengoopta, Chandak (2003), *Imprint of the Raj: How Fingerprinting was Born in Colonial India*, London, Macmillan.
Shaftesbury, Third Earl (1999), *Characteristics of Men, Manners, Opinions, Times* (Lawrence Klein, ed), Cambridge, Cambridge University Press.

Shanley, Mary Lyndon (1989), *Feminism, Marriage and the Law in Victorian England*, Princeton, NJ, Princeton University Press.

Sharma, Sanjay (2001), *Famine, Philanthropy and the Colonial State: North India in the Early Nineteenth Century*, Delhi, Oxford University Press.

Sharpe, Matthew (2006), "Thinking of the Extreme Situation": On the New Anti-Terrorism Laws, Or, Against a Recent (Theoretical) Return to Carl Schmitt, 24 *Australian Feminist Law Journal* 95–123.

Shklar, Judith (1964), *Legalism*, Cambridge, MA, Harvard University Press.

Shy, John (2001), The American Colonies in War and Revolution 1748–1783, in Peter Marshall (ed), *The Oxford History of the British Empire II: The Eighteenth Century*, Oxford, Oxford University Press.

Simmons, John (1993), *On the Edge of Anarchy: Locke's Consent and the Limits of Society*, Princeton, NJ, Princeton University Press.

Simpson, James (2007), *Burning to Read: English Fundamentalism and its Reformation Opponents*, Cambridge, MA, Harvard University Press.

Singh, Jyotsna (1996), *Colonial Narratives, Cultural Dialogues: "Discoveries" of India in the Language of Colonialism*, New York, NY, Routledge.

Singh, Uday Mehta (1999), *Liberalism and Empire: A Study in Nineteenth Century British Liberal Thought*, Chicago, IL, University of Chicago Press.

Sinha, Mrinalina (1995), *Colonial Masculinity: The "Manly" Englishman and the "Effeminate" Bengali in the Late Nineteenth Century*, Manchester, Manchester University Press.

Skinner, Quentin (1980), *The Foundations of Modern Political Theory vol 1*, Cambridge, Cambridge University Press.

Skinner, Quentin (2003), States and the Freedom of Citizens, in Quentin Skinner and Bo Strath (eds), *States and Citizens: History, Theory, Prospects*, Cambridge, Cambridge University Press.

Skorupsky, John (ed) (1998), *The Cambridge Companion to Mill*, Cambridge, Cambridge University Press.

Smith, Adam (1982), *A Theory of Moral Sentiments*, 6th edn (1790) (D Raphael and AL Macfie, eds), Indianapolis, IN, Liberty Classics.

Smith, Adam (1982), *Lectures in Jurisprudence* (22 March 1763) (R Meek, D Raphael and P Stein, eds), Indianapolis, IN, Liberty Classics.

Smith, Alan (1984), *The Emergence of a Nation State: The Commonwealth of England 1529–1660*, London, Longmans.

Smith, Brian (1991), Introduction, in Brian Smith (ed), *The Laws of Manu*, Harmondsworth, Penguin.

Smith, FB (1966), *The Making of the Second Reform Bill*, Melbourne, Melbourne University Press.

Snell, KDM (1985), *Annals of the Laboring Poor: Social Change and Agrarian England 1660–1900*, Cambridge, Cambridge University Press.

Snyder, Alice (1929), *Coleridge on Language and Learning*, New Haven, CT, Yale University Press.

Spear, Percival (1932), *The Nabobs*, Oxford, Oxford University Press.

Stanlis, Peter (ed) (1963), *Edmund Burke: Selected Writings and Speeches*, Washington, DC, Regnery Press.

Starr, Leonie (1992), *Julius Stone: An Intellectual Life*, Sydney, Sydney University Press.

Staves, Susan (1987), Separate Maintenance Contracts, 11 *Eighteenth Century Life* 78–101.

Steele, Ian (2001), The Annointed, the Appointed and the Elected: Governance of the British Empire 1689–1784, in Peter Marshall (ed), *The Oxford History of the British Empire II: The Eighteenth Century*, Oxford, Oxford University Press.

Stephen, James Fitzjames (1967), *Liberty, Equality, Fraternity*, Cambridge, Cambridge University Press.

Stokes, Eric (1959), *The English Utilitarians in India*, Oxford, Oxford University Press.

Stone, Julius (1964), *Legal System and Lawyers' Reasonings*, Sydney, Maitland Press.

Stone, Julius (1966), *Social Dimensions of Law and Justice*, London, Stevens.

Stone, L and J Stone (1984), *An Open Elite? England 1540–1880*, Oxford, Oxford University Press.

Strachey, Lytton (1918), *Eminent Victorians: Cardinal Manning, Florence Nightingale, Dr. Arnold and General Gordon*, London, Chatto and Windus.

Sugarman, David and Ronnie Warrington (1996), Land Law, citizenship and the invention of "Englishness": the strange world of the equity of redemption, in John Brewer and Susan Staves (eds), *Early Modern Conceptions of Property*, New York, NY, Routledge.

Sugarman, David and W Wesley Pue (2003), Introduction: Toward a Cultural History of Lawyers, in W Wesley Pue and David Sugarman (eds), *Lawyers and Vampires: Cultural Histories of Legal Professions*, London, Hart Publishing.

Teltscher, Kate (2000), 'Maidenly and well nigh effeminate': Constructions of Hindu Masculinity and Religion in Seventeenth-Century English Texts, 3 *Postcolonial Studies* 159–70.

Teschke, Benno (2003), *The Myth of 1648: Class, Geopolitics and the Making of Modern International Relations*, London, Verso.

Theweleit, Klaus (1977–78), *Male Fantasies*, 2 vols, Cambridge, Polity Press.

Thompson, Andrew (2005), *The Empire Strikes Back: The Impact of Imperialism from the Mid-nineteenth Century*, Harlow, Pearson Longman.

Thompson, EP (1978), *The Poverty of Theory and Other Essays*, London, Merlin.

Thompson, EP (1991), *Customs in Common*, London, Merlin.

Thornton, Margaret (1998), Techno-Centrism in the Law School: Why the Gender and the Color of the Law Remain the Same, 36 *Osgoode Hall Law Journal* 369.

Tidrick, K (1992), *Empire and the English Character: The Illusion of Authority*, London, IB Tauris.

Tillyard, EMW (1998), *The Elizabethan World Picture*, London, Pimlico.

Tolkien, JRR (1954–55), *The Lord of the Rings*, 3 vols, London, Allen and Unwin.

Toulmin, Stephen (1992), *Cosmopolis*, Chicago, IL, University of Chicago Press.

Trautmann, Thomas (1997), *Aryans in British India*, Berkeley, CA, University of California Press.

Trevelyan, George Otto (1878), *The Life and Letters of Lord Macaulay*, 2 vols, London, Longmans Green.

Tully, James (1995), *Strange Multiplicities: Constitutionalism in an Age of Diversity*, Cambridge, Cambridge University Press.

Turpin, Colin and Adam Tomkins (2007), *British Government and the Constitution*, 6th edn, Cambridge, Cambridge University Press.

Twining, William (1973), *Karl Llewellyn and the Realist Movement*, London, Weidenfeld and Nicolson.

Underdown, David (1996), *A Freeborn People: Politics and the Nation in Seventeenth Century England*, Oxford, Oxford University Press.

Viswanathan, Gauri (1997), Currying Favor: The Politics of British Educational Policy in India 1813–1854, in Anne McLintock, Amir Mufti and Ella Sholat (eds), *Dangerous Liaisons: Gender, Nation and Postcolonial Perspectives*, Minneapolis, MN, University of Minnesota Press.

Viswanathan, Gauri (1998), *Masks of Conquest: Literary Study and British Rule in India*, Delhi, Oxford University Press.

Wahrman, Dror (1995), *Imagining the Middle Class: The Political Representation of the Middle Class in England 1780–1840*, Cambridge, Cambridge University Press.

Waterhouse-Watson, Deb (2007), All Women Are Sluts: Australian Rules Football and Representations of the Feminine, 27 *Australian Feminist Law Journal* 155–62.

Webb, Beatrice (1926), *My Apprenticeship*, London, Longmans Green.

Webber, Jeremy (2006), Legal Pluralism and Human Agency, 44 *Osgoode Hall Law Journal* 167–99.

Weber, Max (1978), *Economy and Society*, 2 vols, Berkeley, CA, University of California Press.

Weiner, Martin (1981), *English Culture and the Decline in the Industrial Spirit 1850–1980*, Cambridge, Cambridge University Press.

White, Edward (1979), *Sir Edward Coke and the Grievances of the Commonwealth*, Manchester, Manchester University Press.

Wik Peoples v Queensland (1996) 187 CLR 1.

Williams, Karel, John Williams and Dennis Thomas (1983), *Why Are the British Bad at Manufacturing?*, London, Routledge & Kegan Paul.

Williams, Penry (1979), *The Tudor Regime*, Oxford, Oxford University Press.

Williams, Raymond (1961), *Culture and Society 1750–1950*, Harmondsworth, Penguin.

Williams, Raymond (1976), *Keywords*, London, Fontana.

Williams, Raymond (1981), *Culture*, London, Fontana.

Wilson, AN (2002), *The Victorians*, London, Arrow Books.

Wilson, AN (2005), *After the Victorians*, London, Hutchinson.

Wilson, Ben (2007), *Decency and Disorder: The Age of Cant, 1789–1837*, London, Faber and Faber.

Wilson, Fred (1998), Mill on Psychology and the Moral Sciences, in John Skorupsy (ed), *The Cambridge Companion to Mill*, Cambridge, Cambridge University Press.

Wilson, Kathleen (1992), *The Sense of the People: Politics, Culture and Imperialism in England*, Cambridge, Cambridge University Press.

Wilson, Kathleen (ed) (1999), *A New Imperial History: Culture, Identity, History*, Cambridge, MA, Harvard University Press.

Wilson, Kathleen (2004), Empire, Gender and Modernity in the Eighteenth Century, in Philippa Levine (ed), *Gender and Empire. OHBE Companion Series*, Oxford, Oxford University Press.

Wilson, Richard (ed) (1920), *Macaulay's Essay on Robert Clive*, London, Dent.

Wolf, Naomi (2007), *The End of America: Letter of Warning to a Young Patriot*, Melbourne, Scibe Publications.

Wolfenden Report (1957), *Report of the Committee on Homosexual Offences and Prostitution*, Cmd 247, London, Her Majesty's Stationery Office.

Womersley, David (1998), *Edmund Burke: A Philosophical Enquiry into the Origins of our Ideas of the Sublime and the Beautiful and Other Pre-Revolutionary Writings*, London, Penguin.

Wormold, Jenny (1980), Bloodfeud, Kindred and Government in Early Modern Scotland, 87 *Past and Present* 54–97.

Yates, Frances (1975), *Astraea: The Imperial Theme in the Sixteenth Century*, Harmondsworth, Penguin.

Yolton, John and Jean Yolton (eds) (1989), *John Locke: Some Thoughts Concerning Education*, Oxford, Oxford University Press.

Young, Robert JC (2008), *The Idea of English Ethnicity*, Oxford, Blackwell.

Zinn, Howard (1980), *A People's History of the United States*, New York, NY, Harper and Row.

Zinn, Howard (1990), *Declarations of Independence: Cross-Examining American Ideology*, New York, NY, Harper Collins.

Zizek, Slavoj (1994), The Specter of Ideology, in Slavoj Zizek (ed), *Mapping Ideology*, London, Verso.

Index

Historiography, Empire and the Rule of Law

Historiography, Empire and the Rule of Law considers the intersection of these terms in the historical development of what has come to be known as the 'rule of law'. The separation of governmental powers, checks and balances, and judicial independence signified something entirely new in the way in which politics was imagined and practiced. This 'rule of law' cannot, as it often is, be traced to the justification and practice of government as originating in a social contract among the governed; but rather, by analogy with a popular conveyancing innovation of the era, to the trust – a device by which the power of ownership of land could be restrained. But how could the restraint of power remain consistent with the avoidance of anarchic disagreement among those granted the task of supervision and restraint? In response, it is argued here, the central legal and political task became one of managing disagreement and change peacefully and constructively – by drawing on a colonial tradition that emphasized civility, negotiation and compromise. And the study of all of these qualities as they evolved, Ian Duncanson contends, is vital to understanding the emergence of the 'rule of law'. *Historiography, Empire and the Rule of Law* will be invaluable for all those engaged in research and the postgraduate study of socio-legal and constitutional studies, and early modern and modern history.

Ian Duncanson is Adjunct Associate Professor at the Sociolegal Research Centre, Griffith University, Queensland and Research Associate at the Institute for Postcolonial Studies, Melbourne University. Ian has been an academic for over 40 years in the UK and Australia, and is internationally recognized for his work promoting multi-disciplinary and contextual approaches to the legal studies discipline.